CW00766434

WE TOGETHER

WE TOGETHER

451 AND 453 SQUADRONS AT WAR

ADAM LUNNEY

Published in 2020 by Tempest Books
an imprint of Mortons Books Ltd.
Media Centre
Morton Way
Horncastle LN9 6JR
www.mortonsbooks.co.uk

ISBN 978-1-911658-35-1

Typeset by Kelvin Clements

Printed and bound by Gutenberg Press, Malta

To Sid, Joe, Alec and Lindsay, and all the rest of the pilots of these fine squadrons, thank you.

CONTENTS

DUTCH LOCATIONS PRONUNCIATION GUIDE

THE DUTCH language is not an easy one for native English speakers; just ask a Dutch person! Having been to many places associated with Operation *Market Garden* over the years, I know my first efforts to explain where I was visiting to any Dutch people I met were somewhat painful to their ears. So, for this book, I have engaged the help of my long-time Dutch friend, Hennie van der Salm, to create a guide to pronouncing many of the towns that appear in this book. I really hope this helps. Don't blame Hennie if you get it wrong. Good luck!

TOWN	PHONETIC PRONUNCIATION
Alphen	Olphen
Amsterdam	Omster dom
Arnhem	Arn-hem
Boskoop	Bos koap
Eindhoven	Eind hoven (soft n)
Gilze	Chilser
Gouda	Chowder
Haagsche Bosch	Harsch Boss
Haamstede	Harm-staider
Hague Duindigt (Racecourse)	Hayg down-dicht
Hilversum	Hilvershum
Huis Te Werve	House ter werver
Ijsselmeer	Eye-sel meer
Leiden	Lye-den
Nijmegen	Nye may (ch)en
Rust en Vreugd	Rhoost en froocht
Staalduines' Bosch	Staal den boss
Uithoorn	Out-hoaren
Utrecht	Oot-reckt
Wassenaar Ravelijn	Wassenaar Raver-line
Woerden	Woooden
Zandvoort	Zund-voort

A NOTE ON DESIGNATIONS

WHILE 'BF 109' (Bayerische Flugzeugwerke) is the correct technical term for the single-seat, single-engine Messerschmitt fighter encountered throughout the Second World War by Allied pilots fighting against the Germans, it was commonly referred to as the 'Me 109'. It is the same aircraft. Where official records, pilots or logbooks are quoted as referring to Me 109s, they have appeared as such in the text. The same applies for the Focke-Wulf 190, whose correct abbreviated form is 'Fw 190' rather than FW 190, as quoted in some Allied records. It should, however, be understood that ensuring consistency in the recording of such relatively minor matters was not the concern of squadron recordkeepers and pilots of the time.

The Australian Department of Defence has not participated in the research or production or exercised editorial control over the work's contents, and the views expressed and any conclusions reached herein do not necessarily represent those of the Commonwealth, which expressly disclaims any responsibility for the content or accuracy of the work.

FOREWORD BY AVM ROBERTON, DSC, AM

IT IS an honour to be able to provide this foreword to Adam Lunney's latest book, *We Together: 451 and 453 Squadrons at War*, covering periods of the history of two of the relatively lesser known, but equally important, RAAF squadrons during World War II. Complementing his earlier book, *Ready to Strike: The Spitfires and Australians of 453 (RAAF) Squadron over Normandy*, Adam's latest work ably recounts the day-to-day events that constituted the operations of both of these Article XV squadrons across a number of theatres during the war.

This book provides a remarkable insight into the operational tempo of both squadrons that, while Australian in name, flew under the control of the Royal Air Force throughout the war and were composed of personnel from throughout the Commonwealth nations.

Adam's work delves into the early operations of 451 Squadron as an army cooperation unit flying over North Africa and the Mediterranean between 1941 and 1943, and the morale issues that confronted the squadron executives at the time. It goes on to explore 451 Squadron's contributions as a fighter squadron to operations over Europe from 1944, including the squadron's involvement in Operation *Dragoon* and the Allied landings in southern France commencing in August 1944. Picking up from his earlier work on 453 Squadron operations over Normandy in 1944, Adam looks at the parallel activities of both 451 and 453 Squadrons from September 1944 in attacking German V-1 and V-2 rocket assembly and launch sites in the Netherlands in the latter stages of the war.

Importantly, in addition to including anecdotes from the indispensable ground crew, this book recounts the personal stories of a number of those pilots who flew in both squadrons during the war. Having personally flown as an RAAF fighter pilot, as well as having held command positions in a number of the recent conflicts in the Middle East to which Australia has been engaged, I am in awe at the tales of these pilots. They seemingly flew every day, taking the battle to the enemy wherever possible while managing their own fears following the losses of fellow squadron pilots in combat or through flying accidents. Some of the stories of these veterans include tales of their capture and incarceration by the Germans in POW camps. The sheer tenacity and survival instincts of each of these pilots is both sobering and inspiring, and a benchmark for our modern Air Force members.

I strongly commend this book to any reader who has an interest in two of the RAAF's Article XV squadrons that, while sometimes operating on the fringes of main events during the war, made extremely important contributions to the outcomes of World War II and the RAAF's history. For our new generation of RAAF fighter pilots and support crews: this is what we must live up to.

Air Vice-Marshal Steve 'Zed' Roberton, DSC, AM

INTRODUCTION

WHEN I set out to write my first book, *Ready to Strike: The Spitfires and Australians of 453 (RAAF) Squadron over Normandy*, I wanted—and needed—to interview Spitfire pilots. Their recollections of experiences bring an authenticity that often trumps the opinions of those who were not there. However, the first pilot I interviewed, Sid Handsaker, flew with 451 Squadron, and I knew little about them at the time. In the time I spent with Sid, I learned that 451 Squadron had not attracted a great deal of attention over the years, and the history of the squadron put together by its veterans, *Bankstown to Berlin*, had a very limited print run and circulation.

Though I only planned to write one book, I discovered in my research that 453 Squadron flew with 451 towards the end of the war, so it was only right that I should continue my work. The history of 453 Squadron had to be completed and 451 Squadron deserved a larger audience. So, while I was writing my first book, whenever matters relating to 451 popped up, I took note and put them aside for later. Later has arrived.

So, here is the history of 451 Squadron, with their Australians (accompanied by British, Canadians and South Africans) and 453 Squadron from September 1944. Sometimes they were at the front and sometimes on the fringes of the action, but they were always ready and willing to represent Australia and the cause for which the squadrons were raised. Two squadrons raised for war, eager to seek out the enemy and bring about victory for the Allies, no matter where they were sent.

The wonderful cover design is not meant to be the recreation of a historical event, it is a tribute to Sid Handsaker and Joe Barrington, who flew together in 451 Squadron at the end of the war. It depicts Sid (NI-D) and Joe (NI-B) flying their Spitfire Mk XIVs over Wunstorf airfield (Germany) after the war.

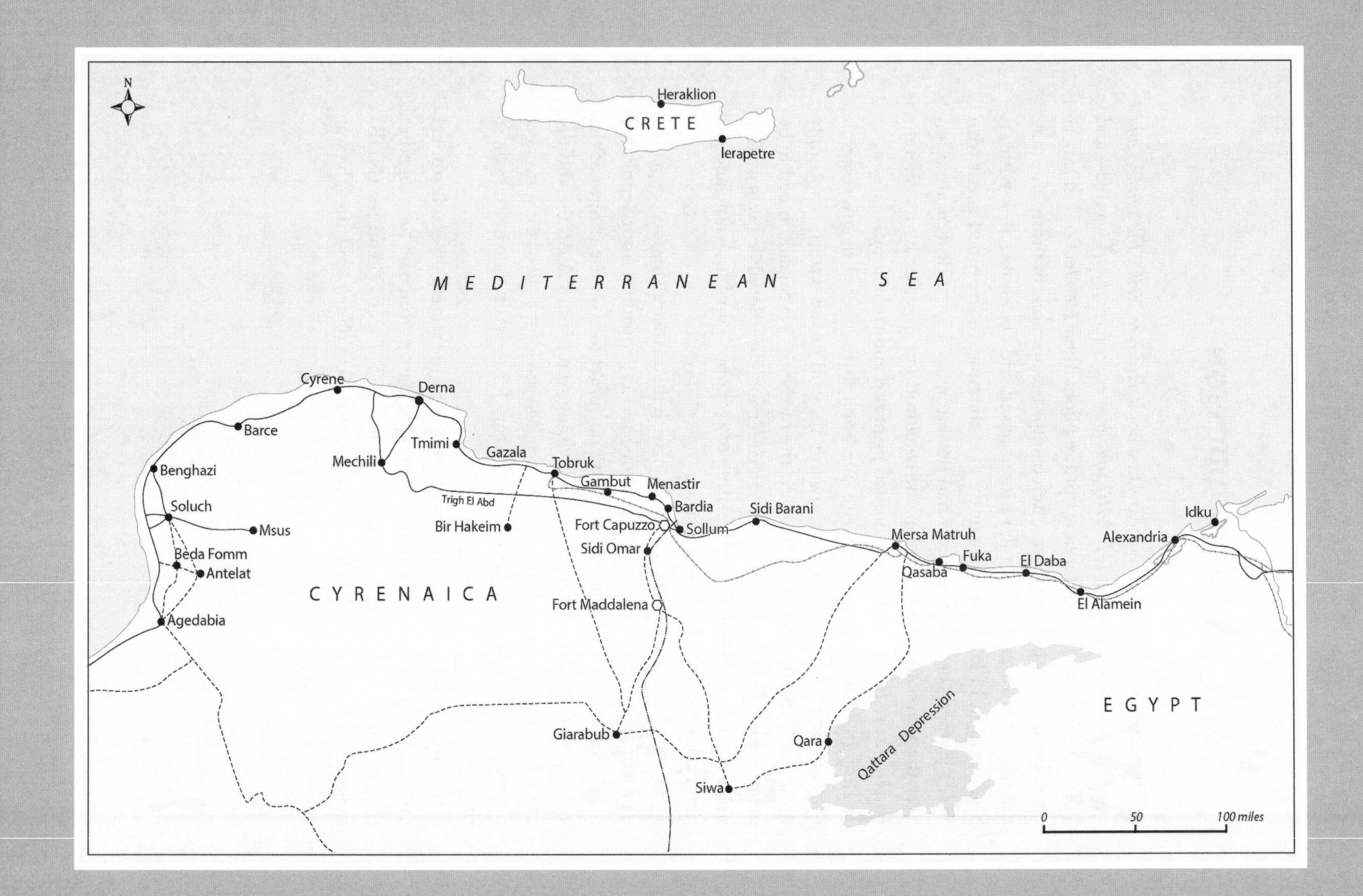
N
Heraklion
CRETE
Ierapetre
MEDITERRANEAN SEA
Cyrene
Derna
Barce
Tmimi
Gazala
Mechili
Benghazi
Tobruk
Gambut
Menastir
Trigh El Abd
Bardia
Sidi Barani
Soluch
Msus
Bir Hakeim
Fort Capuzzo
Sollum
Idku
Mersa Matruh
Alexandria
Sidi Omar
Beda Fomm
Antelat
Fuka
El Daba
Qasaba
CYRENAICA
Fort Maddalena
El Alamein
Agedabia
Qattara Depression
EGYPT
Giarabub
Qara
Siwa
0
50
100 miles

1.

THE DESERT: FORMATION AND EARLY OPERATIONS: SEPTEMBER 1939 TO JANUARY 1942

War doesn't often come as a surprise. An attack may be unforeseen, but the war that follows is usually less so. The British (and others) anticipated the Second World War, but were still rearming when Hitler's Germany invaded Poland on 1 September 1939. But rearmament was not the only way in which the British prepared for the coming war. Air power and air forces had steadily improved since the introduction of fighter and bomber squadrons to the armouries of many nations during the First World War. In this realm at least, a grand plan had been formulated to provide the Royal Air Force (RAF) with the necessary trained air and ground crew for the coming conflict. This plan came to be known as the Empire Air Training Scheme (EATS), and it would see thousands upon thousands of eager young men from Australia, Canada and New Zealand travel across the globe to fight in Europe. The scheme would not only provide men for regular squadrons, but also for what could be described as 'war-only' squadrons, in accordance with Article XV of EATS. These Article XV squadrons had a short life, yet their achievements were many. Though Australia provided the men and framework of the squadrons, it had little capacity to produce any aircraft—let alone military aircraft—in the pre- and early war years; those would have to be supplied from the United Kingdom.[1] But all these things take time, and while these men trained, others fought, so that, hopefully, there'd be something left to defend when the EATS squadrons were ready for war. When the novices arrived, they would be shown the way by the veterans, or so the theory went.

In January 1941, more than a year after war had broken out in Europe, a cable from Australia was dispatched to the United Kingdom. Recent discussions had taken place between the Air Officer Commander-in-Chief Middle East and the General Officer Commanding 1st Australian Corps wherein it was strongly urged that an additional Australian Army Cooperation squadron be provided. The Australian government agreed to form such a squadron but stipulated several conditions:

1. The squadron was to be included as one of the 18 to be formed under Article XV of EATS
2. The aircraft and equipment were to be provided by the RAF
3. Air crews were to be provided directly from Australia and sent to the Middle East
4. Australia would provide the ground crew—with the exception of W/T (wireless/telegraph—i.e. radio) and armourer trades, as none could be spared at the time
5. Financial responsibility for the squadron was to be in line with EATS.[2]

Points one and two were logical enough—after all, what aircraft did Australia possess that were in operational use in a combat zone in the Middle East? Certainly not Hurricanes or Kittyhawks. But the third point guaranteed the squadron would have absolutely no operational experience whatsoever. The same applied for the ground crew.

There was further discussion relating to the issue of these 18 EATS squadrons, and one of many important questions was: what types of squadrons should be formed? As previously stated, such massive international endeavours take time. Pilots must be trained, ground crew must learn their trades, training facilities must be built, and naturally, the planes must be manufactured. The decision was made for squadrons to be formed in stages: the first two by March 1941, with all 18 formed by April or May 1942. For that entire period the United Kingdom would have to hold on, while the RAF expanded to absorb some Dominion pilots, but also those from various conquered European nations, such as Poland, Czechoslovakia and France. Waiting from September 1939 to March 1941 for the first Australian EATS squadron to be formed was surely the perfect argument for having a larger standing military. How much could an enemy achieve while these new squadrons were being brought into service? True, the new EATS squadrons were not the only squadrons of the RAAF, a number of regular pre-war unit were in service, but how long could they hold out?

One very important point was made in the document which outlined the formation and subsequent movements of 451 (RAAF) Squadron:

> Ministry state there is no intention to form special RAAF groups because many groups are now largely homogenous as regards equipment and that segregation [sic] RAAF squadrons in only one or two groups will limit experience. May be possible form RAAF stations in bomber squadrons but this impracticable as regards fighters because squadrons are normally switched about periodically between hot and quiet sectors.[3]

This issue in relation to Australian formations keeping together, in essence, to retain 'national identity' would continue throughout the war. It was something the Canadians often managed to do, and perhaps the Australian government, Australian military commanders, or both, were envious of this. 451 (RAAF) Squadron would suffer from this top-down 'identity crisis' during its early service. They were the Army Cooperation squadron formed as a result of those high-level discussions in the Middle East. The order for its formation was issued on 6 February 1941, their formation date was given as 15 February 1941, their location: Bankstown, New South Wales. Personnel allocated to the squadron upon formation numbered almost 400, of which just 26 were pilots—the remainder included numerous ground-crew trades such as mechanics, carpenters and fabric workers, plus those required to keep the squadron running on the non-operational side, such as the cooks and clerks.[4]

There was no delay in sending the squadron overseas. 450 (RAAF) Squadron, formed at the same time but at Williamtown (near Newcastle) in New South Wales, was to be shipped overseas at the same time. 450 Squadron was designated as a fighter squadron and both 450 and 451 Squadrons would come under RAF command as soon as they disembarked in the Middle East. With the RAAF in such a poor state of affairs equipment-wise (it was not remotely prepared for war), it was only natural that the RAF would be supplying almost every piece of equipment with the exception of uniforms, and only in the circumstances where RAAF uniform differed from the RAF's.[5] But that was not the only difference: pay scales were also different, and all RAAF pay in excess of the RAF rate would be held in Australia for those members as 'deferred pay'. The notice containing these instructions directed that all personnel were to be informed of these (and other) conditions and those not agreeing to such conditions were to be allowed to leave the unit embarking for overseas.[6] Six took up this option immediately and a small number of others left a few days later, with the record noting that they were 'unwilling to accept R.A.F. conditions'.[7] February and March saw staff posted in, posted out, moved around, replaced, and medically assessed for overseas service.

On Tuesday 8 April 1941, 451 Squadron left RAAF station Bankstown and boarded a special train, provided by the army, at Bankstown railway station for the trip to Sydney Harbour where they embarked on their transport, the *Queen Mary*, to the Middle East. The ships sailed around the south of Australia before heading north and across the Indian Ocean. On 3 May 1941, they came under the command of the Air Officer Commander-in-Chief, Middle East. They disembarked on 5 May at Port Tewfik at the southernmost end of the Suez Canal in Egypt and after the usual military messing about, boarded a train to Kasafareet, where they were based for a few days before moving on to Aboukir, near Alexandria, on 11 May.

Scottish-born John Culbert, who was a driver with 451 Squadron at the time, described his first impressions of the Middle East:

> it was a dust hole. There was nothing there, all we seen was just a mass of tents for miles and one railroad track... and in the far distance hills. Everything was just like sand and rock, there was no trees, nothing to break up the area. That's all it was as far as we could see. The canal was a bit over the other side but where we were there was nothing. I thought I hope this improves for the rest of the time we're here.[8]

The next morning the squadron moved to their own area under the command of 103 MU (Maintenance Unit) and Flt Lt (Flight Lieutenant) B. Pelly, a British-born[9] Australian pilot from 3 Squadron, arrived to take temporary command, followed by a number of other experienced 3 Squadron staff, who lent their skills to 451 Squadron for a short time.[10] And it really was only a short time. This could have been handled in a much more efficient fashion if Air Marshal Tedder had been able to apply his solution. At the time he was Air Officer Commander-in-Chief, Middle East and wanted operational Squadrons as quickly as they could arrive. But he was frustrated by Australian policy which, at the time, allowed only temporary postings between regular-RAAF and EATS-RAAF squadrons. He complained in writing to the Australian Air Board: 'Complete segregation of No. 3 RAAF and 450 and 451 Squadrons present insuperable difficulties.'

The Australian Air Board replied the next day:

> Exchange with RAF is difficult and takes time. Number 3 Squadron is a unit of Australia's permanent Air Force serving in the Middle East and while we have no objection in emergency to you attaching personnel from this squadron to other units as a temporary measure it must be understood that such attachments cannot continue indefinitely, and personnel should return to No. 3 Squadron or to Australia as soon as the situation will permit ... Postings between RAF and EATS Australian units is a matter for you and is no concern of ours other than that Australians should be employed when possible in accordance with the arrangements reached.[11]

Since 3 Squadron had been fighting in North Africa for some time and had recently been rested from operations, one-third of the squadron could have been sliced off and given to 450 Squadron and the same could have been done with 451. The vacancies in 3 Squadron could then have been filled with newly arrived staff from those two squadrons, and a moderately experienced wing of three Australian squadrons could have been sent to a less-busy section of the front to build up their experience before moving to the front line proper. But this was not an administrator's war where resources can be moved around at will. For a start, 451 was not a fighter squadron, and for maximum efficiency all three should have been equipped with the same aircraft. In the end, policy was complied with and experienced RAF pilots were posted in. Later developments would reveal that the Tedder option may well have been the wiser choice, for the Australians. From the perspective of the RAF as overall commanders, the RAAF were simply being difficult. If the RAAF was so resistant to British command decisions about how the RAAF squadrons were managed in the Middle East (and elsewhere), then surely it suited the RAF to keep them separated. By doing so the Australians could not so easily band together and form a united front against the British system and commanders in an effort to get their way.

Tedder and the Australian Air Board continued to debate the matter of staff transfers and policy versus practicality, with Tedder pointing out that he had needed to post non-RAAF pilots into 3 Squadron to keep it up to strength as RAAF replacements were slow to arrive. So, if it was permissible to do this, surely it would work both ways? No. It was permissible, but to some it was an extreme measure. Australian squadrons should have Australian pilots, but Australian pilots were not restricted to Australian squadrons. So, to get them into action, Tedder gave 451 Squadron a shove, appointing Sqn Ldr (Squadron Leader) Pope from 204 Group who arrived to take command on 25 June. The next day, an advance party left for El Qasaba OLG (Operational Landing Ground) in the Western Desert to prepare for the handover of the landing ground by 6 Squadron, an RAF Army Cooperation squadron that was based there, and another group was sent to the BLG (Base Landing Ground) at Amiriya on the 29th.

The situation in 451 Squadron at the time was abysmal; when Sqn Ldr Pope took over he was one of two pilots, the other was an RAF bomber pilot who had been a prisoner of the Italians for several months and had no knowledge of, or inclination for, army cooperation work. He needed a rest. The squadron was described as 'keen to a fault without exception, but through their painful inexperience the standard of maintenance was very low'. It didn't help that the BLG and OLG were 200 miles apart and the squadron had to exist divided between the two. 6 Squadron was not at peak performance, especially with regard to equipment; pilots had to share parachutes for the first few months while they awaited delivery of enough to have one each.[12] While 6 Squadron had to give some of their pilots to 451 Squadron, some of these had been posted to 6 Squadron from 229 Squadron just weeks earlier as 6 Squadron had been seriously understrength. 6 Squadron noted: 'They are fighter pilots but can carry out simple tactical reconnaissances[sic].'[13]

The official handover was on 1 July and 451 Squadron was in the war, with the assistance of several 6 Squadron pilots, signal officers, army signal specialists and a medical officer who were posted to them immediately. They joined 253 Wing, which had two other squadrons, 229 (fighter) and 113 (light bomber). All three units were relatively inexperienced, but circumstances dictated their involvement.[14] Presumably 229 Squadron was also understrength, due to their transfer of pilots to 451 Squadron. Since arriving in North Africa many of the ground crew had been detached from 451 Squadron and sent to maintenance units to get experience; there had been no Hurricanes to practise on in Australia. By the time the squadron was back together, Sgt (Sergeant) Neville Guy (Service No. 6720) had assembled Hurricanes and worked under the supervision of experienced staff and was ready to lead his own people with wisdom passed on from the maintenance units.[15] No doubt some of this advice covered how to do the best job with almost none of what they had back in England (or Australia for that matter), such as clean and dry places to work on aircraft—the North African desert is not well-known for an abundance of facilities. According to driver John Culbert:

> we learnt to do things in the desert which normally would have been done in base areas with hangars, dust proof places you know so you could work and we done it out in the open. While the weather was fine you pulled an engine to pieces and put it back together again before anything come through. You didn't have a crane or a truck to lift it up, you had 3 poles and a pulley chain to lift it out of the aeroplane and lower it down onto packing cases or something to work on it. And everyone done the job rough but it was done.[16]

Edward Smith was an armourer with 451 Squadron and arrived in North Africa with them, and had his own thoughts about looking after aircraft in the desert:

> Well you had to be very particular there with the dust and dirt. Because dust storms and everything, sand storms, pretty prevalent. Sometimes sandstorms they'd be that bad you'd be locked up in the tent with all

the things and you wouldn't be able to see more than a few feet. It might go like that for a day or a couple of days. And then be as good as gold and another time you'd get a rainstorm, which seems funny, get floods in the desert, you'd be floating out of your tent trying to stop it. A few days later you'd have a sand storm and wouldn't be able to see for a day...we had to be very particular with the cleaning of the guns. Same as everybody on the aircraft, everything had to be very particular with cleaning and keeping the dust and everything out, it was a big problem...be very, very careful and thoroughly clean them with your petrol and oil and everything and make sure they're all covered properly...you've got your bits of fabric over the front of the main plane so as no dust could get in...Even though the first CO had said we were green and we weren't this and we weren't that. But English squadrons if they had to do an engine change or a main plane change it would be done, back to a RSU...Re-service, Repair and Resalvage Unit...Our fellows would whip up a pair of shear legs or have a crane come and change their own motor. And we'd all get underneath and heave the main plane off and get another one on, bolt it on. And that was all done on site...when we had time we'd do it. But even though he said we were raw and green and everything and I suppose not like permanent RAF blokes at least we could do things in the field that they couldn't do in the field. Cause the Australian usually they're pretty inventive and resourceful really. But that's one thing we use to pride ourselves on.[17]

Tobruk had been under siege since early April 1941 and, the Allies (mostly Australians of the 9th and 7th divisions) were hanging on inside the town and along the perimeter fortifications. This failure by the Axis to take Tobruk meant that they had to ship all their supplies to the front from further west. Tobruk was not a mere inconvenience to Rommel's troops, it was a vital link in the logistical chain for any army operating along the north coast of Africa. It had a deep-water harbour, the only good harbour between Benghazi and Alexandria (over 900 km in a straight line) and subterranean drinking water, ideal for anyone who may be confined there due to siege.[18] 451 Squadron would be the eyes of the army, from behind Allied lines and from within the Tobruk perimeter.

On 1 July 1941, two pilots flew a Tac/R (tactical reconnaissance) sortie in the afternoon: PO (Pilot Officer) Morrison-Bell being escorted by PO Maslen around the Trigh el Abd (an east–west track) and Fort Maddelena areas with 20 vehicles classed as motorised enemy transport (MET—usually trucks) being spotted travelling west. Another sortie was flown the following day, but the conditions were too difficult on 3 July due to the wind and sand, which reduced visibility and resulted in one pilot crashing his Hurricane (Z4765), damaging it badly but luckily escaping injury himself.[19] The desert was not the only danger—flying Tac/R was very dangerous work. It was often done at low level and in straight lines to make observation easier. This also made the Hurricanes easy targets for Italian or German fighters or ground defences. Pilots would make notes on a pad on their knee as they flew and this would be the basis for what they reported when (or if) they returned to base.[20]

The next few days saw reconnaissance sorties flown and these were able to report on the ground situation, but photographic reconnaissance of Tobruk was only successful on the third attempt, the first two being hampered by poor visibility over the target area. On 8 July, PO Whalley was hit by heavy flak over Halfaya Pass (known as Hellfire Pass) and managed to nurse his damaged Hurricane to the front line where he crash-landed and was able to escape uninjured, though the plane was later destroyed by Allied troops due to its proximity to the enemy.[21]

On 10 July, the first three Australian pilots arrived for duties with 451 Squadron. They were POs W.D. Hutley (Service No. 402358), E.E. Kirkham (Service No. 402365) and R.T. Hudson (Service No. 402356). Walter Dean Hutley was a bank officer from South Australia who had enlisted on 19 August 1940 and undertaken his flying in Rhodesia (now Zimbabwe) on Tiger Moths at 25 EFTS (Elementary Flying Training School) Belvedere and Harvards at 20 SFTS (Service Flying Training School) Cranborne. He then travelled to 71 OTU (Operational Training Unit) at Ismailia in Egypt to complete his training on Hurricanes before being posted to 451 Squadron.[22] Edgar Exley Kirkham was a newsagent in Mildura, Victoria, and Ray Trevor Hudson was a salesman from Five Dock, NSW—they signed up on the same day as Hutley, and also trained in Rhodesia before being posted to 451 Squadron.[23]

Reconnaissance sorties continued, results in the area of Capuzzo causing great interest at higher levels, with much attention also being paid to Sollum on the coast and Halfaya Pass, some sorties being directed to fly as low as 40 ft to locate enemy command units. Ed Kirkham, Walter Hutley and Ray Hudson all flew in the first week of their posting at 451, Kirkham force-landing on his first sortie when he ran out of fuel. Visual and photographic sorties filled the remainder of the month and, despite some damage inflicted by flak, all pilots returned safely. During this time Flt Lt Byers arrived from 71 OTU. While flying took up some of the time spent by the squadron, much time was also dedicated to improving the living conditions at their airfield, including acquiring new utensils and fly-proofing the messes (eating areas). The squadron record mentions 'a drastic campaign being waged against fleas and flies'.[24]

August 1941 started as July had ended: reconnaissance of Tobruk, Bardia, Capuzzo, Sollum and Sidi Omar being the priorities. Pilots noted huts, tents, MET, and AFVs (armoured fighting vehicles—tanks and self-propelled guns), some concealed in wadis and others in the open. More pilots were posted in from 71 OTU and commenced operations shortly after arriving.[25] One such arrival was RAF pilot Flying Officer (FO) Geoffrey Morley-Mower. Not content flying biplanes with 5 Squadron in India, Morley-Mower applied for a transfer to the Middle East, hoping for a fighter squadron. He was accepted by Middle East Command, and sent to an OTU where he did his transition from Westland Wapitis to Miles Magisters and then Hurricanes. With just 4½ hours' flying experience on Hurricanes he was sent to 451 Squadron, which was definitely not a fighter squadron, and with the warning that the Australians were a 'tough crowd'. With visions in his mind of the tough and brave Australians at Gallipoli that his father had told him about, the very British Morley-Mower arrived with the gift of a new Hurricane. He was met by Flt Lt Williams who advised him that the RAF was 'not popular in these parts'. He wasn't partnered up with anyone nor made to feel welcome in any special way and so made his home in a tent of his own. One night, on the way back to his tent after using the trench dugout as a toilet, he overheard two Australians speaking in a tent:

> 'Did you see "M squared" with his book of poems? I reckon all the poms are queer.'

The other voice replied: 'Just our luck to miss being with Killer Caldwell and ending up with a bunch of fairy poms who don't know how to fight.'

Yes, the Australians were a tough crowd. To show the Australians that, despite his book of poetry, he was not a 'fairy pom', M-squared (Morley-Mower) decided that he'd fly twice as often as anyone else.[26]

With Tobruk under siege by the Axis forces, it was very difficult to get stores and information to the defenders. However, Sqn Ldr Pope dropped a message and photos to assist the defenders on a landing ground inside the perimeter, crossing the coast at just 1,000 ft with his wheels down to ensure the package hit its target.

On 9 August the elements of the squadron based at the OLG were visited by Air Chief Marshal Sir Edgar Ludlow-Hewitt,[27] and Morley-Mower went for his first escort of a Tac/R sortie. While the squadron records have him escorting Flt Lt Williams, in his own version of events, Morley-Mower describes flying with Flt Lt Malone on this date. Either way, as escort, it was Morley-Mower's role to keep an eye out for fighters while the other pilot took notes of numbers of vehicles, convoys, gun positions or anything else that might be of interest to the ground troops. The information was not transmitted during flight but, upon landing, handed in person to the Army ALO (Air Liaison Officer) on duty with the squadron who would then pass it on to the army for their use and dissemination. To carry out this important work, no cameras were used—it was all visual—and pilots had a notepad strapped to one leg upon which they'd make notes. So, from time to time their head would be down looking at their notes rather than at the sky around them, and this was just one reason why they had an escort.

Morley-Mower recalled on this first escort, while the other pilot flew straight and level through flak so as to make accurate records and visual observations, he was doing no such thing and evaded to the best of his ability, virtually abandoning the other pilot on what he thought was a suicide mission. He eventually reformed with the pilot who apparently hadn't noticed him going missing, and when they landed told him in no uncertain terms that he would never fly with him again. Assuming that the Morley-Mower version is correct and the pilot was Malone, there was no bad blood between them,

Malone simply knew what he had to do and how to do it, and paid little attention to the German (or Italian) efforts to stop him. Malone had the attitude that there was a war on, you did your job, and you did it properly.[28]

On 10 August, Flt Lt Malone and PO Hudson spotted and attacked a Luftwaffe Henschel Hs-126 high-winged reconnaissance plane when about ten miles nor-northwest of Fort Maddalena. When coming down to attack from about 3,000 ft the Hurricanes were sighted by the Germans and the Henschel landed. The crew got out and made a run for it as the plane exploded under Hudson's first burst, which hit the fuel tank. The German aircraft was destroyed and at least two of the three occupants were thought to be dead or wounded.[29]

Another photo drop was made to Tobruk on 12 August using the same successful method of just days before, coming in over the coast. A large effort was put in on 16 August with supporting Hurricane squadrons watching enemy landing grounds while three reconnaissance sorties were flown, with many enemy tents and vehicles being located. On 20 August, Sqn Ldr Pope departed the squadron to take up temporary command of 253 Wing and Flt Lt Beavis took over in his absence. 21 August saw the squadron practise their army cooperation skills, directing an artillery shoot with a battery of Australian 25 pounders and more were carried out the next day. Two more pilots arrived on 25 August, Flight Sergeants L.M. Readett (Service No. 402557) and H.R. Rowlands (Service No. 402404).[30] Leslie Miller Readett was an 18-year-old clerk when he enlisted in Sydney on 16 September 1940. Like many of the early war pilots he trained in Rhodesia at Belvedere and Cranborne before arriving at 71 OTU to learn how to fly Hurricanes. He spent just one week at 6 Squadron before being posted to 451. Harold Rowland Rowlands, a Welshman from Rockdale in Sydney, NSW, was working as a clerk when he enlisted on 19 August, leaving Sydney by ship on 4 November 1940 and arriving in South Africa on 4 December. Rhodesia was also his training ground and he was posted in with Leslie Readett, also having just spent a week with 6 Squadron.[31]

Wing Cdr (Wing Commander) Duncan (RAAF) visited both the OLG and BLG towards the end of the month to check on staff and conditions. Further improvements were made to the base facilities in the month, including the installation of an air raid siren, the laying of some concrete floors, construction of some dugouts and dispersing the various tents. A beach camp was established for those on rest or convalescing.[32]

September 1941 started with the return of Sqn Ldr Pope and the promotion of some pilots and the transfer in and out of others. Photo and tactical (visual) reconnaissance sorties continued, often more than one a day, and on 3 September Readett was attacked by three Bf 109s while escorting PO Charles Edmondson on a reconnaissance of the Sollum area.[33] The two Hurricanes were attacked from almost directly above by one Messerschmitt. Edmondson called a warning when he spotted the shadow of this aircraft on the ground below them whilst looking for enemy positions and vehicles, and they both dived for Sollum, though did not have much chance to gain speed as they were at only 3,000 ft when the enemy was spotted. Two more Messerschmitts joined the battle, and Edmondson engaged these while Readett went after the first. Edmondson had to break off his engagement when his guns jammed after the first burst. He called 'Break away' over the R/T a number of times and headed for the coast in a dive. Seeing two of the Messerschmitts behind him, he pushed the throttle through the gate and got away as fast as he could. He looked back shortly after and saw the Messerschmitts circling a position in the desert. Edmondson flew low along the coast until he found Sidi Barrani then found the ALG and made his report.

Rumours later made it back to Readett's family that he had been made prisoner, and they wrote asking for confirmation of this but this was denied by the Germans, who stated that he was dead. This was not taken to be official and he was listed as 'missing believed killed'. It was not until June 1942 that absolute confirmation of his death was received, when the International Red Cross informed the relevant authorities that German forces had buried a pilot at the airfield located in the Sollum area on the day Readett had been shot down and had retrieved a wristwatch from the body engraved with his name.[34]

On 13 September, Flt Lt Byers and PO Hutley were going to be deployed to Tobruk and had stopped for fuel at Sidi Barrani where they were given orders to carry out a reconnaissance of some Luftwaffe forward landings grounds. Byers took off as scheduled but Hutley had engine trouble and took off ten minutes later. They did not meet up and it was later learned that Byers was shot down and taken prisoner. He was one of many to have fallen under the guns of Hans-Joachim Marseille, the German ace. Though Byers survived the crash, he was wounded and later died as a result of these wounds while in captivity.[35] The details of this became known to the squadron when two low-flying Messerschmitts roared over the landing ground and dropped a note, which may well have been lost had the anti-aircraft guns around the airfield managed to shoot the Germans down before it was dropped. The note reported the shooting down and capture of Byers, and the Messerschmitts returned a few days later with the report of his death. Again, neither of the two German planes was shot down. There was no agreement between the two forces that such things should or could occur; the Germans simply took the risk to pass the message on, much as had been done in the First World War.[36]

In response to German assaults around Tobruk, more sorties were called for and many were flown on 14 September, often spotting 200–300 enemy vehicles on the move. During one of these sorties Hutley and Rowlands were attacked by six Bf 109s of JG27. Fortunately Hutley was able to make a wheels-up forced landing near Allied troops and was picked up by an armoured car, while Rowlands, though shot in the leg, made it back to the ALG (Advanced Landing Ground).[37] On 17 September, Flt Lt Williams and FO Morley-Mower were detached from the squadron to operate from within the Tobruk perimeter, but in the end only Morley-Mower went. He saw it as an opportunity to show the Australians he was up to the job and was offered a Miles Magister for the role. He refused it, because it was just too slow and would make a very easy target, though it would need less room to take off. So, in a Hurricane, he departed for Tobruk, heading out to sea and then coming in to land on the short strip, before being concealed in the camouflaged hangar. During his three weeks there he met General Morshead who said that when not performing Tac/R sorties he'd like him to spot for the artillery. Aerial spotting should use less ammunition and have a better line of sight than posts within the perimeter. In the end he only flew four times, and spotted for artillery just the once, but with good results.[38]

Outside Tobruk, with the rest of the squadron, the ground crew were working hard to keep the number of serviceable aircraft at a maximum—the extra workload had pushed aircraft to their service-due requirements (engine flying hours) ahead of schedule and damage to aircraft meant extra work to get them back in action. On 25 September, the maintenance and administration of the squadron moved from the BLG to an area adjacent to the

OLG where the planes actually flew from. The journey took most of the day.[39]

Around this time the squadron started to receive escorts from 33 Squadron RAF. The escorts of 25 and 26 September were two fighters and one reconnaissance aircraft from 451 Squadron.. On 27 September, Sqn Ldr Pope took A Flight with him to ALG 75 near Bir Mellor to operate more closely with Allied front-line troops. Ground crew left the same day to enable servicing to take place in this forward location. From this date, six aircraft from 33 Squadron operated with 451, in escorts of 'fluid pairs'. However, on 27 September, both FO Graeme-Evans and his escort of one Hurricane from 33 Squadron failed to return and both were listed as missing. Both had been shot down by JG27, and while Graeme-Evans survived, the pilot from 33 Squadron, PO Lowther, did not. It was thought that Lowther may have managed to shoot down a Bf 109 before being killed, but this was not the case: the Germans suffered no losses.[40]

On 29 September, rumblings heard by the army in the front-line area resulted in an emergency recce (reconnaissance) by two aircraft of 451, the fear being that tanks were moving about and possibly preparing for an attack in the vicinity of Capuzzo and Sollum. It was discovered that there was nothing to fear, as the rumbling was explosions from the Allied bombing of Bardia.[41]

At the start of October, Tobruk had been under siege for more than six months. On 6 October, Sgt Neville Guy wrote in his diary: 'Told to pack, we are moving to within 25 k's of the front line.'[42] Reconnaissance (tactical and photographic) sorties with escorts by 33 Squadron continued through the early weeks of October, with the whole squadron moving to ALG 75 on the 10th, pilots maintaining their sortie rate while the ground crew and administrative sections moved everything in a single day. Flt Lt Malone failed to return from an early Tac/R and a later sortie spotted a burning aircraft on the ground with black smoke rising from it, and they thought that this may be his aircraft, downed by flak. They were mistaken though; he'd actually been shot down and killed by a Bf 109 of the ever-present JG27.[43] This was a hard blow for Morley-Mower. A fellow RAF pilot had been killed and while Malone hadn't expressed any ill feelings since their first sortie together and the blow-up after it, they'd never really made up.[44]

Springbett and Ferguson were replaced in Tobruk by Kirkham and Hudson. On 20 October, Sqn Ldr Pope left the squadron for a posting at RAF HQ

Middle East. He was replaced from within the squadron by Sqn Ldr R.D. Williams, and seven South African Air Force (SAAF) pilots were attached from 40 (SAAF) Squadron for escort duties.[45] Their leader was Captain G.M.S Gardner. All the South Africans had operational experience in East Africa and Abyssinia, but in North Africa the intensity was much higher. Murray Gardner had learned to fly before the war, and was hooked from his first flight. Like much of the war in North Africa at the time it was a case of making best use (a sometimes questionable definition) of what was available, so he and his fellow South Africans drove across the desert in a truck with their sidearms and personal belongings to find 451 Squadron and their Hurricanes, though they'd never flown one. They drove all the way from Cairo, where young boys had offered them their 'very hygienic' sisters,[46] but there'd be none of that way out in the desert. Arriving at the airfield, Gardner described it as 'just a bit of desert that nobody else was using'.[47] With a new offensive in the offing there was no time to lose, so each of the South Africans had a very generous two hours on the Hurricane, plus a circular flight before they were declared ready for operations.[48]

One of the seconded pilots was lost on the 23rd when two (Lt J. Thomas and Lt J. Smith) went up on a practice flight and found themselves in enemy territory. Lt Thomas force-landed behind enemy lines due to lack of fuel and Lt Smith returned safely.[49] This is a very simple version of events provided by the squadron records, but there is much more to tell. The two pilots had been bounced by some Bf 109s and had to make a run for it, Smith going one way and Thomas another. Though he was fired on, Thomas's plane was not hit, but when he checked his compass, he found himself flying west instead of east. Perhaps running low on fuel, the Messerschmitts turned and left him alone, and he had to find a place to put the plane down as he too was running out of fuel. This he did safely and without damaging it. He was found by the 11th Hussars, a British unit that patrolled the frontier and often penetrated behind enemy lines. Morley-Mower and some ground crew, with tools for repairs and fuel for the Hurricane, went with the Hussars, crossing the front line during the night to rescue Thomas. They found him in the morning. After inspecting the plane for damage and refuelling it, Morley-Mower took off and flew it back—despite Thomas's protests that he was fit to fly. Thomas and the ground crew returned with the Hussars.[50]

On 26 October, Captain Gardner had his first operational sortie, a photo-reconnaissance of Bardia, Sollum and Halfaya Pass from 18,000 ft. It went well enough and was the first time he'd used oxygen in flight. He returned safely with mind, plane and footage intact. On a later occasion when getting to know the Hurricane in a practice dogfight with Ray Hudson, Gardner attempted to get on his tail but Hudson rolled his Hurricane over and went into a vertical dive and got away from him. While this meant that he had 'won' the fight with Gardner, it didn't teach Gardner anything and gave him no practice. Hurricane dogfighting was about the turning battle; any Hurricane that tried to get away from a Bf 109 by diving was doing the German a favour: the Hurricane could not out-dive a 109, and they'd be shot down in short order.[51]

Mid-October to mid-November saw a build-up to Operation *Crusader*, the attempt to clear the Axis forces out of Cyrenaica and Tripolitania to secure the left flank of the Middle East, in case the Germans broke through the Caucasus. It was also the opportunity for the Tobruk garrison to break out and meet up with the advancing Allied troops. The role of 451 Squadron was to locate any and all enemy forces and report on their position and deployment, as well as traffic on roads and in Axis-held ports. As enemy forces were located, the details were passed on up through the chain of command so targets could be allocated for airstrikes and operational plans amended if required.[52]

This period also saw the arrival of some RAF pilots, two of whom were very bad for morale. In his memoirs, Morley-Mower gives them aliases, 'Whitlock' and 'Dawlish' and perhaps the loss of records during the retreat in late October has concealed their names further. These two were seen by fellow RAF pilot Morley-Mower as cowards and a disgrace, and he even went as far as to approach Sqn Ldr Williams and the medical officer about it in order to have them removed. Morley-Mower had been acutely aware of the RAAF–RAF issues within the squadron when he arrived and had been doing his utmost to show that RAF pilots were working just as hard as the Australians. He knew at least some of the Australians were sick of these two pilots as well when he overheard two Australians talking; one asked, 'You flying today?' and the other replied, 'Nah! I'm going on sick parade with the poms.' At this comment the first laughed, the respect that Morley-Mower and other RAF pilots had been earning was being rapidly eroded.

On another occasion he caught one of these RAF pilots telling a group of assembled Australians how everything the Germans had and did was superior to the Allies, and in front of the group Morley-Mower cursed him to his face, yelling, 'You talk a lot of bullshit. You don't make anyone's job easier by moaning and groaning about dead men. Shut up, for Christ's sake!' He had started to walk off but turned and finished with, 'It'll take a fucking good Jerry to shoot me down.' He plainly hated the two RAF pilots and didn't want them undoing the work he had laid down, nor bringing down the squadron as a whole. When one of these two finally got in a plane to go on a sortie (avoiding sorties was one of their particular skills), he crashed on take-off. Morley-Mower was so incensed he drew his sidearm in front of Sqn Ldr Williams and threatened to 'shoot him like a dog' for deliberately wrecking a plane so he'd not have to fly.[53] But lest anyone think that Morley-Mower was somehow biased against his fellow Brits, Captain Gardner, who held Morley-Mower in high regard, also noted that of the senior British pilots in the squadron at the time 'none ... seemed to do any flying'.[54] Both eventually left the squadron and their fate is unknown.

Another relative unknown is exactly what duties two members of the ground crew got up to when they left the squadron in November. Harry Riley and Arthur Rowe left the squadron together, for 'special duties with Intelligence'[55] and went to the Long Range Desert Group (LRDG), a unit of specialist desert raiding and reconnaissance troops, most of whom were New Zealanders. Apparently only with the LRDG for a short time, it is reported that they participated in these raids but the exact details are not known.[56]

November continued in the way of October, with the pilots of 451 often being escorted on their sorties by the attached South Africans. Neville Guy wrote in his diary:

> We got word to go to LG 75 at 45 miles south of Sidi Barrani ... One plane had a lot to be done, so Taxi, Bert, Rowe, Read and me are being cast off ... FUKA next drome to us had 100 bombs dropped on them, knocked out 6 Hurricanes and a lot of other damage.[57]

On 10 November, FO Walford set off in a Lysander on a special sortie 70 miles west-south-west of Fort Maddalena and found the crew of a Flying Fortress. PO Whalley and Lt Thomas (SAAF) failed to return from their sortie on 12 November and were listed as missing.[58] The battle was coming and, on 13 November, Neville Guy wrote, 'Told to send nearly all our gear to stores at Aboukir, as we will be moving about 80 miles per day.'[59]

On 14 November, the arrangements for the forthcoming battle were set, and 451 Squadron was attached to the Headquarters of XIII Corps.[60] On 16/17 November the squadron advanced to LG 131 and then LG 132 on the 18th, to keep up with the advance, but they were attacked on the ground on 19 November: Axis aircraft strafed the landing ground, damaging three aircraft and wounding three members of the squadron.[61] The landing ground was reinforced on the 20th with the attachment of one flight from 237 (Rhodesia) Squadron. Whilst on a Tac/R that morning, Morley-Mower, being covered by Ron Achilles, used the cloud cover to good advantage, seeking out German formations on the move. They found two Axis airfields and, while over the second, Morley-Mower spotted three Messerschmitts above them. On the call of 'Fighters!' he dived for the ground and opened the throttle up, and Achilles headed east, back to base. Morley-Mower hoped they hadn't been seen, and running was the first natural option for reconnaissance aircraft, even more so in old Hurricanes. Morley-Mower didn't have enough time or power to reach cloud cover safely so he stayed low. He swerved gently from side to side to keep the Messerschmitts in sight before making a steep turn, wings almost vertical. Doing this at such a low level was dangerous business; if he lost lift and went into a high-speed stall (due to the vertical nature of the wings compared to the horizontal wing in regular flight) then he'd go into the ground and that would be it. He knew, however, that the Hurricane could take it, while the Messerschmitt could not. When he felt a slight shudder in the airframe, he backed off the turn a little, in case it was the plane warning him of an impending stall. The Germans came at him one by one, and the first two both took shots at him but missed, unable to get inside his turn for the deflection shot needed. But the second pilot couldn't hold the turn and went crashing into the ground and exploded. Morley-Mower searched around for the next attack and saw the remining two Messerschmitts above him, headed west, so he eased out of the turn and headed for cloud and home.[62]

On return from a sortie on 21 November, another South African was lost when Lt Smith crashed in flames, just a few miles short of the landing ground. His body was recovered and he was later buried and given a proper farewell.

Smith had warned his fellow pilot Campbell not to fly the Morley-Mower 'yo-yo' method of constantly dodging invisible obstacles, nor to dive down too low to get a look at enemy positions due to the high volume of small-calibre anti-aircraft fire. But Campbell had done this on the return leg, diving down to get a look at a position near the frontier wire and, as his cover, Smith was obliged to follow, and this is where he was hit by anti-aircraft fire.[63]

On 23 November, a party left the squadron for Gasr el Arid which was to be the new ALG, and they were followed by Flt Lt Carmichael with another group to prepare the landing ground for use. Four aircraft led by Sqn Ldr Williams took off the next morning for this new base and were met by anti-aircraft fire so they returned to base. He and another pilot tried again later in the afternoon and found it unoccupied, so they landed near XIII Corps headquarters to try and find out what was going on. There they found Carmichael's group, and the squadron assumed the first detachment had been captured. They were right: the army liaison officer, and his codes were 'in the bag', a major coup for the enemy. As a result of the Axis advances, the squadron and attachments moved to LG 128 at Sidi Azeiz, but the administrative elements of the squadron didn't stay long, moving back to LG 75 on the 25th.[64]

Neville Guy kept up his diary, recording on 24 November:

> We passed into LIBYA, we got to our drome at 1600 and told to refuel and be ready to move back at a moment's notice. Jerry tanks have broken through. We watched the tank battles rage 10 to 15 miles away, flares everywhere and at 1730 we were told to move back to LG75.[65]

They did move, and he wrote on the 26th:

> Told that Jerry was only 4 miles off us when we pulled out. Out of his 30 tanks that broke through, 10 have been destroyed, so far, our ALG and OLG are safe in their new positions. We will move up soon, we are on 5 minutes' notice.[66]

Sidi Azeiz was approached by an enemy formation on 26 November, and a number of the squadron retreated in the early morning darkness. PO Maslen remained in the area until first light to report on the enemy, dropping his handwritten report to the 5th New Zealand Brigade. Sidi Azeiz was attacked in strength on the following day and 16 personnel including pilots and photographic interpretation staff were captured, and one killed. This was Corporal Tom Farr, an RAF member of the ground crew, who was said to have been killed whilst firing a machine gun at the assaulting German infantry.

By the end of the month, the squadron and attachments had settled at LG 128. Many of the squadron records were lost, either captured by the Germans or destroyed by the unit when their capture was imminent, on 23 November.[67]

December started with a large number of sorties to keep an eye on Axis movements. Neville Guy wrote, 'Our advance party left for TOBRUK, we are now on ½ a water bottle per day, not much in this heat.'[68] An artillery reconnaissance on 3 December was carried out successfully by Flt Lt Ferguson liaising with 144 Field Regiment and directing their fire on two enemy gun positions while Flt Lt Morley-Mower gave cover. Sqn Ldr Williams was so impressed by the work of his squadron that he wrote to his wing commander for advice on how to proceed: 'I find difficulty in committing to paper the excellence of the work done by pilots of this Squadron. Many of them are doing a very sound job but "highlights" are rare and in comparison with citations I have seen for bomber and fighter pilots, ours are apt to appear rather lame.'[69] Evidently he received good advice and a number of recommendations for DFCs (Distinguished Flying Crosses) and MiDs (mentioned in dispatches) were submitted, and the majority of them were awarded over the following months.[70]

During the first week of December Captain Gardner was on deployment to Tobruk and flew some message sorties and did some artillery spotting for the garrison. On a return flight one morning he noticed a Wellington bomber crashed on the runway and was careful to avoid it. When he mentioned it to the ground crew one replied that he had been most concerned in the morning when Gardner had taken off and nearly hit it. Gardner hadn't seen it at all.[71]

On 6 December, Sgt Ken Watts arrived. Walter Kenneth Watts (Service No. 400827) was born on 10 August 1915 and was working as a butcher in his father's butcher's shop when war was declared on 3 September 1939. He signed up for the RAAF as soon as he could, not because he was a patriot, but because he was an adventurer, and he later wrote that the thought of danger and death lying in wait for him 'never entered my mind'. He was put on No. 9 Course at Somers in Victoria, where the basics of air force life and aviation theory were introduced. In February 1942, he was posted to 3 EFTS Essendon, Victoria, where he learned that he certainly enjoyed flying, but hated to have passengers; he was quite happy just being responsible for his own welfare. By April he was at 2 STFS Wagga Wagga in New South Wales where he flew the Wirraway, and on 13 June, the course lost four trainee pilots when they flew into a hill in bad weather: all gone long before they had a chance to fight. By October he was at 74 OTU in the Middle East, having been shipped over from Australia via Adelaide, Fremantle, Trincomalee and the Suez on the *Queen Elizabeth*. There he had a few short flights in a Miles Magister before taking his first flight in a Hurricane—the one he flew straight to 451 Squadron.[72]

On 8 December the landing ground was attacked, and Neville Guy recorded:

> We got word to move to Tobruk tomorrow. At 1250 Jerry came over, 8 JU88's dropped bombs and just missed us and landed on 237 mess, 4 killed and 8 seriously wounded, about 20 other kites, ME 110s and ME 109s came in behind and strafed us, we were lucky to get off scot free, but 237 were unlucky ... our move is off owing to damage at Tobruk.[73]

Charles Dunger, a ground crew flight mechanic later wrote of this same attack, 'We were all very upset to see one of the 109s shoot down an RAAF Ambulance plane a little further west, it was well marked with red crosses.'[74] The aircraft shot down was a D.H. 86 of 1 Air Ambulance Unit, RAAF, and the attackers were Bf 110s of ZG26. Five of them had formed up behind the slow biplane at a range claimed to be 150 yards, surely close enough for one of them to see the red cross and warn the remainder not to fire, but the Germans shot it down. By some miracle, all the crew survived.[75]

On 9 December, the squadron moved into Tobruk, with all elements in place by the 11th. The enemy had failed to prevent Operation *Crusader* from relieving Tobruk and lifting the siege, and the front moved westwards as Rommel's troops retreated in an orderly manner. The squadron was then directed to focus their efforts in the Gazala area, about 35 miles west of Tobruk. As the battle spread through the desert south of Tobruk, the squadron was directed to other locations, the short range of the Hurricane necessitating the regular moves.[76]

On 12 December, Captain Gardner was flying cover for Lt Campbell from Tobruk when they spotted dust rising from a known Luftwaffe aerodrome. They flew down to the dust, noticing two German aircraft taking off, and Gardner lost sight of them in the dust but found one after he'd turned away from the airfield. As the German plane levelled off, he made an attack from the side to avoid the most heavily armoured parts of the plane, and gave it a three-second burst. It had the desired effect and the plane slowed down and appeared to move and seek out a place to land, but having been on the receiving end of a strafing run at 451 Squadron's airfield shortly before, he wasn't going to give this pilot any chance to get away and attacked again, seeing the plane burst into flames. Campbell was nowhere to be seen; he'd lost sight of Gardner in the attack and, with German fighters about, he'd headed back to Tobruk without delay. Gardner returned safely to Tobruk, submitted his claim of one enemy aircraft shot down and was promptly informed that such activity was 'not the job of Tac R aircraft'.[77]

On 17 December, the squadron set off for LG 131, leaving behind B Flight and a few ground crew to operate from Tobruk. They arrived on the following day and were in operation immediately, performing reconnaissance of battle areas and out to Bardia and over the coast, a submarine being sighted on one occasion. The squadron was moved again, their location dictated by the fluidity of desert warfare, and this time found themselves back at Sidi Aziez, all staff and equipment operating from there from 24 December onwards, now attached to XXX Corps, and with a message of thanks from XIII Corps on their departure.

Many artillery reconnaissance sorties were flown in the Bardia area during the last week of the month—enemy artillery were often the target, though ships in the harbour were also engaged by artillery under 451's direction.[78] On the 19th, Murray Gardner was given the job of finding a submarine (for the army!) reported to be near Bardia. No Fleet Air Arm or Coastal Command aircraft were available (so he was told) so naturally a Hurricane from an army cooperation squadron was the next choice. With weather reported as misty and poor, he took off to the west and, when aligned with Bardia, flew north to the coast, as low and fast as he dared. Low so he could see where he was going, and fast so that if he happened to cross the path of any Italians or Germans he'd be gone before they could line him up for a shot. He crossed the coast, staying low, and through the mist roared a Ju 88 which nearly collided head-on with him. He opened his canopy for a better look at its next manoeuvre and lost his goggles and watch in the process, but it didn't turn on him and he wasn't there to fight it so he closed the canopy again and continued on his way. After a few passes by Bardia harbour he found the submarine hidden in a cove to the west of the town, well concealed, hooked up to hoses and probably unloading fuel for Rommel's tanks. The rifle-calibre machine guns of the Hurricane were not fit for the task of damaging the submarine enough to make it unseaworthy or sinking it, so he left it alone and flew east to find a safe place to cross the coast and return with his report. Something more substantial would have to be sent out to deal with the submarine.

Nearly running out of fuel, Gardner decided to land near a convoy he identified as belonging to the 'right side' to ask for a top up. He put the Hurricane down in a saltpan and fired off a flare to get their attention. Rather than come to his aid the trucks moved off at speed and left him alone. With only hope left he started up again and took off flying as carefully as he could to conserve fuel and made it back to LG 131 with nothing left, landing on the first pass; a second try was not an option.[79]

On 25 December Neville Guy wrote, 'Xmas Day. Camped 10 miles off Bardia, lots of graves here.' and followed the next day with, 'I found a forage cap of one of our fellows taken prisoner here, his number is in it so we are going to check up on it. One of those missing is Don Bailey, he is the next Number to me 6719, I am 6720.'[80] Ted Hirst (Service No. 11586) also made an entry in his diary on Christmas day 1941: 'Three bottles of beer per man, Canadian Black and White Horse, wow, had a kick in every hoof.'[81]

Meanwhile, contradictory command messages arrived from Australia. An instruction, attributed to AVM (Air Vice-Marshal) Bostock, Deputy Chief of Air Staff, RAAF, directed that 450 and 451 Squadrons 'do not themselves form part of the Royal Australian Air Force ... for all practical purposes they should be regarded as R.A.F. squadrons in every way'. The instruction was distributed and caused dissatisfaction amongst the ground crew and aircrew when they were informed. The Air Ministry then countered with a dissemination of their own, 'Cancelling order must therefore make it clear that these are, repeat are, Australian Air Force squadrons.' Administrative arguments followed at higher levels and were not resolved until February 1943, when 451 Squadron's non-compliance with certain administrative and maintenance tasks came to a head and the instruction 'for the purposes of accounting administration No. 451 Squadron should be treated in exactly the same way as an R.A.F. squadron' was issued.[82]

The New Year came and went, and the battles below raged on. Bardia had the squadron's attention for 1 January 1942 and, on the 2nd, the squadron recorded, 'Prisoners being marched in all directions.' Bardia fell that day.[83]

With the fall of Bardia came the release of many Allied prisoners of war—including some of those from 451 who had been captured on 27 November. The three officers who were captured with the group had been taken away to Italy, but the remainder had stayed in Bardia, with little food or water.[84] Neville Guy wrote:

> Bardia surrendered. Major General Schmidt came out to make negotiations, at 1000 hrs officially surrendered 4000 prisoners and 1100 of our own, including our own squadron members. F/L Carmichael was taken to Italy by sub, Cpl Farr was killed. Our boys had their 1st tin of bully beef for 5 weeks, have been poorly fed. One fellow, Cpl Taylor collapsed from weakness, our C/O reported that Bardia would not have fallen only for our squadron. Army officers have been sending us congratulations all along. Major General Schmidt taken away under escort from our drome and General Freyberg went away in a Blenheim. Our planes were congratulated on their performance at the critical time.[85]

Keith Taylor, a transport driver with 451 Squadron was one of those released, and wrote home about his experiences:

> It is with much joy and thanksgiving in my heart that I am able to sit down and write this letter to you. There is no doubt about it you must have had a terrible shock when the cable arrived telling you I was missing. I look back on it as a bad dream ...
>
> ...prior to my capture I was ground strafed at one place, then the

day before early in the morning, in one small ground action. Later in the morning I was shot at by some NZ boys who thought I was a Jerry with my peak cap on and riding a captured motor bike through the camp, lucky for me they were bad shots ... I had just rolled up my blankets at 0645 when the alarm sounded for us to be ready to move, but it had hardly sounded before the fun started and bullets were flying everywhere ... then for the next two hours, during which time we could only lay low and not fire a shot, (that is our own boys—the NZs whom we were with though put up a wonderful show) but we only being armed with rifles could not do anything against tanks, so in the end the NZs C/O gave the order to surrender, and at 0900 on 27/11/41 I was made a Prisoner of War by General Rommel's Panzer Division ...

While sitting round here after being searched was the first view I had of the great General, and that only for a moment as he followed his tanks on ... About 1 o'clock we were all rounded up and started to march and march till 9 o'clock with only a 5 minute stop every ¾ hour, eventually ending up in Bardia about 18 miles away ... we were all that done in we just lay down where we could and shivered ourselves to sleep ... No-one seemed despondent that our boys would be in at any time and have us well out by Xmas for nearly every day our bombers were over doing their job and we could hear the guns in the distance. Later as our food ration was cut down and we were told it was because they were cut off from all supplies and were on short rations themselves, it helped us keep our spirits up ...

About the 22nd, early in the morning, we saw a ship coming in and our spirits sank to zero, but then we saw it was a hospital ship so they rose once more. Then about lunch time they came and read out a list of 300 names to go on board. Darling you have no possible idea of my feelings when I heard my name called, they are impossible for me to write about, I felt as though my life had almost ceased for me ... the Captain of the ship and some high German officer had a pow-wow, then came along and asked us if we felt alright nearly everyone saying yes, and so the captain refused to take us as we were all fit men ...

> ... although we had German guards for the first week or so, they kept telling us they actually had nothing to do with us as we were really Italian prisoners and that if they had the feeling for us we would be treated much better and I really believe we would have been. Most of them could speak English and had no time for the Ities at all ...
> In the morning while lying in front of the tent wondering how we were going to fare for tucker as no rations had arrived, we heard the chap who was acting as interpreter for us come and call for silence, and to our joy and relief he told us that they had given up and that our troops would be in within an hour. My feelings at that moment are impossible to describe, I felt as though God had answered my prayers.[86]

Another prisoner to be released was Don Bailey, and he told a story to a reporter about meeting Rommel, which was published in the *Hobart Mercury* in February 1942. According to his version of events:

> Rommel can handle tanks all right. His own tank was always out in front everywhere. As soon as our guns ceased firing, he whizzed his tanks straight into the fort. He climbed out of the cockpit, and I recognised him at once. He fixed his monocle on his eye and gazed around triumphantly ... "Good morning boys," he said affably in perfect English.[87]

While Rommel was often up with his front-line troops, or even off on his own somewhere, he rarely, if ever, travelled about in a tank, so the story may have to be taken with a grain of salt. However, upon his return to the squadron, Bailey's story quickly spread and he soon became known as 'Shake the Hand Bailey', because to shake his hand, was to shake the hand that shook the hand of Rommel.[88] At least that's how the story went. Rommel's own records place him at the front of troops on the 24th, which may or may not have been a tank, and from late on the 24th he was using a captured British armoured truck, called a Mammoth.[89] Maybe Bailey met some other German officer—do they all look the same in uniform?

As the fighting moved on to Halfaya and Pt. 207, so did the artillery reconnaissance sorties, and fire was directed onto several gun positions over the next two weeks when weather permitted. Ken Watts flew one of these sorties on 8 January, directing the fire of an Allied artillery unit against Axis forces near Pt. 207.[90] On 10 January, Neville Guy wrote, 'No tea tonight, dust storm that bad, cooks couldn't see to cook.'[91] On 15 January, the squadron said farewell to the attached SAAF pilots of 40 (SAAF) Squadron who returned to their unit (Murray Gardner survived the war and retired in South Africa). The Axis forces in the Halfaya and Pt. 207 areas surrendered on the morning of 17 January and 5,500 prisoners were taken. The morning sortie was recalled and the squadron rested for a few days. On 21 January, five Hurricanes were taken to Tobruk and handed over to 238 Squadron.

On 24 January, the squadron moved to Heliopolis outside Cairo, Egypt. The Hurricanes flew via Fuka where they refuelled and the remainder travelled in convoy, arriving on the 27th. Heliopolis turned out to be a disappointment, because it wasn't Heliopolis after all. The town had large modern buildings with facilities, and 451 Squadron was ordered past that—back into the desert out of town. This caused a bit of trouble according to John Culbert:

> But we just drove past the thing another mile out in the desert and that's where we were. So we needed a wash, we'd been grimed up for ages. You were filthy, putting it mildly, and you stank...you smelled. You looked filthy, you felt filthy. So we went down to the barracks to get a shower and the RAF blokes said, "You're not coming in here, not like that. Well, that was another stoush went on. We had a fight to get in to get cleaned up. We took our clean stuff in with us and...we learnt that when you washed yourself you washed your clothes with you. You put them down and you stomp on them, you stomp all the dirt out and rinse them out and hang them out so you wasted no water. In the desert you got a pint a day. Without that pint there was so much went to transport, so much went to the aeroplanes, cook house, and you got the rest, would be a cup full a day, that was your ration. Cup full last you 24 hours. That's when times were hard.[92]

PO Maslen was awarded the DFC on 30 January for 'Courage, determination and devotion to duty'.[93]

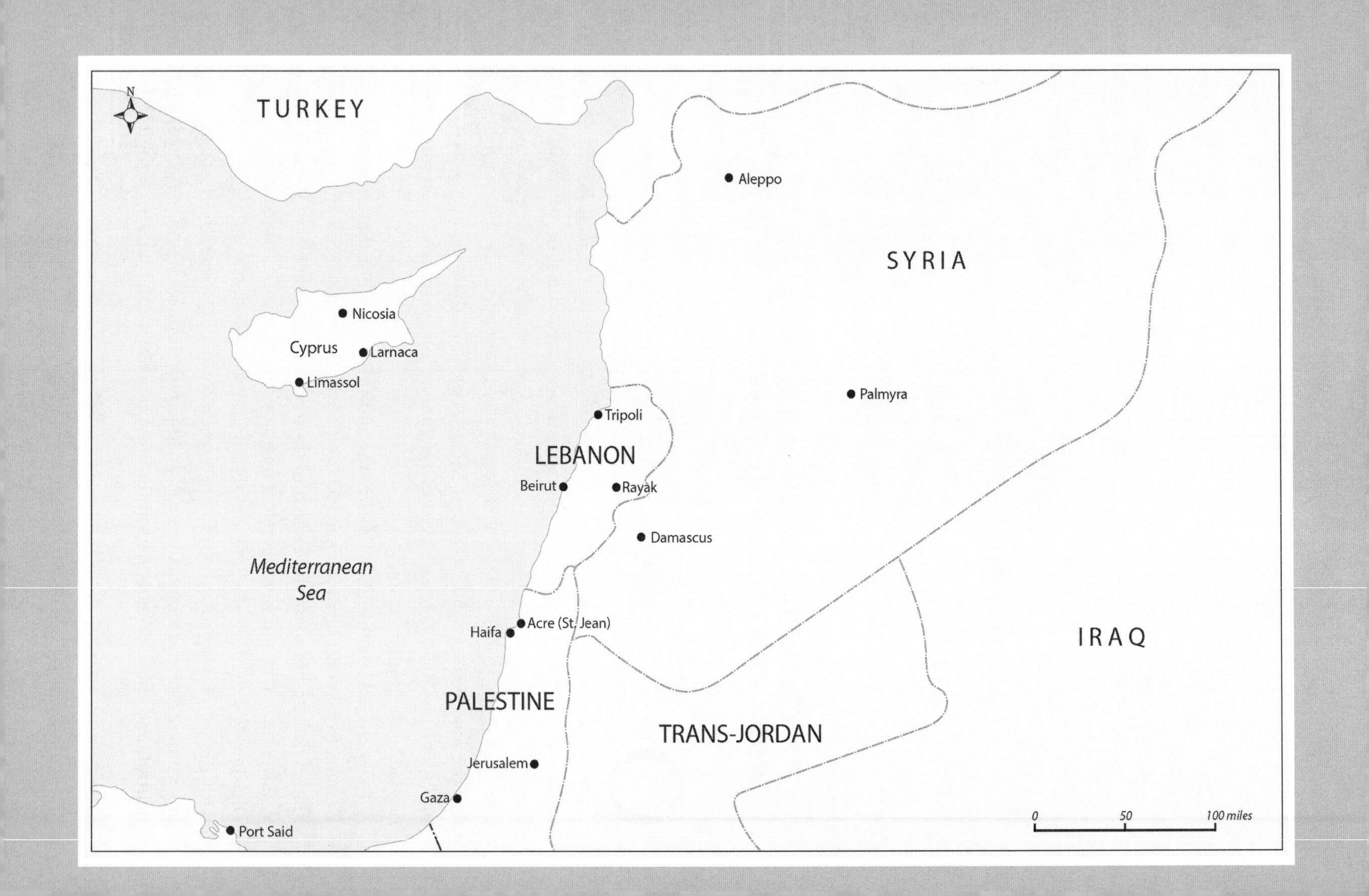
N
TURKEY
Aleppo
SYRIA
Nicosia
Cyprus
Larnaca
Limassol
Palmyra
Tripoli
LEBANON
Beirut
Rayak
Damascus
Mediterranean Sea
Acre (St. Jean)
Haifa
IRAQ
PALESTINE
TRANS-JORDAN
Jerusalem
Gaza
Port Said
0
50
100 miles

FRUSTRATIONS ON THE FRINGES OF WAR: FEBRUARY TO NOVEMBER 1942

On 1 February 1942, Air Marshal Williams visited 451 Squadron and spoke to the personnel regarding their welfare and administration. Ted Hirst wasn't impressed: 'Air Marshal Williams from RAAFHQ Cairo came out and had a talk to us, made no difference, we feel cheated.'[1] However, the question of 'where to next?' was answered when, on 5 February, Flt Lt Ferguson flew to Rayak in Lebanon to inspect facilities while everyone else took short periods of leave and focused on maintaining the Hurricanes and the squadron's ground transport.[2] 450 (RAAF) Squadron had been based in Rayak from mid to late 1941 and supported the invasion there but had since headed to the primary front.[3]

After the end of the First World War and the breakup of the Ottoman Empire, Syria and Lebanon changed from Turkish to French rule but, with France defeated in 1940, the French in those territories sided with the new Vichy government and were therefore hostile to the Allies. The 7th Australian Division, less the brigade defending Tobruk, was tasked with taking Syria, with the support of British and Free French forces. However, the Turkish government was not supportive of Allied operations in Syria and remained neutral, and the Germans had no interest there after the failure of their minor operations in Iraq. Seeing the assembling Allied forces south of the border, the Vichy French in Syria warned that a state of war would exist if the Allies attacked, since the German forces had ceased to use the airfields there and could no longer be used as an Allied justification for action. On 7 June 1941, the Vichy French were warned of Allied intentions and the invasion of Syria and Lebanon took place the next day. By midnight on 11/12 July, a ceasefire was in place, with the Allied forces victorious, and the French troops who surrendered were given the choice of joining the Free French forces or returning to Vichy in western Europe. Only 5,668 of 37,736 chose to join the Free French.[4]

Ferguson returned to the squadron on 7 February 1942, with his favourable report on Rayak (though one member of the squadron later described it as a dump)[5] and the next day the squadron received the warning order to move, with an advance party to leave on the 10th and the remainder of the squadron two days thereafter. It was at this point that Flt Lt Geoffrey Morley-Mower left 451 Squadron, posted to the Aircraft Delivery Unit. He took a Hurricane to India and was married on 7 March.[6] He survived the war and moved to the United States where he became a Professor of English and taught at a university. He had arrived ready to be impressed, and perhaps the behaviour of some RAF pilots made the Australians even more impressive in his eyes. He would later write of his fellow pilots:

> They got into the war as soon as they could and they were so successful that most of them commanded squadrons. When I first encountered them I was taken aback by their obvious excellence … in physique, morale and personal qualities. I already had a high expectation of Australian fighting men, but these boys were amazing.[7]

Ken Watts described Morley-Mower as a 'fine type of gentleman, tall and handsome', which (hopefully) was his honest opinion, and not just because Morley-Mower referred to him as a 'sexy hunk' in his own work![8]

The main body of the squadron travelled from Heliopolis via Ismailia, El Auja and Madera then Beirut, stopping for the night at each location before arriving at Rayak on the afternoon of 16 February.[9] Neville Guy wrote, on the 14th: 'Into PALESTINE, we skirted past GAZA No. 1 AGH. We passed through BEITJIRJA-CASA-GEDERA-RAMLEIGH-REHOVAH-HADERA, we camped in a gum forest for the night. The Jews put on a party, singing and dancing etc, quite good.' On the 15th: 'Passed through HAIFA-ACRE, over a hill into LEBANON, we camped near BEIRUT in a suburb near a racecourse.', and on the 16th: 'Left for RAYAK in Syria, a big airport with brick hangars and brick buildings and barracks, lots of French Airforce here and General De Gaulle.'[10] The aerodrome was about a kilometre from Rayak, which one member of the squadron thought was a shame, not because it was too far to walk, but the town was such a mess that if the aerodrome had been built on top of it everyone would have been better off, and there was very little grass around, one squadron member expressing it as 'the earth in that portion of the world grows little grass but has no trouble in growing rocks'.[11] Regardless, it was someone's home and, shortly after arriving, the Australians found there was trouble between two villages, both apparently being mixed Muslim and Christian communities. To assist in keeping the peace the villagers were separated and resettled, Christians in one and Muslins in the other. All with the help of some of the squadron's truck drivers, who, very unofficially, drove families back and forth, speeding up the resettlement process and earning a bit of money along the way. Some of the boys from the villages worked on the aerodrome in the kitchens and doing other basic jobs, so their families got preferential treatment when it came time to move house.[12]

The next day, the Hurricanes started to arrive, stopping for fuel along the way. A number of pilots were commissioned as officers in the next few days and Sqn Ldr Williams left to take command of 74 OTU, being replaced by Sqn Ldr Ferguson—promoted from within the squadron.[13]

28 February saw the squadron's first operational sortie at the new base, a photographic reconnaissance of the area around Tripoli (about 70 km north of Beirut) carried out by PO Edmondson.[14] While based in the area, the squadron was intended to be used in support of the Ninth Army should the Germans break though the Caucasus and head south to attack the defences of the Suez Canal from the rear.[15] Fortunately, for many reasons, that didn't eventuate.

On 1 March, pilots Springbett, Walford, Robertson and Watts flew from Rayak to Cyprus for temporary deployment there, with a detachment of ground crew following. Part of their role was to be seen by the enemy who would hopefully report the presence of a fighter squadron on Cyprus and curtail their operations accordingly.[16] Though Rayak was a good enough base,

Watts wasn't impressed with the work (nor were many others) and was quite happy to go to Cyprus. He wrote, 'Nicosia is an impressive place, perfumed with Mediterranean jasmine ...'[17] Leonard Hayman was a member of the ground crew who accompanied the detachment to Cyprus and he was a little less complimentary, describing it as 'the hottest place on earth I think. Everything was white. The cliffs, the beach and the only relief was the swimming pool in Nicosia ...'[18]

On 2 March, Rayak was visited by General Catroux, who presented medals to the Lorraine Free French Squadron also based there. Catroux was definitely a name to remember for the squadron: he was de Gaulle's deputy in the Middle East and strongly opposed to the Vichy regime.[19] The following week consisted of photographic sorties looking for suitable satellite landing grounds both in Syria and Cyprus, dogfighting practice, artillery spotting practice and Tac/R practice. The squadron was now a long way from the areas of major action, and ten-day leave passes were organised. During the deployment to Lebanon and Syria, aircraft were sometimes temporarily based at Aleppo, about 300 km north of Rayak.

From 16 to 19 March, the squadron was required, by an order from 213 Group, to conduct 'Showing the Flag' operations over Palmyra, Deir ez-Zor and Aleppo, so seven pilots were temporarily detached to Aleppo for these duties. The squadron also carried out several cooperative exercises with various anti-aircraft units based in the area, so they could practise detecting and tracking aircraft.[20] March also saw a number of staff charged with the loss of their rifles, most likely stolen by locals (and perhaps also used in later fighting between Jewish settlers and the British post-war occupation forces or Arabs). The cost of a rifle was assessed as £6.15s.9d and each member of the ground crew was fined £2 in addition to being confined to camp for 14 days.[21]

These various reconnaissance and army cooperation sorties from Cyprus and Rayak continued through April. News was received on 6 April that two of the squadron's pilots, Flt Lt Morley-Mower and PO Achilles, had been awarded the DFC for 'courage, determination and devotion to duty'. The recommendations for their awards made particular mention of the dangers of flying low-level Tac/R and photo-reconnaissance missions in areas heavily defended by enemy anti-aircraft fire, and the 'dash' sorties flown from Tobruk without any escort to gain intelligence on the Axis formations besieging the town.[22] There was some dissatisfaction within the group regarding the awarding of these medals: for a non-fighter squadron flying fighters, it wasn't necessarily an easy choice—awards couldn't go to whoever shot down the most enemy fighters; that wasn't their job. Nor could they be awarded for ground targets destroyed; that wasn't their job either. So how do you decide who would receive an award when their job was to spot the enemy? It came down to who flew the most sorties. Even though those next in line had flown just three or four sorties fewer than those nominated for the award, the line had to be drawn somewhere, and it was two DFCs for the British and one for an Australian. That the next two in line were both Australian seemed out of balance to Morley-Mower. He also believed that Ray Hudson, who never allowed anyone to misinterpret his thoughts about 'the way things should be', was one of these two who missed out. Had Ray Hudson been a more agreeable type to simply follow the rules, keep his mouth shut and get on with the job he may have had a recommendation submitted.[23]

The Australian 9th Division was also in Syria at the time and a number of exercises were carried out in cooperation with them, as well as some demonstrations. A break from the usual took place in the form of some searches for submarines on 11 and 12 April for the Cyprus-based detachment, but none was found.

On 13 April, Sqn Ldr Ferguson (described as a 'thoroughly decent English gentleman')[24] was posted out to 450 (RAAF) Squadron and Wing Cdr D.R. Chapman arrived to take command of 451 Squadron on the 15th. Assorted sorties continued to the end of the month, and another 'Showing of the Flag' operation took place in conjunction with ground forces at Deir ez-Zor on 27 April. No special mention was made of Anzac Day in the squadron records.

PO J.A. Cox (Service No. 400783) arrived at Rayak on 7 May from 74 OTU. John Allen Cox was from East Malvern in Victoria and, though he had worked as a bank clerk, was listed as an unemployed farmer when he enlisted on 8 November 1940 at No. 1 Recruiting Centre Melbourne, aged 29. He had served with the 2nd Cavalry Division prior to joining the RAAF, so was prepared for the rigours of daily military life. After his introductory enlistment course with the RAAF, he was sent across the sea to Rhodesia for his flying schools—25 EFTS and then 21 SFTS. From there it was up to the Middle East and on to 451 Squadron, his first operational posting.[25]

451 Squadron assisted the army in its training schedule in early May. Their duties included assisting in artillery direction demonstrations and strafing dummy convoys to show the value of spacing and what damage could be done by attacking aircraft. On 11 May, a dinner and concert were held by the squadron to mark the end of their first year of active service in the Middle East.

Staff continued to rotate through Cyprus and the detachment there continued submarine searches and their own cooperative exercises with the island's anti-aircraft defences.[26] Neville Guy wrote on the 15th: 'Jerry radio put over "We have not forgotten RAYAK", our C/O thinks we can expect raids about the 20th'.[27] But there was no raid and on 20 May the Duke of Gloucester visited RAF Station Rayak (to use its formal title) and was met by the Air Officer Commanding (AOC) Air Cdre (Air Commodore) Brown, Wing Cdr Chapman and the Free French commandant, Commandant Huet, and an inspection was carried out of the squadron.[28] Neville Guy recorded, 'No raids. Visit by Duke of Glouchester [sic]. Generals strutting about like peacocks.'[29]

On 22 May, a detachment of aircraft and staff was sent to Forqloss for an exercise carried out with the New Zealand Division, which lasted until 5 June. 451 Squadron's participation in the exercise consisted of artillery shoots, recognition of air and ground forces, R/T communication and message dropping. Some of these exercises involved live ammunition and proved valuable in later operations.[30] During this time Sgt E. Horton of the 26th Battalion, 6th Brigade, New Zealand Expeditionary Force arrived on a one-month posting to conduct lectures and demonstrations of infantry-type skills to the squadron, the first being 'The Principles of Aerodrome Defence'. Towards the end of the month Capt Becourt-Foch arrived on attachment from the Free French Air Force for instruction and experience in army cooperation duties and the squadron received some new aircraft, delivered from Ramat David.[31]

The exercises with the New Zealanders continued through the first week of June 1942, as did reconnaissance sorties from Cyprus by the detachment there. On 4 June, an administrative order was received reorganising the squadron into three operational flights. 5 June saw PO Whalley removed from the squadron strength as his status was updated from missing to presumed killed. Submarine searches continued to feature for the Cyprus detachment and the pilots there also carried out exercises with the 3/1 Punjabs and the

Household Cavalry Regiment on the island. At Rayak, Flt Lt Springbett gave flying lessons to Free French pilots in the Magister, the completion of which allowed them to go solo on the type.[32] In the middle of the month three staff were sent from Rayak to Cairo to attend an Air Photographic Interpretation course and, while they were away, the squadron was visited by ACM (Air Chief Marshal) Ludlow-Hewitt, RAF Inspector-General, who discussed various operational and administrative matters.[33]

On 20 June, several staff received notice that their names would be published as mentioned in dispatches: Sqn Ldr Reid, PO Kirkham, PO Hudson and Sgt Hayes, the first three being pilots and the latter a member of the valuable ground crew. A detachment of aircraft, pilots and the necessary support staff were sent to St Jean/El Bassa near Haifa on 22 and 23 June in response to German success in the Caucasus, though what an understrength Hurricane squadron—considering the Cyprus detachment – could achieve against a German thrust from the north is more than questionable. At this new base the squadron practised interceptions and scrambles. The Cyprus detachment carried out some shipping escorts, though no enemy aircraft or surface vessels were encountered. On 28 June, Flt Lt Springbett was posted out to 3 Squadron (RAAF) for flying duties there, where the promise of action awaited. Finally, on 30 June, Sqn Ldr Young attempted a night interception of a suspected enemy aircraft over Haifa and fired on it, though no results were observed.[34]

The first week of July saw attempted interception of unidentified aircraft from both the Haifa and Cyprus detachments but none was successful. Convoy patrols were also flown, in pairs, and all were uneventful. On 7 July, POs Lomas and Fisher were on patrol at 23,000 ft above Haifa and spotted a Ju 88 above them and chased it to the west for 15 minutes but could not catch it and were forced to return to base without firing a shot. Subsequent patrols were uneventful.

9 July saw overlapping convoy patrols flown in pairs and yet another submarine search, all of which proved uneventful. The 10th was more of the same, but another Ju 88 was spotted near Acre on the 11th by Watts and Fisher, but no interception was made. Watts wrote in his logbook, 'J.U. 88. 24,000' Couldn't catch. Hurry-one.!!!!' Flying a Hurricane Mk I, he certainly didn't need to be convinced the Hurricanes weren't suited for the job. At 1750 on

12 July Watts and Cox took off to intercept a Luftwaffe incursion—four Ju 88s and a Bf 110. As the Hurricanes approached, the Bf 110 fired at Watts's aircraft and the Germans turned and left the area—the Hurricanes couldn't catch them. Intercepts and convoy patrols continued for the next few days, but the only aircraft encountered were friendlies that had previously been identified as unknown.[35]

Two pilots and their aircraft were detached to Gaza on 24 July for local defence. Another Ju 88 was sighted on the 25th but it got away like the rest, and patrols and attempted intercepts continued for the remainder of the month. A promising event was the arrival of AVM Dawson at Rayak on 31 July for an inspection of the workshops and hangar space in advance of possible arrival of United States Army Air Corps (USAAC) forces.[36]

The first week of August 1942 saw the promotion of a number of staff, but otherwise patrols from Cyprus, Gaza and St Jean/El Bassa continued as normal, including an unsuccessful interception of enemy aircraft on the 7th, the aircraft seen over Cyprus and Haifa, but too high for the Hurricanes at 30,000 ft. On 11 August, the squadron was condensed into two detachments—Cyprus and Beirut—in anticipation of supporting naval operations near Greece, but all eyes appeared to be focused on the line at El Alamein where the Axis forces were stopped after a long advance towards the Suez. Convoy patrols and attempted interceptions took place, but no enemy were engaged over the week that followed. Finally, on 21 August, the squadron fired their guns in anger. POs Fisher and Terry, based on Cyprus at the time, intercepted an Italian Cant 1007 bomber in the Larnaca area. It was seen at 25,000 ft heading west. The Australians were spotted but the Cant took no evasive action and continued on its way. The Australians made six attacks out of the sun from the rear quarter of the Cant and received a great deal of fire from the Italian gunner in return. Both pilots used all their ammunition in the attacks with the result that the Cant suffered engine damage and lost height, eventually catching fire and crashing. Of the six airmen on board, three bailed out, but only two parachutes opened successfully and these two were made prisoner. The Australians returned very pleased with their efforts, and a signal was received from Air Cdre Brown, AOC RAF Levant, congratulating the squadron.[37] Convoy and air patrols continued for the rest of the month but the excitement of the 21st was not repeated.

On 4 September, the squadron was divided again—two aircraft, pilots and support staff headed back to Gaza to operate from there. Uneventful patrols continued, and the squadron headquarters moved to St Jean/El Bassa due to malaria concerns about the Estabel area, where they had been based. The squadron strength was further diluted by a detachment of two aircraft, three pilots and support staff to Beyrouth (Beirut) for the defence of that area. Numerous shipping and submarine patrols were carried out but nothing more interesting than dhows and oil slicks were found.[38]

The high-flying Ju 88 returned on 4 October over Cyprus with Kirkham and Goldberg (the first of two Jewish pilots to serve with 451 Squadron) intercepting it near Limassol. Once the aircraft was identified, some shots were taken, but from long range and no claims were made. These Hurricane Mk Is were armed with .303 machine guns and such rifle-calibre ammunition wasn't suitable for long-range shots. Another sighting occurred on 8 October, this time at 35,000 ft and leaving a clear vapour trail for the Hurricanes (Cox and Goldberg) to follow. They failed again though, with guns icing up on one aircraft and the other unable to gain sufficient altitude.[39] These failures had gone on for months, and in 1942 the Hurricane was no longer an effective fighter. The modifications made to subsequent models after the Battle of Britain had allowed it to carry bombs and rockets, and these, along with the upgrade from .303 machine guns to 20-mm cannon gave the plane a powerful punch at low level. What the squadron needed (and they were not the only ones) was Spitfires. Not because of some Spitfire idolisation or fascination, but because it was the best plane for the task of shooting down the high-flying Luftwaffe aircraft that passed over 451 Squadron's area of responsibility on a relatively regular basis. Cleaned-up Spitfire Mk Vs or high-altitude Mk VIIs were the solution, but Fighter Command would not let them go, even two years after the Battle of Britain had been won.

Another interception took place over Cyprus on 9 October, this time by Ahern and Bann, but once again, one aircraft could not gain sufficient height and the other fired a short burst which was ineffective. Other convoy, submarine, and air patrols were uneventful for the remainder of the month, the only aircraft intercepted were all identified as friendly.[40]

On 18 October a new pilot arrived: PO A.F Arnel. Alexander (Alec) Francis Arnel was born on 2 April 1920 and was working as a student schoolteacher when he enlisted on 3 January 1941. When it came to service, the Arnels were a fighting family. Alec's three brothers all served, two in the army and another in the Merchant Navy. His father served in the Australian Army at Gallipoli and on the Western Front in the First World War, had been wounded a number of times and gassed. When war broke out, he advised Alec, 'Lad, don't join the infantry.'

The essential violence of war conflicted with Alec's beliefs: he was a Christian who described himself as 'ardently pacifist'. But when it came down to it, he asked himself a question: what would he do if the Germans invaded Australia and came to his house? A theoretical question for sure, but one that set him on his path. He would fight them, and if he was going to fight them—did it make much difference if he fought them in Australia or somewhere else? His final answer was no, it didn't matter, and he joined the RAAF. Some of his pacifist friends cast him aside when he enlisted, but he admired those who were genuine pacifists and had to put up with the 'ridicule and sniping' that followed. Alec had been inspired by aviation, reading Biggles, and stories of Amy Johnson and Charles Kingsford-Smith—both of whom he met in the pre-war years. Though it was a strong interest, flying was a dream; the average person had no money for that kind of pastime, and he never imagined himself in the RAAF. Without any experience of even driving a car, flying a plane was a world away.

He didn't stop being a pacifist overnight; it was always with him and he was very conscious of it all through his service. A voice in his head kept saying, *You shouldn't be here, you shouldn't be fighting here, attempting to kill people you've never met.* Though chaplains often visited squadrons and other units throughout the conflict, he never once took the opportunity to speak with one and unburden himself of his feelings; he simply suppressed them so that he could get on with the job—feelings would have to wait until the job was done. Alec was one of a few hundred aircrew to be sent to Rhodesia for his flying training and passed through 25 EFTS and 20 SFTS, though he suspected it was by a small margin because he didn't get on with his first instructor, who 'didn't like Colonials'. Arnel's file even recorded the comment: 'A doubtful case who may become wastage at his Service School. He doesn't appreciate discipline and is inclined to be unpunctual and lazy.' The Chief Flying Instructor was much more reasonable though and gave Alec the confidence he needed to pass. All the things Alec felt about his instructor he shouted into the wind as he flew around on his first solo and landed feeling much better. Life with the locals in Rhodesia was agreeable and the trainee pilots were treated well. He even met an Australian family who had set up there and stayed with them from time to time. The weather was perfect for flying.

Alec's first flight in a Hurricane was at 74 OTU and he was taken aback by how fast it was compared to a Harvard. His first operational posting was to 208 Squadron which was equipped with the Hurricane IIC at the time. With just a few hours' experience on a Hurricane Mk I, he found the IIC much heavier, but was more concerned about taking off and landing safely. In a very upsetting experience, Alec was told to give instruction to a pilot who had recently been posted to 208 Squadron. He went through the cockpit drill with the new pilot and made sure to tell him about the differences between a Mk I and Mk IIC—especially regarding the weight—and away the pilot went. Shortly after, the new pilot crashed and died, killed on his first flight. Introducing a new pilot to a new plane should have been the job for a more experienced pilot, but Alec did as he was told, and the consequences could not be undone. Alec Arnel didn't really feel at home with 208 Squadron: the leadership were too distant, and they'd suffered some casualties, but 451 Squadron was different—he was among his own.[41]

November began for 451 Squadron with convoy patrols, submarine searches, friendly interceptions and the Luftwaffe too high to engage. On the few occasions that the Ju 88 (or Ju 86) was low enough to be engaged, by the time the Hurricanes had either scrambled or been vectored onto it (when on a standing patrol), they were spotted far enough away that the German aircraft continued on its way, climbing higher and out of range. The high-flying German reconnaissance aircraft often left vapour trails, also known as contrails, which gave them away, but their superior height and ability to climb away from danger meant that this was not a disadvantage that could be exploited.[42]

On 12 November, a movement order came through—the squadron was moving back to St Jean aerodrome in Palestine, though they would maintain the Cyprus detachment. At the time, the squadron was organised into a Headquarters Flight with the commanding officer and their liaison aircraft (Miles Magister and Gypsy Major) plus three operational flights as follows:[43]

'A' FLIGHT	'B' FLIGHT	'C' FLIGHT (AT CYPRUS)
Pilots Flt Lt R.M. Achilles FO W.D. Hutley FO L.N. Ahern PO R.B. Sneddon PO L.E. Trenorden PO S.J. Archbold PO W.K. Watts FS K.C. Smythe Sgt J.E. Sydney	**Pilots** Flt Lt R.T. Hudson FO C.W. Robertson FO J.E. Schofield PO H.R. Rowlands PO S.J.M. Bartlett PO W.W.G. Gale PO W.E. Goldman PO R.H. Sutton Sgt T.H.S. James	**Pilots** Flt Lt E.E. Kirkham FO C.E. Edmondson FO J.K. Bann PO J.A. Cox PO D.L. Fisher PO R.G. Goldberg PO H.S. O'Donnell PO W.L. Terry PO J.D. Ward PO A.F. Arnel
FS C.A.J. Westbrook plus 24 ground crew	Sgt F. O'Halloran plus 25 ground crew	FS C.F. Best plus 22 ground crew
Hurricane Mk I W9346 W9155 Z4789 V7429 Z4177 V7779 Z4092	**Hurricane Mk I** Z4695 Z4196 Z4100 Z4097 Z4619 Z4779 Z4707	**Hurricane Mk I** Z4554 W9133 Z461 Z4351 W9359 Z4388 V7797 Z4640 Z4424

Shortly after this order was drawn up, PO Purdy arrived from 74 OTU. George Purdy (Service No. 408519) did well at school and came from a musical family. He worked in a number of clerical jobs before he enlisted and spent a few nights a week swimming and doing classes such as Morse code, navigation and mathematics while he was in the Air Force reserve. On 26 April 1941, he was finally able to enlist in the RAAF and on 1 September he was on a ship bound for South Africa, but the ship had thousands of troops on board, so they stopped in Egypt first. On the way the ship travelled at a consistently high speed to minimise the chances a submarine would be able to engage it successfully, and at night they were blacked out. After a short stint in Egypt, George Purdy and the rest of his group finally headed by ship to South Africa, accompanied by 1,500 Italian prisoners. After landing at Durban, they spent two weeks in tents at the racecourse waiting to be told what to do next. Finally, they boarded a train to Rhodesia, where they learned to fly. Like Alec Arnel, George Purdy didn't enjoy the first few hours of flying: his instructor spent the whole time abusing him, swearing at him and cursing him for anything not done perfectly. The instructor refused to fly with him again, which meant he had a new instructor, and this one was far more tolerant and realistic, which Purdy described as 'a breath of fresh air, he was marvellous'.[44] Purdy was described as a 'good reliable type' during his training and was sent to Syria for his OTU training on Hurricanes, holding the rank of sergeant. One of his instructors was Morley-Mower. Purdy was granted his commission after successfully completing a course at the Middle East School of Artillery, where he learned more about army cooperation duties and aerial artillery spotting and correcting, just before he arrived at 451 Squadron along with his mate John (Barney) Wallis, which was their first operational posting. Wing Cdr Chapman was still in charge, and George Purdy didn't have a kind word to say about him.[45]

On 25 November, Hector O'Donnell was killed when his Hurricane (Mk I Z.4554) crashed on a beach in Cyprus. He was on a training flight with two other aircraft (Terry and Edmondson) and flying at about 1,000 ft when they changed course to return to base. He was seen by the other aircraft to begin losing height, and, apparently knowing that he would not make it back to base, attempted a belly-landing on the beach. There was no radio call from him and, upon hitting the beach, his plane burst into flames. He was buried at the Military Cemetery in Nicosia on the 27th. His wife, who lived in Sydney, received a letter from the RAAF Casualty Section in Victoria informing her of the crash and general circumstances.[46]

The squadron lost another member on 28 November when Milton Ifield, a ground-crew armourer, died of cerebro-spinal meningitis whilst in hospital. Milton had applied to join the RAAF in October 1939, a qualified motorcycle engine repairer who wished, like many, to become a pilot. He stated on his application that he had 'studied machine guns to some extent and at the present time [am] working on a gun of my own design' and was assessed on application as being a 'Good type, Keen, Respectful'. He was buried in the military cemetery in Haifa.[47]

At the end of November 1942, the squadron had about 20 Hurricane Mk Is on strength.[48] This was more than two years after the Battle of Britain had been won with this very aircraft.

When would things improve? Alec Arnel recalled, 'While it was a lovely spot, people wanted to get back into operations, they were annoyed at being lost and so on. So we did these tidying up jobs, minor jobs, no satisfaction in them or anything, and you did feel that neglect.' One thing Arnel enjoyed was the view from so far above the desert on the many attempted interceptions. He recalled, 'I have never seen such glorious sunsets. The colours ... at one stage I lost sense of where I was ... it was such a wonderful sight ... it just grabbed me, it was a dangerous moment.'[49]

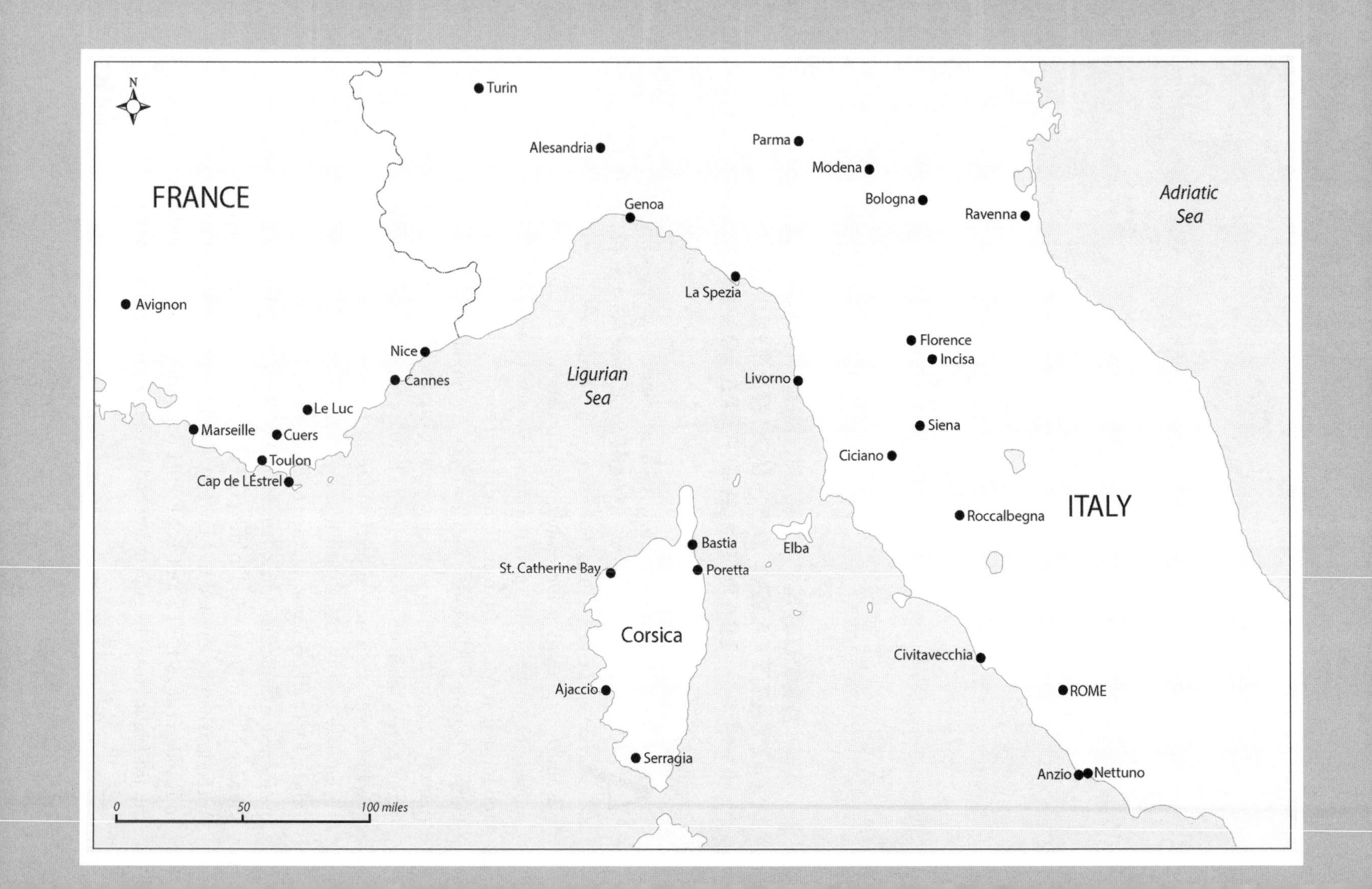
N
Turin
Alesandria
Parma
Modena
Bologna
Ravenna
Adriatic Sea
FRANCE
Genoa
La Spezia
Avignon
Florence
Incisa
Nice
Cannes
Ligurian Sea
Livorno
Le Luc
Marseille
Cuers
Siena
Toulon
Ciciano
Cap de LÉstrel
ITALY
Roccalbegna
Bastia
Elba
St. Catherine Bay
Poretta
Corsica
Civitavecchia
Ajaccio
ROME
Serragia
Anzio
Nettuno
0
50
100 miles

RETURN TO EUROPE: CORSICA, ITALY AND *DRAGOON*: DECEMBER 1942 TO AUGUST 1944

AT THE start of December, A Flight moved to Cyprus (by sea) and C Flight returned to the mainland. Patrols continued, as did the frustration as the Ju 86s passed overhead and out of range. Overall the month was uneventful until 31 December, when orders arrived for the squadron to move back to the front lines. The squadron was to be based together again and located at Mersa Matruh (Landing Ground No. 08—on the coast about halfway between Alexandria and Tobruk). Accompanying this was the news that the squadron was to be re-equipped with the Hurricane Mk IIC, and 18 of these were taken on strength. By 12 January 1943, the squadron was at their new base, with their new aircraft and ready for operations.[1]

The new year brought with it some changes in personnel. The Medical Officer, Flt Lt Blumer, was returned to Australia with the news that he had been mentioned in dispatches. On 19 January PO William Philip Gibson Longbottom (Service No. 416347) arrived from 74 OTU for flying duties. He was a banker in Adelaide when he enlisted in May 1941, and he carried out his flying training in Rhodesia at 26 EFTS and 22 SFTS. Longbottom had previously served in the 3rd Light Horse Regiment but had been discharged to join the RAAF.[2]

Several convoy patrols and scrambles took place at the new airfield in January, but the Luftwaffe weren't to be seen. Aircraft usually operated in pairs and convoy patrols were relieved either by another pair from 451 Squadron or elsewhere (such as Rhodesian or Fleet Air Arm squadrons) along the convoy route. Often convoys would have barrage balloons attached to discourage enemy aircraft from coming down too low when attacking, but the escorts also had to be wary of these, the cables connecting the balloons to their ships would rip a wing off a Hurricane without much trouble. The escorting aircraft had to keep sight of the convoy at all times and they usually flew the escort at about 4,000 ft (low cover), with another pair at 10,000 ft (high cover). If low cloud was about, the low-cover pair would have to come down, perhaps within range of the balloons which were usually at 1,000 ft. The Hurricanes flew numerous times a day on these convoy escorts, and often refuelled at another airfield before returning to Mersa Matruh.

The squadron's stay near the front line did not last for long and, on 4 February 1943, the squadron received orders to move to Idku, (sometimes spelled Edku or even Edcu) about 30 km east of Alexandria. Unfortunately, on 12 February, at the new base, PO Martin Shiels died after suffering serious multiple injuries when his Hurricane (BP 541) crashed while taking off. There was a strong cross-wind as his section took off on an interception. Just after becoming airborne his aircraft struck the buttress (the protective mound) of a dispersal bay which caused his aircraft to somersault and crash. The other three aircraft were recalled and landed shortly afterwards. Before signing up for the RAAF, Shiels had been a real estate salesman and then a manager at the family hotel in Condobolin, western New South Wales. Unlike a number of his fellow pilots, he'd been taught to fly in Australia at 8 EFTS Narrandera before passing his SFTS at Camp Borden in Canada. He'd served about three months with 208 Squadron before arriving at 451 Squadron in January 1942.[3] He was buried on 14 February 1943 at the British War Memorial Cemetery in Alexandria.

On the same day Martin Shiels was buried, the squadron took three Spitfire Mk VC aircraft on strength, the role of this aircraft reserved for intercepting the high-flying reconnaissance aircraft the squadron knew only too well from their time in Cyprus, Palestine and Syria. These Spitfires were BP981, 985 and 987. Spitfire production notes show that BP985 was modified by 103 MU (Maintenance Unit) at Aboukir for high-altitude interception, and the others may have also been modified in a similar fashion.[4] BP985 was modified in a number of ways: the wingtips were extended and brought to a point, all .303 machine guns were removed, the 20-mm cannon were replaced by .50-calibre machine guns, the three-bladed propeller was replaced with a four-bladed one and some fuel and armour were removed to reduce the weight even further.[5] It should be noted here that the Spitfire Mk V was not designed for high-altitude interception; that was the role of the Mk VI and VII, but these were not suitable as they were too heavy to get to the altitudes required in the Mediterranean, so the local forces adapted what they had to suit the circumstances. During this period at Idku, the squadron was reorganised as a two-flight fighter squadron and its role of army cooperation reached a welcome end.

The first recorded flight of the new Spitfires with 451 Squadron was an interception by PO Goldberg in BP 987 on 17 February, which had him ordered to 30,000 ft over Rosetta (Rasheed) to await the Luftwaffe, who made no appearance. Many of these attempted interceptions were done in radio silence so as not to give away the presence of fighters awaiting the Ju 86 reconnaissance aircraft. Convoy patrols continued with the Hurricanes, as did refuelling at bases to the west, along the convoy route, which enabled the squadron to provide cover for longer periods.[6]

On 22 February, PO Wallis, in his Hurricane IIC, was directed to a bandit. His report on the subsequent engagement read:

> Red section was scrambled and I was ordered to 25–28000 ft., on a vector of 360° for a Bandit coming in South. I was given several other Vectors, and when flying at 25,000 ft., I sighted the Bandit 2 miles away to Port at 20,000 ft., and approaching on a parallel course. I turned in towards him and made a port quarter attack from slightly above. I opened fire at 300 to 350 yds., and gave a very short burst. The starboard gun did not fire. I closed in and fired a longer burst with one gun and possibly hit him in the port engine. After my first burst, the enemy did not alter course, but returned fire from a rear gun. Just after my second burst, my port cockpit panel cracked and half blew away. The bandit then went straight down, almost vertically, with one engine smoking. I followed him down and gave another bust going down at longer range. He was gaining on me, and entered cloud

at 16,000 ft. I pulled up over cloud and called the Controller. I was given more vectors and was after him again when I noticed smoke in the cockpit, glycol dripping, and the rad. Temperature was very high, so I decided to return to base. I came back closely, losing height, with the engine throttled back until below cloud base (now about 4,000 ft). The Rad. Temp. went up to about 140° and the engine began to miss cylinders. When nearly over land, the temp dropped back to 100°. It was difficult to maintain height. I sighted Maryiut and decided to land there, but before getting within gliding distance of the 'drome, the engine failed. I could not 'select flaps'. I took away a telephone pole. And crashed in a field. Red 2 was with me up to 20,000 ft., but I lost him 5 minutes before the Tally Ho. Controlling throughout was good. The Bandit was a Ju.88 and appeared to be painted a dark colour—I could see no markings. Claim—One JU. 88 damaged.[7]

March 1943 started off with one of the squadron's busiest days of the year so far, with 36 sorties flown for convoy escorts flown on the 1st. This dropped back to around four to six a day, with Spitfires being sent up on interceptions every second day, but without engaging the enemy. An interception almost took place on 22 March when four Hurricanes were scrambled, but by the time they gained sufficient altitude the intruder had climbed out of range and the Hurricanes returned empty-handed. Two attempted interceptions by Spitfires in the vicinity of Alexandria were thwarted by problems with the oxygen system (BP987 each time) and, despite one aircraft attempting a chase by itself, no combat took place.

On 24 March, two Hurricanes, flown by Terry and Bann, were detailed for an escort of a Lockheed Lodestar carrying King George of Greece. They escorted him east-north-east from Heliopolis and returned after refuelling at Ismailia. There was a successful interception on 26 March by Sutton and Purdy in two Spitfires. Between them the two Australians fired nearly 2,000 rounds of .303 and 160 rounds of 20-mm cannon at the Ju 88 but could not bring it down, though faint smoke was seen to come from both engines, and the Luftwaffe pilots' efforts to evade the two Spitfires was described as 'Violent evasive action and admirable use of cloud cover'.[8] During the Ju 88's attempt to get away, it roared past the Hurricanes of POs James and Goldman, who also made attacks of their own, firing off another 300 rounds of 20 mm for no apparent effect.[9] Another intercept was attempted on the 27th, and though the aircraft turned away before the Spitfires could get to it, it was later shot down by 238 Squadron.[10]

Three new pilots arrived on 2 April from 74 OTU, sergeants P.M. Boulton, R.B. Hudson and A.F. Lane. Alan Frederick Lane (Service No. 409150) enlisted on 19 July 1941, leaving his job as an orchard hand far behind, and left Sydney in November for his flying training in Rhodesia. Though he arrived at 451 Squadron as a sergeant, his commission as a pilot officer came through shortly afterwards.[11] On the same day the newcomers arrived, PO John Cox was listed as missing on an attempted interception of a suspected enemy aircraft while flying Spitfire BP981 north of Rosetta Bay. Trenorden in BP987 lost touch with him when Cox entered a cloud bank. There were no further transmissions and he was not seen again. The squadron flew 26 sorties out over the ocean in search of Cox and his aircraft, in addition to those flown by the dedicated air-sea rescue units, but all they found was a patch of oil. Another Spitfire, BR363, arrived to take the place of the missing aircraft, and yet another, BR114 which was specially modified by the Aboukir engineers, also arrived later in the month.[12]

The change in role to a fighter squadron and the posting to the front out of Syria and Lebanon had raised the squadron's hopes of participating in the real action, but these hopes had been crushed with their move to the Suez. The matter of 451 Squadron and their role in the Middle East was raised in a document to RAAF Overseas HQ in March 1943. While the instruction had come down the line that they were to be converted to a fighter squadron in February 1943, it was pointed out that the squadron had performed that role for the previous nine months, and that army cooperation was the role for which the squadron had been raised 'and proceeded overseas from Australia on loan to the Royal Air Force'.[13] While HQ Middle East wanted the change in role to take place this was challenged by the Australian government, and the opinion of Wing Cdr Chapman was sought. He replied that since the entry of Japan into the war,

> the original desire of all ranks to serve overseas in an active theatre of war has vanished... the personnel of the Unit were unanimous in their natural desire to return... to see action in the defence of Australia.[14]

He thought that the Australian government might, upon seeing that the RAF did not have need of 451 Squadron for army cooperation duties, ask for them to be returned to Australia, as no experienced Army Cooperation squadron existed there. As an alternative, if the squadron were to remain in the Middle East as a fighter squadron, he requested they be moved to the front line, instead of 'being condemned to the morale-sapping permanent duty of defending centres remote from enemy activity'[15] where they would be stuck with 'boring repetition of exercises devoid of any interest'.[16] Subsequent suggestions for a change in role were made at an air force conference in London, but all were rejected.[17]

Clearly a problem with morale and direction were keenly felt by the men and leadership of the squadron, and it was not just a matter of complaining for the sake of it, but an attempt to ensure the squadron was given the opportunity to make a valuable contribution to the war effort—either in the Middle East or back in Australia. They had to fight for the chance to fight, which seems very backwards. Had another (non-Australian) squadron been in their place, it is highly likely that they would have felt the same, and would, perhaps, have been rotated with a front-line unit to give the other a rest. But such things can often be overlooked—451 Squadron was one squadron in a world war, and someone had to be in Syria, or Lebanon, or Cyprus or even all three. These places could not just be abandoned.

Two more pilots, Robert and Kemp, arrived from 74 OTU on 8 April. Several pilots were granted commissions or other promotions, and PO Goldberg left the squadron and was posted to 450 Squadron on 13 April. 20 April saw a visit by AVM Saul, AOC Air Headquarters, Eastern Mediterranean, who inspected the unit headquarters and spoke with all pilots in the operations room. Coincidence or not, two days later advice was received that several pilots had been promoted![18] Convoy patrols varied and ranged from two to 16 per day, east and west along the coast, while repeated attempts to intercept bandits heading to Alexandria all failed.

On 24 April 1943, PO Robert Hudson, who had only been with the squadron a few weeks, was reported missing during a convoy patrol, just two miles from the airfield. There was cloud at 500 ft, so the aircraft had to stay very low to keep visual contact with the vessels, and one aircraft, assumed to be Hudson in BN 162, was seen by a shore-based light anti-aircraft unit to hit the sea.

This was just after the section (Sidney and Hudson) had taken off and after Hudson broadcast a message stating that he may have to belly-land. Exactly why was not stated and Sidney stayed up to search for his No. 2. A further search was carried out, but rescue launches could not get to the area due to engine trouble with the first and the water being too shallow for the vessel that replaced it.

On 25 April, five members of the ground crew were recommended for commissions after appearing before a Command Selection Board. 28 April was the closest the squadron came to a reconnaissance intercept that month when PO Sneddon, in a Spitfire, identified an enemy aircraft he'd been searching for at 30,000 ft, but though he gave chase, he was soon short of fuel and the enemy climbed away northwards. On 30 April, a dinner and concert were held to mark the end of the squadron's second year of service.[19]

On 1 May the squadron was visited by staff from the RAAF Liaison Section of Headquarters, RAF Middle East, and discussed administrative and personnel matters. All they could really do was listen to the men's complaints and concerns, for the RAAF had very little push when it came to how the RAF fought the war, no matter where the squadron felt it deserved to be. Convoy escorts continued and, on occasion, a Hurricane was used as the 'marker' for Spitfires attempting to engage the Luftwaffe, though the Ju 86s simply avoided them by climbing to 40,000 ft. On 4 May Sqn Ldr Paine took over command of the squadron from Wing Cdr Chapman who was to return to the UK, since Air Marshal Sholto Douglas had taken unkindly to Chapman's requests for 451 Squadron to be employed more productively.[20] Prior to leaving, Chapman addressed the assembled staff of 451 and expressed his appreciation for the loyalty and behaviour of the squadron since his arrival. This same day, a dummy convoy patrol was launched, with a single Hurricane flown over the supposed route, perhaps in an attempt to draw down a Luftwaffe reconnaissance aircraft to an altitude where they could be engaged, but the bait wasn't taken.[21]

On 11 May, two Spitfires on an attempted intercept encountered trouble. The first had an oxygen failure and the pilot passed out, only regaining consciousness at 12,000 ft. Due to this being the 'marker', the 'striker' or 'special' had to follow it down, there being no R/T communications. This aircraft also developed an oxygen failure and the plane went into a spin at 27,000 ft when the pilot lost consciousness, fortunately recovering at 4,000 ft and regaining control of the aircraft. It was clearly dangerous business just trying to stay at 30,000 ft and upwards; the Luftwaffe wasn't the only enemy.

On 14 May, several pilots were promoted and, on 17 May, three Spitfires and seven pilots were sent to 123 Squadron (RAF) on temporary assignment, returning on 24 May, though leaving the Spitfires behind. On 19 May, while on convoy escort, Flt Lt Ray Hudson reported engine trouble and then a fire in his aircraft, (BP 518), which he ditched and swiftly escaped, as the aircraft sank immediately. He was picked up by a vessel from the convoy within a short time, suffering minor injuries and burns, and was later admitted to No. 64 General Hospital for several weeks.[22] It was later learned that he had attempted to fire a flare during his patrol (perhaps as a distress signal) but it had gone off in the cockpit and started to burn his parachute, meaning he could not bail out and so he had to go down with the plane.[23]

Convoy escorts continued for the rest of the month, on one occasion using long-range drop tanks, and there was an attempt to intercept aircraft approaching convoys, but no combat took place, and some aircraft turned out to be friendly in any case.[24] It may have been necessary work but mostly it was dull. Between the start of April and the end of May, Alan Lane logged just 15 operational sorties for a total of 17 hours and 20 minutes operational flying time.[25] If he were to make his 200 operational hours before being rested, it was going to take a long time indeed.

June 1943 was a very interesting time for 451 Squadron: three British pilots were posted in to assist in carrying out flight tests of the Hawker Typhoon in 'tropical' conditions. Two aircraft accompanied them, and all pilots seconded for testing were given instructions on the Typhoon by Sqn Ldr Lucas—Hawker test pilot. The squadron was now without any Spitfires, so all operational sorties were flown in their Hurricane IICs. Some very large convoys were escorted during the month, the largest of over 50 vessels, and many overlapping sorties had to be flown from almost dawn to dusk to provide the necessary cover, long-range drop tanks also being used on occasion. On 21 June the Secretary of State for Air, Sir Archibald Sinclair and AVM Saul visited Idku, where they met the CO, pilots and ground staff of the squadron before having lunch in the officers' mess.[26]

Specific orders came through for convoy escorts at the end of June. These related to 'Four convoys of vital importance to the success of certain operations ...'.[27] These were convoys headed west for the first stab at the 'soft underbelly'—Operation *Husky*, the invasion of Sicily. Orders specified the height at which escorts were to be flown and how this might be varied depending on the number of escorts. Low cover was to be flown at 2,500 ft and balloons flown by the ships in the convoys would be at 2,000 ft.[28] No twin-engined aircraft were to approach the convoys lest they be mistaken for Italian or German aircraft and shot down. In relation to anti-aircraft defence of the convoys, the orders stated that 'Particular attention must be directed to the necessity for all pilots not to leave any doubt in the convoy's mind as to their friendly identity.' Radio silence was only to be broken to acknowledge and reply to the Fighter Direction Officer (who may be either in the convoy or on land), in emergency or distress, or upon 'Tally-ho and subsequently until combat ceases'.[29]

The first week of July was a busy one for convoys, with most pilots flying at least once a day. July did find them back in possession of some Spitfires though, Mk VCs again—JK115, JW608 and JW164, but with a Mk VB (ER567) thrown into the mix. Some high-altitude interceptions were attempted but always came to nothing. On 13 July, five officers, two civilians (one from Hawker who manufactured the plane and the other from Napier who manufactured the engine) and 25 other ranks were relocated to LG 105 to commence flying trials with the Typhoons. The officer in charge of the detachment was Flt Lt Hudson, recently returned from his hospitalisation.

The same day, FO Rex Bayly, DFC (Service No. 407416) arrived for flying duties.[30] Rex Howard Bayly was born on 28 May 1918, the son of a reverend, and was employed as a theatre manager when he enlisted on 12 October 1940 in South Australia. He completed his flying at 25 EFTS and 20 SFTS in Rhodesia before passing through 71 OTU and 3 Squadron (RAAF) before a stint instructing at 73 OTU and arriving at 451 Squadron. His DFC citation referenced his 'outstanding keenness and skill, both as a fighter and fighter-bomber pilot', and his one confirmed enemy aircraft destroyed.[31] On 18 February 1942 , Sgt Bayly was charged by field general court martial with two offences—in plain English, flying too low and damaging an aircraft through negligence. This had occurred on 7 January that year in the Sudan, and he was found guilty of the second offence only, severely reprimanded and fined £5, quite a bit of money at the time.[32]

16 July saw yet another visitor: Air Cdre Dunn from Air Headquarters Eastern Mediterranean, who made an inspection of the camp with the CO before discussing squadron requirements. Two Australian padres, McKay and McNamara, visited for four days and a service was held in the airmen's mess. On 17 July, while the squadron was escorting a convoy of 20 ships codenamed 'Burgess', an enemy aircraft thought to be a Heinkel He 111 bomber was seen north of the convoy at 1900, and was chased by FO Terry, who exchanged fire with it over a 25-mile-long chase, but it eventually drew away and he was forced to return without even claiming a 'damaged'. Terry (and the others on that patrol) had been flying a Hurricane IIC[33]—he should have had a Spitfire; Hurricanes were not up to it.

23 July saw the first offensive operations by the squadron in some time. As part of Operation *Thesis*,[34] six Hurricanes (led by Flt Lt Kirkham) were based forward at LG 121, and escorted 38 aircraft of the 'Sidi Barrani Wing' to Crete. Operational orders stated that the intention of the raid was 'To carry out one large scale offensive operation by daylight against CRETE by the simultaneous use of all available aircraft of 219 Group, in conjunction with aircraft from Nos. 212 and 201 Groups'.[35] Most of the Hurricanes were IICs but some IIBs from 74 Squadron were also to be exchanged for 451 Squadron's Hurricane IICs just for the operation, though it is unclear if this actually took place. All were to be fitted with long-range drop tanks. Two additional wings—each of 27 Hurricanes—would also take part, plus 6 Baltimores. Each of the three wings would be led by two Beaufighters from 201 Group, and the return would be covered by Spitfires from 80 Squadron. The approach to Crete was to be made below 1,000 ft and then down to sea level once within 100 miles of Crete, with aircraft timed to arrive on the coast at sunrise. In reality, once the aircraft arrived at Crete, they did some strafing and encountered heavy anti-aircraft fire, but all 451 Squadron Hurricanes returned safely. 238, 74, 335 and 226 Squadrons also contributed.[36] The Baltimores participating in the operation were from 454 (RAAF) Squadron. They bombed and machine-gunned targets at Ierapetra (Italian barracks and soap factory), Pakhia Ammos (small boat), Elownda (causeway and W/T station) and Ayionnis (observation post). These were not targets of any great significance. One aircraft was shot down over the island and another had an engine damaged by anti-aircraft fire: the crew had to throw out the guns and ammunition and even released

their homing pigeon, things were so bad, and they were barely at 150 ft. They broadcast an SOS and prepared to ditch, but were hoping to make a beach in North Africa. Unfortunately, the beach they found had obstacles to hinder landing craft on it, so they had to put it down in the sea and luckily all managed to escape via the top hatches. Bombers not involved in the operation flew sorties in the afternoon in search of their missing comrades, but the five missing aircraft were not found. For 454 Squadron, it was a disaster.[37] In addition to the bombers, 13 Hurricanes were lost.[38] They had a right to wonder if it had been worth it.

George Purdy flew on that operation and gave his opinion on it all when interviewed about his life:

> The big thing about this was they were single engine aircraft over 200 miles of ocean. If something goes wrong you end up in the drink. But the idea was that we just strafed anything we saw on the ground. There wasn't much to strafe to be quite honest, this is why I am critical of the whole thing, and I wasn't the only one. But 454 lost 6 aircraft out of 8 that day, and of the 100 Hurricanes we lost 8 of them. Fortunately, no one from us, my aircraft got hit twice but only minor damage, it was mainly flak, and anti aircraft fire. But as I said the targets weren't worth it. I just think it was somebody who had nothing much else to do and thought up this operation and said, 'Let's go for it'. Because Crete was isolated, it was occupied by the Germans, but I couldn't see much point in it.[39]

Purdy's numbers might be a little off, but the sentiment is right on. No airfields or major surface vessels were attacked, so what was it all about? If aircraft or ships based on, or at, Crete were causing trouble for Allied convoys, then they should have been targeted, and by a substantial bomber force, not Hurricanes. But strafing or bombing barracks and the like was wasteful—the Allies could allow the Germans or Italians to garrison the island with as many troops as they pleased: if troops were on Crete they weren't going to hinder the Allies progress anywhere else in the Mediterranean. Due to Crete's proximity to German-occupied Greece any garrison wouldn't necessarily wither on the vine as quickly as isolated Japanese garrisons in the Pacific, but the Allied focus was up through Italy towards France and Germany, a long way from Crete.

On 24 July, an administrative instruction was issued to all units for the change in command designation: the Western Desert Air Force was to be known as the Desert Air Force from that point onwards.[40] There was a dilution of experience towards the end of the month with FOs Archbold and Goldman posted to 6 Squadron RAF (Hurricanes), FO Schofield was promoted to flight lieutenant and posted to 127 Squadron RAF and FO Bann was similarly promoted and posted to 238 Squadron RAF. This did leave some room for promotions though, Hudson, Kirkham, Newsom making flight lieutenant and James making flying officer.[41]

Now that the squadron was well and truly operational and in an active war zone (again!), standing orders for conduct of the squadron in wartime were issued and these covered all kinds of matters from flying accidents, burials, marriages and how often recommendations for medals should be submitted. Specifically dealing with the matter of marrying a 'local girl' the orders stated, in part:

> Experience in 1914–1918 and subsequently made it clear that marriages between British Soldiers and women of other nationalities domiciled in Eastern and Near Eastern countries often led to unhappiness and disaster that an Order in Council was issued…soldiers desirous of being married to apply to the Commander-in-Chief and of course in the case of airmen, to the Air Officer Commanding-in-Chief…In the past these facilities have been very sparingly granted and then only in cases when the parties were of similar upbringing and in a sound financial position.[42]

Operationally, August started with the usual convoy escorts, the largest of these being 50 and 60 ships. Alan Lane used the quiet time to take a few flights in one of the Spitfire Mk VCs and get used to them before having to fight in one. On 13 August, FO Purdy had a long-awaited encounter with the Luftwaffe high-fliers. He was in a Mk IX Spitfire from 103 MU Aboukir and climbed to 28,000 ft to engage a Ju 88. He fired from 300 yards and then 150–100 yards and hit the port engine of the enemy aircraft, covering his own windscreen in oil. Unfortunately, after this first engagement the enemy aircraft managed to escape, but at least Purdy was able to claim a 'damaged'. There were some other attempted interceptions by the Spitfires, but aircraft usually turned out to be friendly, and some fighter sweeps were undertaken by Hurricanes in conjunction with 238 Squadron. On 14 August Alan Lane (Hurricane IIC BN404) was on convoy patrol with Len Trenorden (Hurricane IIC HL913) for two hours and 45 minutes and wrote in his logbook, 'Too long for convoy'. They flew back and forth while the convoy of 14 vessels made its way westward,[43] becoming dangerously bored. The real action was hundreds of miles away. A few days later, Lane flew another long patrol, this time of 2 hours and 25 minutes with Harry Rowlands, but this time he wrote, '3/10 C. [clouds] at 1500 relieved monotony'.[44]

On 22 August, the squadron had another VIP visitor: AVM Wrigley, Air Officer Commanding RAAF Overseas Headquarters, and accompanying officers, who saw the squadron at Idku, and even stayed the night. The next morning AVM Wrigley spoke to the squadron and addressed concerns in relation to such matters as future operations, promotions and repatriations. Alan Lane continued his do-it-yourself Spitfire training and took a Mk VC up for 30 minutes on 23 August and wrote in his logbook: 'Still trying to fly a Spit accurately.'[45]

On 24 August, the squadron received a movement order to relocate to LG 106, and to be ready for action by the 27th. They were ready, and patrols and sweeps resumed, but no engagements took place.[46] By the end of August a number of submissions were made by the squadron for members of ground crew to be mentioned in dispatches for their ability, devotion to duty and length of service. Not all were awarded, but those who did eventually receive their formal recognition were Sgt Ian Adams (Service No. 26471), Flight Sergeant (FS) Jack Lenney (Service No. 14297), and Sgt Thomas Wilbraham (Service No. 12176).

7 September 1943 saw a change in command, with Sqn Ldr Paine leaving for HQ, RAF Middle East and the arrival of Sqn Ldr Reginald Stevens, DFC and bar. Reginald Noel Basil Stevens (Service No. 404672) was born on 9 September 1917 in Sydney, NSW. He had been working as a clerk and was apparently one of a very few married men when he enlisted on 11 November 1940. He didn't have far to travel, conducting his introduction to military flying at 4 EFTS, Mascot, then moved to 2 SFTS at Wagga Wagga. Once passed, he travelled to the UK via Canada and completed his training at 61 OTU. After 61 OTU he found himself flying Spitfires with 457 (RAAF) Squadron for about ten weeks before they (along with 452 Squadron) were withdrawn from operations and returned to Australia in May/June 1942 to help defend

against the Japanese air raids. He remained in the UK and was later sent to the Middle East, again serving with fellow Australians in 3 Squadron, flying Kittyhawks. While there, he was awarded his first DFC, the citation of which specified 'the squadron was assisting in breaking the Alamein line he displayed most outstanding courage and devotion to duty particularly when leading a formation on raids.'[47] Prior to his arrival at 451 Squadron, Stevens met with Gp Capt Duncan to discuss his posting, and Stevens was told about the low morale in the squadron. Subsequent representations to Group HQ had them lined up to receive Spitfires,[48] but such things did not happen overnight.

Several staff were promoted during September which no doubt pleased all recipients, but they were sobered up on 18 September when Sgt Pennell was killed in an accident whilst conducting shadow firing at LG 106. His Hurricane was seen to flip over onto its back and went into the ground, and he was killed instantly.[49] While this rather simple explanation is how the matter is recorded in the daily records, there was more to it than that, as explained by Sqn Ldr Stevens:

> Any 451 a/c flying in the Sept/Oct intensive training period was liable to be "jumped" at any time. F/L Ray Hudson [Flying one of the 3 Typhoons attached to 451] made a pass at the Sgt's plane who turned into the attack then overcorrected, spun & crashed & burned 20′ from my tent. The subsequent enquiry exonerated Ray Hudson of any liability & quite rightly so.[50]

Using it as an unofficial diary (as many did), Ken Watts recorded the incident in his logbook as '18th. Joe Pennell killed. (Spun in.) Jumped by Ray Hudson in Typhoon. (Long range Hurricane)'.[51]

The squadron also had some staff posted in and out, mainly pilots, those leaving often going to positions of flight commander within operational units. Meanwhile, convoy escorts and fighter sweeps out to sea continued, and now that Sicily had been captured the next move for the Allies was to the boot of Italy, but would 451 Squadron be included in the move and get some of the intensive operations they sought?

It was also about this time that armourer Edward Smith was sent on a course to Heliopolis, for handling chemical weapons:

> I can always remember number 53 Chemicals, Weapons and Warfare Course down to Heliopolis which there's not a lot known about, they reckon there was no gas or anything around but there was plenty of poison gas there. And I did a course there on the use of Mustard gas in containers on planes if it ever had had to be used. And thank heavens that never was used. Whilst there at Heliopolis, I was, we loaded quite a few trucks of everything up of gas that was shipped back here to Australia. I mean it's been denied a lot of times there was no gas, but there was, mustard gas was sent back... We had enormous caves and everything all underground into a big cavern in the hill. An enormous big caverns and caves where all this gas was stored. It was all mustard gas that we were handling... just the container that was to fit under the bomb rack on the plane and it was only just explaining about how to pour it and filling it up and everything and as to how it worked. It was a big canister; big canister and you'd just pour it in so as that the canister was full. It's a liquid. We had masks and full protective clothing and everything... I was the only one from our squadron that went down to the course.[52]

22 September was the last day with 451 Squadron for Ken Watts, now a flight lieutenant, who was posted to 80 Squadron as Flight Commander. Alan Lane wrote that he was 'one of our best pilots'. It would not end well for Watts: on 6 April 1944, flying Kittyhawks with 3 Squadron in Italy (and now a squadron leader with a DFC), his plane was hit by flak and he had to bail out. On the run for only a short time, he was captured within a few days and while being interrogated at Verona by the Germans, took a savage beating about the head with rifle butts when he stood up to his captors and refused to answer their demands for information. This occurred on at least two occasions and finally the Germans gave up asking questions and he was shipped off to Stalag Luft I at Barth on the north German coast, northeast of Rostock. He survived the war but required multiple brain surgeries as a result of the beatings and was confined to a wheelchair before the age of 60 as a result. Perhaps, surprisingly, he held no grudges against the Germans: 'It was kill or be killed, and the more you accounted for the more pats on the back you got! I had the attitude of when or if I was clobbered, I would take what they dish out.' In fact, he accepted

his place as prisoner of the Germans, knowing that, 'Many young airmen paid the supreme sacrifice for helping eliminate Nazi tyranny...oblivion was their constant companion.'[53]

On 26 September, two staff, PO Simmons and FS Waghorn plus a local guide, set off across the desert in a truck looking for an aircraft which was reported to have crashed near El Maghra. After some 50 to 60 miles in the desert south of El Alamein, the guide was classed as 'useless' and they declared themselves lost. The truck then became bogged down. Deciding that the truck was unable to be made mobile, once again they set off on foot. After walking for two days they were picked up by a group of New Zealanders on the afternoon of 28 September. Both suffered terribly in the desert, made even worse by the soft sand which gave way with each step taken. They lacked enough food and water for such a trek and had been found just in time, being described as 'on the point of collapse' when found. There was no further mention of the guide.[54] There were no successful intercepts that month, apart from that of two Italian aircraft on 29 September who wanted to surrender.[55]

October 1943 began with staff posted in and out. Surely the best news was received on 8 October: the squadron was to be re-equipped with Spitfires, with the first four Mk Vs arriving that day from 135 MU. Eight more were delivered by 14 October, and the final four on 17 October, bringing the unit up to their establishment of 16 aircraft. On 23 October, the trial Typhoons were delivered to 161 MU, having been flown by 19 different pilots.[56] Ken Watts had just one flight in a Typhoon, for 80 minutes, and recorded 'Wizard' in his logbook, though also later wrote, 'In flight it was very fast and very heavy on the controls, hopeless in manoeuvrability, and very homesick for the ground. They were totally useless for desert conditions.'[57] Alec Arnel was very happy to get a Spitfire, describing them as 'a gentleman's aircraft ... easy to fly ... lighter on the controls and responsive ... A Spitfire felt like a feather compared to them [Hurricanes]. It was just so beautiful.'[58]

Several Australian pilots were posted over from 238 Squadron, replacing those posted out earlier, and others were sent, one at a time, for a few weeks of gunnery school where they usually flew exercises two to three times a day.[59] In addition to convoy patrols, the squadron somehow became responsible for the official mail run from Cairo to Cyprus and supplied one Hurricane for this task on most days, until they became a complete Spitfire squadron at which time the job was taken off them.[60]

November started with a VIP visit: Air Cdre Rankin and Wing Cdr Wincott stayed for just over two hours and left favourable comments after their inspection. The squadron left their base at El-Daba and moved to 22 PTC (Almaza) on 9 November where they received new vehicles on 11 November which were completely overhauled and camouflaged in preparation for the squadron's move to the front. There followed a messy move, whereby the squadron was divided into a road and rail convoy. The road convoy left on the morning of the 16th and travelled for three days before being recalled.[61] Postings still occurred during this period of annoyance and uncertainty. One such to arrive was FO George O'Neil. George Connor O'Neil (Service No. 403475) was born on 10 November 1915 in Vaucluse, in the eastern suburbs of Sydney, though when he enlisted on 7 January 1941, he was working as a jackaroo in the west of New South Wales. He completed his EFTS and SFTS in Australia and Canada respectively, and prior to arriving at 451 Squadron he had served with 450 and 680 Squadrons. He was quite unique in that he had been awarded the Military Medal, the citation for which read:

> On 25 July, 1942, Pilot Officer [then Sergeant] O'Neil effected a forced landing on Nammon due to engine failure and was successful in making his way back to the British line. After a low level attack on the enemy near Churgia on 13th January, 1943, he was compelled to land many miles behind enemy lines. Despite machine gun fire he penetrated enemy lines and reached our forces three days later. He displayed great courage and resource in evading capture and made a useful report for the military authorities.[62]

Naturally, citations are often short and do not necessarily give a full account of the events which resulted in the presentation of the medal. Upon his return from the crash-landing in January 1943, O'Neil submitted an escape narrative which outlined his actions. On the day in question, he took off at 0750 hours in a formation of Kittyhawks to strafe Tauorga LG but didn't find it, so the formation strafed vehicles on a road instead. He was flying so low that on his second burst, the propeller hit a rise in the ground, badly damaging the blades. He was in no position to bail out so flew south-south-west until the engine overheated and he made a forced landing. He took the emergency rations and water bottle, which was only one-third full and headed south into the desert. He'd only gone a short distance when a truck approached the plane so he crawled away on his hands and knees, taking cover behind camelthorn bushes and slowly making his way further and further from the crash site.

When the trucks finally gave up looking for him, he continued south to a wadi and hid there for a time until he was sure the search was over. In the early afternoon he found a dirty and abandoned Italian position near a road and was able to scrounge some salty water from a damaged vehicle there and topped up his water bottle, dropping the purification tablets in as well. He waited until the sun began to set and moved off to the south-east and found another wadi, and crossed it, avoiding a number of enemy positions and vehicles that had stopped for the night. Though the desert heat can be oppressive during the day, the cold of the night can be just as debilitating and, despite covering himself with sand and a mat and hiding under bushes, he didn't sleep well that first night. He was up early the next morning and crossed more wadis and a road, being careful to avoid trucks on the move. He continued south-east and later came across another traveller whom he thought might be an Arab, but he turned out to be Italian, and quite timid. After a halting conversation in English, Italian and Arabic they parted ways. He watched an aircraft crash and the pilot land in their parachute sometime later, but stayed well away from the area, as a search party was sure to follow—no matter which side the pilot belonged to. He kept an eye out for anything that might be useful and found some hessian which he wrapped around his shoulders so as to give the appearance of an Arab, if seen from a distance. Apparently, it worked well for close-up concealment as he passed a number of German units during the day, sometimes as close as 50 yards, and was not stopped or questioned. Later he passed by some enemy troops constructing fortifications and forced his way through the barbed wire but could not make it through a thicker section. There were too many Germans around to be able to walk up and down the wire looking for a weak spot, so he rested and ate the last of his bully beef and biscuits.

Around 1730, he noticed guards taking up their posts and knew it was time to move, so found a spot and crossed the wire, just a short distance from a German who paid him no attention. He walked directly east, not rushing in order to keep his manner as natural as possible, but after he'd covered about 600 yards, he was fired on by a machine gun from the positions he had passed through. After the third burst he fell in a way that he hoped would indicate he'd been shot, then waited: there was only silence. After five or ten minutes he slid on his stomach for another 50 yards then stayed in that new spot until dark. When he thought it was safe, he got up again and continued east and after an hour or so heard voices and approached slowly until he identified them as friendly. He found infantry of the 7th Black Watch and was taken to a nearby artillery unit who looked after him. During his escape he'd only taken one benzedrine tablet (amphetamines) and recommended them for staying alert, stating that, 'It pepped me up considerably'. The compass was also very useful but the map carried by pilots was not detailed enough to be of much assistance.[63] George O'Neil was not just a fighter, but a survivor. Just what 451 Squadron needed.

On 18 November, Alan Lane took some of the ground crew up in the Miles Magister for short flights and even let them take the controls for short periods.[64] On 21 November, the squadron was detailed to supply an escort to an aircraft carrying a VIP, which Lane's logbook discloses as Churchill himself. However, Lane didn't get to participate in the escort because he pranged his Spitfire while taxiing to the take-off point, and was left behind.[65] By 22 November, everyone, except some aircraft, was back at El Daba. As soon as they arrived, maintenance crews were dispatched to the bases where their Spitfires were temporarily based (Idku and Mersa Matruh). Some convoy escorts were carried out in the first and last weeks of the month, but otherwise it was yet another relatively uneventful month for the squadron.[66] Being split up and moved about had been the lot of 451 Squadron for almost two years. They just wanted to be together and fight together, but no matter how many visits they received from RAAF liaison officers, nothing seemed to get better for any appreciable amount of time.

December 1943 started with a grand claim. The entry in the daily squadron records for 2 December stated, 'In view of recent re-equipping with Spitfire Aircraft it is desired that this squadron in future be referred to by Public Relations as the "First All Australian Spitfire Squadron".' The fact that a Canadian, PO Hough, was still on strength and performing flying duties, did not seem to impact on this decision, nor did the presence of PO Davis, an RAF pilot.[67] They should have asked around: 453 Squadron was 'All Australian' with regards to aircrew in December 1942![68]

On 9 December, Sqn Ldr Kirkham returned to the squadron to take command from Sqn Ldr Stevens who had to return to Australia as his wife had become seriously ill. As the squadron could not support two squadron leader positions while Stevens was away, he had to take a reduction in rank to flying officer, something that later made *The Sun* newspaper in Australia.[69] FO Bartlett was injured on 13 December when his Spitfire overturned after encountering a patch of foul ground whilst landing at Idku. He was taken to 64th General Hospital for treatment to his face and right arm. On 14 December, the squadron was represented by 26 members at a parade held by 219 Group for ACM Sir Sholto Douglas and AVM Saul and congratulations on their performance and bearing were passed on.[70]

On 17 December, PO Henry John Bray was posted in from Abu Sueir. Unlike the early days when 451 Squadron was struggling for pilots with experience, Bray had been around for some time. Henry John Bray was born on 13 March 1919 and was working as a clerk when he enlisted in Queensland on 16 August 1940. Passed medically fit for aircrew he did all his early flying training in Australia at 2 EFTS Archerfield and 3 SFTS Amberley. In May 1941 he sailed from Australia to the UK and arrived at 61 OTU in September, followed shortly afterwards by a posting to 123 Squadron, then to the Middle East, commencing flying with fellow Australians in 3 Squadron in April 1942 where he flew Kittyhawks.[71]

On 25 December, the squadron held a Christmas dinner in the airmen's mess at El Daba and invited some nearby units to attend. In accordance with tradition, the officers and sergeants served the airmen and a grand time was had by everyone. Photographs were taken by the public relations representative present.[72] The menu consisted of soup, roast pork and chicken and pudding with custard sauce, amongst other items. Each menu item had the name or nickname of someone from the squadron added to it, thus Lane's Christmas Pudding and Butcher's Brandy Sauce or Sliced Kirkham Peaches and Aspley Cream. Menus were passed around the squadron—there was a place for autographs on the back page and many signed their name, some including their home address in the hope that, in years to come they could stay in touch.[73] But they had to make it home first.

The next day advice was received that the squadron would be receiving six Spitfire Mk IXs, and these arrived by the end of the month from 80 and 74

Squadrons and 135 MU, the squadron handing over six Mk VCs to keep the books in order. During the month all Spitfires were fitted with bomb racks and pilots were trained in dive-bombing when they weren't carrying out their convoy escorts. Alan Lane took his first flight in a Spitfire Mk IX (MA456) on 29 December and wrote in his logbook, 'Wizard aircraft.'[74] The upgrade of Spitfires and fitting of bomb racks was a good sign—action was surely to follow.

On 3 January 1944, the squadron commemorated their 1,000th day of overseas service. A concert was held in the airmen's canteen and was attended by Padre Davies and FO Robertson from Public Relations. The programme of entertainment went for two hours and everyone had a great time. Meanwhile convoy patrols and attempted interceptions continued. 10 January saw the departure of Canadian pilot T.J. Hough to 22 PTC for redeployment and six days later, Bartlett was taken off strength as he was still in hospital recovering from his crash a month earlier. The same day a detachment of ten Spitfire Mk VCs was sent to Kabrit for Exercise *Tussle* which was conducted with a number of army units. Meanwhile, two of the Spitfire Mk IXs and some ground crew were deployed to Dekheila, just west of Alexandria, for intercepting aircraft approaching that area. The detachment for Exercise *Tussle* returned on 23 January with compliments on their cooperation, and the squadron received notice that it was to be moved to Gamil, Port Said. This was about 150 km east of Alexandria and nowhere near the action. The Spitfire Mark IXs did not return until 31 January and, due to bad weather, the ground party was delayed until 4 February. Bartlett returned on 11 February for ground duties, awaiting approval for him to resume flying duties, while convoy patrols and scrambles continued.[75]

In mid-February a report was created in support of the squadron being returned to Australia for operations in the Pacific. It was created by Gp Capt Duncan, RAAF Liaison Officer and submitted to RAAF Overseas HQ in London. The page-long report stated that, amongst other matters, pilots were required to complete 300 operational flying hours (the standard for UK-based fighter squadrons was 200) which was hard to do when operational sorties were hard to come by, meaning a pilot could be on strength for three years trying to accumulate the required time before being posted out 'on rest'. As a result, both the pilots and ground crew were becoming unhappy and losing enthusiasm for their duties. The report concluded with the paragraph:

> It does not seem necessary to keep the Squadron in the Middle East and it is considered that it can render more useful service in operations against the Japanese. The return to active operations will be welcomed by the aircrew and ground staff. It is requested that you give consideration to the withdrawal of the Unit from Middle East for more active employment elsewhere.[76]

Being unhappy in the Middle East was not unique to 451 Squadron. A newspaper article titled 'Leave for R.A.A.F.' appeared in *The Age* newspaper in Melbourne in October 1943 and was followed by the ominous subtitle 'Discontent Overseas'. It criticised the 'Lack of an Australian policy governing service abroad' as the source of the discontent.[77] The article cited RAF policy for periods of time to be served in the Middle East but stated Australia had no such policy, and followed this up with agitation caused by Australian newspapers arriving in the Middle East reporting that ground crew could return to Australia after two years' service in the region if they applied to do so. Since many had been in there since 1941 or earlier, it caused quite a stir. The pot was stirred more thoroughly when claims were made that some men had received letters breaking off engagements because they had not come home when presented with the opportunity. It was a very damning article that went even further, citing lack of promotion and leave entitlements as additional reasons for dissatisfaction. A reply from Minister for Air labelled the two-year claim as false and said there was no provision within EATS for personnel to be withdrawn after certain periods of service. Given that the claims made in the article may well have been rumours, it shows how putting them into print can be harmful for those serving overseas.[78]

But one thing that often brought joy and comfort to the squadrons during the war was having a dog around, and the mascot for 451 Squadron during the latter part of their time in the Middle East and through Corsica was a dog named 'Hurri', short for Hurricane. They'd found him on Cyprus when a flight had been deployed there in 1942 and begged the farmer who owned him to allow them to adopt him, according to one version of events. Another story states that the dog belonged to an anti-aircraft unit and would go mad any time they fired their guns, so they had to give him away, and the Australians became his adopted owners. He slept in the same tent as George Purdy and

Barney Wallis. Like many of the pilots, Hurri had a narrow escape of his own, but with a friendly aircraft. One day he walked too close to a spinning propeller and it clipped him, the wound requiring a few stitches, but he soon healed, and stayed a bit further away from aircraft afterwards. The squadron also had another dog, a puppy named Mate (or Doughnut, depending on sources)—also thanks to Barney Wallis. Hurri was able to go on the ship to Corsica with the ground crew, but the puppy flew in a kitbag mounted on a platform behind the armoured plate of George Purdy's Spitfire, all constructed and modified by his ground crew, Fred Bonzer and Joe Cross. Though Hurri was healthy and tough enough for the desert, and therefore Corsica, the puppy didn't last long and died of pneumonia a few months later.[79]

On 21 February, the squadron engaged the enemy for the first time in many months. At 0658 Flt Lt Gale and FO Purdy took off in their Mk IXs, scrambled for a Luftwaffe snooper at 30,000 ft. When they reached 28,000 ft, they sighted the Ju 88 and at 0723 attacked. They were spotted and the Junkers turned towards them to head north and went into a dive to get away, but Gale fired on it as it went down and it began to climb again and entered cloud. Gale and Purdy separated a little with Gale waiting beneath the cloud and Purdy above. As anticipated, when the Junkers exited the cloud it was in a steep dive and both Spitfires went after it, each making several attacks, and hitting the plane each time. They followed it all the way down to 300 ft, before it crashed into the sea with no survivors. Despite the Junkers normally being armed with defensive machine guns, no return fire was encountered during the engagement.[80]

On 23 February, advice was received that the squadron would soon be moving to an active theatre of war, and all staff except the pilots (and their aircraft) were moved to 22 PTC in preparation for the big move. Since the ground staff were gone, the aircraft were looked after by 58 RSU. At the start of March 1944, the squadron remained disappointed by delays and was still waiting for news of their redeployment, but Flt Lt Trenorden was posted out to become a squadron leader with 92 (East India) Squadron.[81] More pilots were posted in, including FS Ross Sheppard. Ross Frederick Sheppard (Service No. 417241) was a watchmaker with the family business when he joined the 27th Militia Battalion in 1940, but in January 1942 he left the militia and joined the RAAF, passed his medical for flying training and in June 1942 found himself at 1 EFTS Parafield in South Australia, his home state. His first lesson in a Tiger Moth was on 27 June and after just 7 hours and 15 minutes of flying, he went solo on 6 July. He completed his EFTS with an 'Average +' rating and moved on to 5 SFTS Uranquinty where he was introduced to the Wirraway. He maintained his overall 'Average +' rating and departed Australia on 6 March 1943, leaving behind his wife Joan. He arrived in the UK on 17 April and commenced flying at No. 17 AFU at Wrexham, Wales, where he flew the Master II, then 17 (P) AFU at Calveley, England. In January 1944 he arrived at 71 OTU, Ismailia in Egypt, where, after a few trips in a Harvard trainer he went solo in an old Hurricane Mk I. Now that he was ready to fight, Sheppard was sent to 451 Squadron, and they had Spitfires—of course, you'd send a Hurricane-trained pilot to a Spitfire squadron. The solution to his lack of Spitfire experience was a posting to a training wing in Italy, where after eleven hours and 35 minutes on Spitfire VBs and VCs he was once again declared ready for war and posted back to 451 Squadron to fly Spitfire Mk IXs.[82]

Towards the end of the month orders were received for the big move, and the squadron proceeded by truck and then train to the docks in Alexandria, where they loaded aboard the SS *Samaritan* and HT *Circassia* over three days, the troops in HT *Circassia* departing on 24 March and their equipment on the SS *Samaritan* finally departing on the morning of 26 March with their destination: Corsica. One pilot who would not be accompanying them was Flt Lt Bartlett, who was posted out of the squadron to test pilot duties, though by August 1944 he was back in Australia.[83]

The personnel of the squadron arrived at the Corsican port of Ajaccio on 30 March 1944 and were loaned transport by the Americans so they could make their way to the transit camp, where they waited for their transfer to Poretta. The Spitfires were flown by squadron pilots to Corsica, from Gamil, via Helwan, Marble Arch, El Adem, and Castel Benito, arriving at Poretta on 18 April. After having flown all the way to Corsica, Flt Lt Bayly was promoted to squadron leader and posted out to 3 Squadron (RAAF) as commander. He was able to take another officer with him, and offered the spot to FO Thomas, but he declined, not wanting to give up a Spitfire for a Kittyhawk, and in the end Jack Gleeson went with him.[84] On 20 April, the squadron was visited by the RAAF Liaison Officer and Welfare Officer, who had been visiting other squadrons in the theatre. Staff were spoken to about their needs, and while personal matters were raised, the Welfare Officer agreed to have a supply of cricket balls delivered to them.[85] Herbert Biggs, a member of the ground crew, found Corsica quite agreeable; 'It was Italian French ... coming from the sand and the desert to Corsica was absolutely, hugely, well the opposite. We even had gum trees on Corsica. There were orchards, flowers. It was totally different. It was a green island. It was really great. The people were good. We had no trouble there. They welcomed us.'[86]

Poretta was located on a large flat area with the sea to the east and mountains to the west. There was a river to the south and the airstrip itself was about 4,000 feet long. The locals were described as 'friendly and hospitable' but Allied troops nearby not so, and on two occasions Australians were attacked by the French Moroccan cavalry troops after refusing them cigarettes. Some of the locals were suffering from malaria, but the area had seen almost no rain for six months prior to the squadron's arrival. Food, when cooked, was done in improvised ovens as the unit cookers could not be used, as there was no kerosene available. Breakfast was usually tinned bacon, and other meals were tinned meat of some sort and dehydrated vegetables, with little by way of condiments to vary the flavours. However, unlike the desert from which they'd come, the water was good and unlimited, provided by the Americans who were located less than a mile from the base. A nearby unit of American engineers provided hot showers at negotiated times and laundry was done by the river or by arrangement with the civilian population. Some of the medical supplies left behind by the Germans was added to the squadron stores; especially useful were the anti-malarial quinine tablets.[87]

Where available, commanders appeared to prefer Caucasian British troops to guard their bases—either from the RAF Regiment or an appropriate army unit; but non-whites were certainly looked down upon, not trusted, or both, as shown by this statement in airfield defence orders for 'East African Troops':

> The men of these coys [military abbreviation for companies] while excellent for straightforward guard or labour duties, are of limited mentality. They can be expected to obey simple orders, but to give them any powers of discretion is impracticable, and outside the province of their thoughts.[88]

The documents also contained 'a brief description of the East African to help you understand him'. Though many of the comments made subsequent to this opening line do not align with modern standards, they did conclude with a prescient statement that

> it should be borne in mind that after the war, East Africa will have many important native problems to resolve. The solution of these problems is going to be easier or more difficult according to the way in which the East African is treated during the war.[89]

On Corsica, 451 Squadron was part of 251 Wing, which also consisted of 237 and 238 Squadrons. There was another Spitfire wing on Corsica also, and both belonged to XII Air Support Command of MATAF (Mediterranean Allied Tactical Air Force). Though entirely belonging to Commonwealth nations, 251 Wing was subordinated to the USAAF who, confusingly, also called their command a 'wing', though it was actually the next level higher and in RAF terms would be known as a group. Each evening orders for the next day were distributed by teleprinter and further relevant decisions were left to the formation commanders. Each mission was preceded by a briefing by Wing Cdr Morris or the squadron leader in charge.[90]

Born in South Africa on 6 April 1915,[91] Edward James Morris joined the RAF in July 1937 and was instructed on a Miles Hawk, rather than the usual Tiger Moth. On receiving his wings, he proposed a posting to flying boats but was informed he was to go to fighters. His first operational posting was to 79 Squadron at Biggin Hill in April 1939 which was then equipped with Gloster Gauntlet biplanes. Morris survived a bout of meningitis which kept him out of action for a few months until July 1940, when he was back with the squadron at Biggin Hill, which had now been equipped with Hurricanes. The squadron moved through several airfields during the Battle of Britain and he survived numerous dogfights, a collision with a Heinkel He 111 bomber which resulted in him having to bail out and, on another occasion, make a wheels-up landing in his badly damaged Hurricane. His Battle of Britain ended with him in hospital with wounds sustained in the action that forced the wheels-up landing. By May 1941 he was with 238 Squadron on HMS *Victorious* heading to the Middle East in a relief convoy. There was a sudden change of plans onboard and the warships were detailed to head after the *Bismarck*, which was subsequently sunk, and the fleet returned to Glasgow. From there HMS *Victorious* went to Gibraltar and joined another carrier, HMS *Ark Royal* in

Force H to reinforce Allied formations in North Africa via Malta.[92]

238 Squadron joined with 274 Squadron and the desert conditions shocked Morris, so used to RAF Fighter Command organisation and neatness in England. Though they were equipped with old Hurricane Mk Is, these had been modified locally with extra fuel tanks to give them twice the range of regular Hurricanes. After August 1941 Morris was posted as Acting Squadron Leader to 250 Squadron and AVM Coningham took over what became the Desert Air Force. With new energy radiating from the top of the chain of command, things began to improve immediately. 250 Squadron was equipped with Tomahawks (P-40s) which he described as 'an improvement on the Hurricane in some respects but hardly an improvement in others'.[93] When some of the more experienced pilots were posted out, he had someone promoted from within the squadron, an Australian named Clive Caldwell. Sqn Ldr Morris led 250 Squadron through Operation *Crusader* and in January 1942 was shot down after damaging a Bf 110 which was finished off by the rest of his squadron. He was lucky and found an Allied armoured formation that returned him to his squadron. On 8 April, after the squadron was re-equipped with new Kittyhawks, Sqn Ldr Morris was awarded the DSO 'in recognition of the long and distinguished career as a fighter pilot and leader'.[94]

Morris was then posted to HQ Desert Air Force as an acting wing commander, undertaking the role of Group Training Instructor Fighters. He was 27. After some months he was politely sacked after a disagreement with Gp Capt Broadhurst regarding the performance of some RAAF squadrons. It wasn't the last time that would happen: sacking a subordinate was certainly one way to deal with disagreements. Broadhurst also sacked Wing Cdr Pitt-Brown from 121 Wing in October 1944 after they disagreed about Typhoon operations[95] and, justified or not, it was a method of management and keeping people in line. Morris was assigned the role of air advisor for the 2nd New Zealand Division for their post-Alamein advance on Tripoli. He liked the friendly and casual nature of the New Zealanders but after a month, Morris was posted to Castel Benito as station commander of the former Italian airfield. After his stint there he went on leave to South Africa and returned to be made commander at 71 OTU at Carthago in Sudan, in April 1943.[96] It was a Hurricane OTU, and though they were past their prime, they still had a place in the desert, assuming they were the heavily armed ground-attack versions. As a fighter their place was now in history. 71 OTU was eventually moved 1,500 miles north to Ismailia in Egypt and at the conclusion of that posting, he was given command of 251 Wing. Knowing they were equipped with Spitfires, he used his connections to get some time in a Mk V and Mk VIII, and he flew some operational sorties before arriving to take command.[97] Wing Commander Morris would be leading from the front; there was no doubt about that.

Prior to commencing operations from Corsica, 451 Squadron took part in some practice flying, and on one of these occasions FO Thomas, in his Spitfire Mk IX, had an American in one of their P-51 Mustangs come alongside and

> indicated by hand signals that he would like to try out the Mustang against the Mark IX Spitfire. First we tried straight speed, side by side, and we seemed evenly matched, then we agreed, again by hand signals as we were not on the same radio frequencies, to have a practice dogfight. I really enjoyed this and felt that I had got the better of the deal though it was impossible to tell whether it was because of greater experience, or because I had the better plane. The general impression I gained was that the Mustang and the Mark IX Spitfire were evenly matched.[98]

Alec Arnel also had an encounter with an American pilot, who said they'd never seen a Spitfire up close before. He was invited to sit in the cockpit and he said, 'Oh man, this would not suit me.' When asked why, he replied, 'Well you can't run around, not enough room to run around yelling help!'[99]

On 23 April, 451 Squadron's first operational sortie took off from Corsica. Ten Mk IXs took off as part of an escort, which also included 243 Squadron, for 24 B-25 Mitchells on a bombing mission to Italy. During the mission 14 enemy aircraft were sighted (ten Fw 190s and four Bf 109s) and the squadron went after them, led by Wing Cdr Morris in his personalised Mk IX (MK187) with his markings of TM instead of the usual squadron codes.[100] With three Australians as backup, including Sqn Ldr Kirkham, Morris went after a Bf 109, got on its tail and fired from 200 yds, with hits confirmed. FO Wallis then went in after it, closing to 150 yards and firing three bursts totalling 400 rounds of .303 and 100 rounds of 20 mm, some of which struck the cockpit area, blowing the canopy off and starting a fire. The Messerschmitt rolled onto its back and fell from the sky, the crash being witnessed by three of the squadron.[101] First sortie, first engagement and first claim of an aircraft destroyed, this was the war 451 Squadron had been looking for. Another sortie of eight Spitfires, also led by Morris, carried out an armed recce (split in two: top cover and the attacking section) in the Leghorn (Livorno)–Florence–Siena area later that day. Some railway trucks were strafed in the Siena railway station, but none appeared damaged sufficiently to make any claims.[102]

To keep 12 aircraft in the air at any given time a squadron generally had about 18 aircraft and 25 pilots, which meant that there was usually a pilot available for a task or two. One unofficial, though essential, task was the 'grog run', which involved a Jeep, some jerrycans and a few staff travelling the countryside and visiting the resident farmers to see what could be bought, especially in the way of wine. The Australians would call on a farmer, sample their wares and then negotiate a price and move on to the next, until enough had been bought for the mess to be stocked for a while, at which time another 'grog run' would be put on.[103] If an army marches on its stomach, what does that say about the air force and alcohol?

Operations continued on 24 April, with an escort, led by Sqn Ldr Kirkham, to 24 B-26 Marauders attacking a railway bridge at Incisa (south-east of Florence) followed by an armed recce of the Ciciano–Poggibonsi area, where trucks and railway wagons were attacked with success—all were damaged to some degree, some severely, and one truck caught fire. The following day saw a return trip to Incisa, with heavy anti-aircraft fire over the target and even heavier resistance encountered by some bombers who split off to attack Leghorn, though all bombs fell into the sea. Ciciano–Poggibonsi was in for harassment again and several vehicles were attacked, including trucks and a staff car. One truck was claimed as destroyed. One Spitfire was slightly damaged, but all made it home safely. After bad weather shut down the airstrip on the 26th, another armed recce took place on 27 April, with another Spitfire taking minor damage but all returning safely. The squadron lost another pilot to 3 Squadron on this day, FO Gleeson being promoted to flight lieutenant and posted there to take up duties as a flight commander. Bomber escorts and armed recces continued around the same areas for the rest of the month, and several vehicles were strafed, as were some barges and railway wagons (one of which carried a camouflaged gun), but the Luftwaffe declined to rise and meet them in combat. The Americans, with whom 451 Squadron was based, played two games of baseball with the Australians during the month and each team won a game.

The squadron record included this notable comment at the end of the month:

> In view of the fact that this Unit has not participated in warfare against the enemy to any great extent for a period of over two years, both aircrew and ground personnel displayed the greatest keenness in their duties. The result of the transfer of the Squadron to the present active theatre of war has resulted in great improvement in the morale of personnel.[104]

The squadron had been raised for war, and that's all they were after: to do their part. They were now operating well behind the front line carrying out interdiction sorties. They wouldn't be seen by any Allied ground troops in direct support of their attacks; they operated against the logistics of the Axis forces. Very simply, interdiction affects the ability of the enemy to move and fight, without necessarily causing casualties. If a German position was defended by a company of infantry and a few tanks and Allied troops were set to attack them, direct support would have aircraft attacking those troops and tanks, dropping bombs and machine-gunning them. But interdiction, as carried out by 451 Squadron (and others), meant that when the attack went in against that town the troops defending it might not be able to resist for long because their ammunition resupply had not been able to get through to them—it had been blown up on a train 100 miles away. Maybe it would mean that the German tanks didn't have enough fuel to relocate to better firing positions during the battle because fuel tankers couldn't get across the rivers to make it to the front line because all the bridges had been blown up. Maybe the German artillery wouldn't be able to fire on the attacking Allied troops because they had no ammunition, as they'd used it all the previous day and were waiting for more, and it wasn't going to arrive because the trucks carrying the shells had been strafed and some had exploded, destroying the ammunition. These are basic examples of ways in which interdiction can influence the front-line battle. Naturally, the troops on the front line will still complain that they don't 'see' the air force, which, to them, means the air force isn't contributing anything to their particular struggle. They're wrong, but only because they don't get to see the whole picture.

1 May 1944 started with a weather recce, led by Flt Lt McBurnie in MJ513, followed by a bomber escort to 36 B-25s attacking bridges in Italy during the morning, followed by another bomber escort in the afternoon. Two escorts took place the next day; the first was led by Flt Lt Gale in JL351 to a bridge and the second to railway yards, but cloud on 3 May prevented any bombing. The fighter sweep on the afternoon of the 4th also encountered a lot of cloud and returned empty handed. Another was attempted on 5 May but no enemy aircraft were encountered, and poor weather prevented ops over the next two days. Only three sorties took place on 8 May, single Spitfires going up for weather recces at 0550 (Flt Lt Gale in JL351), 0920 (Flt Lt Gale in MJ513) and 1755 (FO Mercer in JL351). Two more fighter sweeps were attempted on the 9th but only anti-aircraft fire greeted them, and all aircraft returned safely.[105]

10 May was far more productive. Twelve Spitfires, led by Wing Cdr Morris in MK187, went over the triangle of Piombino–Civitavecchia–Orvieto on a fighter sweep and armed recce. The pilots returned with positive results. Two large METs were damaged, and the squadron discovered a dummy airfield and aircraft, which they rated as 'extraordinarily effective'. However, they also found the real airfield and two aircraft under camouflage netting believed to be Fw 190s; after strafing by FO O'Neil, one burst into flames, with the other left smoking. Eighteen railway trucks were also attacked. A bit of anti-aircraft fire was encountered here and there but certainly no coordinated effort was made to fight off the Australian Spitfires. On 11 May, the squadron escorted USAAF bombers on an attack against Ficulle. Since the first target was obscured by cloud only half the bombers attacked, the rest saving theirs for a secondary target in the small port of Piombino. Here a lot of anti-aircraft fire was encountered but it was inaccurate.[106]

12 May saw 12 Spitfires, led by Sqn Ldr Kirkham in JL351, off to Italy again for a fighter sweep which developed into an armed recce when no enemy aircraft appeared. Railway trucks were attacked, as was a large barge. While not a lot of anti-aircraft fire was put up in response, it was accurate enough to damage one Spitfire, which made it home with the others. This effort was duplicated in the afternoon, this time some METs were left smoking, railway wagons were again strafed, and several ships were found. One about 150 ft long was strafed several times by Gale, Mercer, Purdy and Wallis, leaving it immobilised and clearly leaking oil. Later information revealed that the vessel had sunk.[107]

About 2200 on 12 May, the Germans struck back at Corsica. About 25 Ju 88s attacked Poretta airfield. The defending anti-aircraft guns commenced firing at the bombers and soon flares lit up the whole area. Any and all personnel not manning guns took what shelter they could find as the Germans dived down to attack from as low as 300 to 500 ft, and sometimes even below their own flares. Numerous attacks were made on the airfield and sticks of anti-personnel bombs were dropped. The attack lasted for about 25 minutes and the Australian and British medical staff were soon joined by their American counterparts. The Australians suffered many casualties:

SERVICE NO.	RANK	NAME	ROLE	RESULT
403228	Flt Lt	R.B. Sneddon	Pilot	Killed
408177	Flt Lt	J.D. Ward	Pilot	Died of wounds (DOW) 17 May
24205	Cpl	F.E. Bulcock	Fitter	Killed
11204	LAC	A. Ewans	Telephonist	Killed
14436	LAC	S.J. Branch	Fitter	DOW 12 May
30550	LAC	C.A. Conrad	Armourer	DOW 13 May
11963	LAC	H.A. McKay	Fabric worker	DOW 13 May
14675	LAC	D.C. Haggart	Fitter	DOW 1 June
10142	LAC	R.D. Andrews	Instrument maker	Seriously wounded
10063	LAC	J.C. Lewis	Fitter	Seriously wounded
30366	LAC	R.M. Burslem	Driver	Seriously wounded
RAF 1091951	LAC	A.H. Oldridge	Aircraft hand	Seriously wounded
12176	Sgt	T.C. Wilbraham	Cook	Slightly wounded
32669	LAC	S.J. Gabriel	Sheet metal worker	Slightly wounded
RAF 1345016	Cpl	W.F. Hamilton	Cook	Slightly wounded
408179	Flt Lt	R.J. Robert	Pilot	Very slightly wounded
11966	LAC	J. Snowball	Equipment assistant	Very slightly wounded
23143	LAC	J.L. Bellert	Fitter	Very slightly wounded
24412	Cpl	J.H. Buckland	Cook	Very slightly wounded

That night, the squadron's medical officer, Squadron Leader Frances Perrottet, worked on the wounded while the raid went on, and performed several complicated operations afterwards, no doubt saving the lives of several members of the squadron. His worked was praised at the hospital where the wounded were taken and for this, and other work, he was later mentioned in dispatches.[108] An analysis of the casualties showed that those who died were mainly killed by head or chest wounds, and little could be done for them at the time, with some of the anti-personnel bomblets falling directly into slit trenches.[109] Many small-town newspapers carried short articles regarding the death of these Australians, so far from home.[110]

Herbert Biggs was there when the airfield was attacked:

> The old fellas, the old campaigners really felt it on that strike more than the one in North Africa. But to lose mates and that it was pretty tough. The slit trench I was in, there were four of us, and I could hear these bombs screaming down and I was quite interested to see what was going on which was the wrong thing to do. My brother-in-law now, he was the one who dragged me down, and as he did there was one exploded right alongside where I was standing up. It would have been goodnight. The fellas who were caught above ground ... they suffered terrifically really. There were great patches of skin and flesh off their backs ... fragments that small and sharp and it just tore hell out of them. They got over it but a lot didn't. Some of the small bombs landed in the trenches you know. I know one of my mates, one landed on his chest and you can imagine the mess it made. Another fellow in the trench near by ... this chap actually sung out to his mate, are you alright? And apparently he went around and felt for him and all he could find was just blood and everything else. That really got to him because I could hear him screaming you know. Not the best.[111]

The Australians were eager to get back at the Luftwaffe (as were the British and Americans who had also suffered casualties in the raid), and though the damaged Spitfires were ready by noon the next day, it was reported that USAAF P-38 Lightnings had already found the bombers on the ground and flamed 18 of them in strafing attacks.[112] Many of the ground crew spent many hours picking up shrapnel from the airfield, not as souvenirs, but to ensure that it didn't damage any aircraft taking off or landing by bursting a tyre or being taken up in a plane's intake.[113]

Escorts continued on 13 and 14 May, but the frequency of operations was starting to take a toll on the aircraft; magneto problems, rough-running engines and the like all causing some aircraft to return early. Perhaps to help ease the strain on aircraft and the squadron after the losses caused by the bombing raid, 451 Squadron provided only a top cover of six Spitfires for these two days, the remainder of the escort being made up by 237 and 238 Squadrons. Even then, the morning sortie on 14 May only ended up being five aircraft because one crashed before taking off, destroying the plane but leaving the pilot uninjured.[114]

On Sunday 14 May at 1700, the six Australians who had been killed in the raid, or who had died of the wounds they sustained in it, were buried at the US military cemetery near Bastia. The burial service was conducted by Padre Fred McKay who happened to be visiting the squadron when the raid took place; he was assisted by a number of other padres, including Chaplain Connelly who read the Catholic service for LAC Conrad. But it was not only 451 Squadron who suffered: three members of 238 Squadron were also buried, as were 19 Americans. At 2000, a sombre open-air church service was held for the squadron by Padre McKay. Flt Lt Ward was buried alongside them on 19 May after he passed away and Padre McKay again held the service.

Work had to continue—and a weather recce on 15 May, led by Flt Lt McBurnie in MJ203, soon developed into an armed recce when some targets of opportunity arose—a large MET with personnel was destroyed and a 120-ft barge was also strafed and damaged. A bomber escort to the railway bridge and marshalling yards at Orvieto split up when the target was covered by cloud and secondary targets were attacked instead. Similar raids occurred over the next few days, as did armed recces and all Spitfires returned safely, though on the last raid of 18 May, MH574 flown by FO O'Neil was hit by anti-aircraft fire when about to attack a ground target. A 20-mm shell put a hole in his wing root and damaged both fuel tanks (in Spitfires the main fuel tank is located directly behind the instrument panel—the pilot can almost touch it), filling the cockpit to a depth of two inches with fuel. O'Neil didn't panic and flew in this state for 35 minutes, returning to base and landing without further incident.

In a bar in Bastia the Australians found a fellow by the name of Lange Leon, who had been born in Corsica, but had spent 35 years in Australia, living and working in many capital cities and getting himself involved in the racing industry, though the article reporting on his discovery described him as 'unofficially interested in bookmaking'. He'd been in Italy when the war broke out and returned to Corsica to live in his native village, organising bands of patriots to collect information for the Allies and spread pro-Allied propaganda among the Italian and German occupation forces. There was no question of sabotage or sniping though; they had no arms.[115]

On 21 May another special service was held for the squadron, and Sqn Ldr Kirkham read the lesson. Two epilogues were read at this service.[116] The first was read by the ground crew:

> We left Australia together, we arrived abroad together, we lived—we worked—we served together. We were all part of the family of a great Squadron, cemented together by youth, by a sense of duty, and by a common interest. We together faced seen and unseen dangers. We were together when they met their death. Gallant comrades every one: their graves are planted in a land far from home and kith: but their names live on in our hearts, and the unfinished task is in our hands to perform with their devotion and their unselfishness.

This was followed by a reading from the pilots:

> They were members of the team. They had proved themselves by long service and experience. When their hour came in an unexpected way, they gave their lives without murmur, and without shame. Honour is in their laurel for they counted no cost—nor did they question the sacrifice. Greater love hath no man.

Padre McKay stayed until the end of the month and all his services were well attended: the squadron needed a spiritual lift.

The following week consisted of the same types of escorts and recces, and a move for all of 251 Wing on 23 May from Poretta to Serragia, about six miles south, though the squadron personnel continued to live in the same area—about four miles away and in the hills away from the airfields.[117] On 24 May, four Spitfires took off at short notice to escort two Hurricanes of 6 Squadron on an anti-shipping strike. Unfortunately, the Hurricanes disappeared from view on the outward leg—they were down at sea level and the Spitfires were climbing to their cover position and could not see them well enough. However, the

Spitfires continued on their nominated course and flew over the target area a few times, taking note of the shipping along the coast. The Hurricanes were later spotted leaving the target area and everyone made it home safely.[118]

On 25 May, eight Spitfires were tasked to the Viterbo area for a fighter sweep. During the sortie five Fw 190s were sighted with a 2,000 ft height advantage and up-sun going into a line astern formation to attack the Spitfires. The Spitfires turned into the attack and the Germans broke off the dive and fled. While flying over the Roccalbegna area, four Fw 190s were seen 5,000–7,000 ft below the Spitfires. The Australians were not spotted and attacked, the combat resulting in three Fw 190s destroyed and the other damaged for no loss. From the combat report of FO E.C. House:

> While flying as Blue 1 top cover of eight Spits, Green 2 reported A/C at 4 o'clock below. Green 1 and 2 investigated and identified 4 F.W. 190's. I immediately dived to attack, engaged in head on attack. E/A opened fire first at approx. 600 yards. I then opened fire holding attack to 200 yards making E/A give way. No results observed. Attacked again from behind 350 yards approx. 45° opened fire at 30° giving 1 ½ rings at 300 yards. E/A tried to turn inside deflection, but continued to fire at 20° 250-200 yards. Observed strikes on engine which caught fire, pieces falling off fuselage. E/A dived with engine well alight, and observed it hit the ground in flames. Claim: 1 F.W. 190 destroyed.[119]

From the combat report of FO H.J. Bray:

> At approx. 1200 hours while flying at a height of 16,000 ft. to 17,000 ft. heading towards the mouth of the Ombrone River A/C were reported below. I was flying in formation as Green 1 in top cover and on weaving to the left noticed 2 or 3 aircraft pass underneath towards 3 o'clock. On being told to investigate I took my section down out of the sun and approached the hindmost aircraft from 7 o'clock at approx. 10,000 ft and from 500 yards. I identified a/c as enemy and immediately attacked closing to 300 yards. Results unobserved. An aircraft on my left then turned in a climbing turn towards the sun. I immediately climbed and went approx. 1000 ft. above I attacked from 8 o'clock from approx. 300 yds. Closing in to less than 100 yards. Strikes

were observed at the roots of both wings and behind cockpit of the E/A which then rolled slowly on its back, the pilot baling out. I last observed the aircraft diving with large pieces breaking from it. Claim: 1 F.W. 190 destroyed.[120]

From the combat report of Sqn Ldr E.E. Kirkham:

> On sighting E/As by Green 2 of top cover I ordered to top cover to go down and investigate with bottom section following. Green 2 identified a/c as bandits and I immediately went into attack. I followed in and chased 2 F.W.190's without result. At this stage one aircraft dived past me on fire and went straight in. I sighted 1 E/A coming from 2 o'clock below ad turned down into him firing a 3 second burst, with full deflection. I observed strikes on port wing root and behind cockpit, but could not follow up attack as E/A was going up and I was diving down. Shortly after this I saw another E/A crash into the deck. 3 parachutes were seen in the air at the same time by my NO.2 F/ Sgt Stubbs. And one other member of the formation. F/O Minahan. Claim: 1 F.W. 190 damaged.[121]

From the combat report of FO W.W. Thomas:

> While flying as Green 2 in top cover of a formation of 8 Spitfires, I sighted and reported 1 aircraft and 4 o'clock below. On instructions from leader, investigated same with Green 1. I identified 4 F.W. 190's (in lined) travelling West at 7–8,000 ft. South of Grossetto and attacked hind most aircraft which peeled off E. and tried to get away. I opened fire at 400 yards 45° angle off. The enemy aircraft turned left into the attack. I fired 5 or 6 more bursts range 200–300 angle 30°. The E/A the n rolled quickly onto its back and the pilot bailed out. The aircraft went straight in and burst into flames. Claimed 1 F.W.190 destroyed.[122]

Noted for its ability to out-turn most other fighters of the time, in a turning battle it became more than a little bit of work to manage the Spitfire and shoot down the plane in front, and there were moral aspects to be considered. As later reported by FO Thomas:

> Donk was ahead of me at this stage and attacked the leading plane while I took on the second. We were soon in a typical tight circle with Donk on the tail of the first, me on the second, and the third on my tail. I felt quite uncomfortable about this because of my confidence in the ability of a Spitfire to out turn a ME 109. The trouble was though, that while negotiating a practically vertically banked turn, the long nose of the Spitfire obscured the target, so it was a case of easing back until I could see him, drawing a bead through his line of flight, tightening my turn until I estimated I had about the right angle off, and firing blind; ease back to see if he was still there, and if so, which he was, repeat the exercise ... (after the pilot bailed out) ... Completing another circle I found myself bearing down on the parachuting pilot and in accordance with my training I was about to open fire when some instinct made me hesitate ... My hesitation arose from the knowledge that many of the other pilots in the squadron did not have the hard training of the desert, and after all, I had to live with them, and did not fancy the idea of being ostracised ... To settle the question, I called up the C/O. "What about the chaps in the chutes?" The answer came back, "Shoot the bastards" ... Donk Bray called up, "I can't do it boss." That settled it ... It turned out that it was not Ed Kirkham who replied to my query but the Rhodesian C/O of No 237 Squadron who was somewhere within radio range at the time.[123]

Once the dogfight was over the Spitfires headed back to base, low on ammunition and fuel.

From 26 to 29 May, the squadron continued their bomber escorts, sometimes twice a day, and once stopping at Nettuno, inside the Anzio perimeter, to refuel. Unfortunately, on 30 May while on a sweep near Civitavecchia, the squadron's top cover was attacked by a formation of 12 American P-47 Thunderbolts, but the Spitfires managed to get away without any being damaged. Two sweeps on 31 May failed to find any enemy aircraft or ground targets to attack.[124]

May 1944 was also the time of the 'pig hunting incident'. Though Joe Barrington was not with the squadron at the time, he certainly knew about it afterwards:

> What happened, about three of the pilots had observed some pigs in the sort of the woody forest area so they got the rifles out of the armoury and they went after pigs. And they shot several. And immediately the people of the village were up in arms and they called the police because they claimed those pigs were their property. But they didn't pen them, they didn't keep them, they let them roam. It's unusual, very unusual, why would the pig come back? … Now, [the dispute] was never really settled because the pigs were brought back to the squadron and served to the squadron, possession is nine tenths of the law. But the locals countered by making a claim for a huge amount of money and what's more, the claim was made on the Australian government.[125]

It certainly was. On the day in question eight pigs were shot and taken back to the squadron for eating, but a claim for 29 was made by two Corsicans, stating that the Australians had been responsible for killing them all. The pigs were wandering in the forest at the time and the Australians had no reason to suspect they were not wild. A court of inquiry was held and came to the conclusion that eight were killed by the squadron members, no evidence was found to support the higher-numbered claim, the assumption that the pigs were wild was reasonable and the financial amount of the claim was excessive. A subsequent file note recorded that the court was not conducted in a satisfactory manner and the discussion seemed to be distracted by the fact that the incident occurred when the personnel were 'off-duty' and how this should be addressed. This then led to the Australian government declining liability and refusing to pay compensation. In the end, no money was paid, and the matter was not closed until 1949.[126] It was such a relatively small and trivial incident (though, perhaps not for the farmers) in a global war involving so many millions of the world's population, but the matter of a few pigs being shot dragged on for almost five years, illustrating the individual struggles that were often overshadowed by the bigger picture.

Around this time several DFCs were offered to the squadron by the Americans, to be given out to pilots who had shot down an enemy aircraft, but also perhaps in recognition of the numerous escorts the squadron had flown with them over the previous weeks. The offer was rejected by the RAF group commander, stating the pilots had not done enough to earn them.[127] Perhaps by British, RAF, or even Commonwealth standards this was true, but the Americans are known for their generosity, so perhaps they could have been accepted, but then the decision would have to have been made regarding who should receive one. If none was given, then no one would feel left out; they could all feel equally disappointed.

June 1944 began with fighter sweeps and armed recces, usually three or four per day, the first enemy being sighted on 2 June with the squadron attacking railway cars and tankers at Bientina, and three immediately went up in flames. More were attacked at Pontedera, as were scattered METs. The carnage continued that afternoon with an armed recce of 12 Spitfires to the Lucca area. Two staff cars were destroyed, as was a motorbike and sidecar combination, plus some MET damaged. Another armed recce in the afternoon of 3 June saw another staff car destroyed, several MET flamers and a stationary train was given their full attention. Six Spitfires strafed the engine, and when that was left damaged and giving off steam from assorted new holes, the pilots took turns to carry out strafing runs along the full length of the train, all 15–20 wagons considered damaged. Due to being covered by tarpaulins or other material, the exact result could not be ascertained. The squadron was certainly maintaining their maximum effort as another armed recce took place on the same day in addition to a bomber escort.[128]

Another armed recce and bomber escort took place on 4 June. The morning armed recce on the 5th to the Genoa–Savona area found just one staff car, so they went after it, and were satisfied when it exploded. Another sortie in the early evening found a motorcycle and sidecar near Empoli and left it burning, before they found a well-camouflaged tented camp with vehicles. Everyone attacked, leaving three METs burning, another damaged and the tented area a total mess. Weather on 5 June was generally cloudy, some of which obscured the mountaintops, and thus the squadron was forced to stay in the valleys, flying at or below 2,000 ft, and sometimes as low as 500 ft. On 6 June, while the main (Western) Allied force in Europe landed in Normandy, 451 Squadron kept up their attacks, damaging railway trucks, staff cars, METs and even a bus in two sorties totalling 19 aircraft.

7 June was more eventful, with the 12 Spitfires of the morning armed recce, led by Wing Cdr Morris in MK187, finding many MET targets around Vitralla.

All 12 made attacks, with a claim of 14 METs destroyed (some of which were towing trailers) and another 21 damaged. They encountered a moderate amount of small-arms fire in return and two Spitfires were damaged. On the return journey, just 60 miles from Corsica, FO O'Neil's Spitfire's engine caught fire, so he switched the engine off and glided for some distance before bailing out at 4,000 ft, still 15 miles from the coast. He climbed into his dinghy and awaited his rescuers. Two aircraft circled him for only a short time due to a lack of fuel, but FO House in MH547 was sent out from Corsica to replace them and guide in the Walrus for the rescue. The covering Spitfire circled the rescue operation for 30 minutes and when O'Neil was rescued, FO House sank the dinghy as it could not be recovered.[129] At first appearances this might seem wasteful, but each time a dinghy was sighted, aircraft would be diverted to check and see if a pilot was in it waiting to be rescued, so sinking the dinghy would prevent ongoing wasteful diversions from taking place.

The next day on an armed recce, a new type of flak was encountered which was described as 'smokeless, appearing like silver dots or stars coming up in sprays of 20 or 30'.[130] The afternoon sortie went after more railway trucks, MET and yet another staff car. The final sortie of the day, consisting of eight Spitfires, attacked some MET, but just south-west of Poggibonsi, a Ju 88 was seen and chased for 60 miles by Wing Cdr Morris and Flt Lt Sutton. They chased it at low level, and after passing to the south of Siena, carried out a number of attacks, with the satisfying result of the Ju 88's starboard engine catching fire. Its hopes for escape ended there and it commenced a climbing turn to port, perhaps to gain enough height for the crew to bail out, and though the hood came off, it crashed in flames and exploded. Morris and Sutton claimed half a kill each.[131]

More success followed on 9 June. Eight Spitfires, led by Sqn Ldr Kirkham in JL351, were up just before noon on an armed recce in the northern zone allocated to the squadron from Livorno, and enemy aircraft, which later turned out to be three Bf 109s, were spotted behind and 2,500 ft below the Spitfires. The chance was taken, and the Australians attacked, downing all three Luftwaffe aircraft, the claims going to Sutton, Robert and James. While this was going on, four other Bf 109s were sighted passing over a wheat field, which gave them away as their camouflage did not match the terrain. Unfortunately, these were not engaged as the pilot who spotted them, flying as No. 2 to the top cover, could not get through all the radio chatter to report his sighting. He tried five times, and by the time he got through, the Messerschmitts had made their escape.[132]

The three days from 10–12 June saw more armed recces and bomber escorts. The bombers (B-25s) went after bridges, while the Spitfires claimed more MET, motorcycles, staff cars and railway trucks on their attacks. 13 June saw the squadron participate in Operation *Clean Sweep*. This involved much of the Corsica-based fighter force, with 251 Wing (of which 451 Squadron was a part) responsible for the rough square defined by Livorno, La Spezia, Bologna and Florence. 451 Squadron was responsible for the eastern area. 451 Squadron launched two sorties, one at 0600 (eight Spitfires led by Sqn Ldr Kirkham in JL351) and the other at 0615 (four Spitfires led by Wing Cdr Morris in MK187, plus another four from 238 Squadron), which was much earlier than usual. They stayed below 200 ft and when both had assembled, headed to the mainland at low level, not climbing until they made landfall to maintain some element of surprise. The large sortie found only a bus and one MET, both of which were damaged. The smaller sortie did much better: instead of the ground targets they were searching for they discovered an Me 410 flying along a valley. It was promptly shot down by FOs Jones and Mercer and seen to crash in a dry riverbed. FO Jones's combat report read:

> While flying North some 20 miles inland I spotted a military vehicle, which I and my No. 2 went down to strafe. While very low I sighted and reported a twin-engined aircraft some 100 ft. above coming head on, and I identified it as an ME 410. I climbed above the E/A. and was immediately well within 200 yards range, opening fire with cannons, from about a 20° beam attack. The burst of fire was about 5 or 6 seconds duration and strikes were noticed on the back of the cockpit, and port engine nacelle, with small pieces coming off both parts of the aircraft. E/A. then slowly turned towards a narrow strip of land, when my No. 2 made his attack. While the aircraft was still a few feet off the ground, with starboard engine smoking I made another attack from about 40° above closing right in, whereupon he immediately crashed in flames. No return fire was observed. I claim half ME 410 destroyed.[133]

On the return leg of their patrol they attacked a train and engine, with the steam engine destroyed and several railway wagons damaged, and they attacked a second train at another location. The third effort of the day was a bomber escort which failed to make the rendezvous as the Spitfire's take-off was delayed, and another armed recce, this time of 12 Spitfires, led by Flt Lt Gale in MJ903, for the area south of Livorno. This time seven METs were claimed destroyed, 17 as damaged and two dispatch riders were shot off their bikes. A halftrack, in the company of a large tank, was also sighted and attacked. The Spitfires had no weaponry capable of harming the tank, so the flight commander called up some USAAF P-47s carrying the appropriate ordnance. The Americans destroyed the tank and strafed the crew when they bailed out.[134]

14 June started with a top-cover sortie to 36 B-25s of the 321st Bomb Group (though Morris nominates the 340th Bomb Group in his combat report, he was mistaken), consisting of the 445th, 446th and 447th Bomber Squadrons, USAAF. They dropped 1,000-lb bombs on the Borgo San Lorenzo viaducts, claiming several hits, and suffered no losses.[135] The second sortie was top cover again—six Spitfires looking down above 36 B-25s under the close escort of 237 Squadron. In the target area the bombers were attacked by eight Bf 109s diving down on them and the top cover went into action. As the Spitfires chased the Messerschmitts down, four more were seen above the formation, perhaps providing top cover for their own aircraft, so the top cover climbed back up to them and let the close escort deal with those diving down. One of the top Bf 109s was hit by Wing Cdr Morris's cannon fire and rolled onto its back, the engine cowling and canopy flying off. It was last seen in this way hurtling earthwards, and a bomber crew later confirmed the kill. Some of the Bf 109s were chased north-east, away from the bombers but no additional claims were made. The claim by Wing Cdr Morris read:

> On 14.6.44 at approx. 1020 I was leading six aircraft of 451 Squadron as top cover in a bomber escort, the remainder of the escort was made up of 12 a/c of 237 Squadron. We were escorting 36 B25's of 340 Bomber Group. These were spread along a six mile axis. Having seen the leading bomber formation reach the target, I then gave a turn about to cover the remainder of the bombers. Strange aircraft were reported by the rear escort, and I then saw 8 ME.109's diving at about same height, I ordered black section (top cover) to jettison tanks and

> opened up full throttle and boost. We were unable to deal with these 8 a/c and the close cover were left to chase them away. A few seconds later four ME. 109's in fairly tight formation passed about 200 ft, above our section, I turned up and into them, and got a deflection shot at 200 yards, closing, at the starboard outside E/A. I fired two bursts the second at 100 yards or less, in all I observed six strikes on engine and cockpit. The cockpit hood and engine cowling flew off and the last I saw of the E/A. was on his back diving steeply earthwards. Black section then chased the remaining three E/A's towards Bologna. Then we had to return to the bombers. The ME. 109 was observed to crash by the bombers at Q.4397. I claim 1 ME. 109 destroyed.[136]

The final sortie of the day was an armed recce which claimed yet more MET, staff cars, dispatch riders and even horse-drawn wagons. George Purdy felt bad about strafing the horses—they were innocent, not on anyone's side—but they were being used by the enemy, and that made them valid targets. Fortunately, the pilots were too far away to hear their screams, sitting behind a roaring engine and only diving down to fire their guns for just a few seconds before zooming away again, leaving a mess of men and animals in their wake. These operations continued to 17 June, when the squadron's focus was diverted to Elba.[137]

Elba is an irregularly shaped island just 10 km off the Italian coast, with Corsica another 50 km to the west, and measures about 30 km east–west and between 18 and 4 km north–south. The Italian garrison was well equipped, with infantry, machine guns, artillery and anti-aircraft units. After the Italian Armistice, the garrison complied, siding with the Allies and, in mid-September 1943 drove off a number of attempts by the Germans to occupy the island. However, the Germans made a stronger effort on 17 September and occupied the island with paratroops (despite what some claim, Crete was not the last time the Germans dropped paratroops) plus army units brought over in ferries. The Germans took control and transferred the Italian garrison (as prisoners) to the mainland. By May 1944 the garrison consisted of German fortress units made up of soldiers not fit for front-line duty, plus a few hundred pro-Fascist Italians, mainly equipped with the captured Italian equipment. The Free French forces allocated to take back the island included colonial troops from Morocco and Senegal and the assault was given the codename Operation *Brassard*. While the initial reason for the island to be taken was now almost irrelevant due to Allied progress on the mainland (protection of transport routes), the French commander, General Jean de Lattre de Tassigny (later in charge of French forces in Indochina after the war), did not want to cancel the operation. His troops were green, and, to put it very simply, needed practice fighting the Germans.[138]

The first sortie in support of the landings on Elba was made up of eleven Spitfires and was led by Sqn Ldr Kirkham. Gunfire, ship-to-shore and return fire was seen, as was a floating mine and just one armoured car was attacked. During the sortie two of the Spitfires were directed by the fighter control ship for artillery spotting duties. The second sortie attacked several barges and fishing vessels in the mid-afternoon and the last sortie of the day attacked yet another fishing vessel. Sorties in support of the landing continued on 18 June and the squadron was able to track the progress of the land battle. 451 Squadron's last patrol of the day was dived on by eight Spitfires from another squadron as they covered their sector, but luckily there was no firing, and everyone made it home safely. The Spitfires were identified as 'strange' and their squadron was not able to be determined, but they were thought to be based on the mainland as their callsign was not recognised. The final patrols in support of the Elba landings were on the 19th, and the squadron returned its focus to the mainland on 20 June, with MET claims on the first day.[139]

A census was taken by a visiting RAAF officer on 19/20 June, which was essentially research for a repatriation scheme to be implemented at the conclusion of the war. While the end was not necessarily around the corner, the war was going well for the Allies in all theatres and so plans were being made for transporting Australians home in an orderly and manageable manner. The scheme planned for the return of 100 ground crew per month (not per squadron but from the theatre in total) though none was to be returned until replacements had arrived, with preference being given to those with families, married men and consideration for length of service. The squadron diary noted that as a result of the explanations given by the visiting officer and their willingness to explain matters and listen to grievances, squadron morale improved greatly, especially that of the ground crew.[140]

On 21 June, the first of two afternoon sorties attacked the marshalling yards at Alesandria (north of Genoa), where they found about ten locomotives and 50 to 60 railway trucks. The locomotives had priority and five of them were severely damaged, emitting steam and flames. Another train was strafed on the return leg. Operations continued until the afternoon of 22 June and, on 23 June, no flying took place at all due to heavy cloud over the mainland. After returning to operations on the 24th the squadron had the 25th off due to bad weather before providing cover to P-47s on the following day. These were not located so the squadron patrolled the area regardless, and it later turned out that the P-47s were operating on a different frequency, and when they were attacked by German fighters, they could not call on the Spitfires for assistance.[141]

On 26 June, Flt Lt House was posted out to 238 Squadron, as a flight commander. A fighter sweep over the Parma area on 27 June was perhaps the most dangerous to date, with three aircraft hit by anti-aircraft fire from Pescia, one of which had to abort immediately with his No. 2, and they landed on the mainland at Grossetto. On 29 June, the squadron got lucky when they found some Luftwaffe fighters taking off from Caldera di Reno airfield near Bologna. The Spitfires went into the attack, with the Luftwaffe fighters turning left and then left again over the city, and the Australians roaring down after them. One Bf 109 was shot down in flames by FS Vintner and an Fw 190 was hit by FO Bray and crash-landed. A third aircraft—another Fw 190—was hit numerous times by FO Sidney and was last seen with smoke pouring from it, at just 50 ft headed north away from the battle, and this was claimed as a probable. From the combat report of FS Vintner:

> Aircraft reported taking off from BOLOGNA L.G. I was flying position Blue 2 at 16,000 ft, N.W. over BOLOGNA. Lost height in area to 8,000 ft. When flying S-N. over town Blue 1 observed 3 a/c taking off. Bogies turned north and I followed Blue 1 down, and attacked middle a/c. I closed to approx. 200 yards, recognising a/c as ME. 109. The E/A. was flying at high speed at 0 feet, and then pulled up sharply. I opened fire at approx. 150 yards, three quarter port attack, firing a short burst. E/A. burst into flames, and exploded almost immediately, and large pieces of wing and fuselage falling off. E/A. then crashed and burnt out near a road. Claim 1 ME. 109 destroyed.[142]

The engagement was later reported in the *Telegraph* newspaper of Brisbane, Queensland, with the title, 'Got Nazi on First Flight', and under 'Quick Air Victory' in the *Sydney Sun*.[143]

Since there were numerous Luftwaffe aircraft in various stages of taking off and forming up, the Spitfires became separated as they went after different groups and didn't necessarily stick with their flight leaders. Alec Arnel's Spitfire (MJ733) was hit by anti-aircraft fire during this period; the first thing he knew about it was when oil started gushing over his windscreen. He immediately called up to report that his constant speed unit was out of action and he had to return to base but before he could get himself set on a new course the engine went out of control and started screaming. His No. 2, FS Kelly, had lost contact with him for a few minutes so didn't witness the damage to Arnel's Spitfire. Upon the notification of the damage, Kelly paired up with Arnel again, to escort him back to base. Arnel told Kelly to keep a close watch as he thought he might have to bail out at short notice—he was only at 2,000 ft. Shortly afterwards Arnel's Spitfire was seen to be losing glycol—there were large amounts of white smoke—and within seconds Arnel had bailed out. It might have been seconds but certainly felt a lot longer. In preparing to bail out Arnel had forgotten to disconnect the radio from his helmet and was getting tangled up and had to stop and say to himself, *You're the only one here and the only one who can do it, just start again.* It really was a matter of following the procedure. He tried to open the side door but it was jammed shut. He wound the trim full forward, ensured it was staying there and then undid his harness. Normally a pilot in this position would feel the harness holding him in the seat as the plane took a nose-down attitude; with it undone the plane simply flew away from him and he came neatly out of the cockpit. He quickly lost his desert shoes as they weren't done up properly and were torn off. Kelly circled Arnel for a short time as he descended in his parachute but was ordered to rejoin the formation as they had to return to base.[144]

Arnel landed in a cornfield and within seconds shots were fired in his direction. He was still attached to his parachute: there was no hiding or running away, and he was soon the prisoner of some Luftwaffe troops. There was no abuse or threats, he was simply their prisoner. He was taken to a nearby airfield and it was here that he expected things might get a bit rough. He was put in a cell, adjacent to an American who'd been captured sometime earlier. When the airfield was raided later on, they were both taken underground. An Italian girl working in the camp befriended him and gave him some wooden clogs to wear. Arnel's next stop in the process was at Verona, where he was interrogated.

He was 'quite on edge' by this time, but he wasn't abused, unlike some others. His interrogator had a small Hitler-style moustache, which Arnel found quite amusing. He must have let out a bit of a chuckle, because the man roared at him, 'You cannot laugh against us! We are a proud and mighty people!' Arnel quickly settled down; he didn't want to upset his captors. At the Dulag Luft in Germany the interview was much tougher and he was kept alone in a dark cell for days. He was faced with a Luftwaffe pilot who had been grounded due to injury. He was given a Red Cross form to complete, and Arnel gave his name and rank, and the interrogation started. In a series of interrogations over the next few days the officer would offer him coffee or a cigarette, and 'the situation deteriorated' as the questions progressed. Arnel was asked about the Spitfire, what it could do, what he thought of it, but to even admit he flew one was against the rules, and he didn't reply.

In the cell next to him was a New Zealander and one day the Germans came for him. There was much yelling and sounds of struggle, all concluded with a rifle shot. While he didn't know for sure that the New Zealander had been shot, it did put him on edge. Another prisoner he encountered was a high-ranking officer who had been badly beaten and had apparently given up no secrets. He was so severely beaten up he was delirious and described as 'off with the fairies'.[145]

Upon arrival at his camp, Stalag Luft III, Sagan (where the Great Escape took place), Prisoner No. 6492, as he was now known, was interrogated by the ranking officer and 'checked out' to make sure he wasn't a plant, and for some time the other 'Kriegies' (*Kriegsgefangener* is German for prisoner of war) were a bit stand-offish. He thought that he could improve the mood of other prisoners with his news of the progress of the war, but he was disappointed to know they already had all the news from the BBC on a hidden radio. It was a bit of a letdown. He was allocated a hut (all Australians), which was a genuine comfort, and eventually met some people he'd known outside. All this time Arnel's morale had been quite low; he felt that he was out of the war and he would no longer be able to do his part. He'd lost his squadron and his mates. He felt useless, but after a while he came to realise that his chance of overall survival, a chance to make it home at the end, had increased. A friend of his from Bomber Command gave him some advice, saying, 'Look, it might sound to you a bit strange, but I'm relieved. I've had a marvellous run but I feel my number's up. Now I've got a hope for a future. I won't apologise for that.' His friend would no longer have to fly to Berlin and back, or anywhere else for that matter, spending hour upon hour in the dark waiting to be attacked by a night fighter, or flak, or both, as they flew a perfectly straight line to their target on a bombing run. While popular in movies and dramatic stories, interest among POWs in joining actual escape committees was not as high as some might believe. Arnel was certainly not a joiner in this respect. He had seen the terrain on the trip to the camp, and he didn't speak any German, he held out no hope for his chances beyond the wire. He felt the war was going well for the Allies and the end was near, so a few weeks or months as a prisoner was something he could stand. It turned out much longer than that, but some had been prisoners for three or more years when he arrived, so in relative terms he was still hopeful. Some of these other POWs had developed psychological problems and one such prisoner tried to make a break for it by climbing the wire. He stood no chance—the prisoners and guards both knew it—but he was shot anyway. Despite the general misery and boredom of being a prisoner, it did have some lighter moments. The commandant at Sagan was apparently proud of his English and used it to address the prisoners at roll call. However, he didn't always get his colloquialisms correct, such as when he angrily addressed the prisoners on parade. Presumably someone had been up to no good and he'd found out about it, yelling, 'You English, you think I know damn nothing, but I know damn all!' The prisoners couldn't help themselves and burst out in laughter.[146]

In the last days of the war, while being marched from one camp to another to avoid the approaching Soviet forces, they were strafed by Hawker Tempests and several prisoners were killed. The prisoners had been warned to stand still and anyone who moved would be a fair target for the planes, but standing still under fire goes against human nature, so it was only natural that they sought cover. The march commenced in early January 1945; prisoners only took what they could carry, and the first 36 hours was non-stop marching through snow. The guards were not a problem, but any SS encountered had to be treated with great caution. They'd do malicious acts to the prisoners, cutting their bags open with knives or shooting stragglers. Arnel recalled that one German-speaking Australian prisoner stood up for some sick people and demanded medical attention for them and started telling the SS 'some home truths' but had to be held back when they raised their weapons and pointed them at him. There was no point being killed so close to the end.

In the winter the prisoners slept in barns where they could, and Arnel found a spot on the bonnet of a car, and attached his sleeping bag to the windscreen to hold it in place, but froze like 'a block of ice' during the night; a metal surface is no place to rest in a European winter. He was so cold he thought he'd never straighten out again. Part of the journey between camps was made by train, and for almost two days the prisoners, already in bad shape, had no water. Finishing up near Tarmstedt, in early May, the prisoners were liberated by the British. They received Red Cross parcels and enough food to get by, too much and they'd be ill. There were questionnaires about their time as POWs but Arnel had nothing bad to say about the Germans, except of course, for the SS.[147]

Back on Corsica, June 1944 concluded with two escorts which failed to make their rendezvous and uneventful fighter sweeps. 451 Squadron's claims for the month were eight enemy aircraft shot down, one damaged, 110 MET flamers or destroyed, another 154 damaged, 15 railway tankers destroyed and 68 railway trucks damaged, one locomotive destroyed, eight damaged, one ship sunk and four damaged in a total of 1,048 operational flying hours. They were certainly keeping pace with 453 (RAAF) Squadron and their operations in Normandy.[148]

July 1944 continued with success against the Luftwaffe, this time on the ground. The third sortie of 1 July found seven Fw 190s sitting on an aerodrome and strafing attacks left one burning, one smoking and three others damaged. At this time, 451 Squadron received a few Mk VIII Spitfires, including MT546, which Sqn Ldr Kirkham flew most often. So, for some time the squadron operated both Mk VIII and IX Spitfires.[149] Escorts to bombers attacking bridges were a regular occurrence as were fighter sweeps and area cover for USAAF P-47s on dive-bombing sorties. While Spitfires could carry bombs, the bigger P-47s could carry a much heavier payload and were definitely the better choice. The mix-ups between RAF and USAAF units continued—planes taking off early or late or squadrons given incorrect priority led to the escorts not meeting bombers on a few occasions. Sorties took them to their usual zones near Livorno and Florence to the east, and Alessandria and Genoa to the north.[150]

On 7 July, Sqn Ldr Gale took command of the squadron from Sqn Ldr Kirkham who was posted out, along with FO O'Neil; they were tour-expired and were due for a rest. On 8 July, the squadron was moved from Serragia to St Catherine (about 80 km north), with less than two days' notice. When they arrived at the new location later that day, it was clear that there was very little cover and few opportunities for camouflage so everything was widely dispersed—there would be no repetitions of the earlier disaster. A favourable comment was made about the proximity the sea 'where excellent bathing facilities are available. This fact has resulted already in a most beneficial manner upon the health of all personnel'.[151] However, the Americans, with their abundance of resources, dumped rubbish in open pits wherever they chose, and had facilities for protecting staff with their sanitary arrangements, whereas the Commonwealth forces had fewer resources and were therefore more careful about how they disposed of their waste. Once the advance party of pilots and ground crew had the area arranged, the aircraft were flown in, arriving on the 9th.[152]

Three new pilots arrived on 9 July, including Warrant Officer Joe Barrington. Joseph Arthur James Barrington (Service No. 420520) was born Joseph Benjamin on 8 November 1920 in Randwick, NSW, but changed his family name to Barrington (as many of his relations already had) when he enlisted. He left school at 15 and was working as a clerk at the Commonwealth Wool & Produce Co. Ltd. when he enlisted. Prior to enlisting, he would often lie in his bed on his family's open-side veranda and watch the Tiger Moths do their aerobatics, not knowing that he would soon be up there with them. He enlisted on 8 November 1941—his 21st birthday, and would have signed up sooner, but his parents wanted him to finish his qualification as a wool classer before he joined. Not that he regretted this, as art classes were held in the opposite building to wool classing and, if he sat at the right table, he would often be able to see models posing for the art class, which he found 'especially enjoyable'. Joe should not have been accepted for military service in any case as, due to an earlier illness he was unable to fully extend his left arm. To get through the medical assessment he simply bent both arms at the same angle when doing the relevant test and he got through.[153]

After a few months of initial training in the Royal Australian Air Force ways of marching and saluting, Joe Barrington was posted to 4 EFTS at Mascot, just down the road from his home, and arrived there on 2 April 1942. He commenced flying training on 4 April and soloed on a Tiger Moth after just eight hours, recording it with an exclamation mark in his logbook.[154] Next stop was 11 EFTS at Benalla in Victoria, where he spent many more hours on the Tiger Moth, finishing with a rating of 'Average'. Towards the end of June, he was posted to 6 SFTS Mallala in South Australia where he learned to fly Avro Ansons, a twin-engine aircraft used for several tasks, including training potential bomber crews. By the time he finished the course, Joe had over 200 hours' flying experience. He sailed out of Melbourne in January 1943 headed for the UK, where he disembarked on 26 March.[155]

Like many other EATS aircrew, Joe had to wait his turn for a flying posting and did his mandatory refresher on Tiger Moths at 29 EFTS Clyffe Pypard in Wiltshire in May before moving on to the Airspeed Oxford at 20 (P)AFU at Kidlington in Oxfordshire. He then progressed to 1519 Beam Approach Training (BAT) Flight at RAF Feltwell in Norfolk, which trained pilots in 'blind' landing approaches and after this short course he returned to Kidlington for more time on the Oxford. In late July he was posted to the Reserve Flight and then the Night Flight, where his job was to test aircraft to be used by the trainees the next day, and he would often take three or four different aircraft up for 30 to 40 minutes each night, with no co-pilot or navigator.[156] In mid-September 1943, he was taken off this duty and posted to 5(P)AFU at Tern Hill: he was going to be a fighter pilot. Not that he'd asked for it; he was told that his legs were too short for the bombers and so he started back on single-engine aircraft, this time the Miles Master I and II, from which he would advance to the Spitfire. Considering how many casualties Bomber Command suffered during the war Joe believed that this decision saved his life.[157] But it wasn't a short transition. He flew the Master in training until January 1944. In late February he boarded a ship to North Africa where he joined 73 OTU at Abu Sueir in Egypt in April.[158] Planes got so hot during the middle of the day that often, and without operational considerations forcing them to fly at all times, flying practice was done in the mornings before the metal got too hot.[159] Desert flying had a particular set of hazards, and one day his plane was nearly swallowed by a sandstorm:

> I was flying, doing some aerobatics or something well away from the station and suddenly I could see what they called a Khamsin, it's a dust storm and when they come, they just sweep straight in and you can't see a thing. And it was between me and my depot, my base and I knew of another aerodrome that was at Ismailia, very close

to the Suez Canal on the Great Bitter Lakes, so I raced for there and I arrived at the same time as the Khamsin did. And I had to land virtually blind, I couldn't see a thing. Well, I managed to pick out what turned out to be the landing strip and I got down and I just had to get off the runway and just turn my motor off because I couldn't find anything. And I made my way up to the duty pilot tower and there was another fellow there … he'd flown in from Palestine … "Gooday dig," he said. And it turned out when we got talking that he lived in Randwick not far from where I lived. I couldn't get over the fact that we were in the middle of the desert, that we should meet, you know, under those circumstances. But I was fortunate to get in as I did.[160]

The war had well and truly moved on to the mainland of Italy by this stage and the Allies controlled the Mediterranean. On 19 April, Joe Barrington flew his first Spitfire, a very old Mk I, and flew various Mk Is, Vs and VCs until the end of May, when he was transferred to Italy, taking a C-47 Dakota to Naples where he was attached to the Desert Air Force Training Flight at Sinello for a dive-bombing course. Though he was in a training situation, he had an opportunity to take his revenge on the Germans:

I was flying one day and I used to fly over a German POW camp and on this day, there was a long stretch of beach, although they're all pebble beaches there, and all these fellows were swimming. There was a line of them, there must have been several hundred men, and there was a line of them in the surf, and I couldn't resist it, and I went down and I flew as close as I could get to them, right across them. And each one was ducking down under the water …I must have been pretty low but I felt rather good about that because it was the first contact that I'd had with the Germans in any way and I just wanted to sort of give them a bit of curry. I think I was doing about 400 mph then I pulled up, yelling unmentionable words! [161]

It was a telling moment for him. He thought about it later and said, 'I had my guns, I could have shot the lot.'[162]

At the end of the course Joe Barrington was posted to 451 Squadron.[163] Here he was in more danger than the average pilot: he was Jewish. He still celebrated birthdays, Easter and Christmases with everyone the best way they could; he wasn't strict about his faith, he didn't keep up with the Jewish calendar of events or ceremonies—it just wasn't a practical consideration for him. Since a person's religion was stamped on their identity discs, Joe decided he wasn't going to wear his on operations, as being a Jewish prisoner wasn't a fate he was prepared to endure. However, his religion was relevant to him enlisting: 'I didn't join up because I wanted to fly a plane, I did it because I wanted to oppose them [the Nazis].'[164]

Joe was welcomed to the squadron with open arms, but it was time to prove himself. The squadron had 'access' to an old, now 'surplus' B-25 Mitchell for various official and unofficial non-combat duties and since Joe had so much experience on twin-engine aircraft he was soon made second pilot to Bob Milner. They didn't have the usual gunners: it was just the two of them and he enjoyed the various flights they took, including 'picking up grog' from time to time. It was also used to take some of the squadron up to Paris for a very unofficial tour after it had been liberated.[165]

On 13 July, a formation of bombers from 320th Bomb Group (USAF 441st and 444th Bomb Squadrons) was escorted by 451 and 237 Squadrons on a sortie up to Guastalla, northeast of Parma. The bombers were after a bridge and dropped 172 x 500-lb bombs on a pontoon bridge crossing the Po River, destroying an estimated 1,000-ft section. Their navigation must have been off, because they then flew west towards Alessandria, so Wing Cdr Morris, leading the escort, had to suggest over the radio that they go 'home'. In response to this, the bombers turned southeast, which would have taken them down the length of Italy. Morris then told the bombers that the fighters were returning to base—their range was shorter than that of the bombers in any case—and turned for Corsica, at which time the bombers finally took the hint and headed for Corsica also. When the Spitfires crossed the Italian coast at Sestri Levante, Morris decided that the tug and barge moored at the pier could not go untouched and took his section down to attack them.[166] This was Joe Barrington's first operational sortie and he flew as No. 2 to Morris:

I'll always remember that one, I guess everybody remembers their first. But things happened to me on that one, we were escorting American bombers, we did a lot of bomber escorts at that time over the Italian mainland. And we had a long range tank which could be ejected when it was empty and you flew on your long range tanks for approximately an hour and then you'd go on to your mains so you had enough petrol to get there and back from your target. I was giving it every bit of time, I wanted to use it all up and that ... was a great mistake because I should have switched a bit early when all of a sudden, my motor cut out. And the next thing I felt myself going down in a steep dive, the prop was just windmilling, and I was madly pumping ... what was called a wobble pump. I switched on my mains and switched the other one off. And believe it or not ... I'd lost about five thousand feet, the aircraft burst into life. But I thought I was looking at being, at least, a POW. I raced up and I joined the formation, I was flying number two to the Wing Commander and he said, "Where you been Green Two?" And I said, "I ran out of juice, Sir." I wasn't going to go into any explanations ... Anyway, we've completed the task over the target area with the bombers and we came back and we were just crossing the coast ... and all of a sudden the Wing Commander said, "Take over" ... "Number two, follow me, we'll go down and have a look at those ships in the harbour." And he put his aircraft into a steep dive, and I had to follow him. Here I am, I'm congratulating myself that we're on our way home and we're going back in again. I didn't know whether he was doing it for my benefit or ... was just taking the opportunity to have a crack at something. So we dived down and we gave one burst at the ships that were there, they were coastal type ships, you know, and shot off back and landed ... I remember the CO at the time who came over to me and invited me to come and have a drink for my first operation, and we lost him two days later.[167]

Despite carrying 45-gallon drop tanks, the Spitfires returned very low on fuel.[168]

17 July saw the loss of Sqn Ldr Gale. He was one of four Spitfires tasked for a special Tac/R of the Arno River to establish the state of bridges in the area. He was seen by his No. 2, FS Ball, to make two turns, then dive down from 2,000 ft to (presumably) investigate something, and was seen to be firing at the ground, and was hit by return anti-aircraft fire almost immediately. His plane began to pour white smoke. While turning to keep an eye on him, Ball lost sight of him for a few seconds and the next thing Ball saw was a fire on the ground. To see what might be gained as evidence, Ball took a gun-camera run for about eight seconds at the site of the presumed crash, but the attempt was unsuccessful and the footage could not be developed. While no enemy aircraft were sighted,

anti-aircraft fire was attracted throughout the sortie. The loss of Sqn Ldr Gale, who had been with the squadron for just two weeks, saw command passed to Flt Lt McBurnie, though the position was taken over by Sqn Ldr Small, DFC, on 26 July, who made the short move from 238 Squadron.[169]

Gordon Wesley Small, (Service No. 403150) was born on 23 June 1915 and enlisted on 9 December 1940, at which time he was working as a ledger keeper at the Glen Innes branch of the Bank of New South Wales. He lived with his wife Gwyneth in the small town of Guyra. He passed through 5 EFTS at Narromine in New South Wales then headed to Canada for further training at 11 SFTS Yorkton. His next training was carried out in England, after a 22-day crossing of the Atlantic by ship, arriving on 31 August 1941. Unlike many who followed, he didn't wait long for a posting and went to 55 OTU and on 21 October was posted to 232 Squadron before starting with 145 Squadron on Spitfires in November. At 6 ft 4½ inches tall, he towered over many of his fellow pilots who usually stood in the 5 ft 6 in to 5 ft 8 in range and fitted much more comfortably in a Spitfire. When 145 Squadron was transferred to the Mediterranean, he stayed with them until October 1943, during which time he was awarded his first DFC, for 'consistently displaying great courage and devotion to duty'. In addition, he was credited with shooting down three enemy aircraft and damaging at least one other. Small flew with 238 Squadron from May to July 1944, before being posted in to 451 Squadron.[170]

Escorts to bombers attacking bridges continued on and off for the next week, as well as some standing patrols of Spitfires in pairs, guarding against high-level Luftwaffe reconnaissance aircraft, something the squadron had done many times over the years. On 19 July, two public relations officers arrived at 451 Squadron to make records of, and photograph, the unit for publication and historical matters. On the 24th they flew area cover around Turin for some USAAF Mitchell bombers but Joe Barrington, in BQ-K (MJ203), had to return early, noting in his logbook, 'Returned base. Long range tank U/S. Also A.S.I.'[171]

On 25, July FS Sheppard and Joe Barrington were sent out at 1105 on a search for two Spitfires from 237 Squadron. These two Spitfires had been out practising shadow-firing and cine-gun dogfighting since before 0900 and had not returned. The two Australians searched the designated gun range area, but saw nothing, and were then directed out to sea, about eight miles off the coast, where two oil patches had been sighted. This area was then searched with no result and the two Australians were then relieved by two other Spitfires from 451 Squadron who continued the search. The high-speed launch (used for search and rescue) was seen to recover one pilot, dead, and the Spitfires continued their search for the second pilot. On a hunch, they diverted from their zone and found the second pilot in a dinghy. While one circled him, the other returned to the location of the launch and directed it to the surviving pilot.[172]

On 27 July, 12 Spitfires formed part of a bomber escort north of Genoa near the town of Novi Ligure. Anti-aircraft fire was heavy but was focused on the bombers, though no enemy aircraft made an appearance. On the return journey a few aircraft were sighted on enemy airfields, but they did not take off and the Australians did not go down to investigate further. FO John Poate's engine cut out at 15,000 ft on the return journey and could not be restarted. He made a crash-landing on the mainland near Bagnasco and was seen to leave the plane safely and wave to those watching his progress, before heading off into the woods. The plane did not burn, and an attempt was made to strafe it to destroy anything of value, but it was under trees in a steep valley and could not be seen well enough to make a safe run at it, so it was left.[173] Poate must have been on auto-pilot (the human kind) because he had no recollection of getting out of the Spitfire; hitting a tree and going from 80 mph to zero in about two feet was the last thing he remembered and, when he came to, he was all battered and bruised with a bloody face and cuts on his legs from the impact. Around him stood German soldiers. He was made to stand, which caused him a lot of pain, and alerted him to some new injuries, including extreme pain in his lower back. He was first kept in a small house where he was permitted to rest, before being moved by truck in the afternoon to an Italian camp. The next day he was taken to a German officer who asked if he was Canadian, and when Poate replied that he was Australian the German struck him across the face, knocking him to the floor in his weakened state.

Later that day Poate was taken by ambulance to Milan railway station where he was placed in a prison cell. That night he described as 'one of the worst nights of my life'. The cell was wet and dark, the wooden bed sloped, and when he sat on it, he—and his meagre rations—were assaulted by bedbugs. Not small flea-like bugs, but ones 'the size of your middle fingernail'. In desperation he lay on the wet floor to try and relieve some of his back pain but wasn't game enough to eat anything in case he bit into a bug in the darkness. He banged so hard on the metal door for the light to be turned on that, by morning, his hands were cut and bleeding. His next stop was a castle in Verona where he was strip-searched by the SS, and, since he didn't have his identity discs on him (the Australian term for dogtags), he was accused of being a spy. This time he didn't answer back, but kept his eyes and head down, and just gave the usual three pieces of information: name, rank and number. Poate was then taken on an Italian train to the Benner Pass where he changed onto a German train, which was luxurious in comparison with where he had been previously. However, his guards were fully equipped with uniform, great coats and gloves, and John was still in his shorts and shirt and hadn't been allowed to wash since crashing. After arriving in Germany at an interrogation camp north of Frankfurt, he was kept on a starvation diet of bread and water while his interrogator ate good food in front of him, all part of the mental and physical torture designed to break down a prisoner's will and make them say or do anything in return for a bit of food. After a week the Germans received a report on his aircraft, and since it bore the squadron letter code (BQ), the Germans could finally say they were satisfied he was not a spy. He was then read, in perfect English, the German version of the squadron history which Poate found to be 'the most complete history ... that I had ever heard'. After the interrogation camp he was taken to a staging camp and then to Stalag Luft I, up on the German Baltic coast at Barth. While there were many Australian POWs at Stalag Luft III (Sagan), there were only a few at Barth: John Poate was the sixteenth. The night of his move north the train was put in a railway siding near Berlin, where a raid was taking place, which was so loud and frightening that Poate was sure they'd be done for. However, in the morning the train was moved back and forth to get on a functioning line and eventually they arrived at Barth, where he was issued *Kriegsgefangener* number 5184.

It was a while before he was fully accepted by the other prisoners—the Germans would sometimes try and insert a spy into the prison population to discover any plans for escape—so Poate had to prove himself, and a meeting with Ken Watts (even though they did not serve together on 451 Squadron) was enough to clear him. Ken Watts later related to Poate the beating he'd received from the interrogators at Verona. The prisoners kept all the Australians together in a block and called it 'Australian House'. To keep order and give them a sense of purpose they took turns at doing the chores, such as washing the dishes, cleaning etc. Until the end of 1944, Red Cross parcels arrived fairly regularly, with cigarettes and chocolate the camp currency. Raisins and prunes were kept aside for prison 'brew', and the resulting alcohol was quite popular, enough to create a few rowdy evenings which caused the Germans to post notices about the forbidden brewing of alcohol. To pass the time Poate, who spoke fluent French, taught the language to others in the camp, with the aid of a book on French grammar from the camp library, while another pilot ran classes on aeronautics. Sport was restricted to a corner of the camp and if the soccer ball went outside the permitted zone into an area where a prisoner could be shot, they had to get a guard's attention in order to fetch the ball, all the while having a machine gun pointed at them in case it became an attempt to escape. While he didn't ever try to escape from Barth, others did: one pole-vaulted the fence (and was then caught) and another tried to sneak out under a pile of metal cans and was caught when the cans were unloaded by tipping them out onto the ground. Roll call was a daily nuisance for the prisoners, but they made it almost as bad for the Germans and saw it as their job to move about and disrupt the count as often as possible.

Being so close to the sea, there were limited opportunities for digging tunnels, and any attempts had to be made on the landward side. To counter this, the Germans drove a steamroller around the perimeter of the camp to collapse any tunnels. Knowing this, the prisoners dug a tunnel to the fence and hollowed out another section beyond it, so that when the steam roller came around its weight collapsed the roof and it sunk into the cavity, while the prisoners cheered their victory. It took a week for the Germans to get it out of the hole. This was a summer-only event; when winter came the ground was too hard to dig through, and the Germans no longer bothered with the steamroller, but would sometimes send a soldier under the prisoner blocks at night to listen in on their conversations. If they were discovered, the 'spy' would be urinated on through the floorboards of the block.

Part of the role of the POW leaders within the camp was to determine what course of action would be taken if various events took place, such as the Germans leaving. In May 1945 the camp commandant ordered the camp to be evacuated with all prisoners to be marched west to the British. There was no way the Germans were going to surrender to the Soviets if they could avoid it: they knew hard justice was coming for them. The Allied officers refused and said being liberated by the Soviets would be agreeable, as they were allies. In no position to argue, the Germans left, and the prisoners remained in the camp.

Poate was sent into town to arrange some motor transport, which he did, and for the next few days drove work parties around fixing the local water works, and removing bombs from the nearby airfield. He was also detailed to take a group to discover the location of a concentration camp which was rumoured to be in the area. They found it near the airfield, a subcamp of Ravensbrück. There they witnessed the dead and the dying, some too weak to 'move out of their own mess, let alone dispose of the bodies of their own dead'. When the Soviets arrived at Barth, they kept the servicemen locked up in the camp, which was safer in any case, as the Soviets liked to shoot first and ask questions later. In mid-May the camp was evacuated by air, the USAAF providing bombers for the task, each taking about 25 ex-prisoners, and not even stopping their engines during the pickup. Poate and other Commonwealth airmen were taken to Ford on the south coast of England—453 Squadron had operated from here the early stages of the Normandy campaign—where they were sprayed with chemical powder in a 'delousing' procedure, before moving to Brighton and moving into allocated rooms in hotels. They were reunited with their kit, which had been packed away by the squadron after they were declared lost on operations, and then it was time for a big feed at the pub. But, having had so little food for so long, they couldn't manage it, no matter how much time they'd spent dreaming of a big meal during their months or years in the camp. Poate was eventually sent home to Australia on the SS *Orion*, and the Japanese surrendered while they were at sea.[174]

Overall for 451 Squadron, July was very quiet compared to June. But, with Operation *Dragoon*—the landings in the south of France—coming up in August, things were about to get busy once again. Originally codenamed *Anvil*, the name was changed to *Dragoon* on 1 August, but so many orders had been written with *Anvil* in the references that there was no point retyping them all for the name change. So, in 451 Squadron's case at least, 'Operation Dragoon' was typed on a piece of paper noting the amendment and stapled to the top of some documents.[175] Name change done.

The landings in the south of France were first proposed at the Trident conference in May 1943, which was held in Washington D.C. While the landings in Normandy (Operation *Overlord*) were still in the very early planning stages, and the Allies had yet to invade Sicily; such large undertakings had to be planned well in advance. When *Overlord* was set for Normandy in plans laid down during July 1943, simultaneous landings in the south of France were thought to be required to prevent the Germans shifting their forces within France to oppose the Allied arrival. But since this would be an isolated landing, in that the south of France didn't share a front line with any other sector, it could not afford to be a small undertaking. The troops that landed would have to be sustained and then reinforced or else the Germans could simply leave enough troops opposite the landing zone to prevent a breakthrough, resulting in a wasteful stalemate for the Allies, and send the rest of their available forces to Normandy. This plan was named Operation *Anvil* and was to be complementary to the Normandy operation—subordinate to the main operation's needs, yet contributing to the goal of liberating France and the remainder of western Europe. These were general concepts and the primary focus remained on Normandy.

At the end of August 1943, with Sicily now in Allied hands, another conference, codenamed Quadrant, was held in Quebec, Canada, and here *Overlord* was increased in size to five assaulting divisions plus two airborne divisions. Eisenhower stated that *Anvil* should be executed with not less than three divisions, but the increase for *Overlord* meant that it would require more shipping and more aircraft, meaning that fewer resources were available for operations elsewhere, be they nearby in the Mediterranean or on the other side of the world in the Pacific. Shipping, in particular, was at a premium. Thus *Anvil* went up and down in Allied priorities as both the Americans and British proposed varying courses of action for 1944, the Americans generally wanting to get into western Europe as fast as possible and then drive to Berlin, while Churchill seemed to keep proposing action on the fringes, such as Greece and Norway. These fringe operations would require fewer Allied troops and therefore the Americans would not be able to outnumber the British by way of military contribution, meaning they would also not outweigh them (theoretically) when it came to directing the operations themselves. Churchill, and others, were well aware that as the US contribution of troops, of all services, grew, so did their ability to dictate the direction of Allied strategy, and this was natural. The British Empire was in decline, and would not be re-established in the post-war world; colonialism was destined to be a thing of the past.

As time moved on various plans were put forth for various operations across the globe, and *Anvil* was always in the mix, though not always as a priority. In March 1944 a version of *Anvil* consisting of just one division was proposed, which, considering the Allied failure at Anzio in January, was bordering on madness. This was later increased to two divisions (slightly less mad) and given a date of July 1944, meaning that the shipping proposed for *Anvil* could be used in Normandy first. The American Joint Chiefs of Staff insisted on three divisions for *Anvil* and this was the agreed strength in June 1944, as *Overlord* was taking place, and Churchill continued to complain that *Overlord* and Italy should be the focus of Allied efforts now that he'd stopped pushing the Norwegian option. He had however, suggested options for the Balkans, but these were rejected by the Americans.

With *Anvil* on such a short timeline for an actual 'go' decision to be made, the logisticians in the background, whose role it is to provide the troops with the equipment and goods to make these landings happen—had been working on *Anvil* since January 1944. They had the job of determining which ships carried which goods from the US to Europe, which ships and goods had priority at which destinations, and what they would carry on their return journeys, assuming they made it across the Atlantic to start with and weren't sunk by a U-boat. Declaring that an operation will go ahead in two months' time requires more work than those two months allow, so the people in the background were always looking to the future for what would be needed. They performed a generally thankless task that is often ignored in the history books of the battles that took place after the infantry left their landing craft and put their boots on the ground.

While the US and British leaders and commanders debated various operations, including *Anvil*, there was always one extra matter to consider: the French. On 2 July 1944, by which time the Allies had been fighting in Normandy for nearly a month, 15 August was set as the date for *Anvil*. Any later and it would be unlikely to have any influence on events in Normandy, so it was going ahead. Three US infantry divisions would lead the way and these would be followed by a further seven divisions of mainly Free French troops (using American equipment). One division equivalent of airborne troops would take part, a mix of British and American troops; there were very few British or Commonwealth forces involved, relatively speaking. The naval forces would be under the command of the Western Naval Task Force, air operations would be run by XII Tactical Air Command and ground troops were under the command of the Seventh Army. It was much smaller and much less complicated than *Overlord*, though the same planning principles applied. There were some deception aspects to the Allied plan, but nothing as elaborate as those executed for Normandy. The goal was not just to liberate France and keep German troops occupied and away from Normandy, but also to obtain the two large ports of Marseille and Toulon. Getting supplies to the troops, be it in Normandy or elsewhere, was a perpetual problem. Since Normandy had no substantial port on the beachhead, and Cherbourg was sabotaged to such as extent it was unusable for a great deal of time, the Allies had to make do with landing over the beaches and the artificial Mulberry harbours. When these were damaged in the June storm the situation became more pressing. In the south, the Germans were not expected to put up too much of a fight, on land, at sea or in the air, and Allied commanders anticipated the ports could be taken in good time.[176]

As the day of the landings approached, the focus of operations for 251 Wing switched to western Italy and the pre-war French–Italian border areas. The first week of August consisted of bomber escorts and fighter sweeps, sometimes led by Wing Cdr Morris in his usual Spitfire Mk IX, MK187, and conducted in or around Turin, but also as far west as Nice and Marseille. Road and railway bridges were the primary targets—the Allies wanted to keep units in Italy from reinforcing southern France once the landings took place. On 9 August, the squadron flew standing patrols north of Corsica—ready to intercept any Luftwaffe reconnaissance aircraft that might discover the Allied fleet. Additional aircraft were kept ready, with more on 15 minutes' notice. Joe Barrington and Henry Bray were scrambled to intercept an incoming bogey, which turned out to be Sqn Ldr Small returning from his sortie. He had been returning alone as he became separated from his No 2, and he was lucky not to be shot down. Joe recorded in his logbook: 'Second time chased kite back to base—turned out to be the CO!!'[177] Advice was also received on this day that Sqn Ldr Small had been awarded the French Flying Brevet for his work with AFU staff. There were more bomber escorts from 11 to 13 August and two squadron-sized patrols on the 14th for convoys (codenamed 'Baby') passing through the Strait of Bonifacio, the area between Corsica and Sardinia.

Despite what was to occur the following day, 14 August also saw Flt Lt McBurnie posted out of 451 Squadron to 238 Squadron to take over as commander. His position was taken up by FO Bray, who was promoted to flight lieutenant.[178] News of the 24 year-old McBurnie's promotion and new posting were reported in the *Kalgoorlie Miner* on 4 September 1944 under the title, 'An Australian Ace: Command of R.A.F Fighter Squadron', and that he'd been 'one of the original pilots of an Australian Kittyhawk squadron known as the Desert Harassers … '. This was 450 Squadron, and McBurnie had been away from Australia for almost four years.[179]

On the day of Operation *Dragoon*, 15 August, 451 Squadron had 12 Spitfires up at 0540 patrolling a line between Corsica and the French coast, protecting the returning C-47s that had dropped airborne forces at Le Muy. The Luftwaffe was a no-show in this area and all Spitfires returned to base by 0805. The squadron then flew four patrols of six Spitfires each over the beachheads, and again the Luftwaffe failed to show in 451's sectors. The squadron flew in three zones during their time covering the landings, and these were allocated the following codenames:

Apples: Le Luc to Cap de L'Esterel
Pears: Le Luc to Théoule-sur-Mer
Peaches: Le Plan-de-la-Tour to Bormes-les-Mimosas.[180]

Joe Barrington only flew once that day, in Spitfire Mk VIII BQ-B (MT802) from 1340 to 1545 on an 'Apples patrol' and he noted in his logbook, 'Patrolled over troops landing on French Riviera—No E/A's or flak.'[181] That day the Mediterranean Allied Air Force (to which XII Tactical Air Force and therefore 451 Squadron belonged) carried out approximately 900 fighter-bomber sorties and 385 medium or heavy bomber sorties in support of *Dragoon*. As with the Normandy landings, results could have been better but low cloud hampered target identification. Naval gunfire support was provided by a number of ships of various sizes, but special mention must go to the USS *Nevada*, a battleship that was sunk at Pearl Harbor, raised and repaired and sent to Europe where it supported the Normandy landings and then proceeded to the Mediterranean for *Dragoon*. Spotting for naval gunnery was undertaken by US Navy Hellcats, which had twice the endurance of Seafires.[182]

16 August saw patrols flown between Cap Bénat and Sainte-Maxime in the early hours of the morning and three additional patrols, each of six Spitfires, for the remainder of the day, the last aircraft landing at 1830. The weather worsened on 17 August and once again four patrols were flown, including one over the immediate landing beaches. There were no patrols until 1230 on the 18th but this first sortie was recalled due to bad weather, but the next patrol made it to the coast—again no Luftwaffe and no anti-aircraft fire. The last sortie of the day were spectators as the Allied naval forces shelled German positions just west of Cannes.

18 August also saw the first group of 18 ground crew repatriated to Australia, all married men on compassionate grounds, and a farewell was held for them the night before. Rather than feel jealous that they had missed out, those remaining with the squadron felt good to know that the scheme was now in place and their time would eventually come.[183] This had been a long time coming and it was noted that there had been 'Much binding and bitching in this direction from g/staff personnel over a long period'.[184] Their departure from Corsica made the *Daily Telegraph* in Sydney, and a number of the ground crew were named, including sergeants Little of Woy Woy and Atkins of Ballina.[185]

With the Allies landing in the south of France, plus pressure in Italy and Normandy, the Germans could not afford to shift significant forces from any one area to support the other, and while they did benefit from interior lines of communication, the areas behind the front lines were often subject to ongoing Allied air interdiction. Initial Allied progress on the ground was good, and many objectives were taken ahead of schedule, but the ports were the goal.

Alec Arnel was officially reported as a prisoner of war on 19 August, not necessarily welcome news for the squadron, but at least they knew he had survived. For operations, this day saw the squadron run two overlapping patrols to the French coast in the morning and four in the afternoon. One afternoon patrol heard USAAF P-47s on the R/T stating they had encountered Bf 109s north of Marseille, but the Australians didn't become involved. There was some flak, but it was ineffective—and anyone firing at aircraft was liable to bring down more attention on themselves than they could handle. Another saw Allied ships in Toulon harbour and a battleship firing on an inland target. One of these patrols was an escort to a USAAF P-38 (thought to be flown by General Allan) over the Allied landing zones. A similar pattern of four- and six-plane patrols was flown on 20 August, and though some bogies were reported, no interceptions took place. Shelling from Allied ships continued, and this time return fire was observed and one enemy position was noted and passed on.[186] French troops commenced their attack on the port of Toulon on this day as well, and it was captured on the 28th, with 17,000 of the 18,000-strong German garrison taken prisoner. Toulon wasn't expected to fall until D+20 (4 September); now the challenge was to get the facilities into operation.[187]

It was more of the same on 22 August but the next day saw a return to bomber escorts; bridges and roadblocks at Bologna and Voghera in Italy were the targets. On 26 August, it was back to France with escorts, one for bombers attacking positions on the Île Pomègues and Île Ratonneau, two adjacent islands a few kilometres to the west of Marseille.[188] 451 Squadron's arrival in France was noted in the *Perth Daily News* of 22 August when an article titled 'Fliers' Job Eased' mentioned fighter operations from Corsica requiring drop tanks, and that Spitfires were 'now operating from a landing strip in the south of France'.[189]

Originally, the plan had been to move 251 Wing (of which 451 Squadron was a part) to France, with the first group assembling on D+10 and arriving by D+15 or 16, with the main element of the squadron arriving by D+23 or 24. However, the landings and subsequent drive up through the south of France had gone so well that the plan was accelerated and the first group ('A' Party) embarked on D+7 and landed on D+10 (25 August) with the remainder ('B' Party) following on a similarly accelerated timetable. Orders for the move included the instruction that 'Because of the critical shortages of food in target area no local purchase of food will be made by any of the armed forces'.[190] Since there were few British units involved in *Dragoon* (as an overall percentage) and it was mainly an American-supplied operation (the French used American equipment), rations would be provided by the Americans. Vehicles were to be marked with RAF roundels or white five-pointed stars in a white circle and 'patches of gas detection paint will be put on all vehicles on a horizontal surface where it will be visible to the occupants'.[191]

The landings on Normandy might be universally known as 'D-Day', but military operations commence on D-Day, no matter where they occur, and any dates before or after the nominated day are referred to as D+1 or D-1, or whatever number of days the event is before or after the D-Day. For Normandy,

Operation *Overlord*, D-Day was 6 June 1944 and for the south of France, Operation *Dragoon*, D-Day was 15 August 1944. This, in itself, should be sufficient to dispel any myths about those serving in the Mediterranean deserving the title of 'D-Day Dodgers'.[192] They had plenty of 'D-Days' of their own, and many of those serving with 451 Squadron were now entitled to wear the 1939–43 Star (which later became the 39–45 Star) as well as the Africa Star, and had the ribbons sewn onto their tunics.[193]

After landing, A Party moved from the beach area to Cuers, about ten miles north-east of Toulon.[194] It was previously a French Air Force base which had been used by the Luftwaffe so was well established, and the facilities were quickly converted for the use of their new owners. The facilities included an airship hangar and concrete runways. It came complete with German POWs for maintenance of the airship.[195] The accommodation and 'domestic' area was set up in a pine plantation about a mile from the airfield, and everyone was warned about booby traps. All shipping for the move was supplied by the US Navy and all meals and other temporary arrangements were also managed by the Americans. The unit diary recorded the professionalism of the Americans and noted:

> It is desired to record appreciation of the efficiency of the American organisation and the high standard of food provided together with the individual courtesy and cooperation rendered by American Officers and Service Men, there existing a splendid feeling between American and Australian personnel.[196]

The navy always seemed to eat well and the squadron was glad to be benefitting from their facilities, even if for a short time. The Spitfires (all with 45-gallon drop tanks fitted) arrived on 27 August and commenced operations the next day. From 28 to 31 August the squadron flew regular standing patrols from their new base. Patrols were flown along the line Toulon to Cannes or Marseille to Fos (Fos-sur-Mer). The squadron maintained four Spitfires on the ground ready to take off should they be required, but the only aircraft encountered were identified as friendly.[197]

OPERATIONS: AT OPPOSITE ENDS OF FRANCE: SEPTEMBER 1944

FOR 451 Squadron, September started with overlapping standing patrols from Cuers, on the line Marseille to Fos, with other aircraft at readiness. 3 September saw their first armed recce for some time, and some vehicles were attacked, including a staff car which went up in flames, and a diesel locomotive. Flt Lt Sutton's Spitfire Mk VIII was hit several times by anti-aircraft fire, but he returned safely with the others. The squadron was then rested for a few days and held a church service for the entire wing on the 4th for the fifth anniversary of the outbreak of war, no doubt praying for an end to hostilities and a safe return home. For 453 Squadron in Normandy, the answer to these prayers was a way off, but in the south of France the battle was swiftly moving forward, and the Americans advanced their own units as a priority.

Sorties resumed on 8 September with numerous Tac/R sorties flown along the French–Italian border, attention being paid to bridges, roads and railway lines and any traffic upon them. More patrols and Tac/R sorties were flown over the next few days. Again, anti-aircraft fire scored some hits but there was no serious damage, with the exception of FO Thomas's Spitfire which lost its tailwheel, airspeed indicator, all the hydraulic fluid and suffered damage to the flaps—all relatively essential for flying or landing. He stayed calm, lowered his landing gear manually and brought it in safely.[1]

The next few days saw more standing patrols and other patrols to cover shipping, but the Luftwaffe didn't show. WO (Warrant Officer) Hill, in his Spitfire Mk IX, had trouble on the 15th when he returned from a sortie and the undercarriage wouldn't come down. While the others landed, he dropped his long-range fuel tank and climbed to a safe height, rolled the Spitfire onto its back and in this position, was able to select 'down' for his undercarriage. Though he had achieved this feat, after returning to level flight, his engine cut out, leaving him short of the runway at an altitude of just 50 ft with no power on his emergency final approach, causing the aircraft to 'mush in' and inflicting such serious damage his plane was written off. Fortunately, he survived uninjured, but definitely shaken. The next few days saw Tac/R, weather recces and armed recces, some across the Italian border and claims included numerous staff cars, trucks and an electric train and its carriages.

On 17 September, the squadron was addressed by Gp Capt Love, who stated that 451 Squadron would soon be posted to Italy and that the wing might be broken up, with 237 and 238 Squadrons being sent away, while 451 Squadron might eventually be returned to Australia as their work had now been completed, with RAF personnel sent to other squadrons or returned to the UK.

After a couple of days' rest, the squadron resumed patrols and recces on the 21 September. A number of sorties were flown on the 24th, escorting search-and-rescue Walrus and Catalina aircraft that were looking for a Ventura which had reportedly gone down in the sea between San Remo and Corsica. Unfortunately, the rendezvous with the Catalina was not made and the Spitfires searched as best they could while their fuel lasted. The squadron continued to keep four aircraft at readiness with another four on 15 minutes' notice, but none was required.[2]

Despite the surge in operations and the move from Corsica, paperwork and administration continued, and a large number of Good Conduct Badges were awarded to ground crew, who had qualified for the award after serving overseas for three years.[3] The only thing shot down by 451 Squadron on 25 September was a barrage balloon which had broken free of its mooring and had the potential to bring down unwary aircraft. One aircraft was sighted on a patrol carried out on the 26th but it turned out to be a Curtiss SOC-3, an American seaplane usually based on cruisers and battleships. At 1430 two Spitfires were scrambled, backed up by two more at 1440, headed to the coast at 10,000 ft and then 12,000 ft for bandits. Fortunately, 451's pilots approached with caution from up-sun and eventually identified the 'bandits' as USAAF P-47s, and they returned safely to Cuers, landing at 1510. Patrols continued on the 27th, and a Walrus amphibian was escorted in the search for a downed pilot, but he was not located.

Patrols and interceptions continued for the rest of the month, with all intercepts being visually identified as friendly and the Luftwaffe presenting no threats.[4]

When Joe Barrington arrived at 451 Squadron, he was given several jobs, one of which was was messing officer. One part of this role was to 'obtain liquor wherever we could get it':

> The only good thing was we were very close to the Riviera … one occasion about six of us took a wagon … we drove down to Cannes and we stayed for two nights at a hotel there. And that was an eye opener. We had to take all of our own food … that was [a] precaution because we didn't know what we'd get if we didn't. And we handed it in to the kitchen and then we found that the hotel was filled with people who had spent the war there, wealthy, titled … the minute they saw our food coming out they were over at the table to find out could they get some of whatever they thought they might get. Interesting thing, we only took things like bully beef … all tinned stuff and when they brought it out, they brought it out on a silver [plate] and the way it was garnished and everything else, it looked beautiful, but it was the same old food we were getting back at our camp. But that attracted them all. There were all sorts of titled people and they were having parties in the room and inviting us to join them, what they really wanted was to see if they could get something. I was just amazed that that's the life they lived … They could afford … to live there under those conditions and they sat the war out like that … I traded, on one occasion, a couple pair of silk stockings [to a farmer] for big barrel of Brandy. It was pretty dreadful stuff, it hadn't aged enough and we only used it in the bar when we ran out of everything else.
>
> [On another occasion] somebody reported that there was a brewery

operating in Toulon so we immediately got a truck ... found the brewery and loaded case after case of beer. It was stacked high on one of our biggest trucks. And my friend said, "I understand that the Germans have retreated and Marseille has been liberated, let's go and have a look, it's not very far from Toulon to Marseille." ... when we got into the main road through the city ... it was packed with people yelling and shouting and doing all sorts of things that they do under those circumstances. And when we got there, we parked the truck in a back street and when we came into the crowds people were saying "Americans, Americans." Simply because there appeared to be no other troops ... And the things that were happening at that time, everybody's drinking, everybody's offering Champagne to you, all sorts of things. They almost looked on us as though we'd done all this, we were only bystanders. And at the same time you could hear gun shots because there were still some Germans holed up somewhere and the FFI were ferreting them out and that was the shooting we could hear. And they were marching women down the main street that had collaborated with the Germans. They'd picked them out and they'd shaved their heads and that was what happened anywhere where they thought anyone collaborated. Not only in France. So this is happening at the same time and everybody's drinking, it was just an unreal situation We eventually got back ... everybody was around the truck and word got around that we had all this beer. We were more popular than we were in Marseille ... But it was a very interesting day.[5]

***

All 2nd Tactical Air Force (2 TAF) was on the move, trying to keep up with the rapid advance of the ground troops. Running short of fuel, some Typhoons of 245 Squadron landed at an abandoned Luftwaffe airfield about 20 miles on behind the front line. Luckily they were not discovered and the Allied ground forces arrived the next day.[6] Still part of 125 Wing, 453 Squadron, that had covered the Normandy landings, moved to B.11 at Longues-sur-Mer in late June, then B.19 Lingèvres in August, and was still at B.19 at the start of September. The Normandy campaign was now over and the rest of western

Europe awaited liberation. Jack Olver had rejoined the squadron in Normandy after a back injury put him off flying for some time, but with the end of the Normandy campaign, he left the squadron and was posted to 57 OTU at Eshott. With a rating of 'Above The Average' (generous for the RAF) he was selected as a test pilot, and flew Typhoons and Tempests for Napier and Rolls-Royce for the remainder of the war, and a little time after that. He demobbed in January 1946 and returned to Australia with his new wife Jean, a Scottish girl.[7]

On 1 September, the squadron received notice that they were to move to B.40 Beauvais, about 40 km east of Rouen. They made the move on the 2nd, the vehicles leaving Lingèvres at 1600 and driving through the night, while the Spitfires and the squadron's Auster were flown directly to the new base. No sooner had they all arrived than they were directed to move again, to B.52 at Douai, located about halfway between Amiens and the Belgian border. Two patrols were all they managed on the 3rd, a fighter sweep to Ghent and a front-line patrol—both uneventful, though Clifford Taylor, better known as 'CAM' Taylor for his combined initials (Clifford Alan Murray), chased two unidentified planes at about 30,000 ft but could not catch them; he thought they may have been USAAF P-47 Thunderbolts but didn't get close enough for a good look, or to take a shot at them.[8]

On 5 September, the squadron moved up to the Douai area to find that the new airfield was a grass strip formerly occupied by the Germans, and thus equipped with camouflaged hangars and a few office buildings. The airfield was only a short drive from Douai itself and a few members of the squadron visited the town and saw first-hand the carnage dealt by RAF Bomber Command on the railway station and marshalling yards there. They still flew three patrols on 'moving day', each of four Spitfires on the line Brussels–Antwerp, but nothing of interest was seen. Despite this move north-east along the general Allied line of advance (in that area anyway), the squadron diary complained on the 6th that they were 'still too far away from the Front Line'[9]. That day the squadron flew three patrols in the afternoon, each of four Spitfires on the same line as the previous day—and uneventful once again. In addition to flying duties, the squadron busied itself conducting sorties of another kind—trips around the local area to see if they could scrounge any abandoned German vehicles—and they found a small Opel saloon and a Chevrolet truck, which they converted for their own use.[10]

7 September was spent putting these new vehicles into working order, and no flying took place—the front line was just too far away. Somehow, though the front line had not moved, discussions were still being had about whether Patton or Montgomery would get the support to make the next big push. Operational flights resumed on 8 September with several front-line patrols. These were described as 'milk runs' and recorded in the diary as 'a monotonous and regular trip with nothing to report'.[11] More milk runs were flown the next day, but 10 September presented some action. Four Spitfires, led by Flt Lt Vern Lancaster in FU-H, were on an armed recce in the Flushing area, claiming four METs probably destroyed and one damaged, but encountering some accurate anti-aircraft fire and, though Lancaster's plane was hit in the tail, he managed to bring it home safely. Some barges were seen moving north and south across the sea evacuating German troops from the Breskens area, and they were reported for later attention.

Morning mist prevented early flying the next day, but two patrols were flown in the Flushing area in the afternoon. They encountered anti-aircraft fire almost everywhere they went, and the only target they found was a poor dispatch rider, so they shot him off his motorcycle. There was definitely a ferry service working between Flushing and Breskens this time, barges were moving between Flushing and Terneuzen. Another formation of aircraft bombed these barges unsuccessfully, and what was thought to be flak ships were also in the vicinity.[12] In fact, Breskens was used as an evacuation bridgehead for German troops caught between Antwerp and Ostend, since breaking out to the north-east was impractical, the Allies were too strong in that area. Post-war interrogation of German commanders revealed that they evacuated eight understrength divisions via these two towns (Breskens and Terneuzen) using a mixed fleet of civilian and military vessels, some of which could hold up to 18 vehicles. Most of the ferrying back and forth was done at night, but in 16 days the Germans evacuated about 65,000 troops, 750 vehicles, over 200 artillery pieces and 1,000 horses. There was a danger that the Allies would cut these rescued troops off via an assault north from Antwerp towards Bergen op Zoom,[13] but perhaps everyone was looking towards Arnhem. The fighting in this coastal corner carried on into the period when Operation *Market Garden* was launched.

Rusty Leith was now back with the squadron, having crash-landed behind enemy lines in Normandy, hiding with the French until liberated by the advancing Allied troops. He wrote home on 11 September:

> At the moment I am sitting in one of the squadron cars (late of the Hun) with the sun pouring in. I had an uneventful flip back and was pleased to be with the lads again. The first night I was back a whole crowd of us drove into Lille to take part in the City's "Liberation Celebrations." There was no parading in the streets but most cafes had dances and everybody was very gay. The thing that shook me was to see neon signs and decorations in the cafes. As far as the war was concerned the city wasn't touched. Nothing like the places I saw in the south. The people in this part of France are very friendly indeed and yesterday another lad and I went off in one of "our cars" after food for the mess. At every farm we were received with open arms and offered drinks—sometimes beer sometimes port which had been hidden from the Hun. The first place we called at was quite a large place and as soon as we stopped the car and got out we were surrounded by people of all ages and sexes. My French is quite fair and I have little trouble in carrying on a conversation on topical things–farm produce–aeroplanes–Huns etc. The star turn of the trip was our lunch. We called in at this small village not far from Douai and after buying some eggs and a rooster we were invited to lunch by a family who could speak fairly good English. The meal and drinks they turned on was a celebration for their liberation. The army had passed through some days before but did not stop of course. This meant that we were the first of the Allies to come to their house. We began with soup which was followed in turn by fresh tomatoes, veal and saute [sic] potatoes, bread and jam, pears, apples and grapes and coffee. The amazing thing was that in between we had the following drinks—beer, burgundy, port, champagne, Hollands gin (schnapps I think) and cognac. The champagne was absolutely the best and had been well and truly hidden as had some of the other stuff. The meal took just over 2 hours and we were talking all the time. The folk were genuinely pleased to see us and loved the feeling of the party as much as we did. Our experience is typical of what happens to most of the other chaps irrespective of

> whether they are officers, NCOs or airmen. What has happened is that the army has raced through without stopping and so haven't spoiled the district. In other words we are in occupation. Everyone feels quite thrilled that they are here and treated as liberators ... I hear the Belgians are somewhat the same. I hope to be able to visit some of the scenes of the last war but I don't like my chances as we have to keep moving these days. I had quite a laugh in Lille the other night over a round of drinks. Jim Ferguson bought the first drinks. Champagne cost 300 odd francs. Then everyone wanted beer so I bought the round not knowing how much it cost and paid the bill – 10 francs. We all split our sides at the ridiculous price. This place closed at 10 but we left at 12.30 having sampled most of their stock. Well I guess this is all for now. By the way I received a cake the other day but no sender's address. It might be from Meg.[14]

CAM Taylor wrote home on the 12th:

> Still having a whale of a time—for about a week we've been parked near a fair sized town & by now have drunk just about all the champagne that the frogs had hidden from the boche. My French is getting hot and I act as interpreter for some of the boys. By the way I wouldn't send any more parcels over ... this show is just about "Finis" and then hi ho for the return trip to Aussie.[15]

How wrong he was.

Despite the availability of good company and good food, complaints about a lack of action for the squadron resumed on 12 September: 'No-body could find a job for our pilots to do.'[16] On the 13th: 'we appear to be on holiday with no war to trouble us ... ' On the 14th: 'The war has moved too far away from us and our enthusiasts can only occupy their time in searching for derelict enemy transport.' And the 15th: 'We are all getting impatient with this enforced rest.'

Welcome new orders were received on 16 September: the squadron was to move to B.70 outside Antwerp. They would be closer to the front line. The squadron had been welcomed as liberators by the French population—perhaps the army units had moved through the area too quickly. Now 453 Squadron had to move on, and though they complained about the lack of action—moving away from their new friends was difficult. The next day—17 September 1944—would become one of the most well-known dates of the war, because of Operation *Market Garden*.[17]

Operation *Market Garden* was Montgomery's plan to get into Germany via the less wooded area north of the Ruhr, bypassing the Siegfried Line. *Market* was the airborne element of the operation and *Garden* was the ground element. To achieve this goal, Montgomery would have to push his troops across several canal and river lines held by German units of varying quality, strength and effectiveness. They would have little in the way of air support, while the Allies had a relative abundance. To get across these canal and river lines, three airborne divisions would be dropped near—though, in reality, they were often too far from—the bridges, the main ones being at Eindhoven, Grave, Nijmegen and Arnhem. Along this route the ground forces would advance, taking over at each point along the way and breaking out beyond from their narrow corridor to Arnhem. Numerous airborne missions had been planned during and after the Normandy campaign, but each had been cancelled as the front line moved or the situation changed to remove the need to employ airborne troops. The plan for Operation *Market Garden* had specific targets for the airborne element: the US 101st Airborne Division would take the Eindhoven bridge, the US 82nd Airborne Division would take the Grave and Nijmegen bridges and the British 1st Airborne Division would take the Arnhem bridges (road, rail and pontoon). Arnhem was 60 miles beyond the Allied front line. One road lay between it and the ground forces of XXX Corps, their relief.

Even at the beginning, it was known that there was insufficient aircraft to transport all the airborne troops to their various landing zones at the same time, so the 1st Airborne would have to land on two consecutive days. But if the entire 1st Airborne Division was flown in on the first day at the cost of the American divisions, the ability of the weakened US forces to take their objectives would have been drastically reduced, still leaving 1st Airborne in a perilous situation. Another setback for the British was the distance from their landing and drop zones to their objectives—they could not be landed near the bridges and would have to fight their way to them, seize and hold them, while some of their strength would have to be left behind to ensure the ground was held for the reinforcements to arrive on day 2 (18 September). They would start up to eight miles from their objective, and to get to the bridges most would have to travel by foot, only a few Jeeps would make the trip in with them. Their landing grounds were also within a military training zone. Landing south of the bridge was ruled out as the terrain was unfavourable. Knowing that 2 TAF Spitfires and Typhoons would be operating at close to their maximum range, a request was made for the 'maximum number Mustang squadrons be available for operations in the "Market" area'.[18] On 16 September, of the 60-plus squadrons in 2 TAF, about half were in or near either Brussels or Lille, which was 50–100 miles behind the front line. Some of the night fighters were based all the way back at Carpiquet in Normandy.[19] For short-range aircraft such as Spitfires and Typhoons this was just too far away to be effective. So, while XXX Corps was supposed to be carving its way up the highway, over the bridges to be taken by the airborne troops and onwards into Arnhem, 2 TAF would be spending a lot of time just getting to the front and within effective range of the combat zone (as far as the army was concerned). On paper it wasn't terribly promising for 1st Airborne, but the potential the operation held has kept historians in earnest debate ever since.

For 453 Squadron, the move to Antwerp took place on 17 September with the Spitfires taking off from B.52 at 1235 and arriving at B.70 at 1325. The rest of the afternoon was the kind of busy the squadron was after: 32 sorties were flown in support of *Market Garden*. Each consisted of eight Spitfires, the take-offs being at 1425, 1445, 1710 and 1730. The first was led by Sqn Ldr Don Smith in FU-?, and the second by Vern Lancaster in FU-I. Gliders were seen throughout the Arnhem area, as were fires and explosions. The Luftwaffe didn't show but the patrols encountered light-calibre flak from one location which caused them no trouble. That night the squadron was shelled by German artillery just 3,000 yards away, from the far side of the Albert Canal. Fortunately, no one was injured, and no aircraft were damaged. Rusty Leith flew two patrols after the relocation flight, both in FU-S, and recorded in his logbook: 'Cover for large forces of airborne army drop. Opening of big offensive 2nd Army driving from Escaut canal.'[20] Unlike in Normandy, the airborne landings for *Market Garden* were planned to occur during the day, with safety and air superiority the deciding factors. However, rather than arrive at dawn, or even take off at dawn, the first aircraft took off at 0945, after the morning fog had cleared in England. Since the coastal areas of the Netherlands had not yet been cleared of German troops, the airborne armada had to fly over 100 miles of occupied territory to reach their respective landing zones. The Dakotas carrying paratroops and towing gliders had a massive escort—33 squadrons of Spitfires, eight of Tempests and three of Mustangs. No German fighters made it through this cover and into the transports.[21]

On 18 September, 453 Squadron's ground party left Douai and arrived at Antwerp in the afternoon, the drive being described 'like a pleasant peace-time country tour with practically no evidence of the ravages of war'.[22] This was nothing like the battles now being fought along what would become known as Hell's Highway—the road from the Belgian–Dutch border all the way to Arnhem. That road was packed with troops—far too many to be used on a single line of advance. The living quarters allocated to the squadron were some distance from the airfield and consisted of three buildings previously used as a German hospital. The buildings were numbered 11, 13 and 15, but the name of the street they never knew. 453 Squadron's air support for *Market Garden* that day consisted of sweeps up to Nijmegen and back from 1200–1320 and 1700–1815 and were uneventful on both occasions.[23] In England, airborne reinforcements were delayed by fog and did not take off until 1100.[24]

Heavy fog kept the planes grounded on the morning of 19 September, and the squadron only flew once: 12 Spitfires led by FO Ferguson in FU-U on a patrol to Eindhoven which took off at 1705 but was cut short as the weather worsened. The squadron had a broken sleep that night, but surely it was worth it—the Canadians were firing at the German artillery on the other side of the canal. Mist greeted them again in the morning and the rest of the day was taken up with patrols up to Nijmegen, but no enemy were encountered. The squadron reported 8–10/10ths cloud from 3–7,000 ft and thick haze below that.[25] On the ground the road up to and including the Grave bridge had been taken by ground and airborne troops, but the vital bridge at Nijmegen was still in German hands.

German troops attacked the Allied advance at a number of points along the axis of advance—a danger that should have been perceived for such a narrow frontage. Reinforcements for the British in and around Arnhem were postponed and Lieutenant-Colonel Frost and his troops (mainly the 2nd Parachute Battalion) were in Arnhem, and had been since the first day, but they weren't in control of the bridge. Many of them were wounded and they were running low on food, water, medical supplies and ammunition. Many supplies being dropped to the 1st Airborne Division were now falling into German hands as they took back the landing grounds established by the British on 17 September. A request was made by 2 TAF to have night fighters arrive over the battlefield earlier, as on the two previous nights the Luftwaffe had made successful bombing attacks without interference.[26]

Mist was again present on 21 September, and no sorties took place until the early afternoon. The first took off at 1215 and consisted of eight Spitfires led by FO Ferguson in FU-U and another eight took off at 1455 led by FO Baker in FU-F. Two pilots went on leave and Sqn Ldr Smith flew to England to take evidence in a court of inquiry. Sqn Ldr Hilton, an RAAF liaison officer, arrived and spoke with the squadron about operational and personal matters. He hinted that Sqn Ldr Smith would be leaving the squadron and Flt Lt Ernie Esau, who had left the squadron in May 1944 at the same time as Sqn Ldr Don Andrews, would be returning as squadron leader. In addition to this major change, seven other pilots were to be posted out of the squadron for a rest, their operational hours having reached or exceeded two hundred.[27]

On the road to Arnhem, the US 82nd Airborne Division and British 5th Guards Brigade took the Nijmegen bridge, four days too late. UK-based Dakotas and bombers carrying supplies for the airborne troops were denied air cover in the afternoon due to weather grounding the numerous fighter squadrons that had protected them in the days prior. One group of ten Fw 190s shot down seven out of ten resupply aircraft from 190 Squadron alone. At the end of the day 23 resupply aircraft were unaccounted for, representing 20 per cent of the force used, and many more were damaged in aerial combat or by flak, representing 52 per cent of the total force used that day.[28]

22 September provided no better weather—heavy fog again in the morning and the squadron flew just two patrols in the afternoon, with nothing to report on the first and two METs damaged and two gun positions strafed on the second.[29] British troops pushed towards Arnhem from Nijmegen but only made it halfway, being stopped at Elst by determined German resistance—there was no going round it, they had just the one road. The 1st Polish Parachute Brigade was dropped south of the river—on the opposite side to the British troops they were supposed to be supporting. The 1st Airborne were on the north side, fighting hard, but with fewer troops and supplies each minute.[30]

Rain and mist greeted the squadron on the morning of the 23rd. Despite later questions about a lack of air support during *Market Garden*, clearly the weather played a significant role in grounding tactical aircraft that were, by necessity, close to the front lines. Unfavourable weather also delayed airborne reinforcements in England and was another contributing factor to *Market Garden* failing to bring about a swift end to the war. However, basing the airborne force in France instead of England to take advantage of (potentially) better weather as a solution to the delays experienced in reinforcing the British, American and Polish troops on the ground, is another matter entirely. This idea also assumes that somehow those responsible for predicting the weather would have consistently got it right well in advance and knew where in France those forces should have been based. But how many airfields in liberated France were in a fit state to support an airborne battalion, regiment or division, as well as the planes and gliders needed to transport them to the Netherlands? It can make an interesting debate, but if one side is allowed a 'what if' to favour their endeavours, then should the other side also be allowed one? Faster and faster the debate approaches fantasy instead of examining history …

Back to 23 September: although the squadron could not conduct any sorties, things were not boring—the Germans made sure of that by shelling the airfield for three and a half hours in the afternoon. While 453 Squadron escaped unscathed, 121 Wing lost two Typhoons destroyed and others were damaged. Flt Lt Bennett was perhaps bored and wanted to get out and so did an air test, a common excuse used by pilots when they wanted to go for a quick unscheduled flight. He climbed aboard his Spitfire during a lull in the shelling, only to have two rounds land behind him as he was taking off, then he encountered anti-aircraft fire during the 'test' and more shelling on his return.

On the 24th, four pilots arrived: Clemesha, Stansfield, Stewart and Peters all came in from 83 GSU to take the place of Lancaster, Murray, West, Rice, Scott, Daff and Steward. All but Stewart had flown with 453 Squadron previously. Bob Clemesha had been rested just before Normandy and no doubt was happy to be back with the squadron after spending his rest tour at 61 OTU and 3 Flying Instructors School, risking his life with pilots fresh out of training. In August 1944 he was posted to 222 Squadron at Tangmere for a short time flying Spitfire Mk IXs as escorts to bombers, then a week at 83 GSU awaiting a posting to the continent.[31]

Flying for the day consisted of two patrols, one at 0915 and the other at 1440 and no enemy aircraft or vehicles were encountered. On 25 September, came news that the entire wing was to return to England, with a proposed movement date of the 29th. Again, the squadron felt that the war was getting away from them, and now they were being moved further away from it. Their hope was to be there 'at the end' but the end was not to come for some time. Their place would be taken by two squadrons equipped with Mk XIV Spitfires, and two Tempest squadrons. To keep things simple the plan was to have the echelon (ground staff) remain behind and the pilots would simply fly their aircraft back to England. Four patrols were flown over the Nijmegen area, but all were uneventful. The first was of ten aircraft at 0625, followed by four at 0940, eight at 1140 and eight more at 1710. Three patrols were flown on the 26th and the only Luftwaffe plane seen was a Bf 109 which dropped a bomb in the Arnhem area. One of the Spitfires went after it, but it had too much of a lead to be caught.[32]

Market Garden had failed, and on the night of 25/26 September 1944, British and Polish troops were withdrawn from the Oosterbeek perimeter where those who had been unable to get to the Arnhem bridge had been holding on since 17 September.[33] Considering the operations of 453 Squadron during that week it may well appear that tactical air support was underutilised. But with no (or poor) communications with the troops inside the Oosterbeek perimeter and German troops in front of and on both flanks of the Allied thrust along the highway, the battle lines were perhaps not sufficiently well defined to have Spitfires dropping bombs among the villages and woods, or trying to pick the right building within a city block during a mini-siege. 453 Squadron was more suited to interdiction sorties, it had been their bread-and-butter in Normandy, but they didn't get much of an opportunity to apply this in *Market Garden*.

Yet, a 2 TAF report on *Market Garden* written in February 1945 describes it as 'not only the greatest airborne operation to date in history, but unquestionably the most successful'.[34] No doubt the passage of time has seen it judged differently. Regarding the weather, the report states; 'except for some delay caused to the re-supply missions, and the grounding of covering fighters on one day out of seven, the weather did not unduly hinder the operation.' Yet 453 Squadron was grounded for three mornings of the operation, and no doubt many others were too. The operation is assessed in the report as 'two-thirds successful' in terms of ground gained and places the reason for ultimate failure on the failure to capture the Nijmegen bridge on time and the subsequent holdup of units once they did manage to cross the bridge. It also points to the terrain: 'the advance of armour was restricted to the one exposed main causeway, easily dominated by a few well-sited guns.' The problem was not a lack of troops but a lack of available transport aircraft, just as landing troops by sea was always determined by the volume of shipping available. Quite rightly, the report also states, 'Whether the main column, had it reached the south bank of the river at ARNHEM to schedule, could have linked up with the depleted force covering the northern approach and have consolidated the bridgehead, is a matter for military historians to assess.'[35] The matter remains a hot topic for debate and publications.

On the first patrol of the morning of 27 September, six Bf 109s were seen circling at 5,800 ft about ten miles north-east of Arnhem. The Australians charged in and WO Lyall got on the tail of a Bf 109 and shot it down. He recorded this in a very simple entry in his logbook: 'Destroyed 1 Me109. Fired at others.'[36] On the second patrol the flight lost FO Wilson when his plane was hit by flak and he had to crash-land near the front line. He was followed down by WO Stewart. Wilson was seen to crash land but his plane flipped, probably the result of hitting a ditch or the fairings under the wings digging in. Fortunately, he was able to get out and run towards a village. The remaining six Spitfires were attacked by around 50 Bf 109s near Arnhem. Just as they had done on 9 July in Normandy when Sqn Ldr Smith had led just eight Spitfires into a mix of about 50 Fw 190s and Bf 109s, the Australians attacked. From the Personal Combat Report submitted and signed by FO Leith:

> I was leading Blue Section on standing Patrol in the ARNHEM area. On turning West in the ARNHEM area we spotted 50 plus M.E. 109s at about 5000′ N.W. ARNHEM flying S.W. I attacked one of the e/a and using 60 m.p.h. fixed ring on the Gyro sight fired a short burst from dead astern at 800 yards closing to approximately 300 yards seeing strikes around the cockpit and engine. The e/a attempted to dive for cloud but I closed to 500 yards and with another short burst saw more strikes and flames appeared. The hood then came off and as I closed the range still further to 350 yards I saw more strikes and

> flames appear and then saw the Pilot bale out and the e/a crashed a few miles South of Arnhem. I claim this M.E. 109 Destroyed.[37]

Rusty Leith recorded in his logbook:

> Six of us ran into 50+ ME109s S.W. Arnhem. Huns climbed for cloud. I got 1 ME109 (pilot baled out of flamer). F/Lt Bill Bennett (1 Dest. 1 Prob. 1 Dam)—F/O Norm Marsh (1 Dest) W/O Cam Taylor (1 Dest 2 Dam) W/O Johns baled out—OK. F/O Ken Wilson hit by flak—crash landed.[38]

During the dogfight WO Johns was attacked head-on by two Messerschmitts that scored some significant hits on his plane and he had to bail out. Fortunately, he landed behind Allied lines—a feat in itself since the front was so narrow—and returned the same day by Jeep. The other pilots also returned safely after the Germans fled the scene, and that night the airfield was shelled by the Germans, one hitting the officers' billets, but luckily no one was there at the time and only personal property was destroyed.[39]

The airfield was shelled in the early hours of the next morning for almost two hours, but there were no casualties. In the morning the squadron was ordered to hand over their Spitfire Mk IXEs to 126 Wing, and to take their IXBs for the flights back to England. It was definitely an upgrade for 126 Wing.

On the night of 28 September, a party was held, and some of the local civilians were invited. Late in the evening the orders were confirmed: 453 Squadron was off to RAF Coltishall the next day. The Spitfires would be flown by the squadron and everyone else would go by air—their quarters and facilities to be taken over by 80 Squadron. The ground crew, containing some Australians, were to remain behind, though a long explanation was given about the various squadron and ground-crew movements taking place at the time, with the promise that the Australian ground crew would be reunited with their pilots 'when operations permit'.[40] Flt Lt Ernie Esau arrived this same day, his first orders being to get the squadron back to England.[41] Ernie Esau had the nickname 'Screaming Ernie' due to his method of R/T use while flying.[42]

Eight Dakotas arrived the next morning, earlier than expected, and there was a rush on packing to get everything aboard. A single patrol was flown around the Nijmegen area in the early afternoon and is recorded as uneventful in the squadron record, though this clashes with Norm Baker's logbook, who recorded 'Chased—Bounced Jet Job—Too Fast.—Into Cloud.' This was as close as 453 Squadron would ever get to shooting down a Luftwaffe jet.[43] At 1700 Sqn Ldr Esau led a total of eleven Spitfires back to England, leaving WO Carmichael behind to bring over another Mk IXB the next day. The flight to England was directed via Ostend, for some reason. However, on passing over the area, they were met by intense flak and PO Ferguson's plane was hit. He turned inland but a few seconds later his plane exploded; he had no chance to bail out and was killed—or so the squadron thought.

The squadron landed at Bradwell Bay to check for flak damage before refuelling and continuing, but again there was an issue. Flt Lt Norm Baker, known as 'Baker the Escaper' for his time on the run behind enemy lines in Normandy, could not get his undercarriage to lower, so had to come in last and make a belly landing—something he had done before, but in less favourable circumstances.[44]

Rusty Leith wrote home about Jim Ferguson's Spitfire being hit:

> During the week I dashed off an airletter to Mr Ferguson giving him some details of Jim's death. He is only missing believed killed but as a great flash followed by a pall of smoke was seen it seems pretty certain that he blew up in the air. I was flying behind him at the time and when the Huns opened up with light flak I saw the first 20mm shell hit him and as I dived for the deck and passed below him I saw flames licking from his engine as he turned inland. I was pretty lucky as there were about 3 or four guns shooting at me and I could hear the shells exploding beside me. I got so low that I could see the shells ahead and above me. Young Rusty was very scared for a couple of minutes I can tell you.[45]

At the time, a number of ports along the Channel coast were still being held by German forces, and each one was contained by a screen of Allied troops. These were not necessarily strong enough to take the fortress towns, but were strong enough to contain them while the majority of the Allied efforts were focused on the goal of getting into Germany and defeating the remaining German troops. One such location was Dunkirk, and Jim Ferguson was just unlucky enough to fall within the German perimeter and become their prisoner.

As such he didn't go through the normal processing procedures and did not end up in a main prison camp but rather the local prison, where criminals would normally be held during peacetime.

Having lost two aircraft, just nine Spitfires arrived at Coltishall from Bradwell Bay the next day. Norfolk had just five airfields at the beginning of the war, but by the end it had 37 and was home to squadrons of all types, both RAF and USAAF, with the RAF mostly in the north and the USAAF occupying the remainder. Coltishall had seen many famous pilots pass through over the years, including the likes of Douglas Bader, 'Sailor' Malan and Bob Stanford-Tuck. Coltishall was designed to be a Bomber Command airfield but was given to Fighter Command in May 1940, and Matlaske was created as a satellite airfield of Coltishall a few months later.[46]

Another Spitfire Mk IXB was lost when WO Carmichael had to belly-land his due to an engine cutting out, but he did it cleanly and was uninjured. Sqn Ldr Smith rejoined the squadron, as did two pilots who had been on leave—they returned to Antwerp to find the squadron had left, so hitched a ride with 132 Squadron on their Dakotas. Just as 80 Squadron had moved into their area in Antwerp, 453 Squadron moved into theirs at Coltishall, and so the month ended—the same way as it had started—with complaints that the front line was too far way.[47]

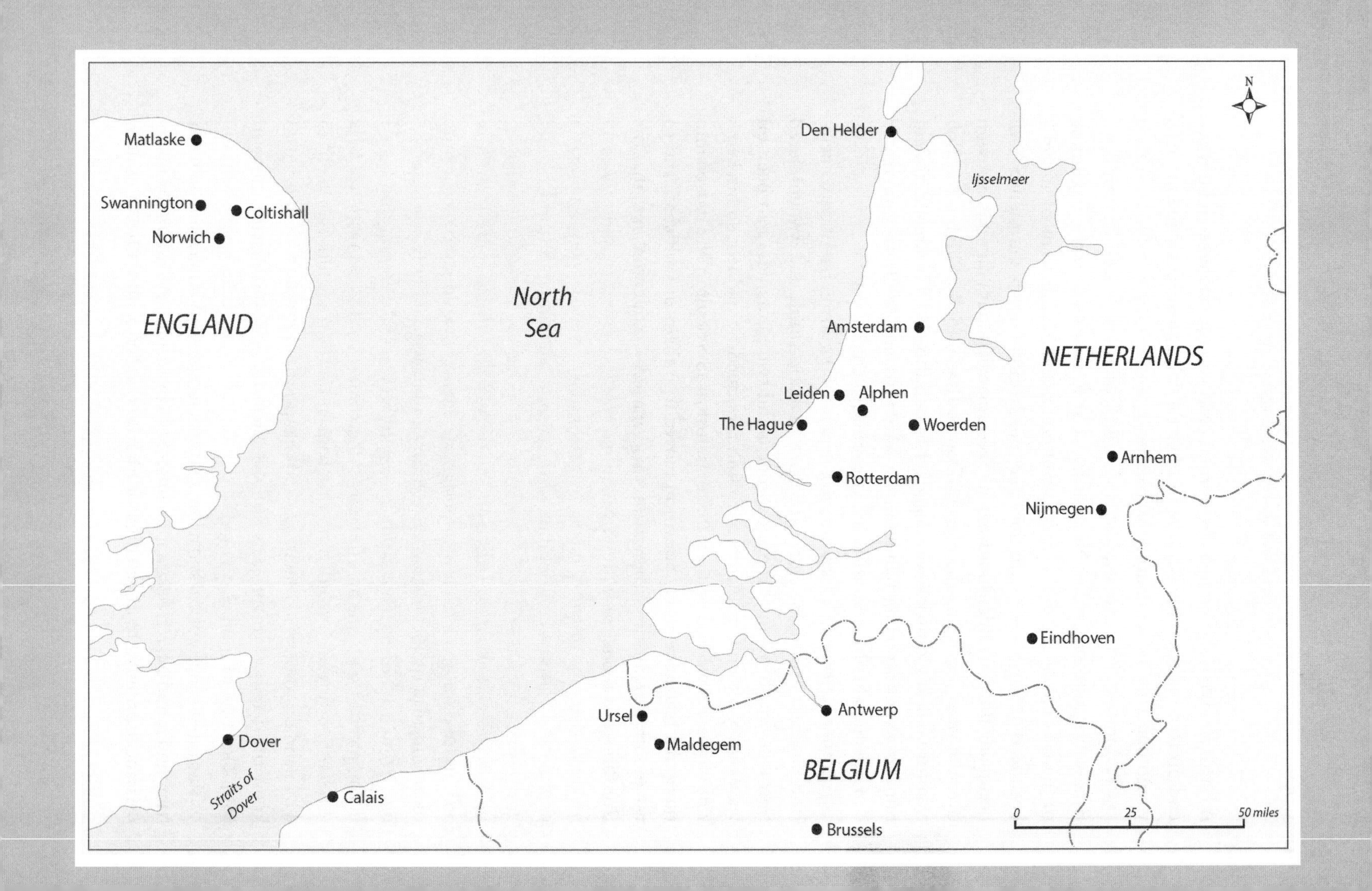
N
Den Helder
Matlaske
Swannington
Coltishall
Norwich
Ijsselmeer
North
Sea
ENGLAND
Amsterdam
NETHERLANDS
Leiden
Alphen
The Hague
Woerden
Arnhem
Rotterdam
Nijmegen
Eindhoven
Ursel
Antwerp
Dover
Maldegem
BELGIUM
Straits of
Dover
Calais
0
25
50 miles
Brussels

OPERATIONS: SHIFTING TASKS: OCTOBER TO DECEMBER 1944

ROCKETRY, as a new weapon of warfare, predated the Second World War, and with the British trying to keep tabs on German developments as they progressed. In 1931 the German Army requested specific rocket designs capable of carrying warheads and, by 1939, a programme was in place and underway. Hitler didn't take a great deal of interest in the project until April 1942, when it was proposed to fire 5,000 V-2 rockets (also known as A-4 rockets) at England. Meanwhile, the Luftwaffe became interested, and began developing their own designs, as rocketry could not be left to the army (due to perpetual inter-service rivalry), and designated their weapon the FZG76, which became commonly known as the V-1. These projects proceeded in competition with one another until Albert Speer became Minister for War Production in March 1943 and concentrated the efforts of the two projects while adding resources of material and manpower. But the Allies needed to know the details of the projects, so used spies and prisoner interrogations to gain what information they could.

This intelligence was backed up by ongoing aerial photography, and between March 1943 and March 1944 approximately 40 per cent of Allied photo-reconnaissance sorties were directed at locating V-1 and V-2 sites. Over a million photographs were taken in an effort to locate the manufacturing, storage and launching facilities of these weapons. In March 1944 the assumption was that the sites would be fixed, and would require heavy bombers to destroy them, but subsequent intelligence, including that gained from the photographic sorties, showed that V-2 sites were a relatively simple square of concrete upon which the portable equipment would be parked for the launch to take place, after which the transporter unit would depart. In July and August 1944 approximately 30 per cent of Bomber Command sorties and tonnage was directed against V-1 and V-2 sites, as was about 20 per cent of US Eighth Air Force sorties and tonnage. Standing instructions set out the code words to be used in reference to the V-weapons:

Crossbow: All general references to long range weapons.
Big Ben: For use in reference to long range rockets.
Diver: For use in reference to pilotless aircraft.[1]

Operation *Hydra*, the raid by 596 RAF bombers (crewed by men from all over the Commonwealth) on Peenemünde in August 1943 alerted the Germans to Allied awareness of their activities and resulted in a dispersal of the facilities, making subsequent raids less effective. That night, 40 bombers were lost, 243 aircrew were killed and 45 made prisoner. To highlight the intensity of Bomber Commands operations, compare this to Fighter Command losing about 537 pilots killed during the Battle of Britain, which lasted almost four months. The loss of one person is not greater than the other, the sacrifice of one no less than the other, but the rate of loss in Bomber Command can often be overlooked. V-1 attacks commenced on the night of 12/13 June 1944 and the Allies instigated a number of countermeasures to complement the bombing raids. The fastest fighters were withdrawn from operations over Normandy, their role being to chase and shoot down the rockets, and a belt of anti-aircraft guns was set up along the coast on predicted routes of approach.

The V-1 attacks against England ceased before Operation *Market Garden*, as the Allies had taken much of the coastal zones where they were primarily based, but with the end of one threat came another, and on 8 September the first V-2 landed in London. Despite the size and speed of this new weapon, the warhead was only as large as the V-1.[2] As the front line moved, so too did the launch sites, and even though England was attacked less often, other targets such as Antwerp and Allied airfields were still within range. By the end of the war, operations against the V-1 sites and their related facilities had cost the Allies 443 aircraft and 2,924 aircrew.[3]

One method which was planned to be used to defeat the V-2 rockets was electronic countermeasures, which consisted of RAF units positioned on the coastal areas with signalling equipment attempting to detect the signals associated with the launch of a V-2 and then trying to jam that signal. It was thought that radio control was only in place for the first 40–70 seconds of the V-2's flight, so any action taken had to be almost instantaneous. These assumptions were based on the method of operating the HS 293 radio-controlled bomb used by the Luftwaffe, which was launched from a bomber then steered onto its target by the bomb aimer. Radio-controlled bombs of varying types were used with some success by the Luftwaffe, including against Allied shipping during the landings at Anzio where LCT *35*, liberty ship *Elihu Yale* and HMS *Inglefield* were all sunk by radio-guided bombs.[4]

While the electronic countermeasures were thought to be of use, one proven piece of technology was radar, which had been used so successfully during the Battle of Britain in 1940. Radar sites along the areas where the rockets were expected to pass were alerted to the potential new threat, and a number of procedures were put in place, one being the shouting of the code word 'Big Ben' when a launch was detected, to set in motion the chain of tasks and communications for the countermeasures to commence. Notification to the Scientific Observers Office was by the codeword 'Fireworks' and if the army units on the continent detected a rocket being fired, they were to use the codeword 'Pop Gun'.[5] Anti-Big Ben exercises were carried out in August 1944 in anticipation of the operation of these long-range weapons. Actual operations included ongoing 'Jim Crow' coastal patrols for spotting V-2 launches, and escorts to the specially modified bombers of 100 Group who would also patrol the area of the coast of the Netherlands in an effort to detect any electronic signals related to the operation of V-2s. However, once the attacks on England had commenced, the rockets turned out to be less deadly than anticipated, and the attacks occurred at a lower rate than anticipated, so some countermeasures (such as equipping trawlers to help spot launches) were reduced or discarded altogether.[6]

While 451 and 453 Squadrons flew dive-bombing missions against the German sites based in and around The Hague, other Australians contributed to operations against the V-weapons, including 456 (RAAF) Squadron. They flew night-interception patrols in their Mosquitos, hoping to find the occasional Heinkel He 111 that launched V-1s from the air.[7] Instructions for squadrons conducting Big Ben operations included:

- not abandoning any escorted bombers for the purpose of attacking a Big Ben site
- not carrying out strafing attacks below 1,000 ft in case the target vehicle being strafed caused a large explosion
- flying patrols at a height out of effective range of light flak, and
- patrolling aircraft to attack other targets of opportunity only after being relieved by the next patrol, ensuring that ammunition was not wasted on targets of little value, since a launch may occur at any time and the patrol should always be ready to attack.[8]

Credit for the idea of using Spitfires as dive-bombers against the V-2 sites is given to a collaborative effort between Sqn Ldr Ernest Esau, of 453 Squadron, and his station commander, Group Captain Arthur Donaldson DSO, DFC, AFC and they took the idea to Air Marshal Sir Roderic Hill, Commander-in-Chief of Fighter Command, who gave them the go-ahead.[9]

* * *

October started with shipping patrols for 451 Squadron and some scrambles to intercept, but no aircraft were ever sighted. A 12-Spitfire armed recce took place across the Italian border on the 5th in the area of Ventimiglia, Cuneo and Imperia, but no movement was seen, and the squadron attracted some anti-aircraft fire, but it was ineffective.[10] With the end of 251 Wing, Wing Cdr Morris moved on to his next posting. He survived the war and ended his service in the RAF with the rank of air commodore in 1968 and retired to South Africa.[11]

On 8 October the squadron was placed under command of the newly formed 340 Wing and told to leave for Foggia, Italy, by the first ship available. The appropriate orders were drawn up, but without a set departure date, and without being delivered to the squadron. Lack of orders, signalling equipment and other ongoing miscommunications led to a very unsatisfactory situation. This was not improved when Sqn Ldr Small asked for maps—essential for the move—which were not delivered. Due to a shipping shortage the squadron was told to merge its A and B parties and, on 13 October, they were ready to move, but excessive rain made it impossible to get their vehicles out of Cuers. The move finally took place on the 14th and the squadron (minus their planes and enough pilots to fly them) waited at an embarkation camp, finally loading aboard LST *665* at Marseille on midnight of the 16th, with everything loaded by 0200. At 0900 the ship left the harbour and the convoy proceeded to Leghorn, Italy, arriving at 1830 on the 19th and where it remained for two days before resuming the journey. Bad weather forced the ship to take refuge in St Stefano for a short time and they finally arrived in Naples at 0730 on 23 October.[12]

The pilots who brought over the Spitfires also had trouble with the weather and were grounded by rain from 6 to 14 October. They got out on the 14th but took a few days to arrive—they went to Foggia, while the rest of the squadron had been told to go to Gragnano, a few hundred kilometres away.

The squadron received three Australian pilots from 238 Squadron on 28 October—FO Kirk, WO Wheeler and FS Pinkerton, but where were they all going anyway? When the CO, Sqn Ldr Small, arrived at Gragnano (he'd flown to Foggia with the rest), he visited Mediterranean Allied Air Forces HQ and was told that the RAF had instructed the RAAF they had no role for 451 Squadron and that they should be returned to Australia. In the Pacific, RAAF units were already complaining of being left out of the action—it was MacArthur's war after all, and Australia was permitted only a small role. Adding another under-employed fighter squadron to the mix would not improve matters.[13]

451 Squadron was in limbo once again, but they had proven beyond all doubt that, given the chance, they would fight and fight well—as evidenced by a newspaper article titled 'All From One Squadron', which pointed out that 451 Squadron (albeit not named as such) had provided eight commanding officers for RAF and RAAF fighter and fighter/bomber squadrons in the Mediterranean.[14]

1 November brought the news confirming that 451 Squadron was definitely moving, but to a different destination: the UK. It was in Italy that the squadron had to leave behind Hurri, their mascot, who was taken in by some RAF Military Police.[15] There were postings out and some new pilots arrived, but all RAF ground crew left the squadron for reallocation, except three who were tour-expired and would return to the UK when the squadron moved. A number of RAF ground crew submitted applications for compassionate leave to return

to England, one because his wife claimed that she only married him out of pity and had since found someone else, and another whose wife was pregnant, even though he had not seen her for more than a year. Such matters could not be resolved by letters[16] and the men involved wanted to get home and sort things out in person, rather than toil away overseas where worry and helplessness would harass them day and night.

In November, Flt Lt Henry Bray had his DFC awarded and gazetted in London and Australia, with a recommendation from Sqn Ldr Small which read:

> This officer was posted to this Squadron on 13th. December 1943, having previously completed a tour of operational flying with No. 3. Squadron R.A.A.F. His record was excellent, and he has since maintained the same high standard. During the hold-up of our Armies in Italy by the GUSTAV and ADOLF HITLER Lines, F/Lt Bray took part in many straffing [sic] attacks on enemy lines of communication in Central Italy from the Squadron base in Corsica. He had marked success, showing great dash and determination. On 25th May 1944, F/Lt . Bray destroyed a F.W. 190 over the OMBRONE RIVER and on 29th. June over BOLOGNA another F.W. 190 fell to his guns. These were the only two enemy machines encountered by this pilot since joining the Squadron, but serve as examples of his skill and aggressive spirit. F/Lt Bray is an exceptional leader, always steady and reliable, but with dash and initiative. He has been a fine example to his Flight and has set a standard for the entire Squadron both in the air and on the ground.[17]

There was another draft of Australians due for repatriation in January 1945, and several personnel were selected for this, and thus remained in Italy to join the rest of the group. On 15 November, the squadron proceeded to Porticci where they waited until the 17th, when they boarded HMT *Alcantara* at Naples for the journey to the UK. They left Naples on the 19th, just them and one escort, arriving at Gibraltar on the 22nd where a couple of personnel were granted a measly three hours' shore leave. They left Gibraltar on the night of the 25th, this time in a convoy, and arrived in Liverpool on the 30th. The squadron disembarked on 2 December and boarded a train, passing through

Addison Road station where they were trucked across to Charing Cross for the train to Folkestone, arriving at 2200. From there they were trucked to RAF Hawkinge and billeted. On 6 December, the good news was received that the entire squadron had been granted 21 days' disembarkation leave.[18] George Purdy and Bob Mercer took advantage of the Lady Rider Scheme and went and stayed with a family in Scotland where they were well looked after—warm beds, a roof over their heads, good food, things they hadn't really experienced for some years.[19]

The last time Joe Barrington had flown a Spitfire was 5 October—he wouldn't be flying again until 31 December.[20] 451 Squadron had once again been left out of the war.

Herbert Biggs appreciated the accommodation in England—billets instead of tents—but it was bitterly cold:

> I had relatives in England. The food was better ... The worst aspect was cold. I have never been so cold in all my life. It was a winter, Christmas when we landed there and it was freezing. It didn't matter what you did, you couldn't get warm. They gave us, I think it was about four blankets and even that was cold ... I scrounged paper and put it in between each blanket, and that stopped the cold a lot. So long as you could get a decent sleep ... You'd go out and there would be snow everywhere. You'd go to your aircraft and be changing a plug or something like that. The spanner would slip, you wouldn't feel it but you would just see bark off your hand. You'd be bleeding. It was that cold. And yet when we got into Spring it was beautiful. Absolutely beautiful. And twilight. Twilight lasted up to about eleven o'clock. That was great.[21]

With Christmas and the poor weather came leave, and rather than risk the V-2s being fired at London, Edward Smith went up north to Scotland, spent his Christmas there, and was lucky enough to see Vera Lynn perform at Usher Hall in Edinburgh. It was his favourite place of all those he visited during the war, and he and his mates would tease the girls at the Forces Club where they stayed just to hear them talk back in their Scottish accent.[22]

The move from the Mediterranean to the UK also saw the squadron change its two-letter identification code from BQ to NI, as BQ was already being used by 550 Squadron (flying Lancasters),[23] but perhaps also to confuse the German intelligence services with regards to the location of 451 Squadron. Considering the file the Germans had on 451 Squadron (as shown to Poate when he was captured) it was unlikely to be effective, but these things have to be done regardless.

453 Squadron knew where they were going. 1 October had them at their new base at Coltishall and they were all given 48 hours' leave—so off to London most of them went. Those who didn't go got comfortable at the new airfield and accustomed to a better class of food and facilities that went with the transfer from 2 TAF to ADGB (Air Defence Great Britain). By the afternoon of the 2nd, those who had gone away for their leave were back and many flew local familiarisation flights to get to know their new area and landmarks, Froggy Lyall recording 30 minutes of 'Sector reconnaissance' in his logbook.[24] Despite the relative new comfort, it was thought that the squadron would go back to cold tents if they could just be a bit closer to Antwerp.[25] But what did Antwerp have that London didn't? Anti-Big Ben operations were not just flown by 451 and 453 Squadrons. The Australians were working with a number of other squadrons, including 26, 124, 303, 602 and 603. V-1 rockets were still being fired from Germany at targets such as Antwerp and Brussels, so launch sites or other facilities associated with these attacks were also sought out, sometimes by Typhoons (2 TAF), Mosquitoes (No. 2 Group) or even heavy bombers.[26] A delayed RAAF media release mentioned Ernie Esau's arrival at 453 Squadron and described him as 'one of the most experienced members of the spitfire squadron' at the age of 25, and that Sqn Ldr Don Smith would soon be returning to Australia.[27]

The first operational flights took place on 3 October, a Ranger across the Channel, led by Ernie Esau in FU-J, which failed to bring the Luftwaffe up to play, so they went looking for ground targets and strafed a number of barges. Bob Clemesha recorded two hours and ten minutes of flying in FU-E as Yellow 3 in his logbook along with the comment, 'Found 8 barges 5 barges damaged.'[28] The squadron also flew overlapping escorts for a B-17 Flying Fortress on a coastal line Haamstede to Zandvoort, described as 'Big Ben Patrols'. Froggy Lyall recorded a patrol of an hour and 35 minutes for 'Escort to Liberator, patrolling at 20,000´ a few miles of [sic] the Dutch coast, bending V2 radio control. Intense cold'.[29]

At 0540 the next morning the squadron was ready for more Big Ben (V-2) patrols, but the first section was scrambled at 0731 to intercept a bogey at 19,000 ft. In the end only Flt Lt Baker took off and was recalled when the bogey was identified as friendly. But there was another Spitfire loss to come—as if the squadron had not lost enough in the last week. Baker was flying FU-A[30] and the engine cut out just before he turned in for his approach and he had to make a forced landing in a field near the airstrip, hitting his forehead on the reflector sight and cutting it wide open.

In the afternoon the squadron flew a Ranger with a destination of Germany —concentrating on the area around Lathen and Lingen just a short distance across the Dutch border and about 45 km north-west of Münster. However, the weather was so poor and the cloud so thick that they turned around after reaching Amsterdam.[31] They tried again at 0940 on 5 October, led by Ernie Esau in FU-H, and all ten Spitfires made it there. They found a long goods train—a locomotive towing 30 goods trucks, strafing the engine to stop the train, but it was not able to stop under control and the whole thing was wrecked.[32] Rusty Leith flew FU-P on this attack and recorded in his logbook: 'Goods train raked and its loco destroyed.'[33]

In the afternoon Gp Capt Edgar and Sqn Ldr Hilton from RAAF HQ visited the squadron and spoke with the pilots about various matters, at the end of which Flt Lt Bennett took off in his Spitfire and did two low-level 'beat ups' to show off to the visitors. The next day saw more success—another locomotive towing 20 railway trucks was wrecked about five miles south-east of Groningen on the northern coastal area of the Netherlands and a nearby stockpile of other railway trucks was also strafed. The gun-camera footage for each of the pilots shows an attack on the engine first, with great billows of steam coming from it, followed by strafing runs down the line of carriages and wagons, often at an angle to the railway line rather than directly down the line.[34] The next sortie was a Jim Crow patrol of two aircraft to the Texel area and a few vessels were sighted and reported off the coast of Den Helder. The rest of the day was spent on uneventful patrols, pairs of Spitfires looking for V-2 launches (they weren't there to try and shoot them down) and two more pilots arrived: FS Lynch and FS McAuliffe.[35] Jim Lynch wasn't new to the squadron—he'd been shot down twice in two weeks over Normandy and, on his second occasion—4 August—had been hospitalised and posted out.

He had hoped to get his spot back and was no doubt happy to be in action once again.[36]

More Big Ben patrols were flown on 7 October and at 0900 a vertical contrail was seen climbing up to about 24,000 ft in the Leeuwarden area and reported. An armed recce was flown in the late afternoon; four Spitfires led by Flt Lt Bennett in FU-H flew over to Vlieland and Terschelling to inspect the island for reported V-2 sites and related activity. While no launches were sighted, a train moving east from Leeuwarden was strafed and the engine blown up. Since it was a passenger train, no attacks were carried out on the carriages as there may have been civilians onboard. The weather quickly deteriorated and stayed that way all the way back to England.

Sorties were planned on the 8th but poor weather forced cancellations in the morning and afternoon. Poor weather also prevented operations on 9 October and the morning of the 10th, but things improved after midday and more Big Ben patrols were flown—all uneventful. Big plans were afoot for the 11th, with 453 Squadron allocated to escort Beaufighters on a shipping strike at Terschelling, but before the Spitfires were airborne it was called off—the target had moved. In an effort to locate the target two Spitfires were sent over the area but with two layers of 10/10ths cloud and only half a mile of visibility at sea level, the Germans appeared to have escaped. Another Ranger of eight Spitfires was sent across the Channel later but the cloud persisted, and they returned empty handed. The same Ranger was attempted on the morning of the 12th but nothing was found.[37]

Big Ben patrols resumed on the 13th and nothing of interest was sighted, but a Jim Crow shipping patrol of FO Clemesha in FU-J and WO Carmichael in FU-F found some minesweepers near the Frisian Islands (which run along the north coast of the Netherlands) before noon and they were reported for later attention. Carmichael recorded in his logbook, 'Lots of ships at Den Helder. Light flak.'[38] Big Ben and Jim Crow made more appearances on the 14th and the only item of interest was the shipping sighted in the Frisians. Another Ranger was flown on the 15th to Groningen and Meppel. As this operation had been flown several times certain features were beginning to stand out. One was described as a 'large red hulk' at Den Helder, which was surrounded by a few smaller vessels, and on this occasion the red hulk had smoke coming from it. Aerial reconnaissance had put the size of the vessel at about 1,000 tons.

453 Squadron was suspicious of it—thinking that it was a flak trap—and they avoided the temptation to go down and have a closer look. With smoke about, they did not have a clear view from the relatively safe heights flown, so going down was the only way to get a good look at the target. Their next sorties were all either or aborted or Big Bens, so they never found out if it was bait or not.

Serviceability of the Spitfires was causing trouble, as the squadron was still operating the older Mk IXBs they'd brought over from Europe. Eight aircraft was usually the maximum the squadron could provide at any one time and they were promised an improvement in matters.

That same day Sqn Ldr Esau and a number of other staff went from Coltishall to Matlaske to inspect their next base and it was described as 'pretty bleak like most satellites, the general impression seems to be that it can be made quite comfortable and homely with a little imagination and some hard work'.[39]

No operational sorties were flown on 16 October and, on this day, Vern Lancaster received his orders for a posting to Australia as a flying instructor. He flew patrols on 17 and 18 October, but that was the end of his time with 453 Squadron. It took him a long time to get home and in the air again, almost a year, and his war was over.[40]

Things livened up on 17 October when, during a Big Ben patrol, the first jet seen by the squadron (since they had relocated to the UK) was sighted above them at 25,000 ft heading west. It didn't turn to engage them, and they could certainly not turn to engage it, so it was reported, and the sortie returned safely. On 18 October, the squadron moved to Matlaske. No other flying took place that day, but Big Ben patrols resumed on the 19th. Bad weather resumed on 23 October and an armed recce on the 24th had to return early due to drop-tank fuel trouble.

Another armed recce was flown on 25 October, and this time they made it all the way to the Netherlands, patrolling around Utrecht and Leiden, but apart from some barges at Rotterdam, nothing was seen. They were fired on by flak a number of times, and though no aircraft took damage, the gunners were persistent and followed them out to sea, their efforts also including the use of orange marker flak to distinguish bursts and range, since all black flak bursts look alike and don't necessarily aid in aiming from one shot to the next if rounds are being fired continuously.

Bad weather aborted a Jim Crow on 26 October and there was no operational flying on the 27th. Three armed recces, each of four Spitfires, were flown on the 28th but there was little to see, one MET claimed as damaged and one vapour trail being the only things to report.[41]

29 October was the nail in the coffin for the Mk IXBs with 453. Four Spitfires, led by Sqn Ldr Esau in FU-?, went on an armed recce to the Netherlands to patrol near Utrecht but though some MET were spotted, no attack was carried out because Sqn Ldr Esau's engine decided it had had enough and packed it in. While this was enough to anger the CO, two of the other Spitfires in the group of four could not jettison their drop tanks, and so they all returned to base, quite slowly, so as not to put stress on Esau's engine when it decided it would run after all. Upon his return, all aircraft in the squadron were grounded and declared unserviceable. Every aircraft was then given a full inspection and the only flying that took place on the 30th was an air test for each aircraft once the full inspection was completed. There was no operational flying on 31 October, and everyone crossed their fingers for better weather and improved serviceability with their planes[42]—or maybe just new ones. Bob Clemesha went to RAF Milfield for a Fighter Leader's course during November and spent the whole month there and returned in December.[43]

1 November saw 453 Squadron return to operations with restored faith in their Mk IXBs. Three armed recces were flown to the area around The Hague. The first returned due to poor weather but the second was more successful. Led by Sqn Ldr Esau in FU-?, they saw some barge activity between Leiden and Amsterdam, and strafed a truck north of Amsterdam, roaring in on a dive from 3,000 ft right to ground level, leaving it smoking and limping for cover under a bridge. They also attacked some railway wagons in Schagen, near where the truck was found. The third armed recce of the day crossed the Channel at a reasonable height but were soon forced down to just 1,500 ft over the Netherlands. At Aalsmeer, south-west of Amsterdam, some barges were attacked in the canals, and more were strafed in the Amsterdam–IJmuiden canal that led to the North Sea. One was strafed so well that it was left burning and sinking. Another six barges were strafed south of IJmuiden on the way out.[44] CAM Taylor flew FU-Z on this final sortie and wrote in his logbook; 'More barges. Must drop a note to the hun about flak.'[45]

On 2 November, the first armed recce of the day, led by FO Leith in FU-S, saw the vertical trail of a V-2 launch as they approached the coast, and searched the area surrounding The Hague for the launch site but to no avail. They then flew north to Amsterdam and strafed two large tugs, coming down as low as 300 ft. One had to beach itself to prevent sinking and the other was left smoking. The section then proceeded to Leiden and attacked another barge. FO Carter, flying FU-D as Red 3, then reported glycol trouble and headed south for Antwerp. The other two Spitfires headed for home, while WO Johns in FU-Z as Red 4 escorted FO Carter. Unfortunately, Carter's plane could not maintain power and gradually lost height and he made a forced landing near the front lines. Carter wasn't seriously injured and he returned to the squadron, which now had one less old Mk IXB to worry about.

A second armed recce in the early afternoon attacked a staff car near Amsterdam, causing it to crash into a canal and sink. The squadron diary recorded 'No swimmers seen.' They then headed out to the coast and attacked some barges at IJmuiden. The third armed recce of the day found a steamer towing two barges on a body of water described as Rijpwetering lake but which could be any of several bodies of water surrounding the town. The section crossed out of the coast at the Hook and here was met with a large volume of anti-aircraft fire, including the marker shells previously encountered. When about halfway home the section spotted another vapour trail from the vicinity of the Hook, and this was reported for later reference, there was not enough fuel to turn around and investigate.

The squadron rested on the 3rd and resumed operations on the afternoon of 4 November, with another armed recce to The Hague. This was led by Wing Cdr Fitzgerald in his personalised Spitfire Mk IXB TBF, following the tradition of wing commanders using their initials for aircraft markings. They found a small troop car and truck and strafed them, but there was little else to see.[46]

More strafing attacks took place on 5 November. The first armed recce was led by FO Baker in FU-L and they caught a staff car in the open and left it burning near Woerden, but a truck attacked nearby gave even more satisfying results when it exploded, leaving a column of black smoke 500 ft high. When they turned back to check on the damage, all they found were a few pieces of burning truck. The second and final sortie of the day found three trucks on the

Amsterdam–IJmuiden road and strafed them, but results were not observed due to a thick haze. The section also attacked a suspected flak position on the same road then returned to base when the cloud became too thick—they had the choice of flying below 200 ft in which case they could see very little and targets would come up too quickly, or above 2,500 ft where they could see nothing on the ground due to the thick clouds.

6 November gave the squadron something a bit more tangible: the first sortie, led by FO Baker in FU-K, attacked a truck north of Leiden, but then saw a V-2 trail originating from some woods south-west of The Hague.[47] The contrail went up to 20,000 ft and the section came down from 10,000 ft to 2,500 ft but despite an additional black cloud of smoke, could not spot any launch site. The second sortie patrolled the same area for a short time then checked Amsterdam, Haarlem and Leiden for activity but returned home empty-handed. The third sortie of the day encountered the usual cloudy weather and some accurate heavy-calibre flak over The Hague, but no targets were spotted, and all returned safely.

On the next day, a single armed recce was flown—once again to the wooded area where the launch was sighted, and the section made a strafing attack from the west, hoping that if there was something there, they might set something off, but no results were seen and they continued home. FS McAuliffe in FU-P had a glycol leak just after crossing the Dutch coast and was directed to Woodbridge, a site further south than Matlaske and closer to the coast. He was escorted back by Carmichael and ended making it just a little closer to home, landing at Debach, a USAAF bomber base about 5 km north of Woodbridge.[48]

More aircraft trouble was encountered on 9 November. The morning armed recce to The Hague lost two of its number when, about 40 miles from the Dutch coast, one aircraft developed oil trouble and another's radio stopped working. Both returned to base leaving the other two Spitfires to carry on. In any case their patrol was cut short due to poor weather.

A Jim Crow of two aircraft took off at 0735 on 10 November for the Frisian Islands. They dodged some storms on the way in and the clouds kept them below 500 ft from Bergen to Den Helder. Just a few outlines of vessels were reported, the weather being too poor to see much else.

There was cause for some celebration on the 11th. There was no operational

Ground crew of 451 Squadron with a Hurricane IIC at Idku in 1943. AWM-MEA0534

Pilots of 451 Squadron with a Spitfire at El Daba, December 1943. AWM-MEA1207

George Purdy (left) and John 'Barney' Wallis as newly commissioned officers, 1942. PURDY FAMILY

1: Alan 'Dusty' Lane posing with a Hurricane, North Africa, October 1943. LANE FAMILY

2: 451 Squadron Hurricane and ground crew, October 1943. Note the long-range tank. LANE FAMILY

3: Barney Wallis (left) and Dave Fisher discussing a sortie, October 1943. LANE FAMILY

4: The remnants: Boxing Day 1943. LANE FAMILY

5: These six pilots from 451 Squadron left Australia together in 1944 and served in a number of RAF squadrons. From left: Fischer, Doddrell, Lane, 'Lyn' Terry, Longbottom and Trenorden. LANE FAMILY

Joe Barrington (far right) and some mates take a camel ride on leave. BARRINGTON FAMILY

On the beach at Calvi, Corsica 1944. 451 Squadron mascot 'Hurri', Barney Wallis, Dick Robert and Ross Shepherd. BARRINGTON FAMILY

451 Squadron mascot wearing a slouch hat, Corsica, mid-to late 1944. BARRINGTON FAMILY

Ed Kirkham. LANE FAMILY

451 Squadron Spitfires at an unknown location, 1944. BARRINGTON FAMILY

451 Squadron rest camp on Albo, Corsica, 1944. BARRINGTON FAMILY

Alan 'Dusty' Lane taking a break from the desert on a trip to the beach somewhere in the Mediterranean. LANE FAMILY

Vern Lancaster in his flying gear, mid-1944. LANCASTER FAMILY

451 Squadron unloading somewhere in the Mediterranean. BARRINGTON FAMILY

Rod Earle and Neil MacKenzie with a P-47 Thunderbolt in front of the airship hangars at Cuers in France, August or September 1944. BARRINGTON FAMILY

Vern Lancaster (centre) with others from 453 Squadron inspecting a damaged Spitfire while based at Douai, September 1944. LANCASTER FAMILY

An RAAF truck of 451 Squadron alongside a captured DAK Kubelwagen. LANE FAMILY

Spitfire Mk XIV at Antwerp aerodrome, 1944. LANCASTER FAMILY

From left: Jim Ferguson, Bill Bennett, Tod Hilton (RAAF Liaison Officer) and Mick West with a French FT-17 tank marked up for use by the German army, Antwerp, September 1944. COWPE FAMILY

From left: Rusty Leith, Jack Stansfield and Norm Marsh with a Spitfire of 453 Squadron, November 1944. OLVER FAMILY

Sid Handsaker as equipped for the infamous defence of the golf course, June 1944. SID HANDSAKER

Pilots of 451 Squadron at Lasham, August 1945. Sid Handsaker is back row middle. SID HANDSAKER

Australian pilots Hulls, Trenorden and Williams with an Fw 190 at Wunstorf airfield in Germany, November 1945. SID HANDSAKER

Sid Handsaker (left) and Bob Green at Gatow, December 1945. SID HANDSAKER

451 Squadron pilots having fun in Berlin. From left: Robertson, Handsaker, Green, Hodges, Hulls, Boulton and Hill. SID HANDSAKER

Don Andrews during his first stint with 453 Squadron, when he introduced the ? to his aircraft. The marking FU-? remained the squadron leader's aircraft until the end of the war. ANDREWS FAMILY

April 1945. Sqn Ldr Ernie Esau (left) and Wing Cdr Don Andrews together again, this time with Andrews leading the wing and Esau in charge of 453 Squadron. Note the Australian flag painted on the Spitfire. AWM-UK2746

From left: Rusty Leith, Ernie Esau and Bob Clemesha with one of their Spitfires – note the Australian flag on the fin – at Matlaske, 1945. LEITH FAMILY

Pilots of 453 Squadron, May 1945. AWM-SUK14387

Pilots of 451 Squadron RAAF, May 1945. Back from left: Clifford Stubbs, Jack Vintner, David Cooper. Middle: David Fisher (poss), Cecil Ball, Bruce Fuller, James Minahan, Joseph Barrington, Arthur Roe, John McDonald, Robert Milner, Ralph Hill, Sidney Handsaker, Bob Field, Unknown. Front: Reginald Sutton, Colin Robertson (Sqn Ldr), Douglas Davidson. AWM-SUK14376

Squadron personnel and a V-1 flying bomb in Germany, 1945. BARRINGTON FAMILY

Lindsay Richards (left) and Sid Handsaker together in Buckeberg. SID HANDSAKER

Sid Handsaker with a Spitfire Mk XIV at Wunstorf, January 1946. He wrote on the back of the photo: 'You get the thrill, and you never tire, when you're flying, that grand Spitfire!' SID HANDSAKER

A Hawker Tempest, photographed by Jack Olver while testing Typhoons and Tempests after his time with 453 Squadron. The name of the pilot responsible for this is not recorded. OLVER FAMILY

453 Squadron Mk XIVs at Wunstorf, Germany. LYNCH FAMILY

Jim Ferguson (second from left) with other staff of the post-war Australian exhibition in France. FERGUSON FAMILY

The Matlaske Airfield memorial in Norfolk. AUTHOR

The memorial plaque to Reginald Mitchell, designer of the Spitfire, mounted on the house where he was born on Congleton Road, Talke, Stoke-on-Trent. AUTHOR

Spitfire Mk XIVE at the Duxford 2015 Battle of Britain Anniversary Airshow. AUTHOR

Hurricane Mk I at the Duxford 2015 Battle of Britain Anniversary Airshow. AUTHOR

Spitfire Mk IX over the fields of Kent in 2015. AUTHOR

Spitfire Mk XVIE at the Duxford 2015 Battle of Britain Anniversary Airshow. AUTHOR

Spitfire Mk XIVE at the Duxford 2015 Battle of Britain Anniversary Airshow. AUTHOR

flying due to bad weather, and the first batch of Spitfire Mk XVIs arrived. The squadron diary recorded:

> To all intents and purposes the Spitfire XVI is merely a cleaned up Spit.IX. with a Merlin Packard engine, bomb racks to carry a 250lb bomb under each wing and .5 machine guns instead of .303's All have the modified pointed tail and some have clipped wings. The pilots are quite happy about their performance against that of the Spit.IX's.[49]

Rusty Leith took a new FU-S up for a short, 30-minute cannon test and was happy, recording in his logbook 'Squadron 1st in country to be equipped with Spitfire XVIs.' His own FU-R arrived a few days later.[50]

Operations resumed on 13 November, with a combined Jim Crow and weather recce in the Den Helder area flown by PO Fuller in FU-F and WO Peters in FU-A. Some small shipping was reported, and the planes were chased by flak around Callantsoog and Haarlem but returned safely, dodging rainstorms. Then followed a week of rain and bad weather where Matlaske approached a swampy appearance and thoughts were given to the squadron operating out of Swannington, located about halfway between Matlaske and Norwich. This was not a popular choice, as crews would have to travel back and forth each day to Swannington in addition to the sorties flown. In the end popularity was not a consideration and 453, 602 and 229 Squadrons all moved from Matlaske to Swannington and all three squadrons were upgraded from Spitfire Mk IXs to Mk XVIs. Matlaske had experienced drainage problems from the time it was constructed, and even an upgrade that took from August 1943 to September 1944 to complete wasn't enough to solve it.[51] The squadron was allocated just one Nissen hut for the pilots and ground crew to use during their stay. Just one sortie was flown—another combined Jim Crow and weather recce taking off at 1421 for Den Helder and returning empty-handed and with no shipping to report.[52]

21 November saw 453 Squadron in action with dive-bombing—their first for some time. At 0804 four of the new Spitfire MK XVIs, with Sqn Ldr Esau leading in his new FU-? took off with bombs for a nominated target, a rocket storage facility at Vreugd-en-Rust, near The Hague. The Spitfires flew via Den Helder to see if they could spot any shipping then patrolled around The Hague to locate the exact spot before diving down from 8,000 ft

to 4,000 ft, eyes always on the target—never on their instruments or the plane in front[53]—and they dropped six 250-lb bombs onto the target. It should have been eight bombs, but one Spitfire was late in taking off and after not being able to catch up with the rest, ditched his bombs in the sea and returned to base. Firing the guns during a dive was not something the pilots were trained to do—they had to focus on getting the bombs on target, so Sqn Ldr Esau came back for a second pass at the site and strafed it well.[54] The RAF issued a press release of this first attack, describing it as 'the culmination of many weeks of practive [sic] by the pilots of the Australian squadron concerned'. Naturally, the RAF release gave coverage to the Group Captain and Commander-in-Chief Fighter Command as much as the Australians. It was quite dramatic in tone, stating:

> As they approached their target, well-concealed in a wood, the Spitfire bombers met intense flak but dived in from 8,000 feet to blast the rocket site and then roared away themselves unharmed. The Nazi personnel who man the rocket sites are specially trained for their task, and are themselves an important target; so the Spitfires returned to shoot up the who[le] area with cannon and machine gun fire.[55]

This sortie was also the focus of a newspaper article in the *Rockhampton Morning Bulletin* of 27 November, titled, 'Australian Airmen's Attack on V2 Site' and mentioned Sqn Ldr Esau who was said to have 'planted his bomb-load smack on target'.[56] More media releases would follow in the months to come, and, propaganda aspects aside, these represented part of the government's efforts to inform the public of their efforts to stop the V-2 attacks on England. CAM Taylor commented in one letter home:

> We made the B.B.C news again tonight 2nd time this week—did you hear it. The Australian Spitfire fighter bomber squadron etc. The papers are full of line shoots about us these days.[57]

Another sortie took off at 1032; four new Spitfires led by Flt Lt Bennett in FU-N, headed to Langenhorst this time for an attack on a rocket depot but the target was obscured by cloud, so they bombed an alternative site. Their attack consisted of a dive from 9,000 ft down to 3,000 ft at which time they dropped their bombs before the massive high-speed pull up, and possible black-out, but at least the plane was headed in the right direction while they regained their sight and wits for the return journey. Unfortunately, no results were observed from the eight bombs dropped, but they did see what appeared to be a V-2 stationary on the ground and this was strafed but did not explode. This sortie encountered heavy flak on the way back out over The Hague, but all planes returned safely. The reason this 'stationary V2' did not explode is revealed in the logbook of Froggy Lyall: it was a monument, and the gun-camera footage of WO Taylor and Flt Lt Bennett reveals how the two could be easily confused when travelling at an angle and well above 300 mph.[58] For a change visibility was very good so another four Spitfires took off at 1326. They patrolled The Hague for a short time then headed to their target, a rocket storage depot in the woods near Wassenaar. Their dive was from 9,000 ft down to 5,000 ft and all eight bombs landed in the target area. The Spitfires then came back for a strafing run into the woods, hoping to hit something of value. They encountered intense light-calibre flak from Leiden and Wassenaar, but all returned safely.[59]

In prison, Jim Ferguson wrote in his diary:

NOVEMBER 21 1944 TUESDAY—54TH DAY

5 mustangs over at 1500´ shot at by light flack [sic] but not hit. Yesterday a Dakota was apparently hit in the port engine but seemed to be OK. No other air activity of any interest. Bread now to last 5 days. Germans say they can last till April and others say 14 days because of food. De Gaulle, Le Clerk [sic] supposed to have told their troops at Lille that they would take Dunkerque in 14–15 days. Went scrounging to our good advantage. Found bars of chocolate. Wacko. Expected visit by the Heinkel did not materialise.[60]

22 November saw just one sortie—an uneventful weather recce, by FO Baker in FU-E and WO York in FU-B. That was until they were about to make landfall in England, they were fired on by Allied anti-aircraft guns while about three or four miles out to sea, perhaps thinking they were V-1 rockets or low-flying intruders. Another weather recce was flown on the 23rd but it was poor, and no follow-up armed recces took place. They didn't even bother with weather recces on 24th and 25th and did local flying and training instead.

In prison, Jim Ferguson wrote in his diary:

24 NOVEMBER 1944 FRIDAY—57TH DAY
WEATHER Overcast but showed signs of clearing at 1600 hours but later developed into rain AIR ACTIVITY Nil GROUND ACTIVITY Light but fairly persistent artillery fire during most of the afternoon and also into the night
MENU: DINNER Pea Soup SUPPER Potatoes and Gravy also Molasses For our private supper bean and pea soup & also porridge made of ground wheat sweetened with molasses. We now seem to have more preserved foods also far more pea soup made out of dried peas also fat and butter ration is almost non-existent.
RUMOURS Practically nil except that General de Galle is said to have spoken over the radio to the French people saying that all France will be free before the end of the year. Let us hope so. The Sergeant Major in charge of the camp was up again to-night for a chat and said that we made 47 attacks in the Rachen area in one day all of which were repulsed. Also Mr Mckenzie King [sic] had resigned and that no more Canadian troops would be sent overseas. More tobacco arrived to-day although in rather small quantity. We now have coal for our fires as wood is said to be short and coal to be had in plentiful supply. Also the issue of chocolate has been increased by 1 to 3 per man. I spent most of the day reading from an "English extracts" a book of the best English poet's authors [sic] for French students of English. It is one of the books we found a day or so ago. The Sergeant Major has promised us sheets for tomorrow. Electric lights went out as usual at 23:00 hrs and I am writing this by the light of a hurricane lamp following our usual practice of sitting up into the early hours of the morning drinking coffee. We find this the best thing to do as we then sleep in until 12:00 hours which saves us spending a hungry morning as there is no breakfast. At the present moment I can hear the whistle and burst of our shells as they land nearby.[61]

26 November saw a return to action with three Spitfires, led by Sqn Ldr Esau in FU-?, taking off at 1015 to hit the Wassenaar site again. Flak from

The Hague was steady as they patrolled the area and the pilots saw two rocket trails commence at 8,500 ft, just 500 ft higher than their patrol altitude. They seemed to come from a few kilometres south-west of The Hague so this area was patrolled for a short time, but nothing was seen. The Spitfires then went back to their original target (just a few kilometres away in any case) and attacked. They rolled onto their backs one after the other and following the next plane down, the pilots pulled back on the stick to bring the nose around and sped down at 70° from 9,000 ft to 5,000 ft, then let their bombs go and climbed away again. Two bombs seemed on target, but the others were off by about 100 yards, and the Spitfires came back for a long strafing run into the woods, again hoping to hit something of value. On the way back to base, the section spotted another V-2 trail from the area of The Hague.

The next armed recce took off at 1230 and also headed for Wassenaar where they dive-bombed and strafed the site; only five bombs were dropped, two were on target, one missed by about 100 yards and the others were not seen due to cloud—the others were 'hang-ups' and didn't release. The pilots turned back to the site and carried out strafing runs into the woods as well. A total of four rocket trails were seen by this armed recce; the Germans were certainly busy. The final sortie of the day was an attack by four Spitfires on a site at Bloemendaal, just a few seconds' flight in from the coast and south of IJmuiden. The planes dived down from north-east to south-west, heading for the coast so they could make a quick getaway if necessary, and all bombs landed in the target area, with two right on target. The woods at Wassenaar were strafed again on the way out and everyone made it home safely.[62]

453 Squadron flew no sorties on the morning of 27 November; the first took off at 1210 for a Jim Crow at Den Helder and armed recce (with bombs) in case the weather was right. Only a few tugs were seen at Den Helder so the Spitfires moved on to The Hague then home. After they'd crossed the Dutch coast, they saw 30 to 40 flashes of flame from a widespread area around The Hague. Seen through the haze it seemed as it the city was being bombed—but they were V-1s being launched. They turned again to check the area for any obvious signs of launchers but none was found so they returned to base.

On 28 November there was no operational flying and the squadron had a few visitors, including official cine photographers to document their activities.

In prison, Jim Ferguson wrote in his diary:

28 NOVEMBER TUESDAY 61ST DAY

WEATHER When I awake at 1200 hours was 10.10 at approx 7–8,000 with slight whispy cloud at approx 500–1,200 feet. Later deteriorating into 10/10 at 300 feet with slight rain.

AIR ACTIVITY Typhoons & Spitfires reported over lines at approx 1100 hrs & stayed from 30 to 45 mins staffing [sic] & apparently bombing judging by explosions they were of large size possibly the 2400 lbs of the Typhoon. No other air activity was noticed owing to the weather.

GROUND ACTIVITY Fairly consistent gun fire from a distance generally in the direction of Rosendale. Mortars mainly also artillery

MENU DINNER cabbage soup SUPPER potatoes gravy molasses fish also

RUMOURS From one of our guards that an attack is going on at the front. He expects to be our prisoner in a very short time. Personally I think there may be small local attacks taking place but there does not seem to be enough gunfire for a general move to take the town. Some of our chaps who were up at the hospital say the German casualties are very heavy as evidenced by the large numbers of wounded arriving at the hospital. A German at the hospital offered to bet one of our fellows that Dunkerque would be finished by Xmas. Bet was to be 100 French francs. Germans are said to be completely out of smokes & are smoking tobacco stems which I know from bitter experience are not the highest quality of tobacco.

GENERAL Day spent as usual except for the tobacco stalk episode when Ted Armitage tried it as a cigarette & Peter Bates and myself in pipes. Either way was far from a success but the pipe was found to be by far the best since coming to prison. I have sundried straw but beech leaves green tobacco dried tobacco leaf tea coffee & also I believe cabbage leaves make a more reasonable smoke, so that appears to be the next step as I much prefer that to the wood as a German is reported to be smoking. English books, good food, plenty of cigarettes & the life of a P.O.W. is reasonable provided he doesn't think too much of home the pleasures of the outside world. German wounded are said to have received 5 cigarettes a piece at the hospital. This rumour is a day or so old so they may have been dropped by the Heinkel.

RUMOUR That Dunkerque has been put at stage 3 in expectation of an attack. The various stages are as follows: Stage 1—a small local attack, Stage 2 –a sizeable attack on one sector only, Stage 3—is an attack along the whole of the front presumably for the purpose of taking the town. So far, with the exception of more men going into the front lines, I have seen no extra preparations although German guns have been remarkably silent during the last few days.[63]

Operations for 453 Squadron resumed on 29 November, with the target for the 0810 sortie being Vreugd-en-Rust, on the west side of The Hague. To avoid flak around the centre of The Hague, the target was bombed from east to west with the bombs landing between 30 and 150 yards of the target. One fire was started by this attack and subsequent strafing runs started another. The woods at Wassenaar were again strafed on the way out, for good measure. At 1035 four more Spitfires took off for Wassenaar but were redirected to The Hague racecourse once they arrived in the target area. This was one of the most heavily defended sites and was the worst of all to dive against when it was active.[64] However, an investigation of the site revealed nothing on this occasion so they returned to their original target and carried out their attacks, then strafed the Te Werve house by the small lake. They also noted the location of some suspicious-looking buildings, one of which appeared to have a bomb-proofed roof, before heading home. The last sortie of the day was at 1354 with eight Spitfires taking off to attack Langenhorst, a site they had not been to for a few days. They patrolled around The Hague for 20 minutes to see if they could spot any launches, but there were none, so they proceeded to the target and carried out their bombing attacks, hitting the site and railway line nearby. They didn't do any strafing and returned to base, harried by flak here and there. Langenhorst and Wassenaar were attacked again the next day, with all aircraft returning safely.[65] New Spitfires were still arriving and being checked out by the ground crew before short test flights by the pilots. Jim Lynch tested the new FU-M on 30 November in a short 20-minute air test and recorded this in his logbook: 'First trip after acceptance check. Sharing "M" with Bruce Fuller.'[66]

December started with some teamwork with 602 Squadron (who were also equipped with Spitfire Mk XVIs), all loaded up with bombs to attack Haagse Bos in The Hague, but when the aircraft arrived there was too much cloud. A few gaps in the cloud were seen but they didn't reveal anything worth attacking so everyone had to ditch their bombs in the sea and return home via B65 Maldegem, where they refuelled.[67] There was no flying on the 2nd and a morning Jim Crow was flown by Peters and Lynch on 3 December to see if the weather was any good so they could try for Haagse Bos again. It was reported as favourable, so the combined formation took off at 1040, but by the time they arrived, the weather had closed in and they had to repeat the performance of the 1st, ditch the bombs, refuel at B.65 and return home. 229 Squadron moved out of the wing to Coltishall and 453 moved in with 602, recording; 'It is good to be back with the 602 boys.'[68]

A third attempt was made on the 4th but again cloud over the target prevented an attack. Other sorties did meet with success though, and Waasenaar was dive-bombed twice in the same day, once in the morning, led by Baker in FU-D, and again in the afternoon, led by FO Cummins in FU-N. After their dive from 8,500 ft to 4,00 ft to bomb, Baker's section was able to come round again and strafe the target, diving down from 6,000 ft to just 1,000 ft, and a car towing a trailer near Leiden endured the strafing, but the afternoon sortie could only bomb, the weather not being favourable for getting down too low on a strafing run. Waasenaar was hit again on the 5th, the section of four Spitfires being led by FO Peters in FU-R, but only two bombs were dropped due to the cloud, though they were judged to be in the target area. A strafing run was also carried out but there were no tell-tale explosions or smoke to indicate any successful strikes.[69]

6 December saw yet another attempt to get at the V-2 site at Haagse Bos and the 453 and 602 Spitfires flew across to The Hague together, each carrying two 250-lb bombs plus a centreline drop tank. Each squadron had provided six aircraft: 453's were led by Flt Lt Bennett in FU-N, and 602's were led by Sqn Ldr Sutherland in SM287. Most aircraft were able to drop their bombs this time. Four bombs from 453 Squadron were right on target and the rest landed in the target area. There was intense flak from the site, which reinforced the

intel that it was a V-2 site, but all aircraft from 453 Squadron escaped unharmed. 602 Squadron was more lucky than unharmed, and Sqn Ldr Sutherland could not jettison his drop tank. This would normally be a perfectly valid excuse not to make an attack, but he dived down anyway and had it shot off by flak, and it went flying out behind him in flames—a very close call indeed. Two trucks were sighted by 453 Squadron in Leiden and were strafed, and on the return journey two V-2 contrails were seen from the Den Helder area. An afternoon armed recce was aborted due to poor weather when it reached the Dutch coast.[70]

Rusty Leith wrote home that day:

> I hope to go on leave about Xmas time again but as yet nothing is definite. This will be the first time I have been away from camp since I have been in England. During the week we had the photographers and public relations fellows up to see us. I figured in a newsreel and also had a still taken. Whether the former will get anywhere I don't know. As you know there has been a lot of publicity of late for the work we are doing. This work gives us a lot of satisfaction as we felt that over here we are out of things as compared to 2nd TAF.[71]

In prison, Jim Ferguson wrote in his diary:

6TH DECEMBER WEDNESDAY—69TH DAY

WEATHER Fine throughout the day but tended to cloud over later in the evening.

AIR ACTIVITY Reported that a/c which flew over here low with lights on was fired at by the heavy flak & apparently brought down.

GROUND ACTIVITY Said to be heavier by working parties in Rosendael Mardyck areas but was not apparent up here except for a few bursts which came near here.

MENU: DINNER bean soup SUPPER cabbage soup, molasses

GENERAL Maurice says the cook rang up here to ask for more flour and was told there was none so he assumes there is no more flour. Personally I think that the place he rang up was out of flour but that they have flour elsewhere as Ted Armitage saw flour going in the direction of the bakery. So we should have bread tomorrow but

> perhaps after that there will be no more. Haven't heard any other rumours today. As the day has been rather quiet & also my fit of despondency still hangs on me.[72]

602 and 453 Squadrons were paired up and ready to go again on 7 December, but weather again interfered so the squadrons were released from ops for the rest of the day. Weather remained poor on the 8th, and the 9th and 10th saw practice flying only, apart from one armed recce which was forced to turn back due to poor weather.[73] It was the European winter, and cancellations and recalls were becoming more frequent. There were fewer hours of daylight in which to fly and bombs were being wasted—the North Sea and Channel must be full of them.

There was at least some good news, a notice from the Air Ministry came through that CAM Taylor was granted his commission to pilot officer, back-dated to 27 October.[74]

Three armed recces were flown on the 11th. The first was led by Baker in FU-M and went to hit V-2 sites in the Hook of Holland but, as usual, there was too much cloud, so after circling for ten minutes the section went after a railway line instead. Some trucks were sighted driving into Hoofdorp but they were safe—the pilots would not risk civilian casualties just to strafe a few trucks. Norm Baker even recorded this in his logbook: 'Intense accurate 20–40mm. Bombed Rlyline as target covered cloud. Saw trucks in street N.E. Leiden but civvies wouldn't move.'[75] There was intense flak from the Hook, but all planes returned safely. The second armed recce was led by Flt Lt Bennett in FU-? and went after Waasenaar and managed to get all bombs in the target area, then strafed a flak train south of Leiden. The return fire was intense, but the Australians had the better of it, hitting a number of carriages and the engine before climbing for height and home. Just after midday a section of two aircraft was scrambled to escort a Spitfire from 602 Squadron home as it was having difficulties and had no accompanying aircraft, and they successfully got it back to Swannington. The afternoon armed recce consisted of four Spitfires, led by FO Adams in FU-K. They each carried two 250-lb bombs, with the target of the Te Werve house, and all bombs landed in the target area. On the way out they flew south of The Hague to check on a ship spotted earlier then returned to base. From 12 to 17 December there was no operational flying except a weather recce on the 15th by Taylor and Mace but this only returned with bad news—it was poor everywhere.[76]

18 December saw a return to action, and rather than send an armed recce of just four Spitfires, the squadron put up 12 aircraft at 1435 with Sqn Ldr Esau back from leave and leading in FU-S. They attacked a V-2 target at Hague Voorde, diving down from 8,000 ft to 3,000 ft on a line south-east to north-west. The squadron was successful: two bombs hit right on target and most of the others in the target area with two hitting an adjacent factory resulting in a large explosion. Light-calibre flak was encountered at the target site but was ineffective, and intense large-calibre flak was encountered near The Hague and the Hook.[77] Bob Clemesha led Yellow section on this sortie in FU-F and recorded, 'Target quite well pranged—2 250 lb bombs used' in his logbook.[78]

Poor weather returned on the 19th, but this day saw a visit from Sqn Ldr Smith, who had last been with them in September and he was entertained in the officers' mess.

The squadron was grounded for the next three days by poor weather but there was at least some good news—five pilots, including Froggy Lyall, received their commissions (all backdated), and three pilots were posted out to 84 GSU: PO Fuller and FS Bundara and FS Pollock.

Weather improved on 23 December, and two weather recces were flown. A three-squadron op was planned, but the recces were needed to ensure it could go ahead; and they weren't going to send everyone over on a 'maybe' only to end up wasting fuel, flying hours on the engines and bombs in the sea. The second recce reported favourable weather, but it was calculated that there was not enough time left to get everyone home safely, so the big op was canned.[79]

Another weather recce was flown at 0825 on 24 December, just FO Carter alone in FU-P, and conditions were perfect, so 453 and 602 Squadrons took off from Swannington at 1025 with 1,000 lb of bombs each (2 x 250-lb and 1 x 500-lb) for a new V-2 target near The Hague. Sqn Ldr Esau led them in FU-?. The target was a large building believed to house technicians who worked on the rockets. Bombing was rated as 'fair to good' with six planes-worth of bombs on or near the target and another six landing short. The Spitfires encountered intense flak in the target area and Flt Lt Bennett was hit on the dive in. His plane burst into flames and disintegrated, but somehow in all this he managed to bail out at about 1,000 ft. His parachute was seen to open and he landed in a forest between the target and a nearby racecourse, though how safely was not known at the time; a letter was sent to his father in Brisbane informing the family of their son being shot down. It was later learned that he was taken prisoner, and he spent the remainder of the war at Stalag Luft I in Germany.[80]

The planes landed at B.67 Ursel to refuel (since they could not carry a 500-lb bomb and a drop tank at the same time) and returned to Swannington at 1450. Fortunately, the weather was poor on 25 and 26 December, so the squadron was able to enjoy their Christmas dinners to the full. The 27th also saw the squadron grounded—too much mist in the UK and too much cloud in the Netherlands.[81]

In prison, Jim Ferguson wrote in his diary:

27 DECEMBER WEDNESDAY

WEATHER Perfect Black frost. Ice throughout the day.

AIR ACTIVITY Not much seen or heard as piano tuning was in progress. Mitchell's (?) 6 of them said to have bombed Rosendael way. At 1410 hrs. One bomb was seen by Lt Mills to have hit or near hit on a Ganachr [sic] near the back of the prison.

GROUND ACTIVITY Usual mortar fire artillery fire were slight. Air bumps were on the programme during the morning.

MENU: DINNER Pea Soup SUPPER Brussels Sprouts Soup.

GENERAL Rumours say that they are building an air strip at Moals Resbans [sic] Don't credit it myself. Said that when the Germans push gets near here 5,000 parachutists will land here & they together with the garrison in here will push out link up with their approaching comrades. Spindlepreis says Dunkerque will be finished within 4 weeks. Johnny said to him "If there was a way out, I would go." Spindlepries said "If there was a way out I would go." He said he had been a good soldier for 4 years but was fed up with Dunkirk. Bread ration for 4 days arrived today. Is or appears to be the same size as previously. A Jerry who was in the bakehouse gave us his last cigarette which we thought was very big of him. We continue to smoke sawdust & much to our disappointment the snuff has given out. The S/M [Sergeant-Major] came across with some tobacco stalks which are more like tobacco trunks than stalks. Still they will all go tomorrow making a smoke.[82]

28 December saw the squadron in action once again. The first sortie was led by Baker in FU-B to Vreugd-en-Rust which was successfully bombed then strafed. During this sortie, the pilots spotted a V-2 contrail from the Hilversum area. There was plenty of flak about, including from some ships in the coastal areas but all pilots and planes returned home intact. The second sortie was led by Sqn Ldr Esau in FU-W and after patrolling, these six Spitfires successfully bombed the Hague Bos woods. This section saw a vertical V-2 contrail, but it seemed to be rising unsteadily, though it made it to at least 30,000 ft. The third attacked Langenhorst and managed to get four out of eight bombs in the target area.[83] Jim Lynch recorded: 'Missed target. Hit railway line just short of target. Heaviest flak since Normandy.'[84] He'd been shot down twice over Normandy—he was the right person to make that assessment. Considering how few V-2s the squadron was actually seeing in place, damaging a railway line was a fairly good result. Each time the Allied pilots crossed the Channel they had to hunt for the V-2 sites instead of hammering fixed sites repeatedly, so impairing German mobility was an acceptable second best.

Somewhat misleadingly, an Air Ministry news service release described the attacks made that day as 'Fighter-Command Spitfire bombers of an Australian Squadron were led by Flight Lieutenant N.K. Baker' and 'Yet another attack was led by Squadron Leader Ernie Esau, D.F.C., of Brisbane, whose formation's bombs ploughed up an area of woodland in use as a V2 storage and launching site.' This wording makes it sound as if there were multiple Australian Spitfire squadrons attacking the sites when in fact both attacks were by 453 Squadron. Yet by doing this and allowing for a little natural misinterpretation, it also boosted the numbers of aircraft and squadrons involved for any Germans who may have read about it or listened to the bulletin being broadcast on radio. It also finished with the very satisfying, 'None of our aircraft are missing.'[85]

A host of VIPs visited 453 Squadron on 29 December: Mr Drakeford (Australian Minister for Air), Air Marshal Williams (RAAF representative in Washington), AVM Wrigley (AOC RAAF Overseas HQ) and the sector commander, Gp Capt Donaldson. The group was late, which didn't impress the squadron, and it rated a mention in one of Rusty Leith's letters:

> Yesterday we had visit from Drakeford accompanied by Air Marshal Williams and AVM Wrigley [AOC in London]. We were expecting

> him at lunchtime but he did not arrive till bout 5.30 when everyone was tired and cold. Well he yarned for quite a while and we all got colder and colder as we were in a tin Nissen hut with a cement floor ... Last night we went to our Hq station for a big party and what a "do". I have never seen so much food before. Of course there was lots to drink but I partook of only a small bit for various reasons with ops the chief one and I was justified. We are having a party in our own little mess here tomorrow night and I think it should be a very pleasant and enjoyable show. As usual there is always a spate of parties over the festive season ... At the moment it is 7.30 and I am still in battledress feeling a bit dirty after a show and the end of the day. I should dress for dinner but I might stay dirty and sneak in late ... On Tuesday I was walking down Kingsway towards the Club when a huge black car pulled up and the chauffeur asked me if I was going to Australia House. When I said "yes" he said "jump in" and drove me there. I enquired as to the owner of the car and was told "The Minister for Air". It was a beautiful vehicle and I knew some "big job" owned it. I appreciated the ride as I had a case. Well family this is all for now and it is feeding time. Well '44 is over and I hope '45 sees us all home.[86]

The Minister for Air also visited 451 Squadron but despite gathering round for photographs, it does not appear to have been a popular visit; it didn't even rate a mention in the squadron daily records.[87] Edward Smith certainly remembered the visit:

> Syria was a highly malarious [sic] place, we had a lot of fellows got Malaria there and we had no such thing as Atebrin or anything. When we were in Corsica, Corsica was very high Malaria but by that time we had Atebrin and we just look like Chinamen. So when we went to England and to Hawkinge, Mr Drakeford came to see us, he was the Minister for Air and we were all there in the thing and Air Marshal Williams was with us, the CO of the RAF Air Base at Hawkinge and Ray Quib was going on about us and some of them were going crook about not being relieved until this. And he started saying this about "Oh yes but the fellows in the Pacific" and everything ... Malaria and

> everything, they all got stuck into him, properly and I know the CO Group Captain said "You can't talk like that." Just a so and so, he's an Australian, we're Australian, we'll speak to him how we like and they really got stuck into him and he turned round and said "Why wasn't I told where this squadron has been, I thought they'd been stationed here in England." We had fellows on the squadron that had two or three relapses of malaria, they're still on it … nobody had told him. So no wonder they got into him … I think he just thought he was talking to a squadron that had been in England all the time as quite a few, 453 and quite a lot of the others and 460 and all those they'd been in England all this time. But he just happened to struck a squadron that had seen quite a bit of service right through the Middle East and through France through Corsica and everything and he didn't know. Till he got well informed though.[88]

On 30 December, 453 Squadron participated in just the one sortie, contributing 12 Spitfires to an escort of 14 Lancasters on a mission to bomb IJmuiden. The rendezvous went to plan but cloud over the target meant there was nothing to aim at, so after one orbit to see if things improved (and the weather did not) the bombers headed for home, 453 Squadron staying with them until they were ten minutes' flying time past the Dutch coast, before heading for their own base. Rusty Leith flew his usual FU-R on this escort and recorded, 'Cloud over Ijmuiden did not bomb.'[89]

The last day of the year had 453 Squadron back to dive-bombing. The first sortie was led by Rusty Leith in FU-D. It was successful, and the target wasn't hidden by clouds, a nice change. It was back to Vreugd-en-Rust, with all bombs landing in the target area, but the two later sorties had to be aborted due to cloud in the target area—ten more planeloads of bombs for the sea. Actual bombs dropped on targets for the month was 136—for a total of 16 tons.[90]

OPERATIONS: JANUARY TO MARCH 1945

WITH EVERYONE rested, 451 Squadron returned to operations in January 1945, in newly assigned Spitfire Mk XVIs. Operations were scarce though, with just two flying dates. On 5 January, six Spitfires took off to assist in the cover of 150 Lancasters returning from a bombing mission. The Spitfires did an escort from Luxembourg to Mons in Belgium before handing over their responsibility to others and returning to base. On this escort Joe Barrington flew NI-G and noted in his logbook, 'Covered Lancasters bombing Ludwigshaven. Nearly died of cold!!'[1]

The second flying day was 14 January, with 12 Spitfires flying a fighter sweep in the area of Frankfurt, which also covered the return of 100 Halifax bombers from a daylight raid in Germany. On the same day a collision took place in heavy cloud between PO Newberry and Flt Lt Wallis over Ostend, killing Wallis, the good mate of George Purdy, who was on his second tour with 451 Squadron. According to Joe Barrington the squadron had been ordered to fly in close formation in 10/10ths cloud and this was what led to the collision. Joe thought it was dangerous and unnecessary.[2]

On 21 January, the squadron was taken out of the front line and declared temporarily non-operational. The end of the month also saw a change in command—Sqn Ldr Small left for HQ Fighter Command on a temporary attachment while awaiting transfer home to Australia and was replaced by Sqn Ldr Robertson.

Colin Walton Robertson (Service No. 400486) was born on 8 December 1918 and was working as a station hand in Jerilderie, New South Wales, when he enlisted on 14 September 1940. He had been serving with 20th Light Horse Regiment when his cross-service posting came through and he was sent to Rhodesia for his flying training. In 1944, while a flight lieutenant with 450 Squadron, he'd been awarded the DFC for attacks on shipping and his 'great courage, skill and resolution'. This was his second stint with 451 Squadron; he'd flown with them from August 1941 to January 1942 and then 450 Squadron from April 1943 to April 1944.[3] Just as Ernie Esau had returned to take command of his old squadron, Colin Robertson had returned to take command of his.

While the squadron was non-operational, they participated in numerous dive-bombing practice sorties, with the instruction in mind that as soon as they were satisfactory in this new task, they would be moving to nearby Coltishall. Joe Barrington logged eight practice dive-bombing sorties in February, as well as another of air-to-ground gunnery.[4]

February saw the posting out of some pilots for their return to Australia and, on 10 February, the squadron received notice that they were to move to Manston. Ross Sheppard wrote in his logbook, 'Sammy Small, George Purdy, Bob Mercer, Jimmy Sidney & Speed James posted home! Lucky Bs!'[5] Had Barney Wallis not been involved in that collision, he probably would have gone with them too. George Purdy and Bob Mercer had arrived in the UK single men, but went home married, to sisters Sheila and Jean, who they'd met at a dance in London. The girls lived with their parents in Putney Bridge and their Australian suitors would stay with them when they had leave. They had a short honeymoon to Cumberland, and Bob Mercer married Jean about six weeks later. George Purdy arrived home in mid-1945; his wife arrived after the war was over and they got on with their new lives in Australia.[6]

The squadron moved to Matlaske on 23 February but, due to Matlaske airfield being unserviceable, the aircrew and Spitfires went to Swannington where they remained until late March.[7] 4 March saw the arrival of more new pilots and the squadron's first operational sorties in some time.

Gordon Lindsay Richards (Service No. 436276) was born on 29 February 1924 and was a junior draughtsman when he enlisted in the army, serving with the 2nd Division and was discharged for enlistment in the RAAF, arriving on 2 December 1942. He was partly inspired by the aviation antics of Australian pilot Goya Henry, who Lindsay watched do aerobatics and sky writing over Sydney in his Tiger Moth in the 1930s. He passed through his flying training in Australia and went direct to the UK and completed his training there at 7(P)AFU and 61 OTU. According to Lindsay, 'When you go to OTU they say, "You have been taught how to fly an aircraft, we are going to teach you how to fight with one!!!" He learned to fly the Hurricane, and while he found it responsive, it was a bit slow, but not compared to the other trainers such as the Tiger Moth and Harvard. The Hurricane was slow compared to the Spitfire, which he described as 'superb'. He also flew the Hawker Typhoon a few times and for him, comparing it to the Spitfire, was 'like a bulldog compared to a greyhound!' He was injured in a crash at 61 OTU in February 1945, when the Spitfire he was flying during formation practice developed a major engine problem, spewing white smoke. He immediately climbed to give himself planning and reaction time should things get worse, and they did. Unable to make the airfield and with zero power from the engine, he searched for a suitable field to land in. Just before he put it down a fire started, but he got down safely and walked away from the crash, a very lucky man with superficial injuries to the face and head. The engine was examined and found to have had an internal glycol leak and a damaged sump which was put down to an engine bearing failure. The wing commander at 61 OTU found that Richards had 'put up a good performance'.[8]

Four Spitfires, led by Sqn Ldr Robertson in SM516, took off at 0905 for an armed recce to the Netherlands. They searched the area around Leiden, The Hague and Rotterdam but didn't see anything worthwhile so headed over to Utrecht and bombed a rail bridge west of the city. After roaring down one after the other, just a few seconds apart, all bombs hit on or near the approach to the bridge and the Spitfires headed for home. The second sortie of the day saw four more Spitfires in the same area, but one had to return early with R/T trouble. Usually someone in trouble received an escort home, but since it was not mechanical perhaps on this occasion, they decided not to worry about it. The remaining three Spitfires, including Joe Barrington in NI-E (SM479), also ended up attacking a railway bridge but, with weather closing in, only two were able to drop their bombs and the third ditched theirs in the Channel on the way back. Joe recorded in his logbook, 'First trip to Holland, dive bombed railway junction N. of Utrecht, near miss. Heavy & Light flak from The Hook & Rotterdam but inaccurate!'[9] The third sortie was warned of the worsening weather as the second headed back so they returned to base before reaching the Dutch coast.[10]

Almost everyone from 451 Squadron was flying on 9 March, the first sortie being led by Flt Lt Bray in SM391 to a road and rail junction at Woerden, about 10 km west of Utrecht. Three out of four Spitfires bombed the target, the fourth having a 'hang up' and later ditching the bombs into the sea on the return leg.

The second of the day was led by Wing Cdr Andrews in his Spitfire marked DGA, the personalised markings being the right of a wing commander. Don Andrews was just 23 years old yet he was a wing commander in charge of two Australian Spitfire squadrons, totalling about 36 aircraft and almost 500 personnel. He'd left 453 Squadron in May 1944, after he'd amassed 320 operational hours, 120 more than the 200 required before a pilot should have been entitled to be posted 'on rest' to a non-operational role.[11] His initial posting had been to 91 Group as a tactics officer, but this wasn't to his liking, and in July 1944 he was posted to the Central Gunnery School at Catfoss, which was much more agreeable. So much so that he wrote, 'Posted to C.G.S. Catfoss Thank Gosh!' in his logbook. There he was back in fighters and had plenty of opportunities to fly, spending time in P-47 Thunderbolts, Mustangs, Typhoons, Tempests and his beloved Spitfires. On leaving CGS, he was given two very favourable reports by his senior officers:

> This officer has at all times shown great energy and perseverance in his duties and set an excellent example in running his flight. He possesses sound judgement and a strong character. A very good officer.

and

> This officer has proved a very capable and reliable flight commander. His keenness and enthusiasm have at all times been maintained on a high level. He possesses a quiet and somewhat reserved manner, but has a strong influence with his brother officers.[12]

Finally, the RAAF had a UK-based fighter wing, albeit at less than full complement. It had taken many years to come together, but when it did, as shown above, they had the right man in charge. At the end of February 1945 Don Andrews was back with the Australians and, for his first local non-operational flight with his wing, took up FU-?, which had once carried his personalised Gremlin marking.[13] Formation of the wing was reported in Australia on 31 March in the *Cairns Post*, under the title 'Australian Fighters—First Wing Formed', and mentioned Don Andrews by name.[14]

Wing Cdr Andrews led three other Spitfires in poor weather across to a bridge south of Alphen on the Rhine (Alphen aan den Rijn) where they made a dive from 11,000 ft down to 4,000 ft. With just a few seconds between them, they let the bombs go then almost blacked out with the G-forces created by their U-shaped flight path, zooming back towards the clouds for height and cover as they left the target behind them. Eight bombs were seen to explode in the target area. While in the area, they saw a rocket trail from the direction of Naaldwijk, on the coast just a few kilometres south-west of The Hague. WO Blake got into difficulties and had to bail out, his chute was seen to open, and the others returned to base. Don Andrews recorded in his logbook, '2 x 250lb bombs on bridge nr. Alphen—lead section 4—lost my no.2 (W/O Blake) parachuted ok.'[15]

In a later report WO Blake wrote:

> After completing the dive I climbed to 8000 ft & then the engine started to cut and blow oil. I tried to get the engine to run long enough to make Belgium but was unsuccessful & I lost height. I bailed out at between 3,500–4,000 ft. Aircraft was under control. The windshield & canopy top were covered with oil & smoke was pouring from the exhaust stubs. The cockpit filled with smoke even with the canopy top open. After I left the a/c it looked as though it caught fire.'

It was his first operational sortie with the squadron, but he was able to evade capture and returned to England in June.[16]

The third sortie of the day included the newly promoted PO Joe Barrington in NI-D (SM199), and they attacked the same target and saw the same rocket trail, with all eight of their bombs also hitting the target area.[17] Joe recorded in his logbook, 'This time picked railway bridge near Alphen. Did some damage. As we crossed coast saw a rocket released leaving a trail of smoke.'[18] Three more sorties were flown that day—each of four Spitfires, attacking road and rail junctions, and abandoning the last sortie while over the Netherlands due to poor weather, and jettisoning their bombs into the sea.[19]

Four afternoon sorties, each of four Spitfires, took off on 10 March, the first led by Sqn Ldr Robertson in TB592 to Woerden where time-delay bombs were dropped on a rail junction, but no explosions were seen despite the pilots staying in the target zone for longer than normal. Though the weather was poor in England, with cloud often down to just 1,000 ft, the sorties went anyway, in the hope that the weather would be better across the Channel. The second sortie attacked a number of road junctions around Gouda and strafed a car on the way out to the coast. The third was led by Wing Cdr Andrews and they dive-bombed a railway crossing west of Boskoop and some explosions from near misses were seen. On the way out to the coast they attacked a troop carrier, seeing those on board run for their lives as the Spitfires roared down to attack, making eight strafing runs in total and causing the vehicle extensive damage so that it emitted a great deal of smoke.

The last of the day was led by Flt Lt Kemp in SM471, and Joe Barrington also flew on this sortie, in NI-B (SM511). They found their target of a road bridge over a railway line at Uithoorn. Due to low cloud they dived down from 4,500 to 2,000 ft before dropping their eight bombs, some of which burst alongside the road and one of which hit right in the middle of the road but about ten yards short of the bridge itself.[20] Hitting a thin railway line with a bomb from a Spitfire wasn't an easy task. Joe Barrington later recalled:

> Well when we approach the target the leader would ... peel off and go down to on about an eighty-degree dive starting at ten thousand and coming down to say five, and you lost a couple of thousand feet in just pulling out, squashed down. That was the most critical time because ... on many occasions I blacked out and so did a lot of others just because in a change of direction at such speed and you were diving at about five hundred miles an hour. And you've suddenly got to pull out and go in the other direction. All the blood rushes from your head and that's where you get the black out. Sometimes it happened and sometimes it didn't, and I found out it just really depended on what you did the night before. What condition you were in to withstand that pressure ... most of the fellows didn't think about the

> next operation you were going to do and whether you should be in bed early, whether you should have a few drinks or whatever. In fact, the latter was more the rule than the exception ... you released your bombs just based on your judgement. It seemed amazing to me that this is what you did ... But this was strictly just selecting your target based on a number of things. It's like anything else, I play bowls and it's just a question of your judgement on when you deliver the bowl, whether you get close to your target or not, it's the same thing. But that's all we had in dive bombing ... we had no instruments, we had no nothing, you just had to try and hit things like railway lines that [were] only a matter of a metre, a couple of metres in width. And sometimes we would get a direct hit. And we'd come back a few days later and they'd been repaired which was very disappointing.[21]

and

> Checking instruments was not done during dive-bombing—there was no time and it certainly wasn't a priority—you had to know your speed by feel and fly in a manner that felt right. A pilot's fitness would determine how long he'd be out if he blacked out.[22]

On 12 March, advice was received that six pilots, including Joe Barrington, had received their commissions. Only two sorties took off that day—both in the afternoon and of four Spitfires each. They attacked their nominated targets and all returned safely. 14 March saw five sorties, each in the afternoon, with the usual four Spitfires heading off to the Netherlands yet again. The first sortie had to wait for other aircraft (453 Squadron)[23] to clear the target area before making their attack on the same racecourse that had been attacked the previous day, with good results observed. The second sortie followed up with an attack on the same location shortly afterwards, but 451 Squadron suffered a loss on the third sortie of the day. Shortly after take-off, Flt Lt Bray, in SM346, complained of oil trouble and turned back. He had to make a forced landing near Swannington, but was killed in the crash. The remainder of his section, including FS Richards in SM362, carried on and made their attacks on their nominated grid references. The weather had been hazy over the Dutch countryside all day, so a high level of accuracy could not necessarily be expected, but the squadron pressed home their attacks rather than drop more bombs into the Channel, and the Spitfires dived down into the haze, sometimes as low as 3,000 ft to get their bombs into the target area.[24]

An investigation into Bray's crash found that he had attempted a wheels-up landing while smoke and flames poured from his engine. During the descent the Spitfire hit a hedge and crashed in the ploughed field beyond it. Bray had jettisoned his bombs but not the long-range tank, and when the Spitfire hit the ground, it did so unevenly, the left wingtip digging in, ripping that wing off and causing the whole plane to cartwheel, resulting in the right wing also being torn off. Had visibility been better (considering the smoke from his engine and haze in Norfolk at the time) and his communications more clear (he apparently did not think his situation too dire—turning back due to engine trouble was a common enough event), he could have been given better directions regarding his position and a suitable place to land (such as at an airfield—it didn't matter if it was his base or not). However, these findings were not upheld by the group captain in charge of the sector. He found that had Bray kept his harness done up he may well have survived the crash, and the fact that it was undone, meant that he may have considered bailing out at some point.[25] The difference between a close call and eternity could be that simple.

15 March saw just a single sortie of four Spitfires, led by Flt Lt Sutton in SM507, with FS Richards as his No. 2 in SM199. They took off at 1300 with haze up to 1,500 ft extending 30 miles out to sea, and saw a V-2 trail from the direction of The Hague as they crossed the Channel. In the target area they encountered 10/10ths cloud, so they looked for targets elsewhere and found a railway line intact east of Leiden. They bombed it with many of the bombs hitting the embankments and cutting the line in at least one section. Ross Sheppard was also on this sortie and he made a note of it in his logbook: 'First bombing trip over Holland. Went for bridge. Missed!!'[26]

17 March was busy with rail interdiction sorties and armed recces, a total of 36 sorties flown between 0915 and 1845. The first was led by Flt Lt Kemp in SM516 and, because they encountered a great deal of cloud over their patrol area, they flew as low as 500 ft to drop their bombs on a railway embankment, with good hits seen. Railway lines around Woerden were attacked by the second sortie, as the weather was too poor any further east. The fourth and fifth sorties were led by Sqn Ldr Robertson with more railway lines hit and

a V-2 rocket launch sighted in the vicinity of The Hague. Railway lines and junctions were attacked on each of the subsequent sorties and several direct hits were observed. Some of these sorties were doubles, in that they landed in Belgium to rearm and made attacks again on the return trip. Ross Sheppard dropped 2,000 lb of bombs in his two trips on the 17th.[27] Sqn Ldr Robertson's encounter with a V-2 rocket was later featured in a newspaper article titled 'Another Jerilderie Airman Prominent', which also featured Don Andrews and Ernie Esau. He was quoted as saying:

> We had just finished bombing and were re-forming when I saw a flash on the ground, and saw the rocket leave at what seemed no more than three or four miles an hour. It wobbled as though it was going to fall over then gained speed and shot up towards us. It passed 500 feet from our formation, and the blast of gases from its tail rocked my aircraft more than any slipstream. Its vapour tail disappeared from sight at 50,000 feet, still going upward.[28]

18 March was even busier, with 38 sorties to the Netherlands, some led by Wing Cdr Andrews, all around The Hague, Leiden, and Utrecht. Road and rail bridges and junctions were again the targets, though anything that drove along the roads was also fair game. A number of trucks and staff cars were strafed, and with little or no flak about, the Spitfires often made multiple strafing runs to ensure their targets were well and truly sieve-looking. Only one V-2 launch was seen, south and inland of The Hague. For his two sorties, Ross Sheppard recorded:

> Bombed r/way line east Utrecht. Cloud 4,500´ B. awful … Lost the boss after bombing run. Strafed truck, bomb blast. No RT! Found Ursel OK. Landed Belgium. Better bombing on return trip. Cut line 2 places. On way out went down to strafe boat off Katwiz [Katwijk] bags of light flak. Hit the deck fast!![29]

Flt Lt Bray was buried in the Cambridge regional cemetery on 19 March with members of the squadron in attendance. The service was conducted by an RAF chaplain and his coffin was covered with a Union Jack. As a result of Bray's loss, Malcolm Kemp was reposted to 451 Squadron, having left them in November 1944.[30]

Operations resumed the next day, with a weather recce taking off at 0705. Not to waste any opportunity, they still carried bombs and attacked a railway line between Leiden and Utrecht, cutting it in two places, with other hits also on the embankment. For good measure, the Spitfires strafed a truck, causing the driver to stop and run away, leaving it smoking on the road. This sortie was followed up by two armed recces of three Spitfires each, then six Spitfires, led by Sqn Ldr Robertson joined six more from 453 Squadron[31] to attack a V-1 site, firstly with bombs then numerous strafing runs. There was one explosion noted, plus another explosion at a large hangar which was hit numerous times in the strafing runs. A later recce by Flt Lt Sutton and FO Cooper saw a V-2 contrail in the vicinity of Zwolle on the eastern side of Ijsselmeer, then found several barges in the harbour at Den Helder. They attacked two trucks travelling singly, the first with four strafing runs and the second with three.[32]

21 March started with two overlapping sorties of four Spitfires sent to assist those of 453 Squadron in their attempt to rescue Marsh who had been in a dinghy off the Dutch coast since the previous day. This would not be the last time the two squadrons would work so closely together. An armed recce later that day saw a railway bridge bombed with hits on the lines claimed and troops carriers and trucks strafed and destroyed. There followed another four armed recces that day, with many hits claimed on railway lines, though no bridges were brought down. A number of vehicles were also attacked and claimed destroyed, and the last sortie thought they may have spotted more midget subs inside IJmuiden harbour, and reported them for later attention. Ross Sheppard flew twice on the 21st, and wrote in his logbook:

> Bombed Hague area saw V2 go up! No flak. No nothin'. Bombed bridge Utrecht area not bad! Landed Ursel rebombed. Took off Ursel, my hood half jettisoned finished trip & did low bomber run on my own. Near miss! Using gas like hell. Landed with 4 gals![33]

When you're using a gallon a minute, landing with only four left is dangerous business. While these sorties were going back and forth across the Channel, Flt Lt Pym (SM394) and PO Roe (SM477) escorted two Mustangs from 26 Squadron to The Hague and back, meeting up with them at Coltishall, crossing the coast north of The Hague and sweeping through the Leiden–Delft area taking note of damage at a V-1 site north of Delft, and then getting the Mustangs safely back across the Channel and leaving them at Felixstowe.

22 March was another busy day, with sorties at 0940, 1040, 1155, 1220, 1330 and 1435. Railway bridges were again primary targets and a number of lines were cut, and though bridges stood strong against the relatively small Spitfire bombloads, trucks and staff cars were no match for their cannon and machine guns.[34]

First up on 23 March was a Ramrod to a V-1 site at Ypenburg, just a few kilometres south-east of The Hague. Twelve Spitfires, led by Sqn Ldr Robertson in TB592, took off at 1150 and, at the target, hurtled down from 10,000 ft to 4,000 ft on a south-west to north-east heading. On this sortie Joe Barrington flew NI-A (SM362), carrying 1,000 lb of bombs for the first time. All bombs were judged to have landed near the ramp with a large explosion creating black smoke up to 3,000 ft. Rather than just head out to the coast though, the Spitfires returned for strafing runs, hitting buildings—including, importantly, a camouflaged building near the ramp. Two cars were attacked at another location on the way out from the site and one burst into flames. Instead of heading back to England, the Spitfires landed at B.67 Ursel in Belgium. There they refuelled and rearmed, and in the words of Lindsay Richards, 'Always a pee and a cup of tea'[35] before taking off again at 1455 for the same target, again diving down from 10,000 ft to 4,000 ft with all bombs landing in the target area. Two sections made strafing attacks down as low as 50 ft on the buildings around the site. Another car was strafed and burned on the road to Rotterdam and a staff car and bus were also attacked but neither burned so were only claimed as damaged. All planes landed safely back in England.[36] Of this major effort Joe Barrington recorded:

> Squadron bombed launching site which was well plastered and then strafed same. Went on down to Belgium & landed at Ursel for first time. Had only 5 gals!! On way saw rocket which threw kite around. Returned to bomb and strafe target nearby.[37]

On 24 March, 451 Squadron returned to operating in sections of four and sent a number of sorties across to the Netherlands, again attacking railway lines, but also some more midget submarines, 30 to 40 miles out to sea. This time the Spitfires were spotted and the subs dived, though the pilots still fired their cannon and machine guns into the water where the subs were last seen, but no claims were made.[38] This may seem to be an action carried out in frustration or desperate hope, but these *Biber* midget submarines were single-man vessels consisting of a hull and very small conning tower, with two torpedos mounted on the outside, the vessel not much longer than the torpedoes. They weren't exactly constructed to the usual high standard expected of the Germans, and some crew were killed by leaking fumes, so taking a run at them with 20-mm and .50-calibre ammunition was definitely worthwhile.[39]

The next sortie was led by Wing Cdr Andrews in DGA (TB520), with Sqn Ldr Donovan (SM480), Flt Lt Milner (SM417) and PO Joe Barrington NI-B (SM511).[40] They bombed yet another Dutch bridge, diving down from 8,500 ft to 3,000 ft and also hit an adjacent factory, then strafed a Jeep-type vehicle before landing at B.67 Ursel at 1140, reloading and refuelling and taking off again at 1225 to head right back to the same target, diving down on a line north to south hitting the railway line in a number of places and claiming it as cut. The next section of four did the same for their target—take off in England—attack—land at B.67—attack again then home. It was tiring, but meant less time going to and from the target than they would have had they returned to England each time. The next section of four did likewise.

The last sortie of the day was across the Channel and back, but they had bad luck. Two returned early—one with mechanical trouble and the other with an unserviceable radio. The other two carried on and bombed their designated railway line, but even this did not go according to plan as one could not jettison its long-range fuel tank, essential for dive-bombing, so had to come in at a shallow dive to drops its bombs. The results were not great, the nearest hit to the railway line being 50 yards away, but a truck was successfully strafed afterwards.[41]

There was no flying for the next few days and operations resumed on 27 March with railway lines again the targets around the usual areas in and around Utrecht. One midget sub was sighted and attacked twice, the first time with success as ricochets were seen but by the time the second pair came down, they could only fire into the water where it was last seen as it managed to dive away, so no claim was made.[42]

30 March 1945 also saw the arrival of two more new pilots, one of whom was Sidney Handsaker. Like many Australians, Sid was not too keen on the strictness of the RAF officers, though he admitted they could certainly run an efficient system. Still, 'What a relief, back amongst your own again, all Aussies. It was great when I got there.'[43]

Sidney Alwyn Handsaker (Service No. 421992) was born on 29 November 1921, in Heaton, near Newcastle, New South Wales. He was working in a protected trade (essential to war) as a labourer machinist making wire rope used in the construction of Beaufort bombers[44], and could have stayed out of the military if he so chose, but he signed up and did his evening classes on Morse and trigonometry to get him up to standard while the RAAF processed everyone ahead of him. But, as his employer wouldn't allow him to join the military in any case, Sid quit his exempt job and joined another he described as 'soul destroying', in the hope that, with his night classes, he would eventually join the RAAF. At this very early stage of pre-enlistment training, waiting for a place to be called up to, everyone had to learn the same subjects. When he became a Spitfire pilot, he only ever used Morse code once

> in England. I was taxiing out in an airfield, night flying, and I taxied out to the end of the runway where the duty pilot was. And you had to flash a signal, and it might have been B, Da Dit Dit Dit and it was the only time I used that Morse code over all those years! And we did course after course learning Morse code, spending hours and hours on it.[45]

On 24 April 1942, Handsaker was posted to 1 ITS at Somers in Victoria, and he didn't expect to be a pilot when he'd finish his initial training:

> they said, "What do you want to do?" and you are standing there at attention, and I had decided because of my education qualification that I wanted to be a wireless air gunner. But just prior to this one day by mistaken identity, and that is all I can put it down to, this civilian teacher that was there came up and he called me Jack. He came from Tasmania and the only thing I can work out is that there was another chap there and his name was Jack and he came from Tasmania and I think he had my papers mixed up and he said to me, "Jack, I noticed you put in for wireless air gunner. Why did you

> do that?" And I said to him, "Because of my education standard, sir, and I thought that is what I would like to do." He said, "If I was you, why don't you go for a pilot?" That was beyond my wildest dreams. I said, "Well, if you think so." He said, "Is it all right with you if I alter it?" I said, "Sure, please." So we altered it ... I snapped out a beautiful salute and I went out and found later was selected as a pilot.[46]

His next destination was 7 EFTS Western Junction in Tasmania where he went solo on a Tiger Moth after nine hours and 40 minutes in about two weeks of instruction.[47] According to Sid, he 'took to it like a duck takes to water. I had never been in a plane before ... I was very lucky I had a really good instructor, Flight Sergeant Johnstone. Lovely man he was ... I couldn't get enough of it, it was incredible.'[48]

Sid Handsaker, like a great many others, not all of whom survived the experience, did some of his training in the Australian-built Wirraway at 7 SFTS Deniliquin. It wasn't always a very popular plane to learn on but Sid found a way to tame it:

> they were a lovely old plane to fly but they had a nasty habit of doing what we call 'flicking', and if you came in and tried to three point land them, and if you held off because of the heat out there, we were out there in the summer time, the air was very thin, and if you held off a shade too long they stalled and they flicked and would want to go into a spin so the wing tips just went bang and hit the ground. And if you did that the common cause was you did a wing tip. The minute you did a wing tip the plane went down and you went round and round ... This is what happened with the other six fellows that I was with, they did wing tips, but me, I worked out quickly that I am not going to three point land. I [was] allowed to come in and land on two wheels so I adopted that policy, so I used to come in and land and low fly, cut the throttle and let it sling down. It wasn't a perfect landing, it wasn't a pretty landing, but it was down, it was right, I had no problem with it.[49]

Someone thought the plane worthy of some poetry, which could be sung or read to the tune of 'Bless 'em All' by the British wartime entertainer George Formby:

Wirraways don't worry me, Wirraways don't worry me
Oil burning bastards with flaps in their wings,
Carboned up spark plugs and buggered up rings,
So we're saying goodbye to them all,
As back to the workshops they crawl,
There'll be no elation and wild jubilation,
When we say goodbye to them all.

They say the Nips have some very good kites,
Of this we are no longer in doubt,
So if you find one of them on your tail,
This is the way to get out,
Be cheerful, be careful, be calm and sedate,
And don't let your British blood boil.
Just open the throttle and go through the gate,
And you will blind the poor bastard with oil.

For the Wirraways now they all have had their chips,
They've blown right out of the sky,
They are not in the race in a fight with the Nips,
But new fighters will help us get by,
So we have sent SOS to the Brits,
And one to the USA too,
Send us a squadron of Hurricanes and Spits,
Or a dozen P40s will do.

Bless 'em all, bless 'em all
As back to the workshop they crawl,
Bless all the sargeants and WO ones,
Bless all the armourers that muck up our guns,
For we are saying goodbye to them all,
They won't fly again at Rabaul,
There'll be only elation and wild jubilation.
When we say goodbye to them all.[50]

Handsaker then had a short stay at Central Flying School Tamworth before heading to No. 1 Bombing and Gunnery School (BAGS) at Evans Head on the north coast of New South Wales, where he reported on 4 May 1943. There he flew Fairey Battles which he described as 'a big overgrown Hurricane'. He had 286 hours on them by the time he finished at Evans Head. As a BAGS pilot, it was Handsaker's job to take trainee gunners up for their air-to-air and air-to-ground gunnery practice:

> each day we had pupils came down and you did two or three trips a day … it was the life. I could live that forever, you'd take off and go out … and head down towards Yamba … and you had a series of exercises … you came alongside the plane (towing the target drogue). Well, if you were doing one particular side, you pulled up alongside … cut the throttle, and the gunners are waiting for the target to come up, and they'd open fire. Then you sink back down again, full throttle, and you go up and do it again … All the shots you fired went out into the ocean.[51]

However, rules did get bent a little from time to time:

> they used to come up, they called you, I was Flight Sergeant and they called you 'Flight'. "Listen, can you get in a bit closer? My score's not real good." Well, you knew what it was like, you'd just been through it, you know. "Yeah, okay we'll get in." And you'd get in and you're supposed to be at a limited distance … and you'd come right in, and they'd get excited and they were supposed to go 'brr brr brr' and you'd hear them go 'brrrrrrrrrrrrrrrrrrrr'. They'd shoot the whole bloody thing … had some good times up there.[52]

Air-to-ground firing was carried out using a 10- or 12-foot-square target along the coastline and well away from houses.

> I did some silly bloody things … I had a friend … He was crowing about this plane he was going to fly … I heard him say this and I liked that plane, and I had an old bloody clapped out thing … And I looked and he hadn't signed for it, he hadn't been down, I thought, well I'll take his plane. I took off, thought no more

> about it, and as I landed, the fire brigade's going, the bloody ambulances are going. The plane that he took, which was my plane, he'd force-landed it, he was doing low-level stuff, and the motor cut out on him, and he stuck it down in the swamp! Lucky me. I apologised to him ... And another silly bloody thing I did when I was up there too. We had a Kiwi used to room with me, a lovely bloke ... But this canny bugger, he had a happy knack of, instead of going back in, he went back into the sun, and back around and, of course, you were with the drogue, you were expecting he's gone, but he hasn't and he comes out of nowhere and comes straight down. Playing bloody bright sparks. I didn't even dream it would come as close as it did so I loaded up the bloody Very pistol ... [and] thought 'this bugger, I'll give him a shock'. Give him a shock alright. As he went underneath me I fired and I hit him right in the front of the bloody board. I could have killed him, and I'm pissing myself laughing, that'll teach you, you bastard. And when I get back, he's shaking and says 'Come and have a look at this'. He took me over and, honestly you could have got an apple and put it where it hit up on the cowling here. You could have got an apple in, I apologised to him. He decided not to talk about it and so did I.[53]

Despite this dangerous behaviour, perhaps due to age more than personality—Handsaker was a quiet type; he wasn't physically large and he didn't try and make up for it with noise and bravado—he just went about his job. His assessment during his posting at BAGS included the comment that he was 'A quiet type who is inclined to be underconfident ... His service outlook is good but he lacks initiative and force of character which however should improve with further experience'.[54] Sid retained that personality for the rest of his life, and when anyone would get too excited about finding out he flew Spitfires he put them in their place and tell them he was no hero; he just did his job.

BAGS didn't last forever, and he found himself at 2 Embarkation Depot Bradfield Park (Sydney) on 18 February 1944, and left Australia from the port of Brisbane on 1 March 1944, crossed the USA by train, buying as much camera film as he could along the way[55] and arrived in the UK on 7 April. He passed the time (deemed by many as far too long) at 11 PDRC and spent many months there mixing with other Dominion aircrew awaiting posting. The New Zealanders made a real impression on him:

> Geez they were well-behaved, well-mannered. Our mob were a rolling rabble, and that's not saying anything unkind, but the Kiwis were just so very English, you know, and I used to look at them and think that I'd like to be like that ... They were really lovable people.[56]

He also did an NCOs course at Whitley Bay, and rather than just rules and regulations, it was more like a commando course. For one exercise those on it were split between red and blue—with one side defending a nominated building against the others. They had denims over the uniform and were equipped with .303 rifles and blanks. He was with another Australian, Norm, who Sid Handsaker described as 'a bloody mystery to himself ... he was the funniest man'.[57] They had been detailed to protect the golf house within the nominated area, but his mate was having none of that and told Handsaker how it was going to be:

> We'll climb out the bloody window. So that's what we did. We climbed out the bloody window of the golf house, made our way up to the pub, and sat up there and had a drink until bloody throwing out time.[58]

But it wasn't over yet. Perhaps inspired by the bottle, Norm led Handsaker off to look for a friend. They found him in his billeted bed at 0300, climbed in and let off their rifles with blank ammunition right next to him and then took off down the street. There they ran into the umpire of the red vs blue exercise:

> Well, we go down the street and are coming back up to our billets and next minute, here's the bloody drill sergeant—we were all above him [in rank] but he was a sergeant. He was a Scotsman. He was only five feet nothing and we all used to treat him as a joke, you know. So down the road comes bloody Jock, and he says, "I thought I heard some shots down there somewhere." "Yeah, we did too." "We think it was down there" we pointed down that way ... So we left him to it. And we'd only just got round the bloody corner and here's the red army, "Ahh, put your arms up!" And of course Normie by this time he's had

a few beers, "Oh, fuck off," he said. "No, no, put em up!" Normie ... he said, "Look, here's my bloody rifle, you can have that." "No, we don't want your rifle." "Well," he said, "tell you what I'll do. You can have my patch." So he took his [blue] patch off and gave it to them. And, he said, "I'll give you the password" and he gave them the password to get into the headquarters! [Handsaker tried to talk him out of it] but he said, "No, no, fuck em" ... So we go back and we're pissing ourselves laughing all the way to the barracks and we don't hear any more. The next day the big conference is on ... Well, I'm sitting in the seat and of course they'd found out ... that the red army had gotten in and captured the place and used the password they knew. Oh Christ! And I'm sitting in my seat and I'm going down further and further and Normie's sitting there with a big smug look on his face. I'm thinking, "you bastard" and he's sitting there pissing himself laughing. And this Wing Commander, boy was he mad! He was hopping mad, he knew somebody did it but he didn't know who it was. Wanted the man to come forward, but not much chance of that.[59]

After these shenanigans, the aircrew received postings to move them through the system and into squadrons. Handsaker was posted to 18 EFTS at Fair Oaks in Surrey where he (and many others) received a Tiger Moth refresher, as they had not flown for quite some time and were out of practice. This time he was allowed to go solo after 90 minutes.[60] Next stop was 5 (P)AFU on 24 October 1944, where he flew the Miles Master II. Of this plane he said: 'The Miles Master was good though, you could just put it down anywhere. They were really good. We did night flying in those. Spitfires were the things that were a menace in the night-time.'[61]

Then it was off to 53 OTU on 16 January 1945, where his course was a real mix of nationalities:

We had the Dutch, we had the bloody Kiwis, there were Englishmen of course, but they had the Rhodesians, Jamaicans, Free French—they were there, and they used to be funny because you had to take a turn being the NCO for the day and you had to read the roll call out, and trying to read the French names out. The minute you got the word out, didn't they get stroppy?! "That's Bogadon, NOT Bogadon!" and

> J'Marais. I used to remember all them. They used to have—instead of drinking tea, they were given red wine. I don't know how they got it ... So I was in the mess there one day and I said, can I have a taste? Oh gee! Shudder! 'Don't know how you can drink that bloody stuff', I said. But they were not real good pilots. In night flying, there were three or four bloody Spits with the nose [down in the ground] and they were all Free French fellows taxiing too fast and up when their nose [hit the ground]. I didn't have much time for the Free French. There were some nice fellows, we had some really lovely officers, but they had this quaint way about them with pronunciation.[62]

Sid Handsaker had a number of good mates, one in particular being Clarence 'Sam' Ford, and Sam wouldn't go anywhere without Sid, but as a stereotypically Australian 'colonial' he wasn't too keen on rules and caused Sid all manner of nervous tension with his behaviour. Clarence became Sam in his youth, when he'd spent a lot of time outdoors and became quite tanned, and so quite brown, which made him 'Sambo' in the language of the time, which became Sam. Not sure about their potential proficiency as fighter pilots, they both put in for PRU training, but Handsaker went down with a cold and couldn't fly for some time, though Ford was due to go:

> they get to him and say, "Well, you're due to go down." "I'm not going," he said, "my mate's not ready." And he wouldn't go! He just wouldn't go until I came out. [I eventually came out] And then ... "Righto, we're going now." So we went down, and when we get down there, what it was, was a big dome ... and they had portholes on one side, and doctors there with white coats and that on, and they were looking in through the portholes, talking to you on the microphone, and you were sitting in the middle on two seats ... and you had probably six at that seat and six at that seat. And then, and the oxygen mask on ... they wanted to show you the effect that oxygen has on you when it's removed ... they simulated the atmosphere in it and they'd say, well we're going to go up to so much—8,000 or 10,000 [ft]. Now, 10,000 you were supposed to put your oxygen mask. So you put your oxygen mask on to get the feel of it, then at 15,000 they'd say take it off and you'd take it off then put it back on again. To go one further

than that they decided that sitting opposite us was these three French fellows ... They said over the loudspeaker, "we want somebody to volunteer to take his mask off". And this little French bloke said, "I will take it off" ... So they said, "Right, there's a little exercise to do" which was to count these peas in a bottle ... and they put a bottle down there with a little neck on it, "And now count the peas." And this is what he said: "One peas in ze bottle; two peas in ze bottle," and he's looking around and smiling, piss easy. "Three peas in ze bottle," and he starts to stagger a little bit. "Four peas in ze bottle." By the time he gets to five and six the bloody peas are going and the next minute, he's out. Of course, I panicked a bit, I thought "shit," you know, he's going to die ... Anyhow, the next thing, the voice comes over and says, "Lean in his pocket and take out his paybook." So they undid his pocket and took his paybook out. "Now, we want you to take his sock off his right foot." So they did that. "Put his shoe back on again." They said, "Alright, so we're going to put the oxygen back on again." And he's there and he's down ... and he goes, "Oh, six peas in ze bottle ... " and he's back on and he didn't have a clue! Didn't have a clue! ... Anyhow, they let him out of it and they said to him, "Where's your paybook?" He said, "Oh, in my pock– it's gone!" His mate's got it. "Why didn't you put your other sock on your other foot?" ... Didn't have a clue ... Didn't have a clue. Maybe a lot of aircrew got out with faulty masks and they went bonkers or just passed out.'[63]

In the end PRU wasn't for either of them and though they had different postings they remained best of friends and kept in touch after the war. Sid put down for Mustangs and Sam put himself down for Spitfires. As it turned out Sid got the Spitfires and Sam got the Mustangs.[64] Handsaker finally arrived at 451 Squadron on 30 March 1945. He wasn't too worried about dive-bombing practice and didn't mind that he scored poorly during training: 'But I remember saying to myself, I'm a fighter pilot, I'm not going to be dive bombing, I don't need to know how to do bloody dive bombing. You wouldn't know it, the first station I went to, they were dive bombing! Luckily I didn't have to go on. I never ever worried about it.'[65]

The last day of March started early for 451 Squadron, with the first section of four Spitfires taking off at 0640 for their attack on a railway line near Utrecht, which they claimed as cut, and strafing a truck and trailer on the return journey for good measure. The next two sorties took place in the early afternoon, but strong winds in the target areas caused their bombs to miss. The last sortie of the day didn't have any such winds to contend with and claimed hits and near misses on their railway bridge target. They declined to attack some trucks as they were seen in built-up areas and the pilots were concerned about the possibility of causing civilian casualties.[66]

In some ways, the war was winding down, and the Luftwaffe couldn't put up the fight it once had but, so close to the end, one pilot could not take it anymore. He spoke with Joe Barrington, who recalled:

> I was on the V2 rockets, dive bombing and I did one of the double operations where we went over to a certain site, rocket site in Holland and then flew down to Belgium, refuelled and rearmed, came back and attacked either that or another one ... And I'd come back and there was a new pilot who'd just come onto the squadron and he came to me and said: "I'm supposed to fly this afternoon, could you do my operation for me?" And I said, "Certainly not, I've just done two not one, so I can hardly go and do another." He'd never flown in operations and this was his first one. And I later learned, when he was no longer on the squadron ... it turned out that he'd asked a number of people to do it. And the reason seemed to be, he'd met a girl ... got married. And the last thing on his mind at that time was flying an operation where he mightn't come back. Now, I only heard that he was called LMF, that expression, Lack of Moral Fibre ... So we never saw him again. But that was the only case I encountered where somebody wouldn't ... didn't want to do what they were supposed to do. I guess it happened, particularly in the bombers but this was fighters. [It was discussed within the squadron which is] how I found out that there were others that he approached ... But that was rare. And the CO was certainly going to hear about that from somebody and take whatever action was appropriate ... But, you know ... it was only the once that it happened. I can understand the reason even if it's not the right reason, but I can understand it.[67]

The pilot in question was James Ware. James Philip Ware (Service No. 420311) enlisted on 11 October 1941 in Sydney at the age of 20 and did his flying training at 8 EFTS Narrandera and 5 SFTS Uranquinty, arriving in the UK in April 1943 and progressing through 53 OTU before being posted to 41 Squadron in October 1944, then 451 Squadron on 2 February 1945. He had flown 50 sorties on V-1 interceptions plus two dive-bombing sorties with 41 Squadron, plus a number of sorties with 451 Squadron before this incident with Joe Barrington. Ware had started complaining of headaches in October 1944, and these were more prominent after flying, and he was grounded that same month, for non-specified, non-medical reasons. He told his flight commander at 41 Squadron that he could not fly more than one operational sortie per day (it should be noted here that dictating your working conditions up the chain of command during wartime was not wise). He was taken off flying duties and underwent a medical examination which found him fit to fly. He resumed flying but returned early on his second sortie and was removed from 41 Squadron. On 10 March he 'came under special observation as a suspected operational failure' when he complained of headaches again and was excused from flying by the squadron medical officer. Sqn Ldr Robertson concluded his report on the matter with:

> During his operational flying duties he has never been engaged by heavy opposition and has never been exposed to stress of any kind. I suspect this pilot of lacking in moral fibre but am unable to confirm the fact that owing to the nature of operations on which he was engaged.[68]

It is probably going a bit far to say that Ware had 'never been exposed to stress of any kind'. After all, simply being in uniform during wartime might be sufficient to cause stress, though with whole nations at war for years this may well be setting the bar far too low. Still, being told the nature of the target may be enough to induce stress, or perhaps sitting in your Spitfire (or any other plane, vehicle or vessel for that matter) and preparing to deliver violence to the enemy might be enough. But in the end, there was a war on, and though it was clear that Germany was on its last legs in Europe, the war in the Pacific still had many months to go, and no atomic weapons had yet been used. The war had to be seen through to its conclusion, and the military could not allow its troops to 'take it easy' as the war approached its end. No one knew exactly how long the war had to run, everyone had to keep pushing right to the end, and hope that with each push, the end came a bit closer. Even the (now) world-famous 'Band of Brothers' E/2/506 took fewer risks towards the end of the war, for which Major Dick Winters was criticised.[69] There's no doubt that infantry units had some troops not fighting as hard towards the end of the war, but it's far easier to be lost in the numbers of an infantry unit compared to a pilot in his own aircraft where individual accountability is much higher.

The headaches returned after Ware joined 451 Squadron. Sinus X-rays revealed nothing on two occasions and the medical report concluded that there was no 'medical cause for the headaches, and in my opinion he is fit for full flying duties'. He had been disciplined for involvement in a brawl, during which he was struck in the face, but this injury was never directly linked to his headaches. Ware was given 24 hours in which to answer the allegations against him by way of statement but he declined, instead asking for an interview with the Group Captain, which was granted. However, this did not have a favourable result; the Group Captain could not determine if the headaches existed or not but he concluded his report with:

> I can say however that this case bears a strong resemblance to all those other cases which I have met where, when a pilot does not like what he has to do, he immediately suffers from headaches or stomach aches or sundry other ailments. I consider that they would all be better employed in the infantry since they are young and apparently "Fighting Fit".[70]

A further report from the Group Air Vice Marshal also came to the conclusion that 'he is lacking in moral fibre' but this came with the provision that it was able to be overturned if 'evidence can be obtained regarding the headaches of which he complains'.[71] Another specialist report was called for, but this found no medical evidence for the headaches, and Ware's categorisation as LMF was supported.

At the conclusion of the matter, Ware was demoted from warrant officer to aircraftman (AC1, the lowest possible) and made to hand in his flying badge. He was later discharged, with the following note made on his file: 'Services no longer required with disciplinary action WEF 22.1.46'.[72] His discharge in this manner meant that he was not entitled to many of the schemes and pensions open to veterans post-war. With this in mind, representations were made on his behalf to have the case re-examined and, while the lack of medical evidence meant that he could not be reclassified, in 1955 the RAAF granted him clemency and the reference to discipline was struck from his record.[73]

***

For 453 Squadron, 1 January 1945 was not the day to be hung over. They flew three sorties against V-2 sites in The Hague area. Bombing appeared good but results were impossible to judge. The weather hindered operations once again, and the first flight was directed to turn around and land at B.65 even though they were 40 miles out to sea. They stayed in Europe for a few days before they could return home.

In prison, Jim Ferguson wrote in his diary:

1ST JANUARY MONDAY

WEATHER Mainly cloudy, but was milder than usual.

AIR ACTIVITY None offensive against this area, although a/c were heard flying over in strength. Also I believe I heard fighters amongst them. Very good story here. A Frenchwoman at Rosendael says she saw a German a/c on the beach at Malo Les Bains. This occurrence took place last night. The a/c is said to have landed & taken off from the landing strip. This event of course developed into the rumour that high ranking German officers are being or are to be evacuated by air. As the a/c is said to have been a small one, I doubt the story in the fullness as it is too small to move many officers & also as the Heinkel is said to have carried extra fuel tanks. I doubt if any small a/c could go the distance on its small petrol tanks. Of course it may have refuelling facilities here. An a/c was heard to fly over here very low & very fast last night at 0200 hrs this morning. It was not a Hun nor did it sound like one of our a/c but it was definitely a heavier a/c than I imagined.

GROUND ACTIVITY Said to have been vicious artillery duels during the night. I slept on. Rather quiet during the morning but artillery fire improved at 1600 hours for an hour or so, but most of the shells were going out, although many were coming in. Rumour from Rosendael says that La Rochelle has fallen. We heard that over a month ago only to have it refuted by the BBC 9 o'clock News. Hitler spoke last night & promised bigger and better victories in 1945 & did not think the war would end this year but would probably finish in 1946. He also said Germany must be strong within herself.

MENU: DINNER Pea and bean soup SUPPER Nil

EXTRAS: HORSEMEAT Private supper of Brussels Sprout soup mixed with the residue of dinner.

GENERAL Once again ate in our private room. We lodged a formal protest against our food rationing. For 3 days now we have only had one meal per day which we believe is less than the German soldiers ration. Johnny wrote a letter to the o/c Prison & gave it to the Sgt Major to deliver. As it so happened the c/m for the area was here (an s/r) & he came up & saw us and really talked, for over ½ hour. We listened to him explaining in German how we were getting the same ration as the German soldiers but it seemed to me that he had been working a racket & was afraid we had caught on. Anyway the next few days should be very interesting. The Frenchmen are eating cats, caught at the hospital which provides a satisfactory answer to what became of "Baldy's" cat. The Frenchman at Rosendale came across to the extent of 3 cigarettes per man, which lasted me approx 2 hours. Peter won the cut for the cigarette to be made of the butt ends. Meanwhile I will rue a smoke made of ground up tobacco stalks, very nice smoke too, especially as Charlie got us some snuff of the S/M. The Jerry c/m who was up to say they have planned their food have planted food and have planned to the extent that he says they have enough to last out this year. Certainly hope he is wrong. Anyway I can't see them being able to plant enough food to keep 12,000 men going as they say they have so many men. George Simpson reports 534 men in Rosendael hospital. As there are other hospitals & hospital bunkers around here the number of wounded & sick must be fairly considerable.[74]

No ops were flown on the 2nd, and two sorties were attempted on 3 January. The first had to attack a secondary target (railway lines) due to unfavourable weather in the primary target area, and the second aborted and returned home for the same reason—more bombs for the sea. Another attempt was made on 4 January, but was aborted for the same reason, and a second sortie, led by FO Stansfield in FU-Q, went after the Huis Te Werve, with several bombs landing in the target area. While in the area, three V-2 contrails were seen, rising from 10,000 ft to 35,000 ft, with the Spitfires close enough to see the actual rockets.

6 January saw an abortive sortie and more bombs for the sea and a patrol by Rusty Leith in FU-Q and Norman Stewart in FU-W for a downed aircraft a 'blue Spitfire', later changed to a 'blue Mosquito' but either way, most likely a photo-reconnaissance version, the patch of oil and a parachute were located but unfortunately no pilot. The fluorescent dye used to show your location if ditched was seen beneath the parachute, indicating the pilot may have been drowned under the parachute. While the two Spitfires circled the area, they spotted three V-2 trails in the sky—all from the direction of The Hague.

In the first week of January the squadron received three new pilots, including WO William Gadd (Service No. 416946), who was an accountant in South Australia prior to enlisting in the RAAF.[75]

7 January was another wasted day—three times the squadron sent out aircraft and all had to abort—more bombs for the sea. On 8 January all the armourers and armourer fitters were posted to 6455 Servicing Echelon to work on 455 (RAAF) Squadron's Beaufighters, and over the next few days others were posted to 461 and 451 Squadrons. The best the squadron could manage up to and including 13 January was a weather recce—and surprisingly, the weather was not suitable for operations.[76]

By 13 January 1945, 460 V-2 rockets had landed in England, or fallen into the sea during flight. A statistical survey from the Air Ministry showed that most were launched between 2000 and 2200 hours and the fewest were launched between 1400 and 1600 hours, when the launch area (The Hague) was most likely to be covered or draw the attention of fighter-bombers operating against the rocket sites. Due to the speed of the rockets, the launch and detonation times were not distinguished, and it was found that the time between a warning being given and detonation was just two minutes and 20 seconds on average, but with a practical action time of 90 seconds, which was perhaps the most frightening aspect of the V-2. This was a practical equivalent to no time at all, especially considering that part of the plan to be enacted in London was to close floodgates within the tube system for those portions of the line that lay beneath the Thames. In addition, assessments of the wrecks of V-2s showed that there were no radio parts as had been previously anticipated, so the electronic countermeasures initiated earlier were reduced, though they continued with their research. With an average approach vector laying about halfway between Chelmsford and the southern bank of the Thames directly south of Chelmsford, when targeting London, this gave some idea about the origin of the rockets. Firing at V-2 rockets with anti-aircraft guns to induce a premature detonation (airburst) had been proposed, but the gunners had to know where to fire and with just a few final seconds to act, assuming they knew where the rocket was headed, just 150 rounds were expected to be fired before the rocket hit its target. When the likelihood of those fired rounds returning to the ground and injuring the population was raised, it was decided it might be a reasonable risk, considering the 30,000 rounds fired per night during the Blitz. A later scientific estimate stated that around 12,000 rounds of anti-aircraft ammunition would have to be fired 'to have a chance of destroying one rocket' and the experiment didn't take place, and the relatively low number of rockets being fired at England and their inaccurate nature would mean that it would take some time to be able to assess the effectiveness of the gunnery.[77]

On 14 January the first sortie aborted and 'bombed the sea' yet again, and the second sortie, 12 Spitfires led by Rusty Leith in FU-R, encountered 10/10th cloud over the Hook of Holland and were on the way back to base when an opportune hole in the cloud revealed a suitable target so this was bombed despite intense flak, and all returned home safely. Leith recorded in his logbook, 'Led Squadron. Good bombing—usual Hook of Holland Flak—Hot. Saw actual V2 missile in the air.'[78] Jim Lynch also saw the V-2 and wrote, '12 plane show. DB target at Hook. Saw V2 break cloud at 1500′. Great sight.'[79] Sqn Ldr Esau went to RAF Banff to advise on tactics and returned the next day.

On 15 January Rusty Leith was promoted to flight lietenant and given command of B Flight. By the end of the month, he had received a DFC for his accumulated efforts in the many months of serving with 453 Squadron.[80] The citation read:

> Flying Officer Leith is now on his second tours of operational duty and has a splendid record of sorties against enemy shipping and

> transport, in addition to completing many bomber escorts and fighter patrols. In addition to the destruction of at least three enemy aircraft, he has also destroyed large numbers of enemy transports, vehicles and trains. This officer has always displayed the greatest keenness and skill as a fighter pilot.[81]

In his thank-you speech Rusty made special mention of the ground crew, saying that the three recent DFCs (for Leith, Cowpe and McDade) 'had been the result of a lot of hard work by a lot of people and that they also had a share in it'.[82] That same day saw three attempts made to bomb and strafe Haagsche Bosch but the best they could manage in the bad weather was attacking some railway lines, but at least they were able to claim 'fair success'. The third sortie hadn't even taken bombs with them, so at least they didn't have to waste them by dropping them in the sea. The squadron did make a successful attack on the 17th, with all eight 250-lb bombs in the target area, but there were no subsequent explosions to indicate any definite results.[83]

19 January saw better weather and an attack against Rust en Vreugd; Sqn Ldr Esau in FU-? led the way, with bombs and strafing against heavy flak defences of all calibres. At 1240 two Spitfires acted as an escort to a PR Mosquito, but on the way across the sea WO Bartels left to escort another aircraft, so FO Stansfield was the sole escort for the Mosquito over enemy territory. After making two runs over the target area (south to north, and east to west) through intense but inaccurate flak, it was lost in the haze when it dived away through a break in the cloud. Unable to find it again, Stansfield returned to base. 453 Squadron also provided two more Spitfires as an escort to Mustangs attacking Haagsche Bosch. The target was covered by cloud, and while the Spitfires patrolled, the Mustangs were lost in the cloud and the Spitfires returned to base; with cloud from 3,000 ft to 20,000 ft it was unlikely they'd be found again.

There was no operational flying on 20 January and the 21st was spent practising dive-bombing, since the squadron had made very few actual attacks in the last few weeks. On 22 January, 12 Spitfires flew to B.67 and later patrolled in sections of four with a Halifax bomber between Antwerp and Nijmegen at 22,000 ft, while it sought to seeking to interfere with V-2 rocket guidance. CAM Taylor flew his usual FU-Z on one of these final sorties and wrote, 'Bloody cold—trouble with Spits.'[84]

The first sortie of 23 January took off at 1005 and, when they reached the target, it was obscured by cloud so they went after a secondary target which was successfully bombed instead. Weather improved even more in the afternoon and an armed recce attacked two trucks and claimed both as damaged, with Norm Baker recording in his logbook: 'No bombs. Shot up beautifully 2 trucks—3 tonners between Gouda + Hague—Left smoking.' It was his last operational sortie with 453 Squadron. He wouldn't have to chance the flak anymore.[85]

FS Lynch was promoted to warrant officer this day and Hec Aldred, who had been with the squadron since January 1944, was posted out to 4 Delivery Flight at RAF Clifton.[86]

The weather remained poor for the rest of the month and only one sortie was attempted, but it had to be abandoned just off the Dutch coast. January was not a successful month for the squadron due to the weather, with only 85 bombs dropped on targets, probably just as many as they dropped into the sea.[87]

February 1945 started with a weather recce—and they found layer upon layer of cloud, preventing any significant operations, but a Jim Crow was flown over Den Helder with no shipping sighted—though two V-2 trails were seen from The Hague. Despite the efforts of 453 Squadron, their fellow Spitfire pilots in 602 and 451, Typhoons and medium bombers from 2 TAF and heavy bombers from Bomber Command, the Germans were still in action. Another Halifax escort was supposed to be flown from Antwerp to Nijmegen but they only managed to contact it on the R/T.

There was no operational flying on 2 February but, on the next day, 453 and 602 Squadrons teamed up to attack the Loosduinen liquid oxygen factory—essential to V-2 operations. 453 Squadron contributed 12 Spitfires to the first attack, led by Sqn Ldr Esau in FU-C, the squadron taking off at 0955. 602 Squadron contributed 12 Spitfires also, their group being led by Sqn Ldr Sutherland. The first attack by the two squadrons saw a number of bombs land short so they went back again in the afternoon and did it all over again—once a target like this had been identified, it had to be dealt with.

Eleven Spitfires from 453 Squadron contributed to the afternoon effort, taking off at 1450, though FO Carter returned ten minutes later. 602 Squadron again put 12 Spitfires into the air for the combined effort, leaving five minutes after the Australians. They travelled to the target area and dropped a total of 39 250-lb bombs in a dive from 9,000 to 3,000 ft. The second effort was better—two bombs from 453 Squadron hit the southern building, between four and six hit the western yards and two more hit another, smaller building. Flak was intense but all Spitfires and pilots came through safely.[88] Rusty Leith rated the bombing of the first attack as 'fair' and the flak as intense light, medium and heavy'. He noted, 'Bombing better—intense flak' for the second.[89] Clearly it was a well-defended target.

The only sortie that took off on 4 February was aborted due to poor weather, but things were better on the 5th. A Jim Crow, led by Rusty Leith in FU-R, was flown from 1150 to 1355 and an armed recce, led by Sqn Ldr Esau in FU-? was flown in the afternoon. The Jim Crow section brought back half of their bombs and dropped the rest in the sea, but the armed recce was able to hit a railway line south-east of Leiden when their main target was obscured by cloud. The next armed recce of the day was aborted and another Halifax escort was flown, the Luftwaffe failing to show.[90]

The first armed recce of 6 February bombed a site near The Hague with two bombs on target and the others landing within a 200-yard radius. Two vehicles were also strafed near Utrecht before the Spitfires returned, though they spotted twin contrails on the way home—possibly caused by a twin-engine jet (Me 262). The second armed recce of the day went after the Hotel Promenade, a target that had been on the list in January but was continually covered by low cloud. Bob Clemesha led the way in FU-M. All bombs fell within 50 yards of the target and FO Emmerson's Spitfire was damaged by flak but all returned safely. Clemesha recorded in his logbook, 'Five bursts of heavy [calibre] flak over target ... All bombs overshot target by 50 yds and set a building on fire.'[91] The third armed recce of the day was led by Rusty Leith in FU-E and went after Huis Te Werve yet again, with bombing appearing to be good. This sortie also left a staff car in flames—they'd found it on the road east of Leiden.

Peters and Lynch flew a Jim Crow on 7 February, looking down on an empty Den Helder from 8,000 ft and Sqn Ldr Esau went to London to make a recording for broadcast about the operations against the V-2 sites.[92]

The liquid oxygen factory was the target again on 8 February, 12 of 453 Squadron's Spitfires joining 602 and 603 Squadrons for the attack. 603 was the follow-up squadron and took off 45 minutes after 453 and 602, which left together. At the target site, when it was the Australians' turn to bomb, cloud had moved in over the target and only four Spitfires made their attack, though ten from 602 Squadron were able to make it down through a hole in the cloud and drop their bombs, but only a few were seen to hit the target area. Seven from 453 Squadron dropped their bombs on a secondary target on the way back to the Dutch coast; the last had to jettison its bombs into the sea. Flak was heavy and bombing results were unobserved but all planes returned safely. As if to remind them that the Germans had not yet given up, two more V-2 trails were seen in the sky. Meanwhile 602 Squadron had gone to Ursel to refuel and attempted to find the target again on the return leg for strafing attacks, but there was not even a small gap in the clouds for them to exploit, so they returned to base without having fired a shot.[93]

A weather recce on the morning of 9 February reported extensive cloud and haze below it, not good for dive-bombing. Other, more favourable reports must have been received because in the afternoon 453 and 603 Squadrons teamed up to attack the liquid oxygen factory again. Each Spitfire from 453 Squadron was loaded with a 250-lb bomb under each wing and a 500-lb bomb on the centre pylon, taking the place of a drop tank, and 603 Squadron was loaded up in the same way. The squadrons flew past the target, which was clearly seen, then made their attacks going down in a gut-wrenching dive from 12,000 ft to 3,000 ft heading from east to west. Many near misses were observed on the target buildings and large explosions were noted from the tram sheds near the main building. Flak was moderate and inaccurate and all planes returned safely. At the time 602 Squadron had two Spitfires escorting PR Mustangs whose role it was to photograph the targets after they had been attacked (bomb damage assessment), and one of the Spitfires, flown by WO Ryan (an Australian), was shot down. His plane had been hit by flak and his engine stopped before he could make it back to Allied lines. He managed to crash-land his plane but was immediately captured and was a prisoner until liberated by the Americans on 29 April.[94]

This was the third time 453 Squadron had attacked the factory and it may be asked, instead of having Spitfires attack it repeatedly with relatively small bombs, could the RAF have sent over a few squadrons of Lancasters with 1,000- and 4,000-lb bombs and smothered the whole area to deal with it in one blow? In theory this could have been done, but the factory was a hostile target in a friendly country. On a number of occasions targets had not been attacked (such as when 453 Squadron refused to strafe trucks near civilians on 11 December) because the Allies did not wish to cause, or risk causing, civilian casualties to a friendly nation (in this case, the Dutch). With cloud obscuring the target on a regular basis, it was far easier to send over some Spitfires at low level than Lancasters at high level—a faster target is harder to hit, and even if the window of opportunity was small (due to cloud—which can vary in location, height and density from minute to minute), the Spitfires were better able to take advantage of a temporary gap, get under the cloud, drop their bombs more accurately (in theory at least) then get out and, if necessary, come back the next day and do it again. They could also defend themselves better than Lancasters—bombers would need escorts while Spitfires did not—if they were attacked, the Spitfires could drop their bombs and transform from dive-bomber to fighter in a matter of seconds.

Between 10 and 14 February, no operational sorties were flown—but the squadron did practise their dive-bombing and gunnery at a nearby range. A Jim Crow was flown for no result on the 15th with multiple layers of cloud preventing any useful observations. On 16 February, Norm Baker left the squadron—posted out to 12 Group as his tour had expired. His place as flight commander was taken over by Bob Clemesha.

Proving that sometimes the brass did listen, on 16 February AVM Wrigley wrote a letter about the poor circumstances in which 453 Squadron found itself. He pointed out that the move from Matlaske to Swannington was only expected to be for ten days but had stretched out to three months and each day pilots and ground crew travelled 15 miles each way between the two airfields. The facilities for 453 Squadron at Swannington were poor, and this was admitted by the CO there, but that person had stated that as 453 Squadron belonged to a different group, he was unable to do anything about improving their facilities, and obviously had not done anything for three months. AVM Wrigley went on to state that 453 Squadron had a 'reputation for being one of the most highly serviced squadrons in Fighter Command' (meaning they had a good record for having a high number of operational aircraft available at any given time) and he thought this might suffer if conditions did not improve. In closing, he pointed out that it had been agreed that 451 and 453 Squadrons should serve in the same wing and therefore be based together at a suitable location.[95] This wing would finally form in March 1945, but it had been a long time coming.

The next operational sorties for 453 Squadron took place on 20 February, but all they could manage were two uneventful Jim Crows—the weather foiled any other plans. Six armed recces were flown on the 21st against the site at Haagsche Bosch. On the second attack WO Carmichael's Spitfire was hit and seen to be streaming white smoke (glycol) after attacking a truck. He bailed out and his Spitfire crashed into the ground near a farm—Vondel's Landleeuw—by the village of Abbenes, the crater quickly filling up with water in the low-lying ground typical of the Netherlands. Carmichael landed near Lisserweg (a road) not far from the crash site and he was surrounded by farm workers and taken away on a pushbike by a Dutch girl. He was hidden by the local resistance and given civilian clothes to replace his uniform, which was burnt, a safer option than hiding it. To reduce chances of his discovery Carmichael pretended to be a mute as Norm Baker had (usually convincingly) in Normandy, so verbal communication was not expected by those not taking care of him.[96]

The fourth attack on the site was the most visually satisfying and a large explosion was seen in the target area. Since he was unable to drop his bombs in the initial attack, WO Gadd bombed a railway line, and his bombs wrecked the line. Shortly afterwards he reported that he had no oil pressure and though his flight lost sight of him, he had an escort and was heard to say he was going to crash land and shortly afterwards reported that he was okay. Two staff cars were strafed near Leiden on this fourth armed recce with one claimed as damaged and the other in flames—destroyed. For a change, the weather was described as 'perfect'.

But on the ground, Gadd had landed safely about 14 miles south-south-east of Carmichael, near Reeuwijk. One of the first Dutchmen he came across wanted to turn him over to the Germans and said as much in English, but the other members of the community prevailed and came to his aid but had nowhere to hide him. He was handed over to the Resistance who took him to the town of Leimuiden, just three miles from where Carmichael had landed. Clearly this area was well organised when it came to helping out Allied airmen. He stayed there for two weeks with one family, then was moved and stayed with another family for eight weeks. There was not a lot of choice when it came to concealing Gadd, but when the building next to where he was staying was taken over by German troops, he was forced to leave, and stayed with yet another family. Allied authorities were notified of the location of both Gadd and Carmichael in the same communication. Discussions between people in the resistance group soon led to the conclusion that the Australians might know each other, and soon they were in touch, but did not stay together. They kept each other's spirits up and maintained their visits and communication until their liberation, when Carmichael rode through the town on the front of a fire engine.[97]

22 February was the busiest day for the squadron in months: 40 sorties were flown. Six attacks were made on Haagsche Bosch. The first flight of four was recalled due to bad weather but the second flight was boosted to 12 Spitfires and they were led by Sqn Ldr Esau in FU-? for an attack on some old film studios north-west of Haagsche Bosch. Bombing was very good with nine pairs of bombs on target and the rest landing nearby. One large explosion was noted and several hits were spotted on the buildings. Rusty Leith flew FU-R on this sortie and recorded: 'Wizard squadron show. Film studio building got many direct hits. Big explosion—building razed to ground—smoke stretched Hague to Leiden.'[98] Bob Clemesha led his section in FU-C and recorded: 'Very good bombing by squadron—one building seen to blow up—Sqn show—2 x 250lb. Complete destruction of the dump given by GRP to the Squadron.'[99]

Heavy calibre anti-aircraft fire from the Hook targeted the Spitfires but all returned safely. Subsequent attacks by other sorties later in the day noted 'huge columns of smoke' coming from the buildings. A midget sub was spotted at 1405 and upon close inspection at almost sea level was observed to have a glass dome and small periscope. The same or another was spotted at 1500 but no action was able to be taken.

No sorties were flown on 25 February, and a section of four Spitfires from 453 Squadron was sent back to Haagsche Bosch on the 26th but it was covered by cloud so they bombed a railway line instead, noting four hits. The squadron returned to Haagsche Bosch and the squadron diary recorded that 'every inch … is being systematically raked with bombs'.[100] The day's efforts were regarded as a success. An American bomber was spotted on the ground about 4½ miles sout-east of Leiden and was later identified as a Liberator; two crew were seen standing next to it. The Liberator was strafed by the fourth and fifth sorties of the day to deny it to the Germans, and it started to burn, just what they wanted.

One pilot, WO Carter, was posted out to 83 GSU on 26 February, and he would later fly with 130 Squadron, then, in 1947, 82 Squadron RAAF on occupation duties in Japan.[101] Another was posted in—FO Francis Noel McLoughlin, who had completed a nine-month tour as a wireless operator/air gunner with 53 Squadron and was now a pilot.[102]

The next day, three sections of four Spitfires went after Haagsche Bosch, but the cloud returned and thwarted their efforts. The first sortie had to return and the second and third went after railway lines near Leiden and Utrecht instead. Two trucks were also strafed. The 28th was very similar—more flights to saturate Haagsche Bosch, but cloud over the target caused the Spitfires to divert to railway targets, including a bridge, instead. Strafing accounted for one vehicle probably destroyed and two lorries and a trailer damaged. Brian Inglis flew twice on the 28th, and encountered flak around Leiden on the second trip. Most of what the pilots had to deal with on this occasion was 40-mm guns, rather than the 88-mm guns that were more feared. The difference between the two guns was evident to the pilots, an '88' left 'a big black cloud'[103] that could rip the wing off a bomber; not much of a Spitfire would be left if that deadly cloud made contact. Rusty Leith was hit by some of the smaller flak in FU-R but returned safely.[104] Monthly totals were much improved from January—411 bombs dropped, approximately 46 tons.[105]

For the Spitfire squadrons, March started with a return to Haagsche Bosch, but due to the weather only one of the two armed recces sent over were able to drop their bombs. The first armed recce had to climb above 14,000 ft of cloud before they broke into the clear and returned home. Jim Lynch flew his usual FU-M on this occasion and recorded a comment in his logbook, 'Climbed through 14,000′ cloud. Clem leading. Didn't see Holland.'[106] The second was led by FO Cummins in FU-? and crossed the Dutch coast at 11,000 ft before diving down to 4,000 ft and dropping their bombs, though some hung up and had to be brought back.

On 2 March, Rust en Vreugd was the target. Twelve Spitfires went over, led by the newly promoted Flt Lt Bob Clemesha in FU-C, but due to the cloud they split up into fours to make their attacks. The Spitfires went down below cloud, coming out into the open at about 6,500 ft then diving down to 3,000 ft and dropping their three bombs—one 500 lb from the centreline and two 250-lb bombs—one from each wing. On landing at B.67 to refuel, FO Marsh in FU-S burst a tyre on the airfield matting and had to taxi on to the grass so those coming in behind could land but, in doing so, he nosed over in the soft ground and damaged the propeller.

The squadron returned to Haagsche Bosch on 3 March, each Spitfire carrying 1,000 lb of bombs. The 500-lb bomb meant they could not carry a drop tank as well, so after their attacks they landed at B.67, refuelled and returned to Swannington. After those Spitfires returned, four more were sent over but cloud obscured the target so they brought their bombs back (for a change) and four others took off, led by FO Grady in FU-R. They also found cloud over the target, so they went after a section of the Leiden–Utrecht railway instead, causing some damage and strafing a truck afterwards. A final section of four, led by Rusty Leith in FU-? was sent over to Rust en Vreugd but bad weather meant they targeted the railway junction at Alphen instead, and the pilots reported fair results.

FO William Ernest Tonkin arrived at the squadron on 3 March from 61 OTU, and there was no time wasted getting him into the action. Tonkin had one day of practise dive-bombing and the next day was his first operational sortie with 453 Squadron.[107]

Two four-plane attacks were made on 4 March, the first through intense flak against Rust en Vreugd and the second with 1,000 lb of bombs per plane against Ockenburgh, right on the coast and south-west of The Hague. There was a lot of cloud, but a convenient gap showed itself and the Spitfires dived through it, climbing back up into the cloud as fast as they could, and not seeing the results of their efforts. One Spitfire, FS McAuliffe in FU-J, nosed over on landing, but the others rearmed with two 250-lb bombs and headed back to Ockenburgh, but they couldn't bomb due to poor weather, so returned to England. There were no operational sorties between 5 and 7 March, and only a few midget submarine patrols were flown on the 8th, and none was spotted.[108]

A new target was allocated to 453 Squadron on 9 March—a V-2 storage depot at Wassenaar Ravelijn. Four Spitfires were led across to the Netherlands by Rusty Leith in FU-C, and this time they were successful, as two bombs struck home. A section of six Spitfires, with 1,000 lb of bombs each, took off at 1115 and dive-bombed Rust en Vreugd with success, rolling into their attacks from 10,000 ft to 3,500 ft then roaring back up into the clouds and heading for B.67. They refuelled and rearmed with a full 1,000-lb load before attacking the target again on the way home. The next section of six made the same initial attack but on their second attempt found their target covered by cloud, so dropped their 500-lb bombs in the sea and brought the smaller ones home. Four Spitfires took off as the last effort of the day but there was too much cloud over the target and they returned to base.

10 March was just as busy but not as successful due to the weather. This time they went after V-2 launch sites at Hague Duindigt and Wassenaar Ravelijn, but cloud meant that all seven of the four-plane sections had to attack railway lines in the Gouda and Utrecht areas instead. One midget sub was sighted off the coast and strafed by the third armed recce, which was led by Dick Peters in FU-A. The Spitfires roared down to sea level, firing as they went, but it submerged successfully so damage could not be assessed; the pilots could only hope it kept going to the bottom of the Channel and stayed there. Two staff cars were strafed by other sections during the day, one claimed as damaged and the other as destroyed.

11 March was a flying training day—with air-to-air firing and cine-gun practice. The squadron returned to Hague Duindigt and Wassenaar Ravelijn on the 12th, but the first attack had to be aborted due to the weather. The second and third sections made their attacks against Hague Duindigt when conditions improved, and they claimed a truck as probably destroyed, also by strafing.

The first section airborne on 13 March was led by Sqn Ldr Esau in FU-? and attacked the Hague racecourse twice—once on the way over and again after refuelling and rearming at B.67. A medium-sized fire was noted in the target area and gave the pilots some evidence of success. Three more attacks were made that day against the same target and all were reported as successful. Rusty Leith flew three of these attacks and recorded comments in his logbook for all three. First, 'With 1000 lb bombs each, wizard squadron bombing' then 'Very good bombing again—fires started' and finally 'Days standard maintained'.[109] CAM Taylor was also pleased and recorded 'Best bombing this year' in his logbook.[110]

Six four-plane sections took off on the 14th, and five of these were sent to the racecourse again. The Spitfires dived down through the intense, small-calibre flak and put many of their bombs in the target area, hitting one of the target buildings, and resulting in 'good dense smoke'.[111] Matlaske was finally fit for operations again so the squadron returned there at the end of the day's operations.

On 14 March, a complaint was raised with the British by the Dutch government, based on evidence from a KLM employee who had escaped the Dutch-occupied zone and contacted his government-in-exile. The complaint covered the period mid-February to 5 March, which was the day the person escaped. The report confirmed the Germans were storing rockets in Haagsche Bosch (Hague Wood), and that a railway line ran from the Queen's Palace in the woods to Haagsche Bosch. The person estimated that 40–50 per cent of all rocket firings were failures and that Typhoon attacks in the region of The Hague and Wassenaar were inaccurate and only caused a 'slight delay' in operations. The inaccuracy of these attacks meant that numerous houses were hit, causing a number of civilian casualties. A subsequent attack by bombers on 3 March took place from high altitude, but low-level winds blew many bombs off course and the suburb of Bezuidenhout was badly damaged and an estimated 100,000 people had to be evacuated. It was estimated that 800 civilians were killed and the number of wounded was 'considerable'. The report also stated that 'The temper of the civilian population has become violently anti-Ally as a result of this bombardment'. A response from Churchill to this complaint, directed to the Secretary of State for Air was not as defensive as might be expected, but pointed out that it 'shows how feeble have been our efforts to interfere with the rockets, and secondly, the extraordinarily bad aiming which has led to this slaughter of Dutchmen'. He pointed out the ability to conduct pinpoint attacks on Gestapo houses and thought a similar level of precision would be able to be applied to Crossbow operations.[112]

Try as they might, the operations of 451, 453, 602 and the other squadrons on operations against the V-2s didn't often lead to any great success, and as can be seen, secondary targets were often attacked due to poor weather over the target areas. The pilots did their best with what they had, but only the ground campaign could make a lasting difference. It is the role of the land forces to seek out the enemy, take ground from them and hold it against attempts to seize it back. Aircraft can assist in this process, but aircraft can't take and hold ground, and denial of launching sites is what really mattered.

Two sections of four went after railway targets on the morning of 18 March, resulting in some tracks being broken up. A full 'squadron show' of 12 Spitfires attacked Hague Duindigt in the company of 602 Squadron in the early afternoon, with results being described as good. While 602 Squadron went after the Shell building, hitting it with a number of bombs from an attack made at lower-than-roof height, 453 Squadron (in the company of 124 Squadron) made a diversionary attack on a nearby rocket site, attracting lots of flak.[113] The 12 Spitfires of 453 Squadron landed at B.67 and attacked again later in the afternoon and it was on this that FO Tonkin in FU-P, flying as Red 2, was hit by flak. He recalled the sequence of events quite well afterwards:

> The outward trip was quite uneventful—we achieved several direct hits on a storage site which blew up very prettily but nobody was hit by the quite intense flak ... the boss decided that this time we would smash a rail junction on the outskirts of a town called Gouda, some 15–20 miles north east of Rotterdam and told us that there was no flak in the vicinity ... on the contrary we ran into the heaviest and most concentrated barrage we had ever seen but I was the only poor blighter who collected anything.[114]

Fortunately, the momentum Tonkin had built up in the dive to drop his bombs enabled him to get back up to 7,000–8,000 ft at which time his engine packed it in. He notified the other pilots of his intention to bail out but was advised to try and get the plane back to friendly territory if possible. Thinking about it, he knew that bailing out would definitely make him a prisoner, but if he got closer to Allied lines then he'd at least be in with a chance if he landed safely and could make a fair getaway. Picking a strip of land between two canals as a relatively safe spot to crash, Tonkin was all lined up when strong winds blew him sideways into the bank of a canal: one wing dug in, the plane flipped and twisted at the same time, facing back the way he came and upside down, with the wings torn off and the cockpit under water.[115] Above, his escort Red 3, Dick Adams in FU-J, stayed in the area for a while, looking for any signs of Tonkin surfacing, but there were none and the squadron wrote him off as unlikely to have survived the crash.[116] They'd lost another pilot, so soon after arrival. Some had luck and others didn't. Or so they thought. Upside-down in his harness, Tonkin was about to drown. The canopy was partly open and water came rushing in. The wings had ripped off and there was nothing to hold the aircraft up. Holding his breath and struggling in his cramped, cold, dark, wet, upside-down cockpit, he fought against his restraints and eventually freed himself. He was exceptionally lucky not to have been stunned or knocked out by the landing or else he would have met the same fate as Henry Smith in the Caen Canal back in June 1944 when he'd become 453 Squadron's first casualty in Normandy. Soaked but alive, Tonkin climbed the canal bank and ran for about a mile before finding a young Dutchman who asked, in quite good English, if he needed any assistance. Tonkin wasn't sure if he could be trusted, but went along with him and soon they were taking cover from a German search party, which passed as close as 100 yards from where they were hiding. Once it was safe, they moved off and he was hidden for two days, then moved away into the care of some farmers. The journey he took with them crossed many canals, some of which they had to pole-vault. There was little talk between them as the new group spoke almost no English and Tonkin didn't have a word of Dutch. Once safely at the farm, Tonkin was shown the cellar concealed under the cowshed, and saw it was full of arms, including Bren guns and Stens. The Dutch were waiting for the right time to bring out the arms and support the advancing Allied armies. Rather than be escorted across the front line, Tonkin was moved around a few times; the last pilot to be assisted across the front line had made it, but the group responsible was discovered and executed. With the war so close to the end in Europe, it wasn't worth the risk, and if Tonkin was safe, he'd just have to wait it out.

This he did, hiding in an attic for six and a half weeks. He only left his hiding place twice, both at midnight, one occasion meeting with the local Resistance and seeing their printing press for their unauthorised newsletters. During this time breakfast consisted of four small slices of black bread, lunch was some boiled potatoes and dinner was five more slices of black bread. For a time they had two hours of electricity between 1600 and 1800 and used this to listen to the illegal radio, with an ear to the speaker and the volume down so low it could not even be heard on the far side of the room. Eventually there was no electricity at all and the radio was run sparingly on accumulators mainly taken from crashed aircraft.

Despite earlier plans to keep him hidden, there were numerous plans to get Tonkin out, but none developed beyond the planning stage. From what he learned with his gradual accumulation of Dutch language skills, there were about 15 airmen hidden within 15 miles of his location. When VE Day came, Tonkin and the family he was with stayed put, gave thanks for the end of the war and shared a bottle of cognac. Soon after, he heard the Canadians were in Gouda, so he recovered his uniform from its hiding place and rode the five miles there only to find the Canadian Army consisted entirely of an army doctor looking for a building suitable for a hospital. The two of them were swamped by the population:

> If we had been Eisenhower, Montgomery or Churchill we could not have been cheered or made more of, to them we were the symbol of all the allied nations … Perhaps the most touching thing was that just to be able to touch us made them supremely happy.[117]

When the Canadian Army arrived that evening, Tonkin was advised to go to Brussels where he could be evacuated to England. He rode a truck there, past thousands of German troops, across broken bridges, through fields and around damaged roadways until they reached Arnhem, at which time they took the highway, noting the damage and destruction to the city. At the end of a 12-hour drive they made it to Brussels, and Tonkin bade farewell to his Canadians. In Brussels he was issued a new uniform and met up with several Australians who'd been prisoners since their capture in Greece, Crete or Tobruk. On 10 May, Tonkin was flown back to England in a Lancaster and sent to Brighton, where he was medically assessed as suffering from malnutrition and put on a month's leave and given an allowance for double rations. While in Brighton, he met Norm Marsh and they returned to 453 Squadron together.[118]

Railways were the nominated targets for 19 March, but the first section was redirected to search for a raft 20 miles north-east of Yarmouth, which they found and circled until the three men onboard were rescued. PO Bartels returned early in FU-W with engine trouble but the others remained. Since they didn't have enough fuel to continue, they returned to Matlaske with their bombs. Three other sections, including one led by the Wing Cdr Don Andrews in his personal DGA-marked Spitfire attacked railway lines in the Leiden, Gouda and Utrecht areas but the last two sections aborted due to bad weather.

20 May was even busier, with eight rail interdiction sorties planned. The first saw a V-2 launch from the area of the Hotel Promenade, the first spotted for some time. The second armed recce was led by Wing Cdr Andrews in DGA and the bombs would have been accurate were it not for a strong wind in the area. FO Marsh in FU-S complained of low oil pressure after his attack, and

headed out to sea. He knew he could not make it all the way back to England so at 4–5,000 ft he bailed out when six or seven miles off the coast. Without smoke or flames or the Luftwaffe to threaten him, it was a fairly easy procedure which he described as disconnecting (his helmet from oxygen and the R/T), standing on the wing and jumping off. He landed in the sea and was seen to get into his dinghy and wave to his squadron mates circling above, but they didn't know the trouble he'd had just to manage that. In full flying gear he had trouble getting into the dinghy, so had to calm himself and go back to procedure, just as Alec Arnel did when he bailed out over Italy. Marsh had attended an Air Search and Rescue course at Blackpool during his training in the UK, and thought back to the methods taught which, when applied, worked perfectly, and he was safely aboard. His mates circled until they were low on fuel and had to land at B.67. There they refuelled and checked on him on the way home. Though no flak was seen, it was assumed that this was what brought him down. Later sections also saw his dinghy and ASR aircraft were directed to his location.[119] Marsh had been flying No. 2 to Don Andrews, so the wing commander had lost two No. 2s in his first month back on operations.[120] Not that it was his fault, but when you were flying with a wing commander as bold as Don Andrews, you were bound to attract more than your fair share of flak and attention.

By the next morning FO Marsh had still not been rescued, so 453 Squadron sent out several patrols to locate him and he was spotted by the first Spitfires which had taken off at 0615, the earliest they could manage. Another dinghy was spotted during their search and since it was obviously unoccupied one Spitfire was detailed to sink it lest it become an ongoing distraction, but somehow it resisted and remained afloat. Marsh was now just two miles south-west of Zandvoort and his mates kept watch over him. The third ASR patrol from 453 Squadron stayed with him until relieved by 451 Squadron. These two Spitfires then flew south to meet a Catalina flying boat and escorted it to the area, but the sea was too rough for it to land.

The last attack of the 20th was a combined effort with 451 Squadron, both contributing six Spitfires for an attack on a V-1 site at The Hague/Vrenburg. The Spitfires crossed the Dutch coast north of The Hague then made a turn to starboard and dived on a line north-west to south-east from 9,000 ft to 3–4,000 ft, with the six from 451 Squadron leading the way. Men were seen to run from the site as the Spitfires rolled and dived down to bomb the target area. Bombing results were described as 'very successful', with a large cloud of black smoke following a large explosion, and further explosions following strafing runs which took the Spitfires down as low as 50 ft.[121]

On 21 March, two overlapping sorties of four Spitfires each provided protective cover for an air search-and-rescue Catalina. The first took off at 0930 and found two dinghies near the Dutch coast and orbited the location waiting for the Catalina to arrive. It landed by a dinghy which was found to be empty, (perhaps the one that was seen by 453 Squadron which they failed to sink by strafing) but the Catalina had to take off immediately as the Germans began shelling it. Two of the Spitfires peeled off and began strafing the German positions, just as the second section of four Spitfires arrived, joining the attack with bombs and silencing the guns. The Catalina returned and was about to land on the sea again when another position opened fire and the Catalina was damaged and had to leave, and the two sections of Spitfires were recalled. The Spitfires complied, but not before attacking another German position, and one just 300 yards away from that with camouflage netting over it. These were both silenced, the first being described as 'wiped off', and then the batteries that had fired on the Catalina on the second occasion were attacked. Though they were seen, the camouflage was enough to prevent the pilots hitting them precisley and they could not be silenced. Not satisfied with this, they then found a midget submarine, thought to be a Biber-class vessel, and they dived down on it, as low as 300 ft, to strafe it numerous times and it 'disappeared in foam in a minute'.[122] The Spitfires circled for a few minutes to see if it would resurface, but it did not, and they all returned to base.[123]

The last ASR patrol took off at 1655 and flew up the Dutch coast looking for Marsh and his dingy but witnessed him being taken on board by a German Red Cross boat—perhaps attracted by the constant circling of Spitfires. He saw the Spitfires and waved to them, but there was nothing more to be done. He went through the usual prisoner of war facilities and ended up at Stalag Luft I, Barth, alongside others from 451 and 453 Squadrons.[124]

Two rail interdiction attacks were made on the 22nd on the Haarlem, Leiden and Gouda areas. Wing Cdr Andrews led the second attack of the day—a full 12-plane effort against the Kurhaus garage, which was suspected of housing trucks used for the V-1 and V-2 sites. A number of bombs were direct hits and some overshot onto a railway line but some hit houses, though if these caused any casualties is not known. The Spitfires rearmed and refuelled at B.67 before attacking the same site again and returning to Matlaske. The Spitfires encountered flak of all calibres but returned safely. WO Lynch was informed of his commission on this day, backdated to 22 February.[125]

Despite the high workload, the 23 March was a training day, and operations resumed on the 24th, with five attacks launched on railway lines around Leiden, Alphen, Gouda and Utrecht, followed by attacks against the railway lines in Amsterdam, Hilversum, Woerden and Utrecht the next day. Hits on the various lines were observed on both days. If the rockets could not make it from the storage sites to the launch sites then that was almost as good as getting the sites themselves. Jim Lynch flew twice on the 25th and made the following entry in his logbook after the second sortie, 'Had crack at bridge. Just missed and got a house.'[126]

Rain grounded everyone on the 26th and into the morning of the 27th, but an armed recce reported just 5/10ths cloud over the usual target areas, and compared to many days, that was good, so the ground crew loaded the Spitfires with bombs and away they went. Four armed recces were sent over to the Utrecht and Woerden areas where they bombed the railway lines successfully, and strafed several vehicles, claiming one destroyed and two damaged.

Weather was poor again on 28 and 29 March, but local flying training was carried out.

The first armed recce of 30 March was very successful for 453 Squadron: Rusty Leith in FU-P led his section dive-bombing a railway bridge, then discovered a possible V-2 convoy consisting of a few truck and trailer combinations travelling together along the Haarlem–Leiden road. The claims were two trucks probably destroyed and one truck and two trailers damaged. Rusty recorded his success: 'My bombs right under bridge. Attacked and damaged V-2 trucks and trailer N.W. Leiden.'[127]

They didn't want the target to get away so, to finish it off, two more Spitfires were scrambled but could not find the target, though they did find a staff car, and this was successfully strafed. Four other attacks were made on railway targets that afternoon, all with 1,000 lb of bombs, the planes refuelling and rearming at B.67 before attacking the same targets again on the way back to England.[128]

30 March saw Don Andrews lead a section from 453 Squadron to the Netherlands, and they attacked a railway junction north of Leiden on the first leg, each dropping one 500-lb and two 250-lb bombs into the intersection, against strong winds which blew them off target. They returned to the same location on the way back, with just the two 250-lb bombs this time but, as Don Andrews recorded, 'Wind blew bombs off target. Cleaned up a farmhouse.'[129]

An ASR scramble was also launched to assist in locating a pilot downed in the North Sea and the 453 Squadron pilots found him, face up and still attached to his parachute, but not showing any signs of life. When the launch arrived to pick him up, they confirmed he was dead. Whoever he was he'd nearly made it: the war had just a few weeks to go.

On the last day of March, the squadron made six attacks on railway targets and some hits that severed the lines were recorded. Some vehicles were sighted and attacked, including an armoured car which was claimed as probably destroyed, plus three staff cars and two trucks as probables. The last armed recce of the day was led by FO Grady in FU-K and they sighted a possible V-1 ramp pointing towards England in the Amsterdam–Schiphol area so made a dummy gun run on it, using just the cine-camera for later viewing and assessment.[130]

453 Squadron flew 659 operational hours in March 1945, and dropped 858 bombs on targets, weighing about 116 tons.[131]

OPERATIONS, OCCUPATION AND HOME: APRIL 1945 TO JANUARY 1946

APRIL 1945 saw a significant drop in the number of operations flown, mostly due to the progress made by the Allied armies into Germany and the Netherlands, which contributed to the issuing of an Air Ministry notice which stated that, in view of the lull in rocket attacks, Fighter Command could use the 'six anti-rocket squadrons' for bomber escorts if they wished.[1]

The first operational sortie for 451 Squadron was flown on 3 April: an armed recce to the Netherlands once again, but cloud obscured the primary target so they went after a railway line instead, claiming near misses and hits. A second sortie also went after a railway line and they also claimed a truck which was left smoking.

453 Squadron flew three armed recces on the same day and also went after the railway lines, but the third was recalled due to poor weather. The first of the 453 Squadron armed recces was led by Sqn Ldr Esau in FU-?. Their bombs cut the railway line and then they went looking for vehicular targets. They strafed one truck and claimed it damaged then found another apparently heavily loaded and going at a high sped towards IJmuiden. The truck was strafed and hit a few times, but it wasn't until Esau fired his cannon and machine guns into it that it exploded in a bright red flash.

On 4 April both squadrons received notification that they were to move from Matlaske in Norwich, down to Lympne in Kent. This was definitely a move away from the operational zone, but there were rumours that the squadrons would move to mainland Europe and, from there, escort bombers into the remaining parts of Germany that were holding out. While the lucky ones took a short flight in their Spitfires, the rest went by rail and air on 6 April.

The only sortie on 9 April was a two-plane weather recce to the Netherlands, returning via Belgium and France.[2] The rest of the two squadrons left Lympne early in the evening for B.90 at Kleine Brogel in Belgium, ready for an escort on the 11th.

In early April, the wing received a letter of thanks from Air Marshal Sir Roderic Hill of Fighter Command HQ for the efforts made by the six squadrons tasked with taking on the V-2s daily. It was passed on to Wing Cdr Don Andrews to be read to all staff. It read, in part:

> With the intermission of V-2 attacks on this country and before the re-deployment of the six Spitfire Squadrons from Coltishall, I should like to take the opportunity of congratulating all ranks of these Squadrons on the outstandingly good work which they put in while attacks were in progress. The Fighter/Bomber attacks carried out in the Hague Area undoubtedly did much to prevent the enemy stepping up the weight of his attack, and thereby achieved a lightening of the burden which the Londoner was called up to bear ... I fully realise that the targets which the Squadrons were called upon to attack day after day, were heavily defended by flak, and I am most pleased in the manner in which attacks between aggressiveness and caution was very nicely struck. This implies both professional skill and good discipline. I consider that the accuracy attainted in bombing was a great feather in the cap of the aircrews, and that the high number of sorties was an achievement on the part of the ground crews ... [3]

The squadrons had a right to be proud, and though the weather had hindered them time and again, and the targets were very hard to find, they did what they could with what they had, risking their lives over and over again.

On 11 April, 451 and 453 Squadrons combined to provide an escort for Halifaxes and Lancasters bombing Bayreuth in Germany. The 451 Squadron contribution was led by Sqn Ldr Robertson in TB592 and Wing Cdr Andrews led 453 Squadron in his personalised DGA. Though the weather was very good, 451 Squadron noted that the bombers arrived five minutes late and their formations were very poor, making them hard to escort in an orderly manner. Bombing results were not seen and the squadrons landed at 1620, having been airborne for two hours and 40 minutes, a genuine stretch for the Spitfire. Fortunately, the Me 262s that were sighted didn't get involved and left the formations alone.[4] Bob Clemesha flew his usual FU-C on this escort and recorded, 'No flak. No nothing. Nurnberg appeared to be burning well as were most of the towns in Germany.'[5]

The next escort took place on 13 April, again from B.90 and the Spitfires were led by Wing Cdr Andrews in FU-?, the markings he had introduced into the squadron back in January 1943.[6] The Australians were on time at the right location, but the bombers were not, so the Spitfires flew to the escort point as if the bombers were with them, then returned to B.90, without sighting the bombers at all.[7]

New Australian pilots continued to arrive at 453 Squadron—six in the first two weeks of April.[8] The war in Europe was coming to a close and Rusty Leith recorded some of his thoughts in one of his many letters home:

> Well I have been really very busy this week and it might surprise you to know that I have been to within sight of the Czechoslovakian border. Since I have been there escorting the heavies the place has been reported captured by the Yanks—really it is almost unbelievable. I have slept on the continent on a number of nights. Really some of the Hun towns are in a mess. I skirted the Ruhr and most of the places are rubble with a few gaunt buildings. Darmstadt is also nicely smashed too. The old Hun is really getting his share this time Dad, and it is no more than he deserves. We have no hesitation in smashing a place however small and that is the correct attitude. Perhaps they will be able to occupy their minds building cities and homes after this instead of a war machine.[9]

More than a week later he wrote:

> In due course you will be seeing pictures which have been published daily this last 10 days or so of some of the atrocities committed by

> the Huns in their concentration camps. Really there are some pretty ghastly sights but it is a good thing to print them and make people realise what the Hun is like. We are much too soft-hearted about the Huns and treat them too well. I don't see why we don't put all of them in cages and let them starve to death. As long as there is one S.S. or Nazi fanatic left he is a menace. I feel very strongly on this and would have no compunction about killing any of them—it's only saving our people's lives. After all if a person commits a murder he is generally executed so why not execute one for one to make up. This rough treatment has not been confined to the foreign slaves but our POWs are known to have had a bad time.[10]

On 16 April, the two squadrons flew to B.86 at Helmond in preparation for another escort. As ever, fuel was an issue and Ross Sheppard nearly didn't make it, recording, 'To B86 nr Eindhoven. Landed last light. Main tanks empty! F. !!'[11]

An RAAF press release on 17 April gave a wonderful statistical summary of the efforts made by 451 and 453 Squadrons against the V-2 operations, quoting a total of 1,328 sorties flown and 2,309 bombs dropped, of which 453 Squadron flew 1,013 sorties and dropped 1,582 bombs. It also made mention of the valuable work of the ground crew, who were so often left out of the limelight, stating, 'The large number of sorties put a big strain on the ground staff, who frequently had to work through the night to get the aircraft ready for dawn the next day.'[12] Poor weather on the 17th delayed operations by a day but on the following day, Sqn Ldr Robertson in SM516 led both squadrons into the air and this time the rendezvous with the bombers was made. The target for the day was the U-boat base on Heligoland, and there were numerous squadrons of Spitfires and Mustangs escorting almost 1,000 Lancasters and Mosquitos.[13] The bombing was noted to be good and four large fires were seen in the target area. Flak was bursting up at 18,000 ft and continued until well after the bombers had turned for home.[14] Joe Barrington flew NI-B on that escort and recorded in his logbook, 'Escorted nearly a thousand Lancasters bombing Heligoland. Gave it a terrific pounding!!'[15] While the flak was aimed primarily at the bombers, some stray rounds—perhaps not set to explode at the correct altitude—made it through to the fighters. One such round exploded underneath Sid Handsaker's Spitfire (NI-K TB744). It was certainly a moment to remember:

> We were posted at 25,000 feet. Looking from 25,000 it [the island] looks as big as your thumbnail … the bombs that missed the island opened up in the water, came up slowly, slowly, like a flower … the Germans they must have had a lot of guts. They had a thousand bombers coming in … between 15 and 10 thousand feet and we were at 25. There was no one up with us, so we thought. One of them [the anti-aircraft gunners] must have put a wrong setting on and hit right underneath me … Just as I should have been changing over [drop tanks], someone said, "There's jets above us." That was those 262's but I didn't see them, never got a chance to have a look … They never came near us and of course, boom there was I going on like that, upside down, 25,000 feet … Everything just stopped … You had to determine first of all what the problem was. So I rolled him straight over onto his back … In the meantime I'm there on my own, they're all gone! I thought 'shit'. I thought straight away, it could be fuel, right down in the corner so you had to get down and change selector valves. Then you got up in your cockpit and set your controls. You set the throttle at a certain thing, your revs, your pitch then when you get everything shipshape just roll it on its back and straight down you go. And when she came up I was so relieved. And when I looked up it [an aircraft coming towards him] looked like a bloody 109, I'd never seen one in the air … But it was one of our own and he gave me a little wings wiggle … In the Spit you had the supercharger came in at 10,000 feet. Well I was well over that, so I just pushed straight through over the gate and I got up alongside and they were like, 'look out!'. There was two squadrons of us. 451 and 453, so I just joined up with one of the closest ones. It was funny, nobody thought anything about it, nobody ever even worried about it. I could have been a dead duck.[16]

Fittingly, the squadron's last operational sortie of the war was on 25 April—Anzac Day. Sqn Ldr Robertson led 451 Squadron one final time, with Rusty Leith in FU-P leading 453 Squadron on an escort to three waves of bombers attacking the seaplane base at Wangerooge Island, about 40 km west of Cuxhaven, and all Spitfires returned safely. One bomber was seen to crash on the island and the Australians watched as another turned for home with at least one damaged engine. There was moderate and heavy flak in a barrage form (i.e. firing into a set area where the planes are expected to fly rather than at specific aircraft) but it caused no trouble for the Spitfires.[17] CAM Taylor flew FU-Z on this escort and recorded two hours and 25 minutes' flying time in his logbook along with the comment, 'Nice to watch big bombs go off.'[18]

Later, 453 Squadron had an ASR scramble for a heavily damaged Mosquito to be escorted across the Channel. It had been hit by flak near Dunkirk and PO Mace in FU-A and PO Johns in FU-D found it struggling along at just 1,000 ft and escorted it back to England where it landed at Manston.[19]

While at Lympne, the squadrons received their next movement order to go to Hawkinge on the 30th, which was later postponed until 2 May.

On 1 May, a memo was issued titled 'Review of "Crossbow" Countermeasures'. It contained just two paragraphs, the second of which read:

> Although it cannot be stated categorically that the risk of further attack by rockets is past [sic] the chance is so remote and the war situation has changed so considerably since the Joint Intelligence Sub-Committee's Appreciation was written, that it is considered that all the "CROSSBOW" countermeasures may now be dispensed with.[20]

The squadrons had stopped their dive-bombing operations shortly before, but it was now official: there'd be no more. Other pilots continued to be posted in and out of 451 Squadron—arriving from Personnel Dispatch Centres or leaving when tour-expired. On 3 May, the two squadrons escorted a Dakota containing Queen Wilhelmina of the Netherlands from England to B.77 Gilze/Rijen. On 7 May, they moved back to Hawkinge.[21]

The end of the war in Europe occurred on 8 May, but didn't even rate a mention in the squadron records. Two days later, another 20 staff were selected for repatriation and their long journey home to Australia commenced. All those selected had been away from Australia since April 1941.[22] What would they find when they arrived home?

Rusty Leith wrote a series of letters home about his London experiences in the celebrations following the announcement of the end of war in Europe:

> I was in London for the Victory (in Europe as they say) Day and celebrations. This victory announcement however, was nothing like

last time as everyone was expecting it for days and the thing came as a bit of an anti-climax at the finish. For all that people enjoyed themselves I think. But to enjoy their success entailed milling around in circles and terrific crowds or walking backwards and forwards from each centre of celebration. A few of the millions were lucky enough to see the Royal Family and the PM but there was no other entertainment. There was a great shortage of beer and spirits hardly went anywhere. After the first day I imagine every place was pretty well dry...
I wandered down the Strand, which ceased to convey traffic, to Trafalgar Square where a mighty throng was assembled doing nothing. They were waving flags, blowing things, wearing hats and decorations of all kinds and singing. Thousands wandered around trying to get a drink or some food but the queues were seemingly endless. On into the Mall I went but right down to the Palace moved a human tide so I decided not to go down into the crush...I am sorry I did not stay till night fall as things livened up a bit I believe...
Of course I saw some amazing incidents, such as a crowd of sailors having a football game with a hat in the middle of the Strand. One would blow a whistle then there would be a wild scramble. Another was a lone taxi vainly trying to drive round the Square with a woman dressed up in the back and she was fit to kill but was obviously a charwoman. The most amazing thing about the whole celebration was the quantity of flags and bunting. Flags appeared in their millions and I have only seen the sight exceeded by Brussels...One thing I did notice was the number of U. Jacks which were put up incorrectly.
In the evening there were lots and lots of bonfires and quite a few coloured lights around gardens and buildings. One thing I think serves to describe this country and its people, what they have gone through and what they are today. It was from the train going between London Bridge and Waterloo—you know the class and type of district. The building was about six stories high. Looking at it it looked a normal dirty building but then I saw the place was a shell no window frames or boarded-up spaces just rectangular holes in a monument of bricks. Then looking up I could see the sky through the roof that wasn't. Surmounting this monument to destruction at the top of the flag pole

a large U. Jack was standing out in the breeze. It was an amazing scene. What struck me was that it would have been understandable to have seen gaunt blackened timber inside the shell, but no, the thing was all tidied up and cleaned out as though well the thing was only a hollow brickwork of peculiar design. No! I think it was definitely a sign of the times. It was as though the people had said: "Well we are a bit battered and shabby but that won't prevent us dressing up and looking happy along with everyone else". Perhaps you don't agree with me but I haven't lived over for over three years and learned nothing ... Really some of the Australian politicians are the dregs. Forde the other day was addressing some WRENS in Plymouth before their departure to Australia and was reported as saying "It is a very good thing Britain has sent a fleet to the Pacific as it will serve to put her [Britain] on the map". Well I ask you imagine saying that in Plymouth of all places which was given a hell of a pasting. The best I can say is I hope it was a bad choice of words or else he meant something else.[23]

Maybe it was a poorly chosen political statement, but this final comment in Leith's letter appears to show that for some people, the continuation, or perhaps even the return, of the 'The war was easy in England' foolishness. Australian aircrew returning from Europe to take up positions in RAAF formations (often fighter squadrons) in the period following the Battle of Britain were given a hard time by those who had stayed in Australia. They implied that it was sausages and eggs for breakfast every day followed by a leisurely flight to the Channel where, after a hearty 'Tally-ho chaps', a hundred yellow-nosed Messerschmitts were shot down in the blink of an eye. Pilots returned with victory rolls, all in time for a trip to the pub for lunch with steak and beer and a liaison with any one of umpteen girlfriends and then the rest of the day was free, so off for a trip to London and see the sights. That wasn't anyone's war, but it didn't stop people believing that those in Europe had it easy. Britain didn't need to be put on the map. The Germans were well aware of where it had been the whole time, right to the end.

Rusty shared thoughts of his European war on 11 May:

Looking back over the ops I can say that the last 12 months were definitely the hardest more dangerous but very interesting and

> exciting. Life on the continent was extremely interesting and I am glad that I did not miss out. The dive-bombing was quite good fun altho' we always had a liberal share of flak. It is interesting to have read lately that the heavies have been dropping food in the exact places we were bombing. I would liked to have been able to visit the Hague and see what the bombing has done.[24]

453 Squadron did some formation flying on 11 May, which Bob Clemesha recorded as 'The commencement of stooge flying' in his logbook.[25] On 12 May the two squadrons flew a low patrol at 1,500 ft above Guernsey and Jersey as British troops arrived to take possession of the Channel Islands once again.[26] From Hawkinge 451 Squadron received orders to move all the way up north to perhaps 453's least favourite part of the UK—Skeabrae in the Orkneys. 453 Squadron was notified that they'd be going to Northumberland, thus signalling the end of the wing. They'd also be filled up with pilots fresh out of OTUs in order for them to gain experience.[27]

451 Squadron's journey north was mainly by train, taking a few days—perhaps some thought that the longer it took the better. It may have been approaching the European summer but the Orkneys was still the Orkneys. Sid Handsaker noted in his logbook: 'Moved with Squadron to Orkney Is. Forced landed at Acklington owing to bad weather. Refuelled. Good trip to Orkneys. What a dump!! No trees?'[28]

On 15 May a special directive was issued by SHAEF regarding the capture and operation of V2 rockets. It noted that capture of V-2 rockets would allow them to be tested and evaluated in Allied hands and allow the Allies to further their own research and countermeasures. This followed an earlier order that any V-2 equipment captured should be kept intact and not tampered with, and that the staff operating the various apparatus associated with V-2 operations should be kept together and not disbanded. The capture of any such personnel was to be immediately reported.[29]

16 May saw 453 Squadron visited by several staff from the Public Relations Section of Overseas Headquarters (RAAF) who were after stories for publication. It was lucky they visited that day for FO Marsh and FO Tonkin had both returned—Marsh from his time as a prisoner, and Tonkin from being hidden by the Dutch. Flt Lt Bennett returned from his time as prisoner of war the next

day, and the squadron was informed they'd be joining 451 Squadron up in the Orkneys. This order was cancelled a few days later and smiles returned to the faces of 453 Squadron. The squadron welcomed back two of their number—WO Carmichael visited the squadron and passed on news that WO Gadd and he had both been hidden by the Dutch, and were close enough to visit each other and keep their spirits up while they waited to be liberated.[30]

On 22 May, 451 Squadron flew over HMS *Rodney* as a salute as she left Scapa Flow and on the 24th the spent much of the day dropping surplus 250-lb bombs into the sea.[31] 451 Squadron didn't stay up north for long and, by mid-June, 451 and 453 Squadrons were transferred from Fighter Command to 2 TAF and relocated to Lasham in Hampshire, minus their Spitfire Mk XVIs. For Wing Cdr Don Andrews it was time to go home, and he was posted to 16 Aircrew Holding Unit (ACHU) to await repatriation.[32] 451 Squadron had to hand their Spitfire Mark XVIs over at Turnhouse near Edinburgh on the way south; both squadrons were based at Lasham by 1100 on the 15th.[33] For the flight from Skeabrae to Turnhouse, Ross Sheppard wrote, 'Squadron moved to Lasham. Flew all kites to Turnhouse. Finished with the old XVIs. Last trip in the beaut old V,' meaning NI-V, the Spitfire he flew most often.[34]

Much of the flying done by 453 Squadron at the start of May was in cooperation with American units, practising dogfighting against Mustangs of the 355th Fighter Group. Sundays became a regular 'day off' but Lasham was not a popular choice of location—everyone was in tents. There was no running water, no heaters, no lighting and no sewers. The Australians were not impressed. The only Spitfires available were those belonging to the base—not nearly enough for two overstrength squadrons. Meanwhile, at 84 GSU, CAM Taylor was flying about in a Spitfire Mk XIV, recording a top speed of 540 mph in his logbook.[35]

On 16 June many of the old hands of the squadron went to Brompton in Middlesex to attend the wedding of Sqn Ldr Esau to an Englishwoman who was formerly an officer in the WAAF. Rusty Leith wrote home about it:

> Last Sat. afternoon Bob [Clemesha] and I were ushers at the CO's wedding and we had a grand time. A very nice service at Holy Trinity, Brompton, followed by a very nice "do" afterwards. June [nee Clapperton of Yorkshire] looked beautiful in white with the bridesmaids in pink.[36]

Two mentioned in dispatches were received towards the end of the month for 453 Squadron: one for PO 'Froggy' Lyall and another for FO Wilson. The end of the month saw the first of the pilots from 451 Squadron posted to 11 PDRC Brighton—the first step for many on the way home to Australia.

The start of July 1945 saw more posted out of 451 Squadron, and eleven men from 453 Squadron—including many of the most experienced pilots, such as Rusty Leith, Froggy Lyall and Jim Lynch. In their place some were promoted.[37] A cricket match was held against the RAF station staff on 2 July and it was a draw, despite the Brits spending days practising.

New Spitfire Mk XIVs finally started to arrive on 18 July, though one of the new pilots, FS Trevorah, had to bail out when his plane developed engine trouble and it was destroyed on hitting the ground. The matter was not judged against him and he was promoted to warrant officer the next day. Sid Handsaker delivered a few himself after being transported to the depot location (Lasham) by Auster.[38] When not testing out the new aircraft and giving instruction to the newer pilots, many games of cricket were held between 453, 451 and the RAF base staff.[39]

Though the war in Europe was over, it was not yet the time to rest easy. Robert Walter Knox arrived at 451 Squadron on 7 July 1945 and had been with the squadron less than two weeks when he was given the job of picking up a Spitfire Mk XIV from Cosford and flying it back to Lasham. In this task he was accompanied by Fred Ebert, who had been posted in on the same day. The distance between the two was not great, but the poor weather made it impractical to return, so they stayed the night and left the next morning after checking the weather report. They took off at 1145 and flew side by side at 1,000 ft south towards Gloucestershire—to avoid hills between Cosford and Lasham—on a slight dogleg course. After a while, they entered cloud, and Knox turned underneath Ebert, apparently still in full control of his Spitfire, and that's the last time Ebert saw him. Shortly afterwards, Knox's Spitfire was seen by civilian witnesses to come down through cloud, apparently looking to check his position, but went into a hill and was killed instantly. This must have happened almost instantaneously, as Ebert's report on the matter stated that he tried to contact Knox on two different radio channels after he saw him make the turn but he didn't ever receive an answer.[40]

On 20 and 21 July, Sid Handsaker and Lindsay Richards took an Auster (DG 566) from Lasham via a number of stops to Montgomery's headquarters in Buckeburg, staying the night at Twente along the way due to the rain. On 21 July their return flight included spending time as passengers in a Dakota which was also transporting '8 pro-German Belgian girls' from Denmark to Brussels.[41]

With few planes to occupy the pilots, some got up to mischief. Though the exact date is not disclosed, it was around this early post-war period that Sid Handsaker and a few others decided to have a bit of fun. Handsaker discovered that he could fit in through a gap in the door to an armoury and helped himself to some .38-calibre revolver ammunition and some flash-bangs (similar to modern stun grenades). He didn't keep this to himself and soon others helped themselves to the RAF stocks, and one evening they attended a local dance equipped with their new toys, concealed under their greatcoats. The bells of Big Ben on the radio preceded a speech by Churchill and someone got a bit bored and went outside, and Sid followed asking what they were going to do. They replied: 'I'm going to let one off.' With little regard for the civilians who had been bombed by the Luftwaffe and subjected to the somewhat random V-1 and V-2 rocket attacks, the airmen let off some of their flash-bangs, with explosions and loud flashes disturbing the peaceful but joyous mood of the night, leaving the frightened screams of the dance attendees behind them.

Having had their fun, the airmen—about eight in all—went in search for a cab and, having found one, all piled in, only to be told that some would have to get out. The Australians objected strongly and threw a flash-bang out the window which was enough to convince the driver to get going, and all the way through the town they heaved them out the windows of the cab, leaving explosions and bursts of light in their wake. After a journey of about eight or nine miles, they arrived at their very well-furnished billet where those who hadn't gone into town were having a nice quiet game of cards. However, one member of the recently returned group had the idea that they should unblock the chimney, and what better way to do it than lowering a stun grenade down from above? Other experiments included dropping the stun grenade into a waterpipe like a mortar shell and putting another can on top, such as a can of shaving cream or even kerosene, to see how far they could be 'fired'.[42]

Charles Allen Hulls arrived at 451 Squadron in July 1945 and thoroughly enjoyed his OTU:

> They just gave you an initial few hours on the Spit there before you went up to the OTU, and that is where you really had to learn to fly, and formation flying and the whole works, gunnery and everything like that. It was much more exciting. We were well out of the way of things. There was a Mustang base a bit to the left of us over in Wales, so if you saw a Mustang you tried out your skills on the Mustangs. You shouldn't have done it either ... it was an unwritten rule that you'd test the Spit against the Mustang. We could always turn inside a Mustang, tighter than a Mustang.[43]

In August 1945 everyone received inoculations against the numerous diseases they expected to encounter in Europe at the time. They expected occupation duties to be rather dull so were very glad when a donation of sporting gear arrived from the welfare section.

On 15 August, Victory over Japan (V-J Day) was announced and, finally, all Axis powers had been defeated and the war was over on all fronts. Many of the Australians headed into London for the city-wide party, and those who remained on base built a large bonfire, perhaps a little too close to the tents, but they survived unscathed and that's what matters most.[44] By 21 August, everyone was sober enough for practice flying to resume.

On 23 August, Flt Lt Clemesha married his English girl, Mary Moore Cartner at Rochford Parish Church in Kent. Two days later, news was received that the squadrons would be moving to 145 Wing at Fassberg in Germany and, on the 27th the ground crew and pilots without aircraft moved to Hornchurch. This was the last day with 453 Squadron for Sqn Ldr Esau who was posted out pending repatriation. His place was taken by Sqn Ldr Davidson from 451 Squadron.[45]

To get to their new base in Germany, the squadrons went via Ostend, Blankenburghe and Hanover. From Hanover all non-flying staff went by truck to Fassberg, arriving on 1 September. The facilities at Fassberg were certainly superior to those in the UK—there were brick buildings with central heating for a start. They shared the base with two French squadrons (no longer 'Free French') and, on 4 September, the Spitfires arrived and the squadron was whole again. AVM Wrigley visited on the 9th and was bombarded with questions about when the squadron would return home, but he wasn't able to give an absolute answer.[46]

On 15 September, already known as 'Battle of Britain Day', the squadron participated in a mass flypast over The Hague, and also received news that they would be sent to Gatow, on the outskirts of Berlin, for a month. The squadron moved on the 16th through Soviet-held territory and arrived at Gatow the same day—the first 'British' squadron to arrive in Berlin. Being a Luftwaffe airfield, there were many aircraft-related souvenirs to be had, and of all the things to find, one pilot brought home a handle from a German parachute, and cut a swastika off a damaged aircraft.[47]

Sqn Ldr Robertson left 451 Squadron in late September and was replaced by Sqn Ldr Falconer, who had flown Hurricanes and Spitfires with 615 Squadron in the Burma campaign. By late September, 451 and 453 Squadrons were separated, with 451 Squadron remaining at Wunstorf as the replacement for 198 Squadron, and 453 Squadron transferring to Gatow. With four squadrons and the attached supporting staff, Wunstorf was home to well over 1,000 RAF staff, including British, Australians, Dutch and Belgians.[48] 464 (RAAF) Squadron was disbanded about this time and a large volume of comfort items previously destined for them were distributed to the two Spitfire squadrons. Gatow was rated by the squadron as 'quite good'[49] and was in good order compared to the rest of Berlin, which was described as 'a mess of ruins'. Flying at Gatow was very limited due to the Soviet restrictions—no aircraft but their own were to fly over the Soviet sector.[50] However, the rules didn't necessarily work both ways. According to Sid Handsaker:

> They flew right over us. I threw a bloody apple at one, one day, a futile gesture. But if you ventured into their territory, boy look out … I found out later, they were not the elite troops that had captured Berlin. They'd replaced them all and had all these farmhands and that sort of thing. And pulling their guns around, they had oxen … They were a nasty bunch because when we went on to this place called Gatow we had women [working at the base] there. They were German women and a few of them had been raped by the Russians.[51]

In October 1945, 453 Squadron received a lot of attention in the press and photos and footage was taken of them flying in formation over Berlin. Many RAF ground crew were posted back to the UK around this time and replaced by RAAF ground crew, who were quite disappointed at being sent to Germany instead of Australia.[52] The two squadrons were reunited at Wunstorf, crowding the airfield with two Belgian squadrons, the four of them making up the ever-changing roster of 123 Wing. While the two RAAF squadrons wanted to stay together, and RAAF HQ in London certainly wanted them together, the whole point of sending two squadrons was to form an 'all Australian Wing' but two squadrons do not normally form a wing; it is a larger formation of three squadrons (or more if it suited the RAF). It was directed by the Air Commander-in-Chief that each squadron was required to spend one month at Gatow in order to 'show the flag', and a copy of the order was sent to Kodak House, for the information of RAAF HQ in London.[53]

CAM Taylor wrote home on 3 October about events at the airfield:

> yesterday we had Pathé Gazette cameramen taking photos of the squadron flying over Berlin—I was in FU-Z...He also took some of us taking off and you should see Z again—and there were a few groups taken on the tarmac...If there is one of a spit doing some inverted flying keep an eye on that too. We are the only squadron on the 'drome here and this morning much to the amazement of the English C.O. of the station about 9 tanks rolled around to our dispersal—we invited them round so that we could have a go. You ought to see me drive a tank boy—they are just the shot for forcing your way around the place...Got some German women here working as batwomen [servants] gosh they're a scream—speak about 2 words of English and are forever screaming in their native tongue about no dropping ash on the floor.[54]

Two planes from 451 Squadron collided on 10 October: Charles Hulls, known by his middle name, Allen, had to bail out:

> The purpose of going across on occupation was to display, we were told, to the general populous that we were there, that we were formidable, but we were on display and so we did basically constant close formation and open formation just to give ourselves a bit of relief, and it was in one of those one of the members of the squadron got out of position and he cut across the back of my path as I was forming up

and cut my tail off. Fortunately we were only flying at about 1,500 feet and I had full motor on to try and catch up and so the aircraft went up rather than straight down. We didn't ever have any formal training as far as bailing out and things of that nature, but they did tell us that we had to remember or work out in our mind and think of a routine that if it did happen what we would do … What you had to do was pull a knob and push the hood away for a start, undo your harness and then lever yourself out and get out … It all happened according to plan and I eventually got out. The only trouble is I forgot to pull out my radio connection and it stretched and stretched and, 'whack', it hit me right across the face and gave me a wonderful blood nose, but by the time the chute opened I decided I'd better have a look where I was going to land, so I looked over and there was a big clump of trees coming up. They'd told us, 'If you pull one side of the chute you can slide your chute and you'll land elsewhere.' and I thought, 'Which one will I pull?' So I gave it a tug and fortunately it went the right way and I landed in a ploughed field … I went down near a little village called Horst in Germany, and all the local kids came racing out. I was pretty shattered by that time and I grabbed one of the kids who had a bike and I put the chute on the bike. I had blood everywhere and we got out on the road and I tried to communicate with them where we are going and so on. So I thought we'd go this way and we headed off, and I looked behind us and coming along is an army truck. I thought, I hope they speak English, and sure enough it was an English army truck and in typical form the fellow on the left hand side leaned out of the car and said, 'What happened mate? Did you fall off your bike?' Well did I give him an earful! … So they took me down to the army depot and gave me a cup of tea which I could hardly hold … and I was eventually picked up and got back to the squadron and found out the fellow who had cut my tail off, I was his second victim … he had knocked somebody else off at another stage in the same way so I didn't see him again. They sent him straight home. Contrary to what happens these days, and I think this is an important point … their theory then was, 'Ok, you've got out of it. Have you still got your nerve? Next morning up you go and away you go.' And that's what happened. There was no counselling or anything of that nature. I didn't go into hospital or anything like that. I had an examination, of course, but I was very lucky I got out quite unscathed.[55]

The same day CAM Taylor wrote a letter home, and highlighted the desperate situation found in a wrecked Germany:

> Been away at a 'drome near Hanover (also smashed to bits) for a couple of days ... Had my last beat up the other day, the day we had the Pathé Gazette cameraman here—told dad about it ... Going to England on Monday for a few days leave by Spit. Like doing these long trips in day time across Europe because in war time you couldn't look around so much ... Weather is getting a bit on the cold side already here so the huns will really be cold in a month's time; probably sell my great-coat for a thousand quid. One of the boys sold some cigarettes for 3/6 each yesterday.[56]

On 12 October, while practising aerobatics, Sid Handsaker took the opportunity for a look at Hanover and described it as 'a clapped out mess!'[57] On 23 October, another batch of pilots from 453 Squadron were posted out to commence the long journey home: Taylor, Mace, Baxter and Peters. They were followed a few days later by Clemesha and Stansfield.[58] Bob Clemesha recorded the event in his logbook, '20-10-45 Posted from Squadron to 11PDRC Brighton and so end of my flying.'[59]

On 24 October, a number of pilots from 451 Squadron, including Joe Barrington, received their orders for home—with the first stop being 11 PDRC at Brighton in the UK.[60] Joe was back in Australian by January 1946.[61]

Before he left, during the squadron's occupation duties, Joe Barrington was given an invitation by the CO, to visit the concentration camp at Belsen:

> I had a particular interest ... being Jewish. So we went down there and the sentry was on the gate and he allowed us to go in but first of all we had to be sprayed, disinfected, both going in and coming out. The place had been cleaned up a bit, they'd left a couple of the huts and they left the ovens ... This wasn't like a big camp, it wasn't like ... some of the other ones that were mass, sort of, destruction, or mass murder.

> And one thing that stood out in my mind, it always will, was a great pile of shoes that were, probably, about twenty feet high, like a pyramid. I remember looking at them and thinking, well they probably got rid of piles like this but they didn't have time to get rid of this one and the powers that be just decided that it should remain there for some time... In the village, just alongside of Belsen, Bergen Belsen it was called, there was still people in their stripe uniforms... maybe they didn't have anywhere to go, they were still walking around in the streets. And the thing that I noticed, that a lot of them had distended stomachs... But for me that was an unforgettable experience, not very nice but unforgettable.[62]

At the end of October there were 21 pilots remaining with 451 Squadron. Non-flying time at Wunstorf was filled with lectures (including one on 'Big Game Hunting') and soccer or hockey matches against nearby army or air force formations. Accommodation was becoming more and more cramped, as the population of the base at Wunstorf had climbed to almost 1,400 by the end of September. Sports continued, with the addition of boxing and rugby.[63]

November 1945 started badly for the Australians in Berlin. According to squadron records, several newspaper articles in Australia stated that the two squadrons were staying in Berlin voluntarily, and that was certainly not the case. Furthermore, this led to some wives and parents writing to the men in the squadrons accusing them of shirking their home and family responsibilities. No information was forthcoming to the squadrons regarding their demobilisation and how long it might take for them to be returned home. They were certainly beginning to think of themselves as the 'Forgotten Legion'.[64] Sid Handsaker wasn't impressed; he'd been away from home for years and was looking forward to going home but, in the end, he assessed it all as being the best thing to ever happen to him.[65] However, 'the biggest worry was always weather because I had been up on trips, even when we got up to Berlin we were out on trips and we were recalled because of bad weather. That was the last time I ever wanted to get killed was when the war was over and I was up flying around Germany, I didn't want to get killed...'[66]

As a follow-up to staff departing their squadrons for home, the squadrons were visited by Wing Cdr Hilton, the RAAF Liaison Officer, to discuss demobilisation and request volunteers to stay an additional 12 months as part of the occupying force. The response was unfavourable and he informed them that should insufficient staff be available, the squadrons would be disbanded. Having said that, pilots were still being interviewed for commissions, so it was not as if the whole system had been put on hold. A newspaper report in Melbourne's *The Age* reported on 15 November, 'Spitfire Groups Not Keen to Stop in Germany' and reported that less than 10 per cent of the ground crew and only about a third of aircrew had volunteered to stay on. The article pointed out that this vote was unfortunate, as the Australian mission in Berlin was due to arrive at the end of the month, and would therefore be expressing opinions without a military presence in the occupying forces.[67]

451 Squadron moved to Gatow on 27 November, and the two Belgian squadrons left Wunstorf, leaving the entire airfield to 453 Squadron.[68] The airmen explored Berlin, as Sid Handsaker later recalled:

> they had bands and the grog was just, particularly champagne, was stacks of it, stacks of it ... you could not describe how, on a moonlight night, driving through the middle of bloody Berlin, nothing—except moonlight coming through all the windows. In every street we went through, and occasionally in the bottom we'd see a little light coming through the windows where somebody was living in the basement, but it was just completely and utterly flattened. But all these buildings were still standing, I went up in one ... and I got all the way up to the top, it must have been 6 or 8 floors up I supposed. And I looked at the top floor, and there was a hole ... in the floor, and it went right through to the bottom. They'd dropped a bomb, and apparently it obviously didn't go off, and it just went the right way through to the bottom. Incredibl ... glass everywhere. It was sad. They had what they called DPs over there, displaced persons and when we were out and around it was sad. But one thing that really saddened me was the kids, little kids, that brought me to tears ... They followed me around, I didn't smoke, but over there you had cigarettes as money, and a cigarette was worth sixpence—five cents. And I didn't smoke so I had an accumulation of wealth and what we used to do was go down to the black market and we'd have a carton of cigarettes here and a carton of cigarettes

> there ... and the Germans would have the right money ready, you'd give them a carton of cigarettes, and you put [the money] in your great coat. And honest to Christ, this day I had my great coat all full of notes, Marks ... But we had all this money left over at the end when we were going home, and a lot of the fellas just left it there on the tables. And my little mate Alan and I, I just couldn't bear to part with bloody money like that. Because when you went over there you were given Marks to the value of something like 25 pounds, and then when you come back, get it back again. We had a stack of them—must have been like several hundred quid.[69]

Whilst in Germany Handsaker didn't spend a penny of his wages; he did all his trading on the black market with cigarettes. He wasn't a smoker so had plenty to trade with.[70]

> The mood of Berlin was very sombre, it was very sad, and looking back on it now I don't think we could appreciate at the time, I didn't, because these Germans had done so much to England and other people, and I think we all felt they just got back what they gave only with more, and we did not have a great amount of sympathy for anybody. We treated them with courtesy, as they treated us.[71]

But it wasn't just drinking, low-flying and trading cigarettes, there was also deer hunting:

> of course the Germans were grateful the RAF liked to put on deer shoots and that sort of thing. And anyhow, Alan and I decided we would do it independently, so we went to his mates in the ground crew of 453, "Can we borrow your .303s?" Unbeknownst to us they'd stuck a couple of bloody tracers in there, you know. So the first day we go out and a great big paddock, the ground ... was frozen, absolutely frozen. And down in the middle of it was a depression but you couldn't tell until you got up there. And up over this depression come two ears like that. "Shit, look at that!" It was a deer. And he sparked up, up he got, and the other one got up and we both fired and we're shooting tracers and they're up jumping ... So we went out again the next night, next afternoon, back over in the bush. So, you know, there

> was nobody around, and these wild deer were roaming around, so we decided to have one. So we sneaked up on this lot, these were about 4 or 5 of them, all grazing... and I said, "Jesus Alan, you go that side of the tree and I'll go this side, and when I say 'fire', fire." So he aims out, and I say, "Ready?" "Yeah" "Fire" Click back. Two bloody deer fell over. Two! I said, "Gee, you got yours, I got mine." He said, "I didn't fire". I said to him, "Bullshit!" He said, "Look" and pulled the thing—hadn't fired! I got two deer with one shot! But the amazing part came about a week later, we're at it again, different tree, different part, we did the same thing again! He's firing, I'm firing, we had four deer with two bloody bullets.'[72]

On 4 December 1945, 453 Squadron participated in a group exercise, carrying out a bombing attack on a dummy target then engaging the defending aircraft—Spitfires and Tempests—claiming one of each 'shot down' when they returned. A similar exercise was carried out on the 18th, but no dogfighting took place as 453 Squadron were able to bomb and get away from the target without being intercepted.[73]

More pilots from both squadrons were posted out to 11 PDRC, and yet others received their commissions in their place, including WO Lindsay Richards of 451 Squadron. Ground staff travelled on 27 December and the Spitfires flew in on the 28th. Flying hours improved with the weather in December and rumours of being returned to the UK for disbanding in the New Year started to spread.[74]

On 4 December, Sid Handsaker took Spitfire Mk XIV NI-B on a 50-minute flight for a 'look see of Berlin' and recorded an extra comment in his logbook: 'Looks clapped out in the snow.'[75] Sqn Ldr Falconer and FO Dunk were injured in an accident in Berlin on 22 December and hospitalised. The run-around was definitely on and, on 22 December, 451 Squadron were told they were to return to Wunstorf on 28 December, which they did, the pilots and planes arriving on the 30th.[76]

Back in Australia, *Smith's Weekly* posted a message in their newspaper for 453 Squadron, acknowledging their Christmas greetings and wishing them home soon so they would 'no longer be "The Homesick Boys in Germany"'.[77] Many had not seen home since 1941, and while many had chosen to stay in

Europe rather than take individual postings to the Pacific, the war was won, and they wanted to go home.

While 451 Squadron was relocating, a shocking incident took place. On 27 December, Leading Aircraftman (LAC) Gibbs, a cook from 453 Squadron, was found dead in his billet with a gunshot wound to the head. The shot came from a Smith & Wesson service revolver, but despite a court of inquiry, no evidence was able to be brought forth regarding his state of mind at the time, though it was found to be a suicide.[78] He was later buried at Neustadt, with full military honours, and is now in the Becklingen Commonwealth Wargraves Cemetery near Fassberg.[79] Perhaps to stave off any other potential suicides due to depression or other related issues, the squadron was addressed by the Officer Commanding 123 Wing in relation to the death of Gibbs and the future of the squadron. He informed them that the move back to the UK was postponed while the Australian government decided on staffing the squadron with volunteers from Australia, since there were insufficient in Europe. While the news was not good, at least there was an update as to where the squadron stood.[80]

Another death occurred on 1 January 1946. LAC Murray of the ground crew was found lying on the main road outside the base with a head injury. Though this early description sounds rather mysterious, it soon came to light that he had been a passenger in a lorry which had overshot a corner in the darkness but fell out while trying to assist the driver with directions and was subsequently run over. He was returned to base by ambulance but died and an investigation was commenced.[81] Murray is also located in the Becklingen CWGC near Fassberg.[82]

On 4 January 1946, 451 and 453 Squadrons participated in another group exercise, dive-bombing ground targets and dogfighting 'enemy' Spitfires. The target for 453 Squadron was just four miles from the Soviet zone, so navigation had to be spot on.[83] On the same day the 451 Squadron diary recorded: 'Information received today by phone from Headquarters 84 Group R.A.F. that 451 and 453 Squadrons and Echelons were to disband on 21.1.46.'[84] Just two days later, Sqn Ldr Davidson, CO of 453 Squadron was killed when his plane crashed on route to England. He was buried in Brookwood Cemetery in England, the funeral service being attended by Sqn Ldr Falconer who was in England at the time.

On 6 January, 453 Squadron received the news of the death of Sqn Ldr Davidson and the next day Wing Cdr Hilton arrived to deliver the news in person and two minutes' silence was held. With disbanding the squadrons not so far away, Wing Cdr Hilton took command for the next few weeks.[85]

On 10 January, a letter was received confirming the orders received by phone for the disbanding of the squadrons, and a memorial service was held for Davidson, Murray and Gibbs.[86] The last day of flying training was 14 January 1946, and the aircraft were serviced and prepared for handover to other units.

Life was not all rosy with the mixed nationalities in Berlin, it wasn't just a matter of staying out of Soviet airspace:

> They were quite hostile. They were the hostile ones when we got there and when we were there ... we used to go into a night club in Berlin where they said we could go and told us we could go. We used to go in by truck from Gatow. It was quite a trip, probably ten or fifteen kilometres in our terms, and there was a lot of traffic on the road and this night one of the trucks going in, it wasn't ours, I think they said it was a British truck, brushed a Russian transport and their transport was very primitive, it was mainly horse-drawn, and apparently that truck didn't stop, so the Russians set up a machine-gun on the back and sprayed the next truck that came through and that is our allies and that is what happened. When we went into town we met the Russians they were in the same sort of places we were. All I could say, and I don't want to be too disparaging, is that they were uncouth and lacked any sort of social skills at all ... They used to wash their hands in the toilet and things like that ... In fact there was quite a bit of animosity between the Yanks. We were all in the same area, the Yanks and the British and the Australians, and we weren't involved in it, but a Russian soldier was killed one night in there, murdered I suppose, so that really heightened the tension too, but we didn't get a really good impression from them at all. But still, you've got to keep it in perspective. They'd had a very rugged time getting through, and they had been hammered down by the Germans.[87]

With generally poor weather and no Luftwaffe to look out for, there was not a lot of flying done, but sometimes an impromptu 'section formation' flight of a few mates would take off and fly around. What they planned was not always known to those higher up. On one such occasion Sid Handsaker and a few friends took off and headed for a hospital he'd been in while recovering from his worst injury during his time in service: a broken ankle from playing sport. He'd met a nurse there and promised he'd fly over the hospital and do a bit of a show when he was better, and now was the time:

> as we got there, there was the big autobahn and ... I got down on the middle [lane], and he got on that one there, and he on that one there, we were down level with the cars! I'll never forget the frightened look of these Germans! They didn't have trucks, they had these bloody tractors.[88]

They had a great time roaring down the autobahn, three Spitfires flying as low as they could go, going for all they were worth and scaring the locals. But when they got back to base all was not well:

> The CO sent for me. I thought, oh geez, I was guilty before I went in. Christ! And he only wanted to see me. He didn't want to see the other two. I was leading them. He called me in, and you know what he wanted to ask me about? Nothing related to that. He didn't even know about it. He said, "I have a report here of you taxiing out and your tail wheel fell off. Is that correct?" And it was. I said, yeah, and I explained to him what had happened ... the weather was so cold that the rivets gave way and just snapped off and dropped so I wasn't able to take off. That's all he wanted to ask me, was just approving that the damage had been done. And he didn't say a thing about the low flying. After that I thought to myself, I wonder what [the nurse he'd been trying to impress] thought about ... I get a letter about a fortnight later—she'd gone back to Scotland! She wasn't even there![89]

Another memory of Sid's is the day he went for a walk, out of the hospital, on crutches. There was snow on the ground outside, and he was in uniform and greatcoat. He came across a one-armed German soldier, with the sleeve of the missing arm pinned to his jacket. Handsaker expected nothing from the encounter but the German snapped him a left-handed salute that nearly sent the Australian over on his crutches trying to salute him back, but soon enough the German was gone before he could compose himself. As Handsaker approached the village, he could see children playing. But in his mind, they were transformed into the children of one of his older brothers. They were not children of the enemy; they were just children:

> I had been taught to hate the Germans for what they did and I had every reason to be that way but when I saw it that way, I couldn't believe it, I didn't go in ... I wanted to go down and meet the people, I just turned around and made my way back to hospital ... I was looking at spitting images of children ... All the killings that had been going on ... if you're going to drop a bomb you can't think about where it's going to go. If you see an aeroplane coming, I never, ever thought of a man being in it ... I always thought of it as a plane ... You shoot the plane down, never, ever thought it was a person.[90]

On 16 January, there was an explosion in the fireplace outside the billets at Wunstorf and three members of the ground crew and a civilian were injured and admitted to hospital. LAC Samuel Thompson Hill (Service No. 61693) was classified as dangerously ill, with multiple wounds in his abdomen, right arm and right leg. It was lucky that more were not injured as several RAAF personnel and German civilians were around the fire at the time. One of the witnesses, LAC Budd Fray (Service No. 64489) gave a statement to the effect that at the time he thought the explosion was too small for a grenade but too large for a .303 rifle round, but that it may have been a 20-mm cannon shell because he 'had previously heard 20 m.m. shells exploding in a fire when [he] was stationed in New Guinea'.[91] Fortunately, Hill recovered from his injuries after a few weeks of hospitalisation and the explosion was found to be accidental, as rubbish was being burned but it had not been thoroughly searched for ammunition before being added to the fire, and it was thought that a 20-mm HE cannon shell had exploded, causing the injuries. RAF Military Police searched the fire and found expended ammunition in it, all of German origin, no doubt left over from the airfield's previous occupants.[92]

On 19 January, documents were signed for equipment returned from the squadrons to their next level of command, 84 Group. All manner of forms and documents had to be accounted for: Servicing echelon documents for aircraft maintenance, copies of the King's Regulations and even typewriters were all signed off as returned. The ground party of 453 Squadron was to leave Wunstorf by rail through Hanover and Ostend, cross the Channel via ship then proceed by rail to 11 PDRC at Charmey Downs.[93] All aircraft were to go to 39 Maintenance Unit or 6 Maintenance Unit but at least some ended up at Brize Norton. Unfortunately, the weather was poor, so the Spitfires only made it from Wunstorf to Manston via Coxyde (Koksijde) in Belgium. In Manston the weather was poor for ten days straight and no flying took place until 29 January when the Spitfires were flown to their final destinations.[94]

Sid Handsaker's last flight was in Spitfire Mk XIV NI-F from Manston in Kent to Brize Norton in Oxfordshire on that day. He recorded in his logbook: 'Definitely the last trip. Flew over London! Delivered kites to M.U. Taking it easy for good!'[95]

While they waited for their turn to be shipped home, Handsaker and a mate took a trip to Ireland and Northern Ireland and had an unpleasant time of it: 'they looked on us as scum ... because we were in uniform.' They had many of their purchases 'seized' by customs agents who somehow knew exactly what to look for:

> they didn't give us a receipt or anything, we asked for it and they wouldn't give it to us. What really bugged me was, there we were in uniform with medals up and everything, and he said, "The trouble is with you guys is that you don't know there is a war on." That really got me, I never forgot that.[96]

451 and 453 Squadrons were officially disbanded on 21 January 1946.[97] They were created for war, and with the war over, and without volunteers to stay away from Australia for yet another 12 months, there was no longer a need for them, so slowly they returned home, via Gibraltar, Suez and India, and got on with their lives as best they could. Two days after they disbanded, a message arrived at Overseas Headquarters RAAF, Kodak House, from Marshal of the Royal Air Force, Sholto Douglas. It was a message of apology and thanks. It read, in part:

> Owing to illness I was unable to visit Nos 451 and 453 Squadrons to say goodbye so ask that you will convey to all ranks my appreciation for their services whilst in BAFO. Although they came to Germany after the war had ended I was proud to have under my command Australian units with such fine operational records. It was a disappointment to me that for reasons I can well understand it was not possible to retain their squadrons as part of the permanent force in Germany. I wish all ranks the best of good fortune and a happy reunion with their own country and families being justly proud of the part they have played whilst fighting side by side with the Royal Air Force.[98]

Alec Arnel returned from the war and continued his service in the RAAF, but his time away had opened his eyes to the world, and his Christian faith only grew.

Joe Barrington lived out his life in Sydney and had several successful business ventures but would never forget his visit to Belsen. He was a witness, and no one can say otherwise.

Sid Handsaker kept his uniform, gloves, boots and goggles for many years after the war, though you won't find that in any official record. Officially, they were all returned, fully accounted for and signed off by the supply officer, 'Ned Kelly'.[99] It's a colonial thing.

Not all Australians went home on the same ships. Jim Ferguson chose to stay on in Europe where he participated in a post-war Australian government exhibition in Paris, which was set up in a department store. The exhibition was open for ten weeks and it was estimated to have been visited by 250,000 people and prompted many applications for immigration—though that was not its intention. The main aim of the exhibition was to educate visitors about Australia's participation in the Pacific theatre of the Second World War.[100]

During his time as a prisoner, Ferguson wrote a list of 'Good and bad intentions for after Liberation day'. He recognised life and the opportunities it offered were not to be wasted. Not everyone he had flown and served with would make it home but, if he did, he was determined to never take life—or freedom—for granted again:

1. Eat as much as required.
2. Exercise by means of walking as often as possible.
3. Buy and read a good French grammar.
4. Read as much of Chas Dickens & other good authors as my spare time allows.
5. Write home more frequently.
6. Take up BK accountancy again.
7. Eat as much chocolates & sweets as possible also as much cake of any kind as possible. Esp. NAAFI tea etc.
8. Get up earlier. Go for early morning walks.
9. Visit as many tea shops as possible esp. Aust. House also sandwiches at Bobby's.
10. Roll my own cigarettes. Never have empty cig case.
11. Eat bread and cheese with meals.
12. Go for walks on clear nights. Wanted to go for one to-night.
13. Read John Ruskin.
14. To often remember I was a P.O.W. & how much I missed things then & so how much things should mean to me. Always to appreciate even the smallest of luxuries & necessities of life.
15. Brush up my physics.
16. Buy browse through a German grammar.
17. Do the little things that people like so much, eg letters of thanks, telegrams on birthdays.
18. Never, never miss breakfast eat it all from porridge to many rounds of toast.
19. Before every meal, cigarette, book, beer or any luxury remember I was in Dunkerque without any such things.
20. Write to Tom Swift.
21. Read daily newspaper right through. Not just glance—read??
22. Enjoy the simple pleasures of life it is those that I miss, eg a good book, a brisk walk, a good meal, a good cigarette.
23. Drink cocoa or hot chocolate as often as possible, especially before retiring.
24. Read Ben Travers esp plays of his such as Rookery Nook, Cuckoo in the Nest.

25. Never procrastinate. If I feel like doing anything *do* it. If I feel something should be done do it. Live for to-day & don't worry about too much about tomorrow it may never happen.
26. Attend church & give thanks to God for my deliverance.
27. Read all the books I bought to read, before buying others, eg read my economics book.
28. Eat Vienna steaks they taste beautiful here.
29. Do daily exercise especially early morning & before tea.
30. Stay at Wilberforce Hotel Oxford if opportunity occurs. Good breakfast toast I had there also good tea shop in Oxford.
31. Feel very sorry for myself to-day. Went for a walk felt so much better. Moral—don't feel sorry for myself.
32. Eat at Railway Refreshment Rooms on pies & buns, rock cakes, tea etc. Was thinking of pies to-night. Go to Kings X especially if necessary.
33. Read up Air Force Law K Rs.
34. Go for walk before breakfast, however short.
35. Eat bags of biscuits. Use points of ration cards for this purpose. Also if I go home via America buy biscuits especially cream centres keep the tin full.
36. Stop feeling sorry for myself. Be natural have no room for self pity.
37. Stay at Australia residential Hotel at Grosvenor Square. Mainly because of meals, especially breakfast.
38. If time allows go with a pal or alone on a Lord Nuffield Scheme.
39. Don't procrastinate in Prison do things at once. Go for walks, no self pity, write read more often.
40. Go for long walks on sunny afternoons, short brisk walks on rainy or dull days.
41. Enjoy life to the full.
42. Visit as many small local pubs as possible for a quiet, repeat, quiet drink.
43. Listen to radio. Any programme will do.
44. Go slow on the Grog but have one or two only at any available opportunity so as to break myself in.
45. Eats bags of bread especially malt or fruit health loaf. Eat bread with every meal.
46. Have a lobster or crab supper. Possibly the Monico or better one of the boys may know a place in Soho.

47. Buy sandwiches at Bobby's & take back to Dunkels flat to eat while smoking, reading paper and listening to radio.
48. Eat while I drink. If a pub has rolls or sandwiches for sale buy & eat them. Get available good counter lunch also the Chelsea (Fleet St) is very good for salad at lunch time. Sausages and meat also there.
49. First opportunity make myself a real pea soup with plenty of spuds & bags of peas. Also mashed potatoes to go with it perhaps mixed in with the soup as Madame used to make.
50. Eat bags of porridge with milk sugar. Remember porridge with of wheat and barley with only salt.
51. Read these notes often to refresh my memory of hardships & good things.
52. Pray at least every night & morning. I do a lot of it here.
53. Be a good officer. Dress well, have uniforms cleaned & clothes washed very often. Carry myself well. No stooped back & keep fit.
54. Buy the best French dictionaries (must have pronunciations). Also if I take up German, do the same here. Foyles probably the best place to buy such books.
55. If possible go for a walk before each meal so as to get a good appetite to appreciate.
56. Pray more often. Give thanks for small as well as big things.
57. Read plenty of History especially if presented in fiction form, eg Margaret Erwin. Also read good Greek history esp one dealing with their heroes and Gods.
58. Sit outside on summer evenings & either smoke, think, smoke or smoke & read. If necessary don't smoke. Beer would go very well with all this
59. When practical buy a good Encyclopaedia.
60. Eat everything which I receive on a plate. Even if I have to eat jam etc with a spoon. Of an evening get a good book to read & stay in my room reading & eating my chocolate, cakes, biscuits, jelly etc. Also Oxo Gloten use before going to bed.
61. Buy any books of Everyman's Library. They are usually all good stuff. Read much of their poetry especially plays.
62. A wise man makes more opportunities than he finds—Bacon.
63. (crossed out) Buy and use very good open razors with strap. Buy only the best of all things as I have the money for a change.

64. Go to Edinburgh esp to see castle relating to Mary Queen of Scots. May be done with Lord Nuffield scheme.
65. Eat anything fried. Miss my fat very much in here.
66. Use brushless shaving cream, in the morning so as to appear shaven & neat.
67. Look for and appreciate beauties of nature and manmade edifices.
68. Don't smoke too much but smoke enough so that I get the full enjoyment from each cigarette. Think about a cigarette then don't have one for 5 or 10 minutes is good for the palate. Do other things the same way, esp chocolate, meals.
69. Visit lavatory at least twice a day. Preferably early late.
70. Don't waste time do something, even if only thinking what to do next.
71. Go often to the Films especially in Australia & also perhaps America.
72. To study with condensed notes on post cards for memory training.
73. Never carry too much money on me. One or two pounds should suffice on station. £5 or £10 should do on leave.
74. Always read paper at breakfast.
75. Read at least 2 or 3 books of any kind per week.
76. Get stuck into Bookkeeping Accountancy work until 12.00 pm if necessary but keep at it & to a system. If at all possible eat while working.
77. Have a few lunch time sessions.
78. Take my mother out more often. Also stay home occasionally or go out with the family especially father or mother.
79. If I go to America eat, eat & still eat, go to cheap places for good solid food rather than fancy stuff, but still eat plenty.
80. Never miss N.A.A.F.I. up.
81. Buy new dressing gown slippers also any other clothes I need.
82. Laugh more often especially at myself.
83. Concentrate!!
84. Don't be self conscious, have confidence in myself.
85. Go to all places of Historical interest, esp St Pauls, Tower of London, Westminster Cathedral.
86. Always give thanks to God for all the good things in life. For my meals etc, Have faith in God. He will provide. He has always done so here I'm thankful to Him for it. Be so outside.

87. If any of my pals suggest going for a meal go with them to the place they [choose]. Find out new places to eat.
88. Have 2 battle dresses so as to have one for dry cleaning.
89. Fly as often as possible 4 or 5 hours a day if possible. Would love to fly again here. Fly in early morning if possible. Get up to early breakfast to fly especially in summer. Don't waste time at disposal, read or study. Read paper if possible.
90. Play patience rather than do nothing. It helps to pass the time.
91. Bags of fresh air. Keep room well–aired and sleep with open window.
92. Keep my wits about me. Reason thinks things over more often.
93. Write more letters not only home but to other people. Appreciate letters I receive far more than I usually did.
94. Brush up my Latin. Also read an English dictionary occasionally especially with 5 minutes time to keep.
95. Do at least 5 to 10 minutes exercises every day so as to help myself regain my fitness. Preferably done early before open window and/or before retiring.
96. Always be willing to try or do something new. Also to go somewhere new if so suggested.
97. Invest my surplus cash with Saving Certificates War Bonds, Savings Bank.
98. Always read with a dictionary handy.
99. Cross out these resolutions as they are done or become a habit.
100. Johnson: "Read the book you can honestly feel a curiosity to read."
101. To write letters of reasonable length and to make them very interesting.[101]

This list is a reminder to us all of the value of the simple things in life, the importance of not wasting opportunities, and of celebrating the very act of survival.

451 SQUADRON LOSSES JUNE 1941–JANUARY 1946

NB: The raid on Corsica occurred on 12 May 1944. Some of those injured later died of their wounds.

DATE	NAME	SERVICE NO.	CIRCUMSTANCES
3 September 1941	Readett, L.M.	402557	Shot down by Bf 109
13 September 1941	Byers, P.	RAF	Shot down by Bf 109
10 October 1941	Malone, L.F.	RAF	Shot down by Bf 109
12 November 1941	Whalley, K.	RAF	Shot down by Bf 109 (probable)
12 November 1941	Thomas, T.	SAAF	Shot down by Bf 109 (probable)
21 November 1941	Smith, J.	SAAF	AA fire
18 September 1942	Pennell, J.	RAF	Flying accident
25 November 1942	O'Donnell, H.S.	403226	Flying accident
28 November 1942	Ifield, M.R.	15775	Cerebral meningitis
12 February 1943	Shiels, M.D.	403536	Flying accident
2 April 1943	Cox, J.A.	400783	Possibly shot down
24 April 1943	Hudson, R.B.	409142	Flying accident
12 May 1944	Branch, S.J.	14436	Luftwaffe raid on Corsica
12 May 1944	Bulcock, F.E.	24205	Luftwaffe raid on Corsica
12 May 1944	Ewans, A.	11204	Luftwaffe raid on Corsica
12 May 1944	Sneddon, R.B.	403228	Luftwaffe raid on Corsica
13 May 1944	Conrad, C.A.	30550	Luftwaffe raid on Corsica
13 May 1944	McKay, H.A.	11963	Luftwaffe raid on Corsica
17 May 1944	Ward, J.D.	408177	Luftwaffe raid on Corsica
1 June 1944	Haggart, D.C.	14675	Luftwaffe raid on Corsica
17 July 1944	Gale, W.W.B.	406243	AA fire
14 January 1945	Wallis, J.D.	408541	Flying accident
13 March 1945	Bray, H.J.	404324	Flying accident
20 July 1945	Knox, R.W.	436001	Flying accident

453 SQUADRON LOSSES SEPTEMBER 1944–JANUARY 1946

DATE	NAME	SERVICE NO.	CIRCUMSTANCES
27 December 1945	Gibbs, W.	145684	Suicide (probable)
1 January 1946	Murray, J.W.	66911	Motor vehicle collision
6 January 1946	Davidson, D.M.	402321	Flying accident

EPILOGUE: THE PLANES THEY FLEW: HURRICANES, TYPHOONS AND SPITFIRES

REGINALD JOSEPH Mitchell was born on 20 May 1895 at 115 Congleton Road, Butt Lane, Stoke-on-Trent.[1] He would not live to see the full extent of his influence upon the world, nor to hear the praise of the thousands who flew his Spitfire and the millions more who wished they could. As a child, he had an interest in planes and, in 1911, at the age of 16, he left school and started working at the locomotion engineering firm of Kerr, Stuart and Co.[2] After workshop training, he moved into the drawing office. He then took up a job at Supermarine as personal assistant to the owner, Hubert Scott-Paine and, in 1918, at the end of his first year with the company, was promoted to assistant works manager which was followed by a promotion to the technical directorship in 1927.

From similarly modest beginnings, Sidney Camm was born on 5 August 1893 at Alma Road Windsor in Berkshire. He left school aged 15 to become an apprentice carpenter and, in the years leading up to the First World War, he was a shopfloor carpenter at Martin and Handasyde Company. By 1921 the company was bankrupt and he went to work for Hawker Engineering, where, by 1923, he was a senior draughtsman. His boss was his boyhood hero, Tom Sopwith, previously of the Sopwith Aviation Company, who manufactured a number of famous aircraft during the First World War, notably the Sopwith Camel and Sopwith Pup.[3]

Supermarine and Hawker were both involved in the Schneider Cup seaplane races, the first of which was held in 1913.[4] The races were put on hold during the war years and resumed in 1920, with the British winning the cup outright on 13 September 1931 when the Supermarine S.6B flew the course with a new record average speed of 340.08 mph.[5] The development of engines and aircraft in these races was an important part of aviation history, but exactly how important could not be known at the time. During these racing years, Sidney Camm had advanced to Chief Designer at Hawker (1925)[6] and Reginald Mitchell was made Director of Supermarine in 1927.[7] They would prove to be the right men in the right jobs at the right time, but they had yet to design their iconic planes.

While the Schneider seaplane races were taking place, development was going ahead in the realm of land-based fighters. In 1930 the British government issued a request for designs for a day/night fighter in specification F.7/30.[8] Mitchell's submission, known as the Type 224, was not selected, nor was the submission by Hawker—Camm's PV3—which was a biplane. Both lost out to the Gloster Gladiator, which was the last biplane purchased by the RAF.[9] Though the Hawker design lacked innovation, Camm submitted a design for spec F5/34 which was issued for the companies of Gloster, Westland and Bristol. Though Hawker was not one of the companies invited to participate in F.5/34, the Air Ministry liked Camm's design and so issued another spec just for it, with the reference F36/34. The prototype aircraft was issued serial K5083.[10] Meanwhile, disappointed but not discouraged, Supermarine and Rolls-Royce designed a new fighter and, in response to this (instead of the other way around), the Air Ministry issued specification F.37/34.[11] This plane was known as the Type 300, and was fitted with a better engine, the PV-12 by Rolls-Royce (the PV standing for Private Venture, 12 representing the number of cylinders). Both the Hawker and Supermarine designs were to be fitted with Merlin engines, but also eight machine guns, instead of the previously specified four.[12] The Hurricane and Spitfire were about to be born.

However, the need for eight machine guns meant that, in the thin wing of the Spitfire, they had to be spaced out, leaving no room for additional fuel in the wings.[13] This lack of fuel reduced the range of the Spitfire and was forever its weakness. Director of Vickers, Sir Robert McLean, named the Supermarine design the Spitfire. This was in reference to his daughter Ann, whom he considered a 'little spitfire'[14]. It was a good choice, though Mitchell wasn't impressed; he thought it silly.[15] The name was officially approved on 10 June 1936.[16] At this time and for some years after, the rule of alliteration generally applied, thus the Gloster Gladiator, the Hawker Hurricane, the Fairey Fulmar and the Supermarine Spitfire.

Though the Hurricane may have lacked innovation in its design, it was always easier to build than the Spitfire, and on 6 November 1935 the Hurricane prototype took flight, with test pilot Paul 'George' Bulman at the controls.

The Air Ministry allocated serial number K5054 to the Type 300 Spitfire prototype and its test flight was on 5 March 1936 at Eastleigh and Captain J. Summers, the chief Vickers test pilot had the honour.[17] The flight lasted just eight minutes.[18] The test pilots' often-quoted advice: 'Don't touch a thing' was really more an instruction to leave the controls alone than a request to not change the design.[19] However, the *Summary of Flying Qualities for the Handling Trial of K-5054* starts with the sentence: 'The aeroplane is simple and easy to fly and has no vices', and the same wording was used to describe the Hurricane.[20] Britain had its fighters, but now the race to production was on. In March 1936 a provisional order for 600 Hurricanes was placed, and this order was confirmed in June when 310 Spitfires were also ordered.[21]

During this whole process, Mitchell had been battling bowel cancer, having first had surgery for it in August 1933, resulting in a colostomy. Sir Henry Royce also had a colostomy as a result of surgery due to cancer of the intestine sometime around 1912,[22] so Mitchell shared both the highs and lows of life's fortunes with his partner in racing and design. Not only did he have this to contend with, but the Type 224 and 300 were not the only projects he was working on. He also designed what became the Walrus amphibian, a seaplane that had its first sale to Australia, and one which would serve in the Second World War, rescuing many pilots from the English Channel, including many who flew Spitfires and Hurricanes.[23] Despite flying to Vienna for specialised treatment in April 1937, it was not successful and he returned to Britain to see out his final days. He passed away on 11 June 1937, just 42 years old,[24] never to know the greatness of his achievement.

The Hurricane led the Spitfire in production by about six months, the first production Hurricane being completed on 8 September 1937 with the serial L1547, and the first squadron to receive an operational aircraft was 111 Squadron at RAF Northolt on 15 December 1937. Upon receiving Hurricanes at 32 Squadron, pilot Pete Brothers recorded his opinion that it had a 'solid, rugged feel' and 'inspired confidence'.[25] On 15 May 1938, the first flight of a production Spitfire (K9789) took place and it was delivered to 19 Squadron at Duxford on 4 August that same year. Joe Smith took over the position of Chief Designer at Supermarine after Mitchell's death, and he saw to it that the Spitfire evolved as the Second World War progressed.[26]

Due to production difficulties with the highly specialised Spitfire, 300 additional Hurricanes were ordered, plus another 1,000 on 1 November 1938. By the end of 1939, 731 of the total order of about 2,000 aircraft had been manufactured.[27] On 1 September 1939, Germany invaded Poland and, on 3 September, Britain and much of the Commonwealth, including Australia and

New Zealand, declared war on Germany. On this day, 2,160 Spitfires were on order and 306 had been delivered, of which 187 were operational in ten squadrons.[28] In comparison there were 16 operational squadrons of Hurricanes with 280 aircraft available.[29] There was a lot of catching up to do.

The Spitfire evolution mainly involved changes to the propeller and engine. The first propeller was a fixed-pitch, two-bladed wooden version paired with a 1030-hp Merlin II engine providing a top speed of 347 mph, one of the last combinations being a five-bladed propeller matched with a 2,035-hp Griffon 65 engine, giving a top speed of 439 mph. Rolls-Royce produced about 60 per cent of all British aircraft engines during the First World War;[30] however, it was the American Curtiss 12-cylinder engine (though not a V-12) which was sent to Rolls-Royce for evaluation that really put them on a path to success. After examining the American engine, they produced the Kestrel, all Rolls-Royce engines being named after birds of prey. The Kestrel ultimately evolved into the famous Merlin. The Merlin was seen as such an excellent engine (one for a Spitfire or Hurricane, four for a Lancaster) that, during the war, plans for it were sent to the United States for safekeeping.[31]

Due to the location of the wheels, the Spitfire had quite a narrow track when taxiing and, when flying, the wheels folded outwards into the wings. By comparison, the Hurricane had wheels that retracted inwards, which necessitated them being placed further apart and provided a wider and more stable wheelbase. A beneficial design concept of the Hurricane was the two windows in the cockpit floor which enabled the pilot to see if the undercarriage had been retracted or not. This small piece of innovation (contrary to the previous comments about the Hurricane lacking innovation) was described as 'an excellent feature'.[32] The Hurricane also had better landing characteristics than the Spitfire and settled down quickly after landing and stayed down, whereas the Spitfire tended to bounce.[33]

Building the Spitfire was not an easy task, however—certainly not as easy as building a Hurricane.[34] Every Spitfire was tested by a pilot at the factory, first at Southampton, then, when that was bombed in September 1940,[35] Castle Bromwich. Spitfire marks progressed in Roman numerals up to XX and, from that point onwards, Arabic numbers were used. Unlike many other aircraft, the letter following the mark designation referred to the type of wing armament fitted. Thus, while the P-51D was the D model of the P-51, the

Spitfire Mk IXE was the Spitfire, Mark nine, fitted with the E-wing armament. However, according to Fred Cowpe, who flew with 453 Squadron in the UK and Normandy: 'You can't take notice of the numbers ... the Mark VIII was a more modern aircraft than the XVI.'.[36] The wing designations were as follows:[37]

- A-Wing: Eight machine guns (.303). The Mk IA had 300 rounds per gun, later marks had 350 rpg.
- B-Wing: Two 20-mm cannon (60 rpg in Mk IB and 120 rpg in later marks) plus four machine guns (.303) with 350 rpg.
- C-Wing: Universal-type wing able to be fitted with A or B combinations, or four 20-mm cannon. C-Wings can be distinguished from others by having the outboard cannon mounts plugged.
- E-Wing: Two 20-mm cannon with 120 rpg plus two machine guns (.50 calibre) with 250 rpg.

These wing armaments were combined with a gunsight which also evolved as the war progressed. The success of a pilot in combat, in addition to the often-wished-for 'luck', also relied on their skill in the art of deflection shooting.[38] In very simple terms, deflection shooting involves firing not directly at a target, but at the location in space where the target will be, so that when the bullets and cannon shells arrive there, so too will the enemy aircraft. Early gunsights consisted of an illuminated fixed ring, and pilots would aim off a certain amount of 'rings', leading to comments in Personal Combat Reports such as 'I gave him three rings of deflection'. Later gyroscopic gunsights were estimated to have doubled gunnery effectiveness. As the aircraft turned after a target, the gyroscope also tilted the mirror and therefore the projected image of the illuminated ring, which could also be set for the wingspan of particular aircraft.[39] This combination of factors was then expected to enable the pilot to get his rounds on target with greater consistency and remove some of the human error that naturally occurs in the heat of combat. While the gunsights were not popular with the aces, because they obstructed the view forwards, aces do not win wars by themselves. Therefore, the increase in effectiveness of the average pilot was what really mattered.[40] The gunsight's effectiveness could be undermined easily though, and pilots were advised to not use the sight as a support when entering the cockpit, as the frame could be easily bent, throwing off the accuracy of the device. A memo was sent round 83 Group in February

1944 pointing this out after a pilot had to return early from an operation as his guns were out of alignment with harmonisation (the point in space at which the firepower of the guns converge).[41]

A total of 1,566 Spitfire Mk Is and variants were made, and it was in this first mark that one of the identifying traits of the Spitfire was introduced: the bubble canopy, which replaced the previous flush canopy which had blended more smoothly with the fuselage, but cramped the taller pilots.[42] These early Spitfires had a two-bladed, fixed-pitch wooden propeller, later replaced with a three-bladed, constant-speed propeller, providing the Spitfire with a higher speed above 20,000 ft, a higher service ceiling and a shorter take-off, all just in time for the Battle of Britain,[43] which is generally accepted as having commenced on 10 July 1940.

However, the beginning of the Spitfire's role as a fighter in operational service was not highly praised. The first aircraft shot down by Spitfires in air-to-air combat were two fighters on 6 September 1939, just days after war was declared, but unfortunately it cost the RAF two Hurricanes.[44] It was more than a month later that Spitfires had their first encounter with the Luftwaffe, with two bombers being shot down on 16 October.[45] The first Luftwaffe aircraft to be shot down by a Hurricane occurred two weeks later on 30 October when 1 Squadron claimed a Do 17 near Vassicourt in France.[46] Though Spitfires were generally kept out of France as much as possible, the experiences of the Hurricane squadrons in the Advanced Air Striking Force would lead to improvement for both aircraft, including the introduction of armour plating for the pilot and rear-vision mirrors.[47]

While the Hurricane was the more numerous of the two fighters during the Battle of Britain, (making up 63 per cent of Fighter Command),[48] the Spitfire could sometimes reach the Bf 109s flying above 28,000 ft during the later stages of the campaign when these aircraft were used as fighter-bombers on hit-and-run raids. The Hurricane could not reach these altitudes and was therefore less effective during these later operations. The Spitfire was also twice as likely to survive contact with the enemy due to an overall superior performance and smaller silhouette.[49] While this is certainly a technical measurement of survivability, anecdotal evidence from ground crew and pilots rated the Hurricane as being much more sturdy than the Spitfire.[50] However, one major drawback at this early stage of development was that the Merlin engine (fitted to both the Hurricane and Spitfire) would cut out when inverted, whereas the fuel injected engine of the Bf 109 did not, enabling to German fighters to dive away without much fear of effective pursuit.[51]

The armament of the Spitfire Mk IB was upgraded to two 20-mm cannon but the aircraft trialled by 19 Squadron suffered frequent stoppages. This was caused in part by the mounting of the cannon on their sides as the wing of the Spitfire was too thin for a standard mount.[52] After complaints about these cannon-armed Spitfires, 19 Squadron got their Mk IAs back. Knowing that the weight of fire produced by the Spitfire and Hurricane was less than that of the cannon-armed Messerschmitts, a Hurricane equipped with four 20-mm cannon commenced trials in June 1940, but the cannon-related issues were not resolved until February 1941.[53]

Turning was one of the main tactics of the Spitfire (and Hurricane) in dogfights throughout its service, and early model Spitfires had a shudder that would give warning of the coming stall.[54] This stall would result in the aircraft falling from the sky, a move that was virtually impossible to follow, the near-vertical wing position removing all lift properties of the aircraft. Spin recovery was then necessary to get back into combat or withdraw.[55] In fact, the British tested a captured Bf 109E loaned to them by the French in May 1940 (they didn't get it back) against a Spitfire Mk I and the Germans tested a captured Spitfire Mk I against a Bf 109. Both air forces found that their own aircraft was superior to the captured model, which certainly implies a degree of home-side bias on everyone's part.[56] A Hurricane was also tested against a captured Bf 109 by 1 Squadron during their time in France. The Bf 109 was found to be better when taking off and the initial rate of climb was better, as was the start of a dive. In a straight line the Messerschmitt was better by 30–40 mph, but when it came to the dogfight, the Hurricane could out-turn it and no matter how hard they tried, the pilot in the captured Messerschmitt could not shake the Hurricane.[57] Upon flying a Spitfire and Hurricane captured in France, the German ace Werner Molders described the Hurricane as a 'tugboat ... easy to fly ... particularly good natured, steady as a rock in the turn ... The Spitfire is one class better ...'[58] Despite all the pro-Messerschmitt performance claims, fellow Ace Adolf Galland did ask Göring for an 'outfit of Spitfires' during the Battle of Britain.[59]

But while the Germans said theirs were the best and the British made the same claim of their own aircraft, a bias arose which, in some ways, remains to this day. It is sometimes known as 'Spitfire Snobbery' and certainly does not just apply to British propaganda and the Battle of Britain. It was the grace and looks of the Spitfire that appealed to the public, as it still does. But while the Hurricane may have done most of the work, it was the Spitfire that the government and the population wanted more of. 'Spitfire funds' were created, and Spitfires could be bought and 'donated' to the government with the name of the donor's organisation painted near the cockpit. The plane might be wrecked on its first flight, but that wasn't the point. It is estimated that 1,500 were paid for by people or organisations. To 'buy' a Spitfire, an organisation or group had to raise £5,000, compared to the actual cost of manufacturing one at the time of about £7,500.[60] One example of these Spitfires is memorialised in London at the Spitfire Mk Vb W3311 Gate at the Old Spitalfields Market. The Market's fruit and vegetable traders pooled their funds and bought the Spitfire in 1941, naming it 'Fruitation'.[61] Its service was short, lasting barely a month, with pilot Sgt Smith of 611 Squadron shot down and captured while escorting bombers on 6 July 1941.[62] The feasibility of a similar 'presentation' scheme was raised in Australia in mid-1941 but was rejected on the grounds that 'any such funds would really amount to contributions to the British Treasury, and they could not be authorised'.[63] Even the Germans favoured the Spitfire—one Luftwaffe pilot shot down during the Battle of Britain refused to believe he could have fallen to a Hurricane and insisted to his captors that he was shot down by a Spitfire. Surely it was more honourable to be shot down by one of the best aircraft of the war (at that stage at least). Even when confronted by the pilot of the Hurricane who shot him down, he refused to believe it.[64]

The Type 329 Spitfire Mk II was fitted with a Merlin XII engine producing 1175 hp. Seven hundred and fifty Mk IIAs and 170 Mk IIBs were built. These were fitted with a three-bladed propeller, as were later production Mk Is.[65] In June 1940 the Nuffield factory at Castle Bromwich began to mass-produce the Mk II, the first of these being delivered to 611 Squadron in August 1940, with three more squadrons equipped by September.[66] After the Battle of Britain, in November 1940, metal ailerons were fitted, replacing the fabric ones which were found to balloon at high speeds, thus increasing high-speed handling.[67] The LR (Long Range) Mk II, with a fixed fuel tank under the port wing, was introduced in an attempt to alleviate the limited range of the Spitfire highlighted during the operations covering the evacuation from Dunkirk. At the time, the RAF did not use drop tanks. However, the development was not popular, and the aircraft handled poorly in comparison with the non-LR marks. Upon his first inspection of an LR Mk II and, being told that the external tank could not be jettisoned, one pilot replied in horror, 'My God!' To take off, the pilot had to apply full right rudder with full right stick and only take off into the wind.[68] The modification was not brought in during the Battle of Britain, though some were deployed in 1941 as bomber escorts.[69] The first Spitfires issued to EATS squadrons were delivered in April 1941, going to 452 (RAAF) Squadron and 485 (RNZAF) Squadron, the Canadians of 403 (RCAF) Squadron following a month later.[70]

With 3,857 Hurricane Mk Is produced, the Hurricane also advanced into a Mk IIA model, with an improved Merlin XX engine producing 1,480 hp and armed with eight or 12 .303 machine guns. There should have been 12 in all production aircraft but there was a shortage at the start of the production run. Four hundred and fifteen of these Mk IIAs were built and the first went to 111 Squadron in September 1940. The IIA was followed quickly by the IIB in November 1940, all of which had the 12-gun configuration and almost 3,000 of this model were built. Despite what might be assumed based on their large production numbers, the IIB was not popular and the extra weight of the four additional machine guns and the ammunition had a detrimental effect on performance, including rate of climb and roll. Where the earlier eight-gun Hurricanes had them clustered in groups of four closer to the fuselage, the two extra machine guns and their ammunition (per wing) had to be spread out towards the wingtips where their weight became a disagreeable hindrance. While the developing Hurricanes were weighed down with more machine guns, the 20-mm cannon being produced were kept aside for the newer Spitfires (Mk V) and Beaufighters. As a form of compensation, the Hurricanes had priority for the Merlin XX engines,[71] as they needed the extra power to prevent the aircraft falling too far behind in performance with the added weight of the extra machine guns and ammunition.

The Type 349 Spitfire Mk V was a real improvement over the earlier models and was the first to feature another identifying Spitfire feature, the clipped wing. While the large elliptical wings were a signature of the Spitfire from the beginning, the clipped wing was just as distinctive, and was introduced to improve performance at low levels. The clipped-wing Mk Vs were often referred to as 'clipped, cropped and clapped'. 'Clipped' for the wings, 'cropped' for the modified supercharger, and 'clapped' meaning clapped out, as they were often fitted with overhauled engines rather than brand-new ones. While they were designed for low-level work, they were still used for escorting bombers across the Channel on circuses and other sorties. Their performance at the altitudes required on these sorties was sub-standard and, generally, pilots were glad to see them go. Engine life for a Spitfire was generally about 240 hours, (about nine months' flying time) assuming they survived that long. After this, they were sent to a maintenance unit where they would be refurbished and sent on to another unit, who had no doubt hoped to be equipped with brand-new Spitfires, not those already worn in (and out).[72]

The first time Sid Handsaker flew a Spitfire was in a Mk V, and, compared to the planes he'd flown in training, the acceleration was what really struck him.[73] According to Sid, before you knew it, you'd taken off and were away. He loved the Spitfire:

> When you get in that plane, no other plane is like it. And whatever you do, whatever you think you might do, the bloody plane will do it for you ... I used to think to myself when I was in England, 'Oh, I wish my family could see me here!' I'd be doing slow rolls and everything and flying the best plane in the bloody world and here I am, coming from nothing into that ... What I used to love to do was bring it up almost to the stall and then let it fall and then go down with it and then give it a bloody burst and then come up, do a loop and roll off the top, come out that way ... That's living.[74]

Models of the Mk V designed for use outside Europe, such as in the Mediterranean or North Africa, featured an engine intake dust filter under the nose, which also appeared on the Mk VIII used in the Pacific. There were two versions of the filter: the larger, prominent and pouting Vokes filter for the Mk VC and the smaller 'Aboukir' filter fitted to a smaller number of Mk VCs and the Mk VIII. By May 1941, eight squadrons were equipped with Mk Vs[75] and 6,693 of the Mk V (though some sources quote a figure of 6,787) were produced, including unarmed photo-reconnaissance models.[76] The Spitfire Mk V claimed a number of firsts, including the first Spitfire to be fitted with a bomb, the first with a drop tank (also called 'slipper' or 'jet' tanks) and the first to operate in the desert.[77] The 30-gallon tanks gave an extra 30 minutes' flight time but reduced speed by 10 mph. Considering that the tanks were dropped as soon as the fuel was used or prior to combat, this speed reduction was not a great disadvantage, assuming that the tanks did in fact jettison correctly.[78]

By February 1941, the Hurricane had advanced again, but almost for the last time. The Hurricane IIC was armed with four 20-mm cannon and, by 1944, 4,711 had been manufactured.[79] But what Hawker really wanted was to produce a new aircraft altogether and shake off the 'lacking innovation' criticism. In this respect the company had been working on an aircraft—the Tornado/Typhoon. Design work had actually started on these aircraft before the war, but when France fell and it became obvious that volume production of existing aircraft was what was needed the most, work was put on hold until after the Battle of Britain was over.

The difference between the Tornado and Typhoon was the engine: the Tornado had the Rolls-Royce Vulture and the Typhoon had the Napier Sabre. It might be assumed that Rolls-Royce produced the better engine, but in this case the Tornado was a failure, and so the Typhoon went into production, and struck a number of immediate problems. These included too much weight towards the front, engine failures and short engine life (not even 20 hours) and major vibrations.[80] Despite this, the aircraft proceeded to production and the Typhoon IA was produced, carrying an armament of 12 .303 machine guns in a typically thick Hawker wing, powered by a Sabre 1 engine. Early complaints from Typhoon pilots included the restricted cockpit view, engine problems and the armament.[81]

A thousand Typhoons had been ordered, so major work had to be done to get a worthwhile aircraft into the hands of the RAF. The first Typhoons went to 56 Squadron at Duxford in September 1941 but it was eight months before operational sorties were flown and, even then, restrictions were placed on the aircraft—they were not to cross over to the far side of the Channel. By this stage the Typhoon Mk IB was in production—the canopy had been modified as had the armament, which was now four 20-mm cannon.[82] But there remained problems, and they were fatal. During flight, the tail section sometimes broke off, causing the aircraft to lose control and usually the pilot died. Early operations were not overly successful either: other pilots were not familiar with the new shape and some were shot down by Spitfires, including during the Dieppe raid. But it was the tail section that caused the most problems and, though over 300 aircraft were modified in an effort to correct this, it still happened from time to time, the investigation of the issue lasting from April 1942 to October 1943. Hardly a reassuring timeframe for the pilots.

Five Typhoon squadrons were moved to the southern parts of England to defend against the Luftwaffe tip-and-run raids. These raids were carried out at low level and attacked targets that varied from railway engines to 'gatherings of people' or even flocks of sheep. The Typhoon was well-suited to low-level operations, but being new to the RAF armoury they had black and white stripes painted on them to aid in identification (preceding those used for Operation *Overlord* by about 18 months).[83] By December 1943, 1,756 Typhoons had been delivered, yet only 412 were operational with squadrons.[84]

The Typhoon didn't perform well as a high-altitude fighter and was retained for low-level operations, with the Typhoon wing at Duxford being disbanded in September 1942.[85] The squadrons equipped with the aircraft started specialising, some in carrying rockets, others with bombs, and a very few used both, though switching between the two weapon fittings often took too long to be practical once in the field,[86] such as the landing grounds in the Normandy beachhead. One Typhoon pilot stated that the plane needed 'due respect. You didn't pay much respect to a Hurricane because she was a lady but with the Typhoon you had to obey all the rules if you wanted to live'.[87] Another pilot said, 'As a flying machine I preferred the Spitfire because it was lighter and you felt more a part of it but in the Typhoon you were controlling it but you didn't feel as if it was part of you.'[88] Compared to the Typhoon though, the Spitfire was described as 'very tiny' and the Hurricane was 'a beautiful aircraft to fly although she was terribly slow ... Compared to the Hurricane the Typhoon was a horrendous beast, much bigger and much heavier'.[89] However, in comparison with the Spitfire, the Typhoon had the thick and stable Hawker wing with four 20-mm cannon, one pilot recalling that it was 'a very much better gun platform, in that you could almost write your name with the guns, because the wings didn't flex and you could shoot pretty straight'.[90]

451 Squadron had a very close connection to the Typhoon, though they never flew them operationally. Backed up by 103 Maintenance Unit, the squadron participated in trials of the Typhoon Mk IB in North Africa in the second half of 1943 to test the engine filter. The test involved three aircraft (serials

R8891, DN323 and ES906) and these were accompanied by representatives from Hawker and Napier, some ground crew with Typhoon training as well as an experienced Typhoon pilot, FO Myall. The aircraft were flown from Casablanca, Morocco, to Aboukir, Egypt, in stages for a total of about 12 hours' flying time,[91] definitely a test in itself.

The pilots from 451 Squadron flew the Typhoons from LG 106 Idku, gradually getting to know the aircraft and their handling characteristics. They were made aware of the directions from Fighter Command regarding proper use of the aircraft, one document containing the line 'Remember the Hun is no fool. He will get you unless you use all the advantages God and Hawkers have given you.' This was followed a few sentences later by 'A note of warning. Remember that you are flying a heavy aircraft. Violent manoeuvres at low level are not, repeat not, encouraged. The country would like some value for the time and money expended.'[92] Presumably they were referring to pilots as well as the aircraft.

Flt Lt Ray Hudson was given command of the detachment from 451 Squadron and was accompanied by FOs Bann, Schofield and Thompson, FSs Davis and Hough and Sgt Pennell.[93] During the trials, the Vokes air filters fitted in the UK were found to be unsuitable as they tended to become soaked in fuel and/or oil, and therefore catch fire whenever the engine blew back, and this could happen on the ground or during flight. Local alterations to the filters requiring testing were made at Aboukir (famous for the Aboukir filter fitted to Spitfires). By late August over 164 hours of flying had been done with the three Typhoons and several filters had been tested, with some found to be satisfactory and others not. A report submitted by Flt Lt Hudson on 13 August 1943 concluded that 'In general, the Typhoon appears to be a very suitable aircraft for work in the Middle East theatre'. A later report submitted on 21 August 1943 stated:

> The aircraft have been reasonably trouble free during the trials and two have flown approximately 100 hours each in Africa ... Performance is up to the standard obtained in U.K. The general condition of the a/c is quite good, and the exterior finish seems to last longer in this climate than in U.K.[94]

However, only one of the three aircraft was serviceable at the time of submission. Testing of the aircraft also included firing the cannon in desert conditions and several stoppages occurred. An inspection of the weapons and ammunition found them to be poorly maintained and a written complaint was made through the chain of command, stating that even though the aircraft were not in an operational squadron, they still needed proper weapons maintenance. As a result of the complaint, an additional warrant officer from the Armament Inspection Unit was posted to the trial section to ensure proper standards were maintained. During the trials the engine of EJ906 reached an oil consumption of about 150 per cent expected and the aircraft was not used past that point.[95]

In the end, the Typhoon was kept in North-west Europe and had a standout role to play in Operation *Overlord* and the follow-on operations across Europe to the end of the war, though pilot casualties and aircraft losses were very high: almost 70 aircraft were lost in June 1944, with just under 60 lost in July followed over 90 in August. In late 1944 and early 1945 volunteers were called for from Spitfire squadrons—the experienced pilots in Typhoon squadrons were being lost at an incredible rate, but no one wanted to switch jobs and trade their nimble, high-flying Spitfire for a big and heavy anti-aircraft magnet.[96] By September 1945 though, no Typhoon squadrons remained within 2 TAF. The last of the 3,317 Typhoons built was delivered in November 1945.[97]

While the Hurricane and Spitfire defeated the Luftwaffe during the Battle of Britain, the war at sea posed another challenge. A short range was not a great handicap for a purely defensive fighter when based on land, but how could aircraft with such short ranges be useful elsewhere? The Seafire and Hurricat were proposed solutions to that problem. The first to enter service was the Hurricat, the name modified to represent its method of operation—it was launched from a catapult off specially modified freighters. The 200 Hurricanes modified to carry out this role were formed into the Merchant Ship Fighter Unit (MSFU), a unit controlled by the Fleet Air Arm (FAA) and carried aboard Catapult Assisted Merchantmen (CAM). The first CAM was operational in May 1941 and the first Hurricat victory took place on 3 August that year when an Australian pilot, Lt Robert Everett, shot down a Fw 200 Condor.[98] Piloting a Hurricat was brave work—there was no landing back on a merchant ship, the pilot had to ditch as close to the vessel as they could (assuming it survived the attack the Hurricat was launched to intercept) and then get out of the plane and be taken aboard, rather than sink to the bottom with the plane. The Hurricat was a one-shot weapon.

Fortunately, they were only a temporary measure, and CAMs were phased out from mid-1942 onwards as more aircraft carriers, in the form of converted merchantmen, became available. The Sea Hurricane Mk IB was introduced in July 1941 and was followed by the Sea Hurricane Mk IC with four 20-mm cannon in 1942, and then the Sea Hurricane IIC. But, like the Seafires, they were never really suited to the role, though to make up for their short range, they were regularly fitted with 44-gallon drop tanks under each wing.[99] In total 537 Sea Hurricanes were made or modified, the last being withdrawn from service in April 1944.[100]

At the time of Operation *Husky*, the invasion of Sicily in July 1943, more than two-thirds of Spitfire squadrons in the Mediterranean and North Africa were still operating Mk Vs.[101] From the Mk V also came the Seafire, and though its narrow undercarriage was a disadvantage when landing on aircraft carriers, its performance in the air was what mattered most, initially at least. The Seafires first saw action during Operation *Torch* on 8 November 1942 during the invasion of North Africa, and they were backed up by Sea Hurricanes.[102] While five squadrons supported Operation *Torch*, 106 flew from five aircraft carriers on the first day of the Allied landings at Salerno in Italy on 9 September 1943. Within two days, 42 had been lost to landing accidents.[103] It was usually the case that more Seafires were lost due to damage during landings than enemy action and, especially at the end of the war, the British Pacific Fleet fared much better with the heavier and sturdier F4U Corsair. The first unit to be equipped with Seafires was 807 Squadron Fleet Air Arm, and, while it was a relatively popular plane, it just did not have the flight-time endurance required of fleet planes and so failed to shake off one of the most common criticisms of the Spitfire.[104] The first real Seafire was built in April 1943, all previous Seafires being Spitfire conversions. In total 25 Fleet Air Arm squadrons were equipped with Seafires from 1942 to 1950.[105]

Pre-Mk VII Spitfires can also be identified from underneath or from the front by the radiator underneath the starboard wing in a rectangular fairing and the tubular oil cooler under the port wing, whereas Spitfires from the Mk VII onwards had rectangular fairings under both wings.[106] The starboard fairing held the radiator while the other contained the intercooler and oil cooler. While giving a more symmetrical view of the Spitfire, the twin rectangular fairings were also found to balance the Spitfire when diving, reducing the yaw experienced in earlier marks.[107] It is also noteworthy that Spitfire marks did not always progress in numerical order as some developments were long-term plans and others (such as the Mk IX) were pushed through, while some features, such as the broad chord rudder were applied to later productions runs of the same aircraft. Thus, early versions of the Mk IX can be distinguished from the later ones. The early batches of Mk IXs were in fact modified Mk V airframes, and retained the rounded rudder of the Mk V, the later Mk IXs having the broader and more pointed rudder common to later Spitfires. The Mk V was also the first Spitfire to be fitted with a 50-series Merlin, those having the negative-g carburettor which ensured that the engine did not cut out if the aircraft flew upside down for a few seconds or nosed over into a dive, referred to as 'bunting'.[108]

Outside the UK, the greatest need for the Spitfire was on Malta, where Hurricanes had been operating since August 1940,[109] but it was not until 7 March 1942 that the first Spitfires, all Mk VBs, arrived after launching from the aircraft carrier HMS *Eagle*.[110] This first batch of 16 Spitfires was steadily reinforced until there were five squadrons on the island by the end of May. Only in June 1942 did the first Spitfire squadron (601) transfer from Malta to North Africa, and even then only because the situation in North Africa was so desperate, with the loss of Tobruk and the Afrika Korps on the advance again.[111] Two squadrons of Mk Vs had arrived in Egypt in April 1942, and even 42 of the 48 Spitfires destined for Australia were diverted to North Africa in an attempt to save the situation.[112] This reluctance to send Spitfires overseas was certainly a detriment to the forces serving outside the UK. For many months—and even longer in such places as Malta—the Hurricane had to bear most of the burden.

With consideration to the desert, certain additions were made to Mk V Spitfires sent there. They were fitted out with emergency rations, a drinking-water tank and water bottle, screwdriver, adjustable spanner and pliers, Very pistol and flares, signalling strips and a mirror. The cockpit was modified with an additional ventilator for use when flying at low levels or during taxiing or take-off.[113]

One argument put forth by Fighter Command was that the Spitfire was not tough enough to withstand conditions outside the UK.[114] Spitfires were needed for the Circus operations over France, a faulty, not-quite Battle of

Britain in reverse. But the Luftwaffe was not targeting the UK, they were in Soviet Untion and the Mediterranean, so keeping extra Spitfires at home was not going to help the war effort. However, Fighter Command kept the Spitfires largely to itself, and when it came time for aid to be sent to the Soviet Union, they mainly sent Hurricanes, 2,952 all told and, while the Soviets appreciated them, they really wanted Spitfires, and when they did get some Spitfire Mk Vs, they were reconditioned, not straight from the factory.[115] And yet the Hurricane was tougher than the Spitfire. A New Zealander fighting with the RAF in India, Flt Lt Lawrence Weggery, wanted a Spitfire but was told that the temperatures in which they were operating were too high for the Spitfire to cope with. The Hurricanes his squadron was equipped with blew air through the radiator to help keep the glycol temperature down, whereas the Spitfire did not do likewise as the radiator for the Mk V then available was under the starboard wing and received no such benefit.[116]

One aspect where the Hurricane outclassed the Spitfire in the early to mid-part of the war was in weight of armament. Already armed with four 20-mm cannon in the Mk IIC, and carrying bombs for ground support operations in 1941, Sidney Camm and the Vickers company conspired to add a 40-mm cannon under each wing to create a tank-busting Hurricane, later designated the IID. These were fired via a button on the throttle, rather than the usual button on the control column. Only the thick wing of a Hurricane could stand such an additional load, and a total of 800 were built, serving primarily in North Africa, where pilots were instructed to make their attacks at a height of just 15 to 20 ft.[117] Not satisfied with this, rockets were also tested on a Hurricane in 1942, and these were in operation by June 1943, though they only served with a few squadrons and were replaced by the much-improved Hawker Typhoon.[118] But the thick wing also meant that the Hurricane was a more stable gun platform overall, Douglas Bader had flown both early models of Hurricane and Spitfire and favoured the Hurricane in this regard.[119] In fact, Denys Gillam rated the Hurricane 'the finest gun platform of them all'. In his mind there was no doubt that 'plane for plane it was the stronger aircraft.'[120] The clustering of the machine guns together towards the centre of the aircraft, compared to the spread of those fitted to Spitfires, meant that the weight of fire was greater, as the Spitfire's wings flexed more easily and therefore the rounds fired by the outer machine guns were less likely to be on target.

The Hurricane Mk III should have followed but was not developed and so next came the Mk IV which was a dedicated ground-attack aircraft with two 40-mm cannon, two .303 machine guns and options for bombs or rockets on the wings. The Mk IV was powered by a Merlin 27 engine and the plane was fitted with extra armour, protection for the pilots during the low-flying missions for which the plane was designed. Five hundred and twenty-four were built and operated in Europe, the Mediterranean and the Far East.[121]

The Mk VII was a purpose-built, high-altitude version of the Spitfire, designed to shoot down Luftwaffe reconnaissance aircraft and bombers harassing the British at home and in North Africa (they carried only one bomb and never ventured over in squadron strength). It was built with a pressurised cockpit and wingtip extensions, giving them a distinct point at the tips.[122] In addition, the Mk VII featured a retractable tail wheel (for better aerodynamics) and an additional internal fuel tank, with consumption being higher in the climb to altitudes over 40,000 ft. A few Mk VIs (from which the Mk VII was developed) were sent to Egypt but they were too heavy for the task, so a few Mk Vs were modified and stripped down of everything except the essentials. After first operating singly, they modified their tactics and eventually operated in pairs—one serving as 'Marker' (who was in radio contact with ground control), and the other as 'Striker' (waiting higher and off to one side away from the target).[123] About 100 Mk VIs were built between April and October 1942. While only 140 Mk VIIs were built, the last being delivered in May 1944, its thunder was stolen by a modified Mk IX (no Mk VIIs were operationally ready at the time) which took credit for the highest aerial combat of the war.

On 12 September 1942, FO Emanuel Galitzine engaged a Ju 86R at 43,500 ft in the lightened Mk IX, and had one of his cannon not jammed, he may well have shot it down. But, despite some damage, it returned safely to base in France.[124] This engagement proved that these high-altitude flights were no longer risk-free for the Luftwaffe. The Mk VII was withdrawn from service in January 1945.[125] Perhaps the worst feature of the Mk VI and VII was that, to ensure the cockpit maintained its cabin pressure, the canopy had to be bolted on when the pilot got in.[126]

The Type 360 Mk VIII was equipped with either a Merlin 61 (1,565 hp) or 63 (1,710 hp) engine and was paired with a four-bladed propeller.[127] It was essentially a Mk VII but with regular wings and cockpit. The first of 1,652[128] was built in November 1942 and, due to their longer range, were all sent to squadrons operating outside the UK.[129] They were modified for tropical use and these replaced the earlier Mk VCs in service with Australian and British squadrons operating against the Japanese from Darwin—245 of which (plus a single Mk VB) had been delivered to Australia from August 1942 onwards. The Mk VIII was a welcome replacement in Australia. When a Mk VIII and Mk IX (both fitted with Merlin 63 engines to minimise obvious performance issues) were tested against each other in July 1943, the difference was found to be largely negligible, though the Mk VIII performed slightly better at higher altitudes and the Mk IX had a better roll, as the Mk VIII wing had shorter ailerons.[130]

The capture of an Fw 190A belonging to JG26 on 23 June 1942[131] led to the production of the Type 361 Mk IX Spitfire. This had a strengthened airframe, a four-bladed propeller and a 60-series Merlin engine. Several variants were produced, including a low-level, clipped-wing version and a high-level version with extended wingtips.[132] The 60-series Merlin necessitated a slightly longer nose, but this was not an issue[133] and the improved engine more than made up for any other concerns. These 60-series Merlins also had a two-speed, two-stage supercharger for increased performance and there were more settings and tailoring options.[134] The plane could also carry an additional ten gallons of fuel, increasing the range a little more[135] and 5,665 of them were built. While early Spitfires used A and B to differentiate between the wing armaments, for the Mk IX, A and B referred to the installation of different models of Merlin.[136] Don Andrews described the Mk IXA and B as 'both glorious aircraft to fly', and overall the Spitfire 'was a magnificent aircraft, you felt so much in command of it'.[137]

The first operational squadron equipped with Mk IXs was 64 Squadron in July 1942.[138] Fortunately for those flying the Mk IX, it replaced the Mk V which was being outperformed by the Focke-Wulfs in the cross-Channel fighter sweeps both sides were conducting. This led to the Luftwaffe being surprised on several occasions, expecting Mk V performance but being on the receiving end of a Mk IX, there being very little to distinguish the two until well within firing range. Thus, the German pilots had to make a decision: to warily treat all Spitfires as Mk IXs or risk a beating by assuming that they were up against the inferior Mk Vs and only learn the truth when it was too late. The Allies, on the other hand, had no such issues, as an Fw 190 and Bf 109 were quite different in appearance and combat could be declined if the Allied pilots were in an inferior position.[139]

In that same month, a Mk IX with a 61-series Merlin was flown against the captured Fw 190A. The test found that at varying altitudes, the speed difference was not more than 10 mph and the Spitfire was usually superior, but only by a small margin. In a climb, the Fw 190A was slightly better due to its superior acceleration, but not remarkably so, while in a dive the Fw 190A was better, especially in the early stages. The roll of the Fw 190A was far superior to that of the Mk IX, and the overall manoeuvrability was superior, except in the case of turning circles, where the Mk IX could get inside the Fw 190A for the all-important killing shot. However, the ability of the Spitfire to turn was one of its most well-known traits, and experienced Luftwaffe pilots would likely have avoided this at all costs in any case. One noticeable advantage of the Fw 190A was its ability to get away from a Spitfire by doing a flick-roll in the opposite direction to the angle of attack and then diving away, so Allied pilots were warned to expect this move.[140]

An instruction was issued to all Spitfire pilots in August 1942 giving advice on dealing with the new threat from the cockpit of a Spitfire. Paragraph two of the document included the instruction: 'To defeat this aircraft and to avoid casualties on our side, our aircraft must fly as fast as possible whenever they are in the combat zone.' The document recognised that pilots had previously been instructed to economise and save fuel 'but it is essential, as soon as they are liable to be detected, that they open up to maximum power for duration flying'. Pilots were reminded that the Spitfire's acceleration is relatively poor, and they should avoid cruising when there was a possibility of engagement. The instruction continued with safety tips, concluding with: 'when in the vicinity of Huns, fly maximum everything and in good time'.[141] A notice distributed to Spitfire Mk V pilots in the Middle East titled 'Who's Afraid of the Little Focke Wulf' echoed these instructions and emphasised the turning ability of the Spitfire against the Focke-Wulf: 'The Spitfire V's only tactical advantage over the F.W. 190 in the air is its ability to turn in a smaller circle, but that's a lot'.[142]

The first Mk IXs were delivered to squadrons based in the Mediterranean and Middle East in January 1943.[143] Often in the role of a fighter-bomber, the Mk IX had the capacity to carry bombs but it was not permitted to do so in combination with a centreline bomb or the 90-gallon 'jet' or 'slipper' tank. In September 1944 this restriction was removed, provided that the Mk IX was upgraded with Mk VIII wheels and tyres and with take-off at a maximum weight of 8,700 lb from a smooth surface only. The instruction also reminded pilots that flight with the drop tank remained 'limited to straight and level' and that the drop tank should be jettisoned before attempting dive-bombing.[144]

The Mk IX seems to be regarded by many pilots as the peak of Spitfire development. AVM 'Johnnie' Johnson was quoted as saying 'fighter pilots of every nationality thought the Spitfire Mk IX was the best close-in fighter of them all'.[145] Another pilot, in correspondence with AVM Johnson was quoted as saying: 'I flew most of the various marks of Spitfires, but I felt sort of invincible in the Spitfire Mk IXB. It was a beautiful aeroplane and I was very happy to fly and fight with her.'[146]

Joe Barrington flew with 451 (RAAF) Squadron from Corsica supporting operations in Italy and later the landings in the south of France for Operation *Dragoon*. He'd learned on old Mk I and V Spitfires at Abu Sueir in Egypt, but was introduced to the Mk IX on Corsica—his logbook recording his first flight in one on 11 July 1944 with the note 'Very Nice'.[147] Of the Spitfire (generally) he would later say:

> It was such a manoeuvrable aircraft, you could do anything with it but you're not worth a stamp as a fighter when you're carrying bombs ... the greatest pleasure was to go up when there was a blue sky, full of towering cumulus clouds which looked like mountains and valleys to fly around, and for sheer pleasure was to fly around for pleasure, not for war.

However, for war:

> They taught me in OTU, if somebody got on your tail, the best way to avoid it, if you could, was you go into a tight turn, you try and turn out of his range and if you go into a very tight turn where you've got no real support to the aircraft, it stalls. It's called a high-speed stall, and one wing drops down and you're spinning off. Now if somebody's trying to get you in his sights, this is something he never expects and you're out of trouble, instantly.

Fortunately, he never had to use it.[148]

The Type 366 Mk XII was fitted with a Griffon II or IV engine of 1,720 hp and most were clipped-wing models. The higher speeds and performance of the clipped wing at low levels made them very effective at intercepting the V-1 buzz-bombs, also known as Doodlebugs or Divers, launched at London from Europe.[149] Though this was their role from 1944 onwards, they were initially ordered as a counter to the tip-and-run campaign[150] waged by the Luftwaffe against coastal towns from March 1942 to June 1943.[151] The Mk XII entered service in early 1943, though the first came off the production lines in August 1942.[152] Griffon-engined Spitfires can be differentiated from those powered by Merlins by the additional fairing above the six exhausts on each side of the fuselage. The first batch delivered to 41 Squadron were quite troublesome, being converted Mk Vs and there were many engine and fuel problems, the squadron being given six weeks to acclimatise themselves and become operational before moving to the south-east of England, where most of the action was. Later Mk XIIs were converted from Mk VIII airframes and this was a much more agreeable state of affairs. It was a good plane to fly and had a slightly better forward view than Merlin-equipped Spitfires. While operating in the south-east against the tip-and-run raids, they did have run-ins with Typhoons,; apparently anything with a square-cut wingtip was automatically identified as a Bf 109 or Fw 190.[153] Unfortunately for the RAF, one pilot was shot down and captured in mid-1943 whilst in possession of the manufacturer's handling notes for a Griffon II engine, and a series of memos were distributed reinforcing the requirement that no such documents be taken on flights which may result in a pilot being captured. Indeed, all pilots were reminded to empty their pockets of all unnecessary documents prior to flight.[154]

The Type 373 Mk XIV was based on the Mk VIII and had a Griffon 65 engine of 2,035 hp with a five-bladed propeller and a larger fin and rudder. Early production models had the regular Spitfire bubble canopy, while later models had a teardrop canopy that gave better all-round vision, similar to the Hawker Tempest and P-51D Mustang.[155] They were first operational with 610 Squadron in January 1944, but were not operational in the Far East until August 1945 and saw no action there.[156] In early 1944 the Air Fighting Development Unit at Duxford tested a new Mk XIV against a Mk IX, Bf 109G and Fw 190A. Against the Mk IX it was judged to be an overall improvement and 30–35 mph faster at all heights and turns to port were noticeably better than those to starboard, though the longer nose hindered the forward view. Against the Fw 190A it was judged to be better, and estimated to be equal to the Fw 190D, with a speed advantage of 20–60 mph depending on altitude. In typical Spitfire fashion it was able to out-turn the Fw 190A, but had to be wary of the flick-roll and dive getaway tactic that the Fw 190A's superior roll gave it. Against the Bf 190G it was 10–40 mph faster depending on altitude and could out-turn, out-climb and out-roll this ageing rival.[157] Though not identified by mark number, the arrival of the Mk XIV in RAF service was announced in Australia in the *Sydney Morning Herald* on 9 March 1944 with the article 'Powerful Spitfire'. The Griffon was described as having a cylinder size 23 per cent greater than that of the Merlin but the horsepower was not divulged and was described as 'still a secret', the new Spitfire being described as 'the most powerful of all Spitfires'.[158]

The Type 361 Mk XVI was the last of the Merlin-powered Spitfires and consisted of a US-built Packard-Merlin 266 (equivalent to a Merlin 66) and the airframe of a Mk IX. One thousand fifty-four were built in two different models, a XVIC, with a clipped wing, standard canopy and rounded, early IX-style fin and the XVIE with a regular wing, teardrop canopy and late Mk IX pointed fin.[159] Sid Handsaker first went solo on a Mk VB in January 1945 at 53 OTU in Kirton-in-Lindsay. These were old training aircraft and when he arrived at 451 Squadron in April they were equipped with Mk XVIs. After his third flight in one he recorded in his pilot's logbook: 'Much heavier a/c than Mk V. Lovely to fly.'[160] The Mk XVI was first delivered to squadrons in October 1944, 453 and 602 Squadrons being two of the first, and they were used primarily to dive-bomb V-2 sites.[161]

These Spitfires were also fitted with a special two-way automatic bomb distributor. This switch had two settings. In the 'up' position, marked 'Single & Salvo', all bombs were released simultaneously. In the 'down' position, marked Port and Starboard, the port and centreline bombs were released 0.3 seconds before the bomb on the starboard rack. This produced a greater spread, the spread increasing in proportion to the speed of the aircraft,[162] and hopefully increasing the chance of an effective hit, especially on the narrow railway lines that led to a number of the V-2 sites.

The Packard-Merlin 266 in these MK XVIs had sparkplug trouble though, which caused rough running of the engine. An instruction was issued that they should be changed during the 20-hour inspections instead of every 40 hours. To reduce the possibility of sparkplug trouble, the whole set was to be changed on each occasion. To prevent the engine fouling that had caused issues with the Mk XVIs, pilots were instructed to run the engines up to 2,350 rpm with +9 lb boost and, during flight when practical, to clear the engines every 15 minutes by opening up to a minimum of 2,650 rpm with +7 lb boost.[163] This resulted in a stream of black muck being thrown out of the exhausts and formations opened up when this procedure took place so as not to soil the windscreen of nearby aircraft, or have the engines of fellow pilots ingest what had just been thrown out of the plane in front.[164]

Photo-reconnaissance (PR) developed slowly in the interwar years but accelerated with the onset of the Second World War, and both the Hurricane and Spitfire played their role. However, since flying straight and level (regardless of altitude) was the order of the day, speed was much prized. In that speed lay protection. As previously mentioned, the Spitfire was held back in the UK from overseas deployment, so in North Africa, it fell to the Hurricane to carry out this dangerous task. But speed was not a primary attribute of the Hurricane.

These early photo-reconnaissance Hurricanes were operated by a few squadrons, including 451 Squadron. They were otherwise standard Hurricanes fitted out with three extra cameras. This meant they were heavier, and therefore slower. In 1941 the Hurricane fitout consisted of three cameras in the fuselage behind the pilot—one facing directly down, and the others angled out to each side to create a wide area of coverage. To operate them the pilot pressed a button, that was all. But the weight was a problem, and dragged the tail of the aircraft down, so that to compensate for this the squadron fitted elastic cords to hold the stick forwards and take some of the strain off the pilot. As the Hurricanes were so (relatively) slow, they took along an escort whose job it was to keep an eye out for Axis aircraft and, if necessary, fight them off. Other Hurricanes were subsequently modified, including one designed to fly at 30,000 ft with extra fuel tanks in the wings to give it a longer range, but it really was a task for another aircraft.[165]

A few PR variants of the Spitfire were built, many of which were unarmed. Early versions of these were converted Mk Is and the Spitfire PR Mk IV was built with extra fuel capacity and no armament whatsoever.[166] An Australian, Wing Commander Sidney Cotton, paved the way for Spitfire PR operations, having done much of his own freelance work, essentially spying on the Luftwaffe before the war started.[167] The unit he commanded went by a number of titles, such as No. 2 Camouflage Unit, which were designed to distract from their true role. They eventually became designated as Photographic Reconnaissance Units (PRUs) and it was in these units that the white, pink and blue Spitfires originated. An early, armed Spitfire could barely reach Paris from England but, by comparison, an unarmed Spitfire with 90 additional gallons of fuel could reach Sweden, Berlin or Italy. Though not equipped with Spitfires from the outset, once they were the mainstay of the unit, Cotton noted that it was easier to train a pilot to fly a Spitfire than to get a Spitfire pilot with the 'wrong' attitude to do PRU work well.[168] Later marks of PR Spitfires carried some armament, but fuel was one of the most important considerations, as reconnaissance had to cover as much of Europe as possible.

The PRU Spitfire had to make it back to base to be of any value. If any other plane was shot down after it had dropped its bomb on a bridge, that was totally different—the bridge might be destroyed and the sortie was done but, until the film was developed from the PRU Spitfire that made it home, nothing had been achieved. Flying PRU sorties also included finding the contrail layer—that point of altitude where a plane leaves a trail behind it, which a PRU aircraft could not afford to do—then climbing up or dropping down another thousand feet to provide a buffer zone. Mirrors on PRU Spitfires weren't for looking out for other aircraft, they were for spotting your contrail.[169]

The Type 509 Trainer Mk IX was actually built after the war ended and had a second seating position behind and slightly higher than the normal pilot's position. The timing of the arrival of this mark is important and gives an indication of the difficulty of flying a Spitfire for the first time. Despite all the ground training, cockpit familiarisation and taxiing practice, the first time a pilot flew a Spitfire (or Hurricane for that matter) they were on their own! Spitfire modifications and marks progressed throughout and beyond the Second World War, but they became less Spitfire-like. The final three marks of Spitfire, of which the Mk 21 was the first, were all armed with four 20-mm cannon, two in each wing, but fewer than 500 were made of all three marks.[170] A Mk 24 was judged to be too heavy and unbalanced compared to previous marks and, while it flew well enough, it had perhaps progressed too far for some.[171] Likewise, a Mk 21 flown by Sir Brian Inglis (who joined 453 Squadron just before Normandy) was judged to be not as good as earlier marks, though with a Griffon engine he stated it was possible to take off without full throttle, something he hadn't done previously.[172]

In total, some 22,789 Spitfires of all marks and variants were built, plus 14,533 Hurricanes of all marks, some of which were manufactured in Canada.[173] The last Hurricane (PZ865) was completed on 12 August 1944, and Sidney Camm was present for the event.[174] The Hurricane had long since passed its prime, but made a steady contribution to the war effort, and remained in service until 1947.[175] In comparison, Spitfires continued to be manufactured until February 1948, when the last Spitfire built was delivered to the RAF. The FAA took delivery of the last Seafire in January 1949.[176] These aircraft would continue to serve for a number of years, but the jet age had arrived and, eventually, most would be scrapped.

Sidney Camm passed away on 12 March 1966, though not before contributing to a new generation of aircraft: designing the Hawker Hunter and the Hawker Siddeley (later British Aerospace) Harrier.[177] Both he and Reginal Mitchell had truly made their marks on aviation—and world—history. Group Captain W.G.G. Duncan Smith DSO DFC, a Battle of Britain veteran who went on to fly Spitfires in the Mediterranean later in the war, perhaps summed it up best when he wrote:

> If it had not been for men such as Camm and Mitchell the outcome of the war might have been very different. No praise is too high for them and their chief test pilots, Philip Lucas and Jeffrey Quill. Their Spitfires and Hurricanes have assured them of an honoured place in history.[178]

AIRCRAFT STATISTICS AND FEATURES[179]

MARK	ENGINE	STATISTICS	DESIGN NOTE
Spitfire Mk IA	1,030-hp RR Merlin II, III	Wingspan: 36 ft 10 in Length: 29 ft 11 in Ceiling: 34,500 ft Max speed: 362 mph at 18,500 ft	8 x .303 machine guns (A Wing)
Spitfire Mk IB	1,030-hp RR Merlin III		Initially equipped with 2 x 20 mm but then upgraded to 2 x 20 mm and 4 x .303 (B Wing)
Hurricane Mk I	1,030-hp RR Merlin III	Wingspan: 40ft Length: 31 ft 6 in	8 x .303 machine guns
Spitfire Mk IIA	1,175-hp RR Merlin XII		Produced at Castle Bromwich
Spitfire Mk IIA (LR)	1,175-hp RR Merlin XII	Max speed: 328 mph at 16,500 ft	30-gal fuel tank fixed under port wing; not a popular decision with pilots
Spitfire Mk IIB	1,175-hp RR Merlin XII		B wing version of Mk II
Hurricane Mk IIA	Merlin XX	1,480 hp	8 x .303 machine guns
Hurricane Mk IIB	Merlin XX		12 x .303 machine guns
Hurricane Mk IIC	Merlin XX		4 x 20-mm cannon
Spitfire F. Mk VB	1,470-hp RR Merlin 45 1,415-hp RR Merlin 46	Wingspan: 36 ft 10 in Length: 29 ft 11 in Ceiling: 37,500 ft Max speed: 371 mph at 20,000 ft	Merlin 46 for higher altitudes
Spitfire LF Mk VB	1,585-hp RR Merlin 45M		Merlin 45M for lower altitudes; some LFs were 'clipped'
Spitfire F. Mk VC	1,470-hp RR Merlin 45, 50, 50A, 55, 56		Universal Wing (C Wing); 84 gals of fuel carried internally

MARK	ENGINE	STATISTICS	DESIGN NOTE
Hurricane Mk IID	Merlin XX		2 x .303 machine guns and 2 x 40-mm cannon under wings
Hurricane Mk IV	Merlin XX		2 x .303 machine guns and 2 x 40-mm cannon or rockets
Typhoon Mk IB	Napier Sabre II	Max speed: 376 mph at 8,500 ft 394 mph at 20,200 ft	4 x 20-mm cannon; additional bombs or rockets depending on squadron task
Spitfire Mk VI	1,415-hp RR Merlin 47	Wingspan: 40 ft 2 in Ceiling: 39,200 ft	Pressurised cabin; 4-bladed propeller
Spitfire Mk VII	1,710-hp RR Merlin 64		Pressurised cabin and 2-speed, 2-stage Merlin
Spitfire F.Mk VIII	1,565-hp RR Merlin 61 1,650-hp RR Merlin 63 1,710-hp RR Merlin 63A 1,720-hp RR Merlin 66		120–123 gals of fuel of which 26–27 were in wing tanks (figures vary)
Spitfire F. Mk IXC	1,565-hp RR Merlin 61 1,650-hp RR Merlin 63 1,710-hp RR Merlin 63A	Wingspan: 36 ft 10 in Length: 31 ft 4 in Ceiling: 43,000 ft Max speed: 408 mph at 25,000 ft	
Spitfire F. Mk IXE	1,565-hp RR Merlin 61 1,650-hp RR Merlin 63 1,710-hp RR Merlin 63A		2 x 20-mm cannon and 2 x .50-cal machine guns (E Wing)
Spitfire Mk XII	1,735-hp RR Griffon III, IV	Max speed: 393 mph at 18,000 ft	Griffon rotated in opposite direction to Merlin

MARK	ENGINE	STATISTICS	DESIGN NOTE
Mk XIVC	2,035-hp RR Griffon 65	Wingspan: 36 ft 10 in Length: 32 ft 8 in Ceiling: 43,000 ft Max speed: 439 mph at 24,500 ft	C Wing
Spitfire FR Mk XIVE	2,035-hp RR Griffon 65	Max speed 448 mph at 25,400 ft	Teardrop canopy like Typhoons and Tempests; armed reconnaissance version fitted with camera
Spitfire LF Mk XVIE	1,580-hp Packard Merlin 266		Packard-Merlins were manufactured in the USA.
Spitfire Mk 21	2,035-hp RR Griffon 61		
Spitfire PR (Photo Recon) Type A	1,030-hp RR Merlin III		
Spitfire PR Type B	1,030-hp RR Merlin III		Extra 30 gals of fuel behind pilot
Spitfire PR Type C	1,030-hp RR Merlin III		Additional fuselage fuel as in Type B plus port wing tank as in Mk IIA (LR)
Spitfire PR Mk X	1,475-hp RR Merlin 77		Pressurised cabin and 2 speed, 2 stage Merlin
Spitfire PR Mk XIX	2,035-hp RR Griffon 65 or 66	Max speed 445 mph at 42,600 ft	254-gal fuel capacity plus optional drop tank
Spitfire Seafire Mk IB	1,470-hp RR Merlin 45 1,415-hp RR Merlin 46		Conversions from Mk VB
Spitfire Seafire Mk F.III	1,470-hp RR Merlin 55		Folding C Wing
Sea Hurricane	1,030-hp RR Merlin III		Wings did not fold

NOTES

CHAPTER 1: THE DESERT: FORMATION AND EARLY OPERATIONS: SEPTEMBER 1939 TO JANUARY 1942

1. Douglas Gillison, *Australia in the War of 1939-1945, Series Three: Air Volume I: Royal Australian Air Force 1939-1942*, Australian War Memorial, Canberra, 1962, p. 62.
2. NAA: A1196, 36-501-160.
3. NAA: A1196, 36-501-160.
4. NAA: A1196, 36-501-160.
5. NAA: A1196, 36-501-160.
6. NAA: A1196, 36-501-160.
7. NAA: A9186, 136.
8. AWFA: John Culbert.
9. Personal File – Pelly (NAA: A12372, R/210084/H).
10. NAA: A9186, 136.
11. John Herington, *Australia in the War of 1939-1945, Series Three: Air, Volume III: Air War Against Germany & Italy 1939-1943*, Australian War Memorial, Canberra, 1954, p. 97.
12. 451 Squadron Association, 451 Squadron R.A.A.F. Middle East Forces 1941 – 1946 Anecdotes, (2002), p. 69.
13. TNA: AIR 27
14. NAA: A9186, 136 and Herington, *Air War Against Germany & Italy 1939-1943*, pp. 98-101.
15. 451 Squadron Association, 451 Squadron R.A.A.F. Middle East Forces 1941 – 1946 Anecdotes, (2002), p. 23.
16. AWFA: John Culbert.
17. AWFA: Edward Smith.
18. John Delaney, *Fighting the Desert Fox: Rommel's Campaigns in North Africa April 1941 to August 1942*, Cassell & Co, London, 1998, (1999), pp. 28-29 and Peter Cochrane, *Tobruk 1941*, ABC Books, Sydney, 2005, p. viii.
19. NAA: A9186, 136.
20. Author interview.
21. NAA: A9186, 136.
22. Hutley – Personal File and Kirkham – Personal File
23. Kirkham–Personal File and Hudson – Personal File
24. NAA: A9186, 136.
25. NAA: A9186, 136.
26. Geoffrey Morley-Mower, *Messerschmitt Roulette*, Phalanx, St Paul, 1993, pp. 1-17.
27. NAA: A9186, 136.
28. Morley-Mower, *Messerschmitt Roulette*, pp 27-33.
29. NAA: A9186, 136 and NAA: A9652.
30. NAA: A9186, 136.
31. Readett–Personal File and Rowlands – Personal File
32. NAA: A9186, 136.
33. NAA: A9186, 136.
34. Personal file – Readett.
35. NAA: A9186, 136 and Christopher Shores, Giovanni Massimello, and Russell Guest, *A History of the Mediterranean Air War 1940-1945 Volume One: North Africa June 1940–January 1942*, Grub Street, London, 2012, pp. 259-260.
36. Morley-Mower, *Messerschmitt Roulette*, pp. 62-63.
37. NAA: A9186, 136 and Shores *et al*, *A History of the Mediterranean Air War 1940-1945 Volume One: North Africa June 1940 – January 1942*, pp. 263-264.
38. Morley-Mower, *Messerschmitt Roulette*, pp. 68-79.
39. NAA: A9186, 136.
40. NAA: A9186, 136, TNA: AIR 27 and Shores *et al*, *A History of the Mediterranean Air War 1940-1945 Volume One: North Africa June 1940 – January 1942*, pp. 268, 270.
41. NAA: A9186, 136.
42. 451 Squadron Association, 451 Squadron R.A.A.F. Middle East Forces 1941 – 1946 Anecdotes, (2002), p. 23.
43. NAA: A9186, 136 and Shores *et al*, *A History of the Mediterranean Air War 1940-1945 Volume One: North Africa June 1940 –January 1942*, p. 275.

[44] Morley-Mower, *Messerschmitt Roulette*, pp. 90-91.
[45] NAA: A9186, 136.
[46] IWM: 8199.
[47] IWM: 8199.
[48] IWM: 8199.
[49] NAA: A9186, 136.
[50] Morley-Mower, *Messerschmitt Roulette*, pp. 93-97.
[51] IWM: 8199.
[52] Herington, *Air War Against Germany & Italy 1939-1943,* pp.193-196.
[53] Morley-Mower, *Messerschmitt Roulette*, pp, 99-115.
[54] IWM: 8199.
[55] NAA: A10605 1036/2.
[56] AWFA: Leonard Hayman, Personal File – Rowe and M. Baudot, H. Bernard, H. Brugmans, M. Foot, and H. Jacobsen, *The Historical Encyclopaedia of World War II*, Facts on File, New York, 1980, p. 306.
[57] 451 Squadron Association, 451 Squadron R.A.A.F. Middle East Forces 1941 – 1946 Anecdotes, (2002), p. 23.
[58] NAA: A9186, 136.
[59] 451 Squadron Association, 451 Squadron R.A.A.F. Middle East Forces 1941 – 1946 Anecdotes, (2002), p. 24.
[60] Herington, *Air War Against Germany & Italy 1939-1943,* p. 198.
[61] NAA: A9186, 136.
[62] Morley-Mower, *Messerschmitt Roulette*, pp. 131-134.
[63] IWM: 8199.
[64] NAA: A9186, 136 and Herington, *Air War Against Germany & Italy 1939-1943,* p. 202.
[65] 451 Squadron Association, 451 Squadron R.A.A.F. Middle East Forces 1941 – 1946 Anecdotes, (2002), p. 24.
[66] 451 Squadron Association, 451 Squadron R.A.A.F. Middle East Forces 1941 – 1946 Anecdotes, (2002), p. 24.
[67] NAA: A9186, 136 and 451 Squadron Association, 451 Squadron R.A.A.F. Middle East Forces 1941 – 1946 Anecdotes, (2002), p. 61.
[68] 451 Squadron Association, 451 Squadron R.A.A.F. Middle East Forces 1941 – 1946 Anecdotes, (2002) p. 24.
[69] NAA: A11305 79-P1 pt 1.
[70] NAA: A9186, 136.
[71] IWM: 8199.
[72] Ken W. Watts, *One Airman's War: An Australian Fighter Pilot's Experience of a Lifetime*, Perfect Print, 1988, pp. ii-5, and Personal File–Watts
[73] 451 Squadron Association, 451 Squadron R.A.A.F. Middle East Forces 1941 – 1946 Anecdotes, (2002), p. 24.
[74] 451 Squadron Association, 451 Squadron R.A.A.F. Middle East Forces 1941 – 1946 Anecdotes, (2002), pp. 24 and 61.
[75] Shores *et al*, *A History of the Mediterranean Air War 1940-1945 Volume One: North Africa June 1940 – January 1942,* pp. 372-375.
[76] NAA: A9186, 136.
[77] IWM: 8199.
[78] NAA: A9186, 136 and Herington, *Air War Against Germany & Italy 1939-1943,* pp. 207, 209.
[79] IWM: 8199.
[80] 451 Squadron Association, 451 Squadron R.A.A.F. Middle East Forces 1941 – 1946 Anecdotes, (2002), p. 25.
[81] 451 Squadron Association, 451 Squadron R.A.A.F. Middle East Forces 1941 – 1946 Anecdotes, (2002), p. 26.
[82] Herington, *Air War Against Germany & Italy 1939-1943,* pp. 120-121.
[83] NAA: A9186, 136.
[84] NAA: A9186, 136 and Herington, *Air War Against Germany & Italy 1939-1943,* p. 210.
[85] 451 Squadron Association, 451 Squadron R.A.A.F. Middle East Forces 1941 – 1946 Anecdotes, (2002), p. 25.
[86] 451 Squadron Association, 451 Squadron R.A.A.F. Middle East Forces 1941 – 1946 Anecdotes, (2002), pp 75-78.
[87] NLA: Trove – "Taken By Rommel" Hobart Mercury 10 February 42.
[88] AWFA: John Culbert.
[89] B.H. Liddell-Hart, (ed), *The Rommel Papers*, Da Capo Press, New York, 1953, pp. 163-168.
[90] Logbook – Watts.

[91] 451 Squadron Association, 451 Squadron R.A.A.F. Middle East Forces 1941 – 1946 Anecdotes, (2002), p. 25.
[92] AWFA: John Culbert.
[93] NAA: A9186, 136.

CHAPTER 2: FRUSTRATIONS ON THE FRINGES OF WAR: FEBRUARY TO NOVEMBER 1942

[1] 451 Squadron Association, 451 Squadron R.A.A.F. Middle East Forces 1941 – 1946 Anecdotes, (2002), p. 35.
[2] NAA: A9186, 136.
[3] NAA: A9186, 135.
[4] Christopher Shores, *Dust Clouds in the Middle East*, Grub Street, London, 1996, (2016), pp. 198-205, 261-262 and Gavin Long, *The Six Years War, Australia in the 1939 – 45 War*, Australian War Memorial, Canberra, 1973, pp 80-81.
[5] 451 Squadron Association, 451 Squadron R.A.A.F. Middle East Forces 1941 – 1946 Anecdotes, (2002), p. 160.
[6] NAA: A9186, 136 and Morley-Mower, *Messerschmitt Roulette*, p. 187.
[7] 451 Squadron Association, 451 Squadron R.A.A.F. Middle East Forces 1941 – 1946 Anecdotes, (2002), p. 54.
[8] Watts, *One Airman's War*, p. 72.
[9] NAA: A9186, 136.
[10] 451 Squadron Association, 451 Squadron R.A.A.F. Middle East Forces 1941 – 1946 Anecdotes, (2002), p. 26.
[11] 451 Squadron Association, 451 Squadron R.A.A.F. Middle East Forces 1941 – 1946 Anecdotes, (2002), p. 161.
[12] 451 Squadron Association, 451 Squadron R.A.A.F. Middle East Forces 1941 – 1946 Anecdotes, (2002), pp. 160-161, 175.
[13] NAA: A9186, 136.
[14] NAA: A9186, 136.
[15] NAA: A9695-1000.
[16] NAA: A9186, 136 and Herington, *Air War Against Germany & Italy 1939-1943,* p. 250.
[17] Watts, *One Airman's War*, pp. 12-13
[18] AWFA: Leonard Hayman.
[19] Long, Gavin, *Greece, Crete and Syria*, Collins, Sydney, 1953, (1986), pp. 321-322.
[20] NAA: A9186, 136
[21] NAA: A10605 1036-2 pt 1
[22] NAA: A9186, 136 and NAA: A11305 79-P1 pt 1
[23] Morley-Mower, *Messerschmitt Roulette*, pp. 177-178.
[24] 451 Squadron Association, 451 Squadron R.A.A.F. Middle East Forces 1941 – 1946 Anecdotes, (2002), p. 162.
[25] Personal File–Cox
[26] NAA: A9186, 136.
[27] 451 Squadron Association, 451 Squadron R.A.A.F. Middle East Forces 1941 – 1946 Anecdotes, (2002), p. 26.
[28] NAA: A9186, 136.
[29] 451 Squadron Association, 451 Squadron R.A.A.F. Middle East Forces 1941 – 1946 Anecdotes, (2002), p. 26.
[30] J. L. Scoullar, *Official History of New Zealand in the Second World War 1939–45: Battle for Egypt The Summer of 1942*, War History Branch, Wellington, 1955, p. 43.
[31] NAA: A9186, 136.
[32] NAA: A9186, 136.
[33] NAA: A9186, 136.
[34] NAA: A9186, 136.
[35] NAA: A9186, 136 and Logbook – Watts.
[36] NAA: A9186, 136.
[37] NAA: A9186, 136.
[38] NAA: A9186, 136.
[39] NAA: A9186, 136.
[40] NAA: A9186, 136.
[41] Author interview and Personal File – Arnel.
[42] NAA: A9186, 136.
[43] NAA: A11305 7-6-AIR.
[44] AWFA: George Purdy.
[45] Personal file – Purdy and AWFA: George Purdy.
[46] NAA: A9186, 136 and Personal file – O'Donnell.
[47] NAA: A9186, 136 and Personal File – Ifield.
[48] NAA: A9695 1004 and Herington, *Air War Against Germany & Italy 1939-1943,* p. 393.
[49] Author interview.

CHAPTER 3: RETURN TO EUROPE: CORSICA, ITALY AND DRAGOON: DECEMBER 1942 TO AUGUST 1944

[1] NAA: A9186, 136.
[2] NAA: A9186, 136 and Personal File – Longbottom.
[3] NAA: A9186, 136 and Personal File – Shiels.
[4] Spitfire Aircraft Production, viewed 20 August 2019, < http://www.airhistory.org.uk/spitfire/production.html>.
[5] Price, Dr Alfred, Tomasz Drecki, Robert Gretzyngier and Wojtek Matusiak , *Aircraft of the Aces: Men & Legends, Volume 13: Spitfires Over the Mediterranean & North Africa,* Del Prado, Madrid, 2000, pp. 38-39.
[6] NAA: A9186, 136.
[7] NAA: A9695 1004 and A9652.
[8] NAA: A9652.
[9] NAA: A9186, 136 and NAA: A9652.
[10] NAA: A9186, 136.
[11] Personal File – Lane.
[12] NAA: A9186, 136 and Spitfire Aircraft Production, viewed 20 August 2019, < http://www.airhistory.org.uk/spitfire/production.html>.
[13] NAA: A9695 1004.
[14] NAA: A9695 1004.
[15] NAA: A9695 1004.
[16] NAA: A9695 1004.
[17] NAA: A9695 1004.
[18] NAA: A9186, 136.
[19] NAA: A9186, 136.
[20] Herington, *Air War Against Germany & Italy 1939-1943,* p. 394.
[21] NAA: A9186, 136.
[22] NAA: A9186, 136.
[23] 451 Squadron Association, 451 Squadron R.A.A.F. Middle East Forces 1941 – 1946 Anecdotes, (2002), p. 52.
[24] NAA: A9186, 136.
[25] Lane – Logbook.
[26] NAA: A9186, 136.
[27] NAA: A11305, 7-1-AIR pt 2.
[28] NAA: A11305, 7-1-AIR pt 2.
[29] NAA: A11305, 7-1-AIR pt 2.
[30] NAA: A9186, 136.
[31] Personal file – Bayly.
[32] Personal file – Bayly.
[33] NAA: A9186, 136.
[34] NAA: A11305, 7-1-AIR pt 2.
[35] NAA: A11305, 7-1-AIR pt 2.
[36] NAA: A11305, 7-1-AIR pt 2.
[37] NAA: A9186, 140.
[38] Herington, *Air War Against Germany & Italy 1939-1943,* p. 579.
[39] AWFA: George Purdy.
[40] NAA: A11305 7-6-AIR.
[41] NAA: A9186, 136.
[42] NAA: A11305 13-4-AIR.
[43] NAA: A9186, 136 and Logbook – Lane.
[44] Logbook – Lane.
[45] Logbook – Lane.
[46] NAA: A9186, 136.
[47] Personal file – Stevens.
[48] 451 Squadron Association, 451 Squadron R.A.A.F. Middle East Forces 1941 – 1946 Anecdotes, (2002), p. 128.
[49] NAA: A9186, 136.
[50] 451 Squadron Association, 451 Squadron R.A.A.F. Middle East Forces 1941 – 1946 Anecdotes, (2002), p. 129.
[51] Logbook – Watts.
[52] AWFA: Edward Smith.
[53] NAA: A9186, 136, Logbook – Lane, and Watts, *One Airman's War*, p. I, 22-51, 72-74.
[54] NAA: A9186, 136.
[55] NAA: A9186, 136.
[56] NAA: A9186, 136.
[57] Watts, *One Airman's War*, p. 6.
[58] Author interview.
[59] Logbook – Lane.
[60] NAA: A9186, 136.
[61] NAA: A9186, 136.
[62] Personal file – O'Neil.
[63] AWM66-97 Escape narratives.
[64] Logbook – Lane.
[65] NAA: A9186, 136 and Logbook – Lane.
[66] NAA: A9186, 136.
[67] NAA: A9186, 136 (he left the squadron in January 1944).
[68] NAA: A9186, 139.
[69] NAA: A9186, 136, Personal File – Stevens and NLA: Trove – "Famous Pilot's Drop in Rank" Sun (Sydney) 19

September 1944.
[70] NAA: A9186, 136.
[71] TNA: AIR 27 and Personal File – Bray.
[72] NAA: A9186, 136.
[73] NAA: A11335 207-1-AIR.
[74] NAA: A9186, 136.
[75] NAA: A9186, 136.
[76] NAA: A9695-1005.
[77] NLA: Trove – "Leave for R.A.A.F." Age (Melbourne) 28 October 1943.
[78] NLA: Trove – "Leave for R.A.A.F." Age (Melbourne) 28 October 1943.
[79] NLA: Trove – "Airman's Mascot" Newcastle Sun 8 February 1944, NLA: Trove – "Close Shave" Telegraph (Brisbane) 21 February 1944, AWM: MEA1154 and P00869.105, AWFA: George Purdy, and Author interview.
[80] NAA: A9186, 136 and NAA: A11335 207-1-AIR.
[81] NAA: A9186, 136 and Personal File – Trenorden.
[82] Personal file – Sheppard and Logbook – Sheppard.
[83] NAA: A9186, 136.
[84] 451 Squadron Association, 451 Squadron R.A.A.F. Middle East Forces 1941 – 1946 Anecdotes, (2002), p. 138.
[85] NAA: A9186, 136.
[86] AWFA: Herbert Biggs.
[87] NAA: A11305 18/MED.
[88] NAA: A11305 24-AIR.
[89] NAA: A11305 24-AIR.
[90] IWM: 8231.
[91] M B Barrass, Air of Authority–A History of RAF Organisation, viewed 20 August 2019, <http://www.rafweb.org/Biographies/Morris_EJ.htm>.
[92] IWM: 8231.
[93] IWM: 8231.
[94] IWM: 8231.
[95] Christopher Shores, and Chris Thomas, *2nd Tactical Air Force: Volume 2 Breakout to Bodenplatte, July 1944 to January 1945,* Classic Publications, Surrey, 2005, p. 334.
[96] IWM: 8231.
[97] IWM: 8231.
[98] 451 Squadron Association, 451 Squadron R.A.A.F. Middle East Forces 1941 – 1946 Anecdotes, (2002), pp. 137-138.
[99] Author interview.
[100] IWM: 8231.
[101] NAA: A9186, 136 and NAA: A9652.
[102] NAA: A9186, 136.
[103] 451 Squadron Association, 451 Squadron R.A.A.F. Middle East Forces 1941 – 1946 Anecdotes, (2002), pp. 146-147.
[104] NAA: A9186, 136.
[105] NAA: A9186, 136.
[106] NAA: A9186, 136.
[107] NAA: A9186, 136.
[108] NAA: A11305 79-P1 pt2.
[109] NAA: A11305 18/MED.
[110] NLA: Trove – "Death on Service" Age (Melbourne) Port Macquarie News and Hastings River Advocate 20 May 1944, NLA: Trove – "Died of Wounds" Advocate (Burnie) 24 May 44, NLA: Trove – "Another Singleton Man Makes Supreme Sacrifice" Singleton Argus 7 June 1944, NLA: Trove – "Details of Don Haggart's Death in Action" Singleton Argus 24 July 1944.
[111] AWFA: Herbert Biggs.
[112] 451 Squadron Association, 451 Squadron R.A.A.F. Middle East Forces 1941 – 1946 Anecdotes, (2002), p. 164.
[113] AWFA: Herbert Biggs.
[114] NAA: A9186, 136.
[115] NLA: Trove – "Australian Led Corsican Patriots" Townsville Daily Bulletin 8 August 1944.
[116] NAA: A9186, 136.
[117] NAA: A9186, 136.
[118] NAA: A9186, 136.
[119] NAA: A9652.
[120] NAA: A9652.
[121] NAA: A9652.
[122] NAA: A9186, 136 and NAA: A9652.
[123] 451 Squadron Association, 451 Squadron R.A.A.F. Middle East Forces 1941 – 1946 Anecdotes, (2002), p. 140.
[124] NAA: A9186, 136
[125] AWFA: Joseph Barrington.
[126] NAA: A705 42/3/388.
[127] 451 Squadron Association, 451 Squadron R.A.A.F. Middle East Forces 1941 – 1946 Anecdotes, (2002), p. 145.

[128] NAA: A9186, 136
[129] NAA: A9186, 136
[130] NAA: A9186, 136
[131] NAA: A9186, 136 and NAA: A9652.
[132] NAA: A9186, 136
[133] NAA: A9652.
[134] NAA: A9186, 136
[135] The 57th Bomb Wing Association, Accessed 17 October 2018, <http://57th-bombwing.com/321stHistory/321_BG_1944-06.pdf>
[136] NAA: A9652.
[137] NAA: A9186, 136 and AWFA: George Purdy.
[138] J.P. Pallud, 'The Invasions of Elba Island', *After The Battle*, No. 173, August 2016, 2-36, pp. 4-36.
[139] NAA: A9186, 136
[140] NAA: A9186, 136
[141] NAA: A9186, 136
[142] NAA: A9652
[143] NLA: Trove – "Got Nazi on First Flight" Telegraph (Brisbane) 7 August 1944 and NLA: Trove – "Quick Air Victory" Sun (Sydney) 7 August 1944.
[144] NAA: A9186, 136 and Author interview.
[145] Author interview
[146] Author interview, Personal File – Arnel and 451 Squadron Association, 451 Squadron R.A.A.F. Middle East Forces 1941–1946 Anecdotes, (2002), p. 121.
[147] Author interview and Personal File – Arnel.
[148] NAA: A9186, 136.
[149] Spitfire Aircraft Production, viewed 20 August 2019, < http://www.airhistory.org.uk/spitfire/production.html>.
[150] NAA: A9186, 136.
[151] NAA: A11305 18/MED
[152] NAA: A9186, 136, NAA: A9695 1004 and A11305 18/MED.
[153] Author interview.
[154] Personal File – Barrington and Logbook – Barrington.
[155] Author interview, Personal File – Barrington, AWFA: Joseph Barrington and Logbook – Barrington.
[156] Author interview and Logbook – Barrington.
[157] Author interview.
[158] Logbook – Barrington.
[159] Author interview.
[160] AWFA: Joseph Barrington.
[161] AWFA: Joseph Barrington and Author interview.
[162] Author interview.
[163] Logbook – Barrington.
[164] Author interview and Sydney Jewish Museum interview – Barrington March 2010.
[165] Author interview and AWFA: Robert Milner.
[166] NAA: A9186, 136 and 320th B.G. Reunion Association, Accessed 17 October 2018, <http://320thbg.org/1944_missions.html>
[167] AWFA: Joseph Barrington.
[168] NAA: A9186, 136.
[169] NAA: A9186, 136.
[170] Personal File – Small.
[171] Logbook – Barrington.
[172] NAA: A9186, 136.
[173] NAA: A9186, 136.
[174] 451 Squadron Association, 451 Squadron R.A.A.F. Middle East Forces 1941 – 1946 Anecdotes, (2002), pp. 189-200, United States Holocaust Memorial Museum, Accessed 5 September 2019 <https://encyclopedia.ushmm.org/content/en/article/ravensbrueck> and Barth City History, Accessed 5 September 2019, <https://rathaus.stadt-barth.de/geschichte.php>.
[175] NAA: A11305 1-9-AIR.
[176] Jeffrey J. Clarke and Robert Ross Smith, *Riviera to the Rhine*, Centre of Military History United States Army, Washington, DC, 1993, (1995), pp. 3-48 and Samuel Eliot Morison, *History of United States Naval Operations in World War II, Volume 11: The Invasion of France and Germany*, Naval Institute Press, Annapolis, 1953 (2011), pp. 28 and 227-229.
[177] Logbook – Barrington.
[178] NAA: A9186, 136.
[179] NLA: Trove – "An Australian Ace" Kalgoorlie Miner 4 September 1944.

[180] NAA: A9186, 136.

[181] Logbook–Barrington

[182] Clarke and Smith, *Riviera to the Rhine*, p. 97 and Morison, *History of United States Naval Operations in World War II, Volume 11: The Invasion of France and Germany*, pp. 86, 265, 279-281.

[183] NAA: A9186, 136.

[184] NAA: A9695 1004.

[185] NLA: Trove – "R.A.A.F. Party on way from Corsica" Daily Telegraph 24 September 1944.

[186] NAA: A9186, 136.

[187] Clarke and Smith, *Riviera to the Rhine*, p. 51, 139-140.

[188] NAA: A9186, 136.

[189] NLA: Trove – "Fliers'Job Eased" Daily News (Perth) 22 August 1944.

[190] NAA: A11305 1-9-AIR.

[191] NAA: A11305 1-9-AIR.

[192] Lloyd Clark, *Anzio: Italy and the Battle for Rome – 1944*, Atlantic Monthly Press, New York, 2006, p. xiii.

[193] NAA: A11305 79-P1 pt 1 and North East Medals, Accessed 18 September 2019, <https://www.northeastmedals.co.uk/britishguide/hmso/campaign_stars_defence.htm>

[194] NAA: A1196, 36-501-160 .

[195] Author interview.

[196] NAA: A9186, 136.

[197] AWFA: Herbert Biggs, NAA: A9186, 136 and NAA: A11305 1-9-AIR.

CHAPTER 4: OPERATIONS: AT OPPOSITE ENDS OF FRANCE: SEPTEMBER 1944

[1] NAA: A9186, 136.

[2] NAA: A9186, 136.

[3] NAA: A11305 134-P3 pt 5.

[4] NAA: A9186, 136.

[5] AWFA: Joseph Barrington.

[6] Shores and Thomas, *2nd Tactical Air Force: Volume 2 Breakout to Bodenplatte, July 1944 to January 1945*, p. 281.

[7] Olver – Personal file and Logbook – Olver.

[8] NAA: A9186, 139 and Logbook – Taylor.

[9] NAA: A9186, 139.

[10] NAA: A9186, 139.

[11] NAA: A9186, 139.

[12] NAA: A9186, 139.

[13] Canadian Military Headquarters (CMHQ) reports 1940 to 1948, Canadian Participation in the Operations in North-West Europe, 1944. Part IV: First Canadian Army in the Pursuit (23 Aug – 30 Sep), Accessed 12 October 2019, <https://www.canada.ca/en/department-national-defence/services/military-history/history-heritage/official-military-history-lineages/reports/military-headquarters-1940-1948.html>

[14] Leith letter home dated 11 September 1944.

[15] Taylor letter home dated 12 September 1944.

[16] NAA: A9186, 139.

[17] NAA: A9186, 139.

[18] TNA: AIR 37-615.

[19] Shores and Thomas, *2nd Tactical Air Force: Volume 2 Breakout to Bodenplatte, July 1944 to January 1945*, p. 289.

[20] Logbook – Leith.

[21] TNA: AIR 37-615.

[22] NAA: A9186, 139.

[23] NAA: A9186, 139.

[24] TNA: AIR 37-615

[25] NAA: A9186, 139.

[26] TNA: AIR 37-615 and Antony Beevor, *Arnhem: The Battle for the Bridges, 1944*, Viking, Milton Keynes, 2018, pp. 228-229.

[27] NAA: A9186, 139.

[28] TNA: AIR 37-615.

[29] NAA: A9186, 139.

[30] TNA: AIR 37-615.

[31] Logbook – Clemesha.

[32] NAA: A9186, 139.

[33] Beevor, *Arnhem: The Battle for the Bridges, 1944*, pp. 328-329.

[34] TNA: AIR 37-615.

[35] TNA: AIR 37-615.

[36] Logbook – Lyall.

37 TNA: AIR/50/156.
38 Logbook – Leith.
39 NAA: A9186, 139.
40 NAA: A2217 22-36-ORG.
41 NAA: A9186, 139.
42 Cyril Ayris, and Russell Leith, *Duty Done*, Cyril Ayris Freelance, West Perth, 2001, p. 188.
43 Logbook – Baker
44 NAA: A9186, 139 and Logbook – Baker.
45 Leith letter home dated 9 October 1944.
46 Graham Smith, *Norfolk Airfields in the Second World War*, Countryside Books, Newbury, 1994, (2014), pp. 23, 39, 66.
47 NAA: A9186, 139.

CHAPTER 5: OPERATIONS: SHIFTING TASKS: OCTOBER TO DECEMBER 1944

1 John Herington, *Australia in the War of 1939-1945, Series Three: Air, Volume IV: Air Power Over Europe 1944-1945*, Australian War Memorial, Canberra, 1963, pp. 67-171, 184 and TNA: AIR 20-2302
2 Herington, *Air Power Over Europe 1944-1945*, pp 160, 170, 186 – 187, Steve Bond, Steve Darlow, Sean Feast, Marc Hall, Robert Owen, and Hoard Sandall, *V-Weapons Bomber Command: Failed to Return*, Fighting High Ltd, China, 2015, p. 6 and John Terraine, John, *The Right of the Line*, Wordsworth, 1985, (1997), p. 219.
3 Bond et al, *V-Weapons Bomber Command: Failed to Return*, p. 121.
4 Samuel Eliot Morison, *History of United States Naval Operations in World War II Volume 9: Sicily-Salerno-Anzio*, Naval Institute Press, Annapolis, 1953, (2011), pp. 363, 366.
5 TNA: AIR 20-2302.
6 TNA: AIR 14-2923, AIR 37-533 and AIR 16-446.
7 Herington, *Air Power Over Europe 1944-1945*, pp. 192-193.
8 TNA: AIR 37-647.
9 AWM65: 2010.
10 NAA: A9186, 136.
11 IWM: 8231.
12 NAA: A9186, 136 and NAA: A11305 1-9-AIR.
13 NAA: A9186, 136 and Herington, *Air Power Over Europe 1944-1945*, p. 257.
14 NLA: Trove – "All from one Squadron" Age (Melbourne) 12 September 1944.
15 AWFA: George Purdy.
16 NAA: A11305 134-P3 pt 5.
17 Personal File – Bray and AWM: 79-P1 pt 2 and Australian War Memorial, Accessed 3 October 2019, <https://www.awm.gov.au/collection/R1522898> and NAA: A11305.
18 NAA: A9186, 136.
19 AWFA: George Purdy.
20 Logbook – Barrington.
21 AWFA: Herbert Biggs.
22 AWFA: Edward Smith.
23 M B Barrass, Air of Authority–A History of RAF Organisation, viewed 1 September 2019, <http://www.rafweb.org/Squadrons/Sqn541-598.htm>.
24 Logbook – Lyall.
25 NAA: A9186, 139.
26 TNA: AIR 16-966 and AIR 37-370.
27 AWM65: 2010.
28 NAA: A9186, 139 and Logbook – Clemesha.
29 Logbook – Lyall.
30 Logbook – Baker.
31 NAA: A9186, 139.
32 NAA: A9186, 139.
33 Logbook – Leith.
34 IWM: CGE 10881, 10882, 10884 and 10885.
35 NAA: A9186, 139.
36 Logbook – Lynch.
37 NAA: A9186, 139.
38 Logbook – Carmichael.
39 NAA: A9186, 139.
40 NAA: A10605 Vol 2 and Logbook – Lancaster.
41 NAA: A9186, 139.
42 NAA: A9186, 139.
43 Logbook – Clemesha.
44 NAA: A9186, 139.

45 Logbook – Taylor.
46 NAA: A9186, 139.
47 Logbook – Baker.
48 NAA: A9186, 139, Logbook–Carmichael and 493rd Bomb Group Museum, Accessed 20 August 2019, <http://www.493bgdebach.co.uk/index.php>.
49 NAA: A9186, 139.
50 Logbook – Leith.
51 Smith, *Norfolk Airfields in the Second World War*, pp. 164, 168.
52 NAA: A9186, 139 and NAA: A2217 22-36-ORG.
53 Author interview.
54 NAA: A9186, 139.
55 AWM65: 2010.
56 NLA: Trove – "Australian Airmen's Attack on V2 Site" Morning Bulletin 27 November 1944.
57 Taylor letter home dated 26 November 1944.
58 NAA: A9186, 139, Logbook – Lyall and IWM Combat Film FC 11198 and FC 11199.
59 NAA: A9186, 139.
60 Diary – Ferguson.
61 Diary – Ferguson.
62 NAA: A9186, 139.
63 Diary – Ferguson.
64 AWFA: Joseph Barrington.
65 NAA: A9186, 139.
66 Logbook – Lynch.
67 NAA: A9186, 139 and Logbook – Carmichael.
68 NAA: A9186, 139 and Douglas McRoberts, *Lions Rampant: The Story of 602 Spitfire Squadron*, William Kimber, London, 1985, pp. 207-208.
69 NAA: A9186, 139.
70 NAA: A9186, 139 and TNA: AIR 27.
71 Leith letter home dated 6 December 1944.
72 Diary – Ferguson.
73 NAA: A9186, 139.
74 NAA: A9186, 139.
75 Logbook – Baker.
76 NAA: A9186, 139.
77 NAA: A9186, 139.
78 Logbook – Clemesha.
79 NAA: A9186, 139.
80 Personal file – Bennett.
81 NAA: A9186, 139.
82 Diary – Ferguson.
83 NAA: A9186, 139.
84 Logbook – Lynch.
85 AWM65: 2010.
86 Leith letter home dated 30 December 1944.
87 NAA: A9186, 136 and AWM: UK2395.
88 AWFA: Edward Smith.
89 Logbook – Leith.
90 NAA: A9186, 139

CHAPTER 6: OPERATIONS: JANUARY TO MARCH 1945

1 Logbook – Barrington.
2 NAA: A9186, 136, Personal File – Wallis and Author interview
3 Personal file–Robertson
4 Logbook – Barrington.
5 Logbook – Sheppard.
6 AWFA: George Purdy.
7 NAA: A9186, 136.
8 Personal file – Richards and Author interview.
9 Logbook – Barrington.
10 NAA: A9186, 136.
11 Adam Lunney, *Ready to Strike: The Spitfires and Australians of 453 (RAAF) Squadron over Normandy*, Barrallier Books, West Geelong, 2018, p. 202.
12 Personal file – Andrews.
13 Logbook – Andrews.
14 NLA: Trove – "Australian Fighters" Cairns Post 31 March 1945.
15 NAA: A9186, 136 and Logbook – Andrews.
16 Personal file – Blake.
17 NAA: A9186, 136.
18 Logbook – Barrington.
19 NAA: A9186, 136.
20 NAA: A9186, 136 and Logbook – Barrington.
21 AWFA: Joseph Barrington.
22 Author interview.
23 NAA: A9186, 139.
24 NAA: A9186, 136.

[25] Personal File – Bray.
[26] Logbook – Sheppard.
[27] NAA: A9186, 136 and Logbook – Sheppard.
[28] NLA: Trove – "Another Jerilderie Airman Prominent" Jerilderie Herald and Urana Advertiser 26 April 1945.
[29] Logbook – Sheppard.
[30] Personal File–Bray and Personal File – Kemp.
[31] NAA: A9186, 139.
[32] NAA: A9186, 136.
[33] Logbook – Sheppard.
[34] NAA: A9186, 136 and TNA: AIR 16-966.
[35] Author interview.
[36] NAA: A9186, 136 and Author interview.
[37] Logbook – Barrington.
[38] NAA: A9186, 136.
[39] Jak P. Mallmann Showell, *Companion to the German Navy 1939 – 1945*, The History Press, Stroud, 1999, (2009), pp. 164-166.
[40] Logbook – Barrington.
[41] NAA: A9186, 136.
[42] NAA: A9186, 136.
[43] AWFA: Sidney Handsaker.
[44] Author interview and AWFA: Sidney Handsaker.
[45] Personal file – Handsaker and Author interview.
[46] AWFA: Sidney Handsaker.
[47] Personal File – Handsaker and Logbook – Handsaker.
[48] Author interview and Logbook – Handsaker.
[49] AWFA: Sidney Handsaker.
[50] S. Handsaker, 'Wirraways', in *Spitfire News: Journal of the Spitfire Association*, No. 86, March 2007, p. 24.
[51] Author interview.
[52] Author interview.
[53] Author interview.
[54] Personal File – Handsaker.
[55] Author interview.
[56] Author interview.
[57] Author interview.
[58] Author interview.
[59] Author interview.
[60] Logbook – Handsaker.
[61] Personal file – Handsaker and Author interview.
[62] Author interview.
[63] Author interview.
[64] Author interview.
[65] Author interview.
[66] NAA: A9186, 136.
[67] AWFA: Joseph Barrington.
[68] Personal file – Ware.
[69] Stephen E. Ambrose, *Band of Brothers*, Touchstone, New York, 1992, (2001), pp. 253-254.
[70] Personal file – Ware.
[71] Personal file – Ware.
[72] Personal file – Ware.
[73] Personal file – Ware.
[74] Diary – Ferguson.
[75] AWM65 – 2230.
[76] NAA: A9186, 139.
[77] TNA: AIR 16-446 and AIR 20-2653.
[78] Logbook – Leith.
[79] Logbook – Lynch.
[80] Ayris, and Leith, *Duty Done*, p. 196.
[81] Leith – Personal File.
[82] Leith letter home dated 28 January 1945.
[83] NAA: A9186, 139.
[84] Logbook – Taylor.
[85] Logbook – Baker.
[86] NAA: A9186, 139 and Personal File – Aldred.
[87] NAA: A9186, 139.
[88] NAA: A9186, 139.
[89] Logbook – Leith.
[90] NAA: A9186, 139 and TNA: AIR 27.
[91] Logbook – Clemesha.
[92] NAA: A9186, 139.
[93] NAA: A9186, 139 and TNA: AIR 27.
[94] NAA: A9186, 139, TNA: AIR 27, and Personal File – Ryan.
[95] NAA: A2217 22-36-ORG.
[96] NAA: A9186, 139 and AWM: PR 04441.
[97] NAA: A9186, 139, AWM: PR 04441, AWM65 – 2230 and Personal File – Gadd.
[98] Logbook – Leith.
[99] Logbook – Clemesha.
[100] NAA: A9186, 139.
[101] Personal File – Carter.

102 NAA: A9186, 139 and Personal File – McLoughlin.
103 Temora Interview – Inglis.
104 Logbook – Leith.
105 NAA: A9186, 139.
106 Logbook – Lynch.
107 AWM: PR 03203.
108 NAA: A9186, 139.
109 Logbook – Leith.
110 Logbook – Taylor.
111 NAA: A9186, 139.
112 TNA: AIR 20-2653.
113 Logbook – Leith and TNA: AIR 27.
114 AWM: PR 03203.
115 AWM: PR 03203.
116 NAA: A9186, 139.
117 AWM: PR 03203.
118 AWM: PR 03203.
119 NAA: A9186, 139 and Temora Interview – Marsh.
120 Logbook – Andrews.
121 NAA: A9186, 139.
122 NAA: A9186, 136.
123 NAA: A9186, 136.
124 NAA: A9186, 139 and Temora Interview – Marsh.
125 NAA: A9186, 139.
126 Logbook – Lynch.
127 Logbook – Leith.
128 NAA: A9186, 139.
129 Logbook – Andrews.
130 NAA: A9186, 139.
131 NAA: A9186, 139.

CHAPTER 7: OPERATIONS, OCCUPATION AND HOME: APRIL 1945 TO JANUARY 1946

1 TNA: AIR 20-2653.
2 NAA: A9186, 136.
3 NAA: A11305 300.
4 Logbook – Barrington.
5 Logbook – Clemesha.
6 Logbook – Andrews.
7 NAA: A9186, 136 and NAA: A9186, 139.
8 NAA: A9186, 139.
9 Leith letter home dated 15 April 1945.
10 Leith letter home dated 23 April 1945.
11 Logbook – Sheppard.
12 AWM65: 2010.
13 Logbook – Handsaker.
14 NAA: A9186, 139, Logbook – Handsaker and Logbook – Barrington.
15 Logbook – Barrington.
16 Author Interview.
17 NAA: A9186, 136, NAA: A9186, 139 and Logbook – Leith.
18 Logbook – Taylor.
19 NAA: A9186, 139.
20 TNA: AIR 20-2653.
21 NAA: A1196, 36-501-160.
22 NAA: A9186, 136.
23 Leith letters home (numerous) dated 10 May 1945.
24 Leith letter home dated 11 May 1945.
25 Logbook – Clemesha.
26 NAA: A9186, 139.
27 NAA: A9186, 139.
28 Logbook – Handsaker.
29 TNA: AIR37-657.
30 NAA: A9186, 139.
31 Logbook – Handsaker and AWFA: Sidney Handsaker.
32 Logbook – Andrews.
33 NAA: A11335 551-6-ORG.
34 Logbook – Sheppard.
35 Logbook – Taylor.
36 Leith letter home dated 24 June 1945.
37 NAA: A1196 36-501-160, A2217 22-36-ORG, A9186, 136, and NAA: A9186, 139.
38 Logbook – Handsaker.
39 NAA: A9186, 139.
40 Personal File – Knox.
41 Logbook – Handsaker.
42 Author interview.
43 AWFA: Charles Hulls.
44 NAA: A9186, 139.
45 NAA: A9186, 139 and NAA: A10605 Vol 2.
46 NAA: A9186, 139.
47 Author interview.
48 NAA: A1196 36-501-160, TNA: AIR26-183 and Personal File – Falconer.
49 NAA: A9186, 139.
50 NAA: A9186, 139.
51 Author interview.

52 NAA: A9186, 139.
53 NAA: A2217 22-36-ORG.
54 Taylor letter home dated 3 October 1945.
55 AWFA: Charles Hulls.
56 Taylor letter home dated 6 October 1945.
57 Logbook – Handsaker.
58 NAA: A9186, 139.
59 Logbook – Clemesha.
60 NAA: A9186, 136.
61 Logbook – Barrington.
62 AWFA: Joseph Barrington.
63 TNA: AIR26-183.
64 NAA: A9186, 139.
65 Author interview.
66 Author interview.
67 NLA: Trove – "Spitfire Groups Not Keen to Stop in Germany" Age (Melbourne) 15 November 1945.
68 NAA: A1196, 36-501-160, TNA: AIR26-183 and NAA: A9186, 139.
69 Author interview.
70 AWFA: Sidney Handsaker.
71 AWFA: Sidney Handsaker.
72 Author interview.
73 TNA: AIR26-183.
74 NAA: A9186, 139.
75 Logbook – Handsaker.
76 NAA: A9186, 136.
77 NLA: Trove – "Acknowledgement." Smith's Weekly (Sydney) 22 December 1945.
78 NAA: A9186, 139 and NAA: A11335 605-2-P1.
79 NAA: A9186, 139 and Commonwealth War Graves Commission, Accessed 16 May 2018 <www.cwgc.org> .
80 NAA: A9186, 139.
81 NAA: A9186, 139 and NAA: A11335 605-2-P1.
82 Commonwealth War Graves Commission, Accessed 16 May 2018 <www.cwgc.org> .
83 TNA: AIR26-183.
84 NAA: A9186, 136.
85 NAA: A9186, 139.
86 NAA: A9186, 136, NAA: A9186, 139 and TNA: AIR26-183.
87 AWFA: Charles Hulls.
88 Author interview.
89 Author interview.
90 Author interview.
91 Personal File – Hill.
92 NAA: A9186, 136 and Personal File – Hill.
93 NAA: A11335 553-1-ORG.
94 NAA: A9186, 136 and Logbook – Handsaker.
95 Logbook – Handsaker.
96 AWFA: Sidney Handsaker.
97 NAA: A1196, 36-501-160.
98 TNA: 37-674.
99 Author interview.
100 NAA: A1066, E45/13/39.
101 Diary – Ferguson.

EPILOGUE: THE PLANES THEY FLEW: HURRICANES, TYPHOONS AND SPITFIRES

1 Mitchell, Gordon, *R.J. Mitchell: Schooldays to Spitfire*, The History Press, Stroud, (1986), 2009, p.27.
2 Mitchell, *R.J. Mitchell: Schooldays to Spitfire*, pp. 29–31.
3 McKinstry, Leo, *Hurricane: Victor of the Battle of Britain*, John Murray, London, 2011, pp. 21-24.
4 Mitchell, *R.J. Mitchell: Schooldays to Spitfire*, p. 42 and 127
5 Mitchell, *R.J. Mitchell: Schooldays to Spitfire*, p. 118.
6 McKinstry, *Hurricane: Victor of the Battle of Britain*, p. 25.
7 Mitchell, *R.J. Mitchell: Schooldays to Spitfire*, p. 93.
8 Mitchell, *R.J. Mitchell: Schooldays to Spitfire*, p. 141.
9 Stewart Wilson, *Spitfire*, Aerospace Publications, Fyshwick, 1999, p. 12 and McKinstry, *Hurricane: Victor of the Battle of Britain*, pp 27-29.
10 McKinstry, *Hurricane: Victor of the Battle of Britain*, pp. 30, 37-38.
11 Mitchell, *R.J. Mitchell: Schooldays to Spitfire*, pp. 142–143.
12 Mitchell, *R.J. Mitchell: Schooldays to Spitfire*, pp. 142–145 and Appendix 3,

p. 314.

[13] Jonathan Glancey, *Spitfire: The Biography*, Atlantic Books, London, 2007, p. 39.

[14] David Curnock, *Little Book of Spitfire*, G2 Entertainment Limited, United Kingdom, 2011, pp. 20–29.

[15] Curnock, *Little Book of Spitfire*, pp. 20–29.

[16] Wilson, *Spitfire*, p. 56.

[17] Mitchell, *R.J. Mitchell: Schooldays to Spitfire*, pp. 149–150.

[18] Glancey, *Spitfire: The Biography*, pp. 42–43.

[19] Curnock, *Little Book of Spitfire*, pp. 32–33.

[20] Martin Robson, *The Spitfire Pocket Manual*, Conway, London, 2010, p. 44, McKinstry, *Hurricane: Victor of the Battle of Britain*, p. 52.

[21] McKinstry, *Hurricane: Victor of the Battle of Britain*, p. 52 and Mitchell, *R.J. Mitchell: Schooldays to Spitfire*, p. 153.

[22] Mitchell, *R.J. Mitchell: Schooldays to Spitfire*, p. 236.

[23] Mitchell, *R.J. Mitchell: Schooldays to Spitfire*, pp. 135–136 and 142.

[24] Mitchell, *R.J. Mitchell: Schooldays to Spitfire*, pp. 191–195.

[25] McKinstry, *Hurricane: Victor of the Battle of Britain*, pp. 65, 73.

[26] Mitchell, *R.J. Mitchell: Schooldays to Spitfire*, pp. 204 and 213.

[27] McKinstry, *Hurricane: Victor of the Battle of Britain*, pp. 78, 83, 88.

[28] Wilson, *Spitfire*, p 65.

[29] Martin Robson, *The Hurricane Pocket Manual*, Conway, London, 2016, pp. 8-9.

[30] Curnock, *Little Book of Spitfire*, p. 50.

[31] Curnock, *Little Book of Spitfire*, pp. 50–58.

[32] McKinstry, *Hurricane: Victor of the Battle of Britain*, p.53.

[33] Andrew Thomas, *Osprey Aircraft of the Aces: Volume 87, Spitfire Aces of Burma and the Pacific,* Osprey, Oxford, 2009, p. 28.

[34] Robson, *The Spitfire Pocket Manual*, p. 8.

[35] Wilson, *Spitfire*, p. 15.

[36] Temora Interview – Fred Cowpe.

[37] Wilson, *Spitfire*, p. 15.

[38] Dr Alfred Price, *Osprey Aircraft of the Aces: Volume 5, Late Mark Spitfire Aces 1942 – 45*, Cadmus Communications, USA, (1995), 2010, p 70.

[39] Mitchell, *R.J. Mitchell: Schooldays to Spitfire*, p. 71.

[40] Mitchell, *R.J. Mitchell: Schooldays to Spitfire*, p. 71.

[41] NAA: A11335 Z2

[42] Curnock, *Little Book of Spitfire*, p. 39.

[43] Dr Alfred Price, *Aircraft of the Aces: Men & Legends, Volume 1: The Legendary Spitfire Mk I/II 1939–1941*, Del Prado, Madrid, (1996), 1999, p. 18.

[44] Price, *The Legendary Spitfire Mk I/II 1939–1941*, pp. 7–8.

[45] Price, *The Legendary Spitfire Mk I/II 1939–1941*, p. 10.

[46] McKinstry, *Hurricane: Victor of the Battle of Britain*, pp. 99-100.

[47] McKinstry, *Hurricane: Victor of the Battle of Britain*, pp. 128-129.

[48] Robson, *The Hurricane Pocket Manual*, p. 5.

[49] Dr Alfred Price and Tony Holmes, *Aircraft of the Aces: Men & Legends, Volume 17: RAF Aces of the Battle of Britain,* Del Prado, Madrid, (1995), 2000, pp. 45–47

[50] McKinstry, *Hurricane: Victor of the Battle of Britain*, p. 100.

[51] Price and Holmes, *RAF Aces of the Battle of Britain,* p. 19.

[52] Price and Holmes, *RAF Aces of the Battle of Britain,* pp. 50–52.

[53] McKinstry, *Hurricane: Victor of the Battle of Britain*, p. Hurricane p. 132.

[54] Price and Holmes, *RAF Aces of the Battle of Britain,* p. 55.

[55] Author Interview.

[56] Price, The *Legendary Spitfire Mk I/II 1939–1941*, p. 61.

[57] McKinstry, *Hurricane: Victor of the Battle of Britain*, pp. 159-160.

[58] McKinstry, *Hurricane: Victor of the Battle of Britain*, p. 150.

[59] Adolf Galland, *The First and The Last*, Readers Book Club, London, 1956, pp. 92-93.

[60] Mitchell, *R.J. Mitchell: Schooldays to Spitfire*, pp. 225–227.

[61] Old Spitalfields Market, Accessed September 2015, <http://www.

oldspitalfieldsmarket.com/the-market/the-history-of-the-market>

62 Spitfire Aircraft Production, viewed 20 August 2019, <http://www.airhistory.org.uk/spitfire/p012.html> .

63 NAA: A2676, 1115.

64 Douglas Bader, *Fight for the Sky*, Pen & Sword, Barnsley, 1973, (2008), pp. 185-186.

65 Curnock, *Little Book of Spitfire*, p. 40.

66 Price, *The Legendary Spitfire Mk I/II 1939–1941*, p. 21.

67 Price, *The Legendary Spitfire Mk I/II 1939–1941*, p. 46.

68 Richard C. Smith, *Hornchurch Eagles: The Life Stories of Eight of the Airfield's Distinguished WWII Fighter Pilots*, Grub Street, London, 2002, p. 145.

69 Price, *The Legendary Spitfire Mk I/II 1939–1941*, p. 46.

70 Wilson, *Spitfire*, pp. 76–77.

71 McKinstry, *Hurricane: Victor of the Battle of Britain*, pp. 229-231 and Mike Williams and Neil Stirling, *WWII Aircraft Performance,* Accessed 5 May 2019, <http://www.wwiiaircraftperformance.org/Aircraft_Engines_of_the_World_Rolls-Royce_Merlin.pdf>.

72 T.F. Neil, *From the Cockpit: Spitfire*, Ian Allan Ltd, Shepperton, 1980, pp. 35–36.

73 Author Interview

74 Author Interview

75 Price, *The Legendary Spitfire Mk I/II 1939–1941*, p. 49.

76 Glancey, *Spitfire: The Biography*, p. 96.

77 Wilson, *Spitfire*, p. 17.

78 Neil, *From the Cockpit: Spitfire*, p. 40.

79 McKinstry, *Hurricane: Victor of the Battle of Britain*, pp. 232-233.

80 Graham A. Thomas, *Firestorm: Typhoons over Caen, 1944*, Spellmount, Stroud, 2006, p. 64.

81 Thomas, *Firestorm: Typhoons over Caen, 1944,* pp. 64-65 and Norman Franks, *Typhoon Attack*, Stackpole, Mechanicsburg, 2003, (2010), p. 14.

82 Franks, *Typhoon Attack*, pp. 12-13,19 and Thomas, *Firestorm: Typhoons over Caen, 1944,* pp. 65-66.

83 Chris Goss with Peter Cornwell and Bernd Rauchbach, *Luftwaffe Fighter-Bombers Over Britain: The Tip and Run Campaign, 1942–43,* Stackpole Books, Mechanicsburg, 2010, pp. 136, 165.

84 Thomas, *Firestorm: Typhoons over Caen, 1944,* p. 66, Franks, *Typhoon Attack*, pp. 21-23 and Chris Thomas, *Osprey Combat Aircraft: Volume 86, Typhoon Wings of 2nd TAF 1943-45*, Osprey, Oxford, 2010, pp. 8, 14.

85 Franks, *Typhoon Attack*, p. 26.

86 Thomas, *Typhoon Wings of 2nd TAF 1943–45,* p. 16.

87 Thomas, *Firestorm: Typhoons over Caen, 1944,* p.70.

88 Thomas, *Firestorm: Typhoons over Caen, 1944,* p. 178.

89 Thomas, *Firestorm: Typhoons over Caen, 1944,* pp.108-109.

90 IWM: 10049.

91 NAA: A11305-7-8-AIR.

92 NAA: A11305-7-8-AIR.

93 NAA: A11305-7-8-AIR.

94 NAA: A11305-7-8-AIR.

95 NAA: A11305-7-8-AIR.

96 Thomas, *Typhoon Wings of 2nd TAF 1943–45,* pp. 63-64, 69.

97 Franks, *Typhoon Attack*, p. 252.

98 McKinstry, *Hurricane: Victor of the Battle of Britain*, pp. 238-241.

99 Robson, *The Hurricane Pocket Manual*, p. 102.

100 McKinstry, *Hurricane: Victor of the Battle of Britain*, pp. 243-244.

101 Price, et al, *Spitfires Over the Mediterranean & North Africa,* p. 45.

102 Glancey, *Spitfire: The Biography*, p. 108 and Robson, *The Hurricane Pocket Manual* p. 16.

103 Wilson, *Spitfire*, p. 102.

104 Mitchell, *R.J. Mitchell: Schooldays to Spitfire*, Appendix 11, pp. 363–364.

105 Wilson, *Spitfire*, p. 23.

106 Curnock, *Little Book of Spitfire*, pp. 40–42.

107 Robson, *The Spitfire Pocket Manual*, p. 116.

108 Wilson, *Spitfire*, p. 16 and 80.

109 McKinstry, *Hurricane: Victor of the Battle*

of Britain, p. 248.

110 Price, et al, *Spitfires Over the Mediterranean & North Africa,* p. 9.

111 Price, et al, *Spitfires Over the Mediterranean & North Africa,* pp. 16–17.

112 Price, et al, *Spitfires Over the Mediterranean & North Africa,* pp. 24 and 37 and NAA: A5954, 23111.

113 Pilot's Notes Spitfire VA, VB and VC – Air Ministry 1st Addendum

114 McKinstry, *Hurricane: Victor of the Battle of Britain*, p. 265.

115 McKinstry, *Hurricane: Victor of the Battle of Britain*, pp. 276-277, Albert Axell, *Russia's Heroes 1941 – 1945*, Robinson, London, 2002, pp. 52-53 and Alfred Price, *The Spitfire Story*, Arms and Armour, London, 1982, (1992), pp.139-140.

116 Malcolm Laird, and Steve Mackenzie, *Spitfire – The ANZACS*, Ventura Publications, Wellington, 1997, p. 40.

117 Pilot's Notes Hurricane IIA-B-C-D and IV, para 28 and Robson, *The Hurricane Pocket Manual*, p. 133.

118 McKinstry, *Hurricane: Victor of the Battle of Britain*, pp. 287-288.

119 Bader, *Fight for the Sky*, pp. 20, 22.

120 Bader, *Fight for the Sky*, p. 126 and IWM: 10049.

121 McKinstry, *Hurricane: Victor of the Battle of Britain*, pp. 288-289.

122 Price, *Late Mark Spitfire Aces 1942 – 45*, p. 9.

123 Price, et al, *Spitfires Over the Mediterranean & North Africa,* pp 37–39.

124 Price, *Late Mark Spitfire Aces 1942 – 45*, p. 13.

125 Price, *Late Mark Spitfire Aces 1942 – 45*, p. 20.

126 McRoberts, *Lions Rampant: The Story of 602 Spitfire Squadron*, p. 190.

127 Curnock, *Little Book of Spitfire*, p. 42.

128 Wilson, *Spitfire*, p.20.

129 Price, *Late Mark Spitfire Aces 1942 – 45*, p. 20.

130 NAA: A11093 452/A58 Part 1.

131 Dominique Breffort, *German Fighters Volume II: Bf 110 – Me 210 – Me 410 – Fw 190 – Me 262 – Me 163 – He 162*, Histoire & Collections, Paris, 2014, p. 10.

132 Curnock, *Little Book of Spitfire*, p. 43.

133 Robson, *The Spitfire Pocket Manual*, p. 114.

134 Wilson, *Spitfire*, p. 18.

135 Robson, *The Spitfire Pocket Manual*, p. 114.

136 Price, *Late Mark Spitfire Aces 1942 – 45*, p. 14.

137 Temora Interview – Don Andrews.

138 Price, *Late Mark Spitfire Aces 1942 – 45*, p. 9.

139 Mitchell, *R.J. Mitchell: Schooldays to Spitfire*, p. 214.

140 Price, *Late Mark Spitfire Aces 1942 – 45*, p. 87.

141 NAA: A11093 452/A58 Part 1.

142 NAA: A11093 452/A58 Part 1.

143 Price, et al, *Spitfires Over the Mediterranean & North Africa,* p. 41.

144 NAA: A11335 Z2.

145 Mitchell, *R.J. Mitchell: Schooldays to Spitfire*, Appendix 9, p. 349.

146 Mitchell, *R.J. Mitchell: Schooldays to Spitfire*, Appendix 9, p. 348.

147 Logbook – Barrington.

148 Author Interview.

149 Curnock, *Little Book of Spitfire*, p. 44.

150 Price, *Late Mark Spitfire Aces 1942 – 45*, pp. 28–29.

151 Goss, Cornwell and Rauchbach, *Luftwaffe Fighter-Bombers Over Britain*, pp. 15–16.

152 Glancey, *Spitfire: The Biography*, p. 111 and Wilson, *Spitfire*, p. 21.

153 Neil, *From the Cockpit: Spitfire*, pp 64–68.

154 NAA: A11335 Z2.

155 Curnock, *Little Book of Spitfire*, p. 44.

156 Price, *Late Mark Spitfire Aces 1942 – 45*, pp. 32–33.

157 Price, *Late Mark Spitfire Aces 1942 – 45*, p. 88.

158 NLA: Trove – "Powerful Spitfire" Sydney Morning Herald 9 March 1944.

159 Wilson, *Spitfire*, p. 20.

160 Logbook – Handsaker.

161 Wilson, *Spitfire*, p. 113.

162 NAA: A11335 Z2

163 NAA: A11335 Z2

164 Author Interview.

[165] McKinstry, *Hurricane: Victor of the Battle of Britain*, pp. 289-291.
[166] Wilson, *Spitfire*, p. 16.
[167] Wilson, *Spitfire*, p. 67.
[168] Herington, *Air War Against Germany & Italy 1939-1943*, pp. 31–32.
[169] Price, *The Spitfire Story*, pp. 104, 106.
[170] Wilson, *Spitfire*, pp. 22–23.
[171] Mitchell, *R.J. Mitchell: Schooldays to Spitfire*, Appendix 2, p. 300.
[172] Temora Interviews – Sir Brian Inglis.
[173] Mitchell, *R.J. Mitchell: Schooldays to Spitfire*, p. 203 and McKinstry, *Hurricane: Victor of the Battle of Britain*, pp. 3, 288.
[174] McKinstry, *Hurricane: Victor of the Battle of Britain*, p. 304.
[175] McKinstry, *Hurricane: Victor of the Battle of Britain*, p. 318.
[176] Wilson, *Spitfire*, pp. 123–124.
[177] McKinstry, *Hurricane: Victor of the Battle of Britain*, pp 320-321.
[178] W.G.G. Duncan-Smith, *Spitfire into Battle*, John Murray, London, 1981, (2002), p. 82.
[179] Robson, *The Spitfire Pocket Manual*, pp. 12-15, Glancey, *Spitfire: The Biography* pp. 221-230, NAA: A11093 452/A58 Part 1, Wilson, *Spitfire*, pp. 21-22, Price, *The Spitfire Story*, pp. 81-248 and Robson, *The Hurricane Pocket Manual*, pp. 19, 69, Jeffrey Quill, *Birth of a Legend: The Spitfire*, Quiller Press, London 1986, (1987), p. 156, and Mike Williams and Neil Stirling, *WWII Aircraft Performance*, Accessed 5 May 2019, <http://www.wwiiaircraftperformance.org/typhoon/typhoontest.html>.

GLOSSARY

AC	Air Commodore
ACM	Air Chief Marshal
ADGB	Air Defence Great Britain
AFC	Air Force Cross
AFU	Advanced Flying Unit
AFV	Armoured Fighting Vehicle (tanks)
AGS	Air Gunnery School
Air Cdre	Air Commordore
ALG	Advanced Landing Ground
ALO	Air Liaison Officer
AOC	Air Officer Commanding
ASI	Air Speed Indicator
ASR	Air Sea Rescue
AVM	Air Vice-Marshal
BAFO	British Air Forces of Occupation
BAGS	Bombing and Gunnery School
BAT	Beam Approach Training
Bogies	Unidentified aircraft
BLG	Base Landing Ground
Brevet	An award of a higher rank but without pay
CAM	Catapult Assisted Merchantmen
CO	Commanding Officer
Cpl	Corporal
DFC	Distinguished Flying Cross
DOW	Died of wounds
DSO	Distiuished Service Order
EATS	Empire Air Training Scheme
E/A	Enemy Aircraft
EFTS	Elementary Flying Training School
ENSA	Entertainments National Service Association
FAA	Fleet Air Arm
FFI	French Forces of the Interior (i.e. the Resistance)
Flt Lt	Flight Lieutenant
FO	Flying Officer
FS	Flight Sergeant
Gp Capt	Group Captain
GSU	Group Support Unit
HQ	Headquarters
ITS	Initial Training School
LAC	Leading Aircraftsman
LG	Landing Ground
Lt	Lieutenant
MATAF	Mediterranean Allied Tactical Air Force
MET	Motorised Enemy Transport (e.g. a truck)
MiD	Mentioned in dispatches
MSFU	Merchant Ship Fighter Unit
MT	Motorised transport
MU	Maintenance Unit
NCO	Non-Commissioned Officer
OLG	Operational Landing Ground
OTU	Operational Training Unit
PDRC	Personnel Dispatch and Reception Centre
(P)AFU	(Pilot) Advanced Flying Unit
PO	Pilot Officer
PR	Photographic Reconnaissance
PRU	Photographic Reconnaissance Unit
PTC	Personnel Transit Centre
RAAF	Royal Australian Air Force
RAF	Royal Air Force
RCAF	Royal Canadian Air Force
Recce	Reconnaissance
RSU	Repair and Salvage Unit
R/T	Radio/telephone
SFTS	Service Flying Training School
Sgt	Sergeant
SHAEF	Supreme Headquarters Allied Expeditionary Force
Sortie	One operational flight by one aircraft
Sqn Ldr	Squadron Leader
Tac/R	Tactical reconnaissance
TAF	Tactical Air Force
U/S	Unserviceable
USAAF	United States Army Air Forces
Wing Cdr	Wing Commander
WO	Warrant Officer
W/T	Wireless/Telephone (radio)

BIBLIOGRAPHY

THE NATIONAL ARCHIVES (TNA KEW)

AIR/27 series squadron records.
AIR/50 series Combat Reports
AIR 20/2653: Operation "Crossbow": Counter-measures against "Big Ben".
AIR 37/657: 2ND TACTICAL AIR FORCE: Anti-"Big Ben" organisation.
AIR 24/653: Statistics of Combats and Casualties in ADGB., Fighter Command and 2 TAF.
AIR 37/370: 2ND TACTICAL AIR FORCE: Enemy long range weapons: S.H.A.E.F. daily summaries.
AIR 37/674: 2ND TACTICAL AIR FORCE: Messages of congratulation and appreciation.
AIR 37/615: 2ND TACTICAL AIR FORCE: Operation "Market".
AIR 16/966: Operation "Big Ben".
AIR 26/183: Operations record book 123 Wing.
AIR 20/2302: Operations "Bodyline", "Big Ben" and "Crossbow": operational instructions.
AIR 37/533: ALLIED EXPEDITIONARY AIR FORCE: Operation "Big Ben".
AIR 14/2923: "Big Ben" countermeasures: No 80 Wing progress reports.
AIR 37/647: 2ND TACTICAL AIR FORCE: Operation "Big Ben": air defence of Great Britain instructions.
AIR 16/446: "Bodyline", "Big Ben" and "Crossbow".

IMPERIAL WAR MUSEUM (IWM LONDON)

Oral Histories:
Denys Gillam (10049)
Private Papers:
Air Commodore EJ Morris CB CBE DSO DFC (8231)
Wing Commander C M S Gardner OBE DFC (8199)
RAF Gun Camera Footage—ADGB:
Series CGE 10881 to 11427.

REPUBLISHED AIR MINISTRY DOCUMENTS

Air Publication 1564 B&D Pilot's Notes, *Hurricane IIA, IIB, IIC, IID and IV Aircraft*, HMSO, 1940, (Crecy)

Air Publication 1565 B Pilot's Notes, *Spitfire IIA and IIB Aeroplanes*, HMSO, 1940, (Crecy)

Air Publication 1565E and 2280 A, B & C, Pilot's Notes, *Spitfire VA, VB and VC aircraft and Seafire Ib, IIC and III Aircraft*, HMSO, 1941 (Crecy)

AUSTRALIAN WAR MEMORIAL FILES

AWM65 series personnel records
AWM66-97 Escape narratives
AWM online photographic collection
AWM PR 03203 (Tonkin)
AWM PR 0441 (Carmichael)

AUSTRALIAN NATIONAL ARCHIVES

A705 series Casualty Records
A1066 series Department of External Affairs
A1196 series Squadron Records
A2217 series RAAF WW2 records
A2676 series War Cabinet Minutes
A5954 series assorted documents relating to the defence of Australia
A9186 series Unit Histories (Operational Record Books)
A9300 series Personal Records
A9301 series Personal Records
A9652 series Squadron Records
A9695 series Squadron Records
A11305 series Squadron Records
A11335 series Squadron Records

INTERVIEWS WITH THE AUTHOR

Alec Arnel
Joseph Barrington
Sidney Handsaker
Lindsay Richards

INTERVIEWS HELD AT THE TEMORA AVIATION MUSEUM

Don Andrews
Fred Cowpe
Sir Brian Inglis
Norman Marsh

BOOKS AND ACADEMIC JOURNALS

Ambrose, Stephen E., *Band of Brothers*, Touchstone, New York, 1992 (2001).

Axell, Albert, *Russia's Heroes 1941–1945*, Robinson, London, 2002.

Ayris, Cyril and Leith, Russell, *Duty Done*, Cyril Ayris Freelance, West Perth, 2001.

Bader, Douglas, *Fight for the Sky*, Pen & Sword, Barnsley, 1973, (2008).

Baudot, M., Bernard, H., Brugmans, H., Foot, M., Jacobsen, H., *The Historical Encyclopaedia of World War II*, Facts on File, New York, 1980.

Beevor, Antony, *Arnhem: The Battle for the Bridges, 1944*, Viking, Milton Keynes, 2018.

Bond, Steve, Darlow, Steve, Feast Sean, Hall, Marc Owen, Robert and Sandall, Howard, *V-Weapons Bomber Command: Failed to Return*, Fighting High Ltd, China, 2015.

Breffort, Dominique, *German Fighters Volume II: Bf 110—Me 210—Me 410—Fw 190—Me 262—Me 163—He 162*, Histoire & Collections, Paris, 2014.

Clarke, Jeffrey J. and Smith, Robert Ross, *Riviera to the Rhine*, Centre of Military History United States Army, Washington, DC, 1993, (1995).

Clark, Lloyd, *Anzio: Italy and the Battle for Rome—1944*, Atlantic Monthly Press, New York, 2006.

Cochrane, Peter, *Tobruk 1941*, ABC Books, Sydney, 2005.

Curnock, David, *Little Book of Spitfire*, G2 Entertainment Limited, United Kingdom, 2011.

D'Este, Carlo, *Fatal Decision: Anzio and the Battle for Rome*, Aurum Press, London, 1991, (2007).

Delaney, John, *Fighting the Desert Fox: Rommel's Campaigns in North Africa April 1941 to August 1942*, Cassell & Co, London, 1998, (1999).

Duncan-Smith, W.G.G, *Spitfire into Battle*, John Murray, London, 1981, (2002).

Franks, Norman, *Typhoon Attack*, Stackpole, Mechanicsburg, 2003, (2010).
Galland, Adolf, *The First and The Last*, Readers Book Club, London, 1956.
Gillison, Douglas, *Australia in the War of 1939–1945, Series Three: Air Volume I: Royal Australian Air Force 1939-1942,* Australian War Memorial, Canberra, 1962.
Glancey, Jonathan, *Spitfire: The Biography*, Atlantic Books, London, 2007.
Goss, Chris with Cornwell, Peter and Rauchbach, Bernd, *Luftwaffe Fighter-Bombers Over Britain: The Tip and Run Campaign, 1942–43,* Stackpole Books, Mechanicsburg, 2010.
Herington, John, *Australia in the War of 1939-1945, Series Three: Air, Volume III: Air War Against Germany & Italy 1939–1943*, Australian War Memorial, Canberra, 1954.
Herington, John, *Australia in the War of 1939–1945, Series Three: Air, Volume IV: Air Power Over Europe 1944-1945*, Australian War Memorial, Canberra, 1963.
Laird, Malcolm and Mackenzie, Steve, *Spitfire—The ANZACS*, Ventura Publications, Wellington, 1997.
Long, Gavin, *Greece, Crete and Syria*, Collins, Sydney, 1953, (1986).
Liddell-Hart, B.H.(ed), *The Rommel Papers*, Da Capo Press, New York, 1953.
Long, Gavin, *The Six Years War, Australia in the 1939–45 War*, Australian War Memorial, Canberra, 1973.
Lunney, Adam, *Ready to Strike: The Spitfires and Australians of 453 (RAAF) Squadron over Normandy*, Barrallier Books, West Geelong, 2018.
McKinstry, Leo, *Hurricane: Victor of the Battle of Britain*, John Murray, London, 2011
McRoberts, Douglas, *Lions Rampant: The Story of 602 Spitfire Squadron*, William Kimber, London, 1985.
Mitchell, Gordon, *R.J. Mitchell: Schooldays to Spitfire*, The History Press, Stroud, (1986), 2009.
Morison, Samuel Eliot, *History of United States Naval Operations in World War II, Volume 9: Sicily–Salerno–Anzio*, Naval Institute Press, Annapolis, 1953 (2011).
Morison, Samuel Eliot, *History of United States Naval Operations in World War II, Volume 11: The Invasion of France and Germany*, Naval Institute Press, Annapolis, 1953 (2011).

Morley-Mower, Geoffrey, *Messerschmitt Roulette*, Phalanx, St Paul, 1993.
Neil, Wg Cdr T.F., *From the Cockpit: Spitfire*, Ian Allan Ltd, Shepperton, 1980.
Price, Dr Alfred, *Aircraft of the Aces: Men & Legends, Volume 1: The Legendary Spitfire Mk I/II 1939-1941*, Del Prado, Madrid, (1996), 1999.
Price, Dr Alfred, Drecki, Tomasz, Gretzyngier, Robert and Matusiak, Wojtek, *Aircraft of the Aces: Men & Legends, Volume 13: Spitfires Over the Mediterranean & North Africa,* Del Prado, Madrid, 2000.
Price, Dr Alfred, and Holmes, Tony, *Aircraft of the Aces: Men & Legends, Volume 17: RAF Aces of the Battle of Britain,* Del Prado, Madrid, (1995), 2000.
Price, Dr Alfred, *Osprey Aircraft of the Aces: Volume 5, Late Mark Spitfire Aces 1942—45*, Cadmus Communications, USA, (1995), 2010.
Price, Dr Alfred, *The Spitfire Story*, Arms and Armour, London, 1982, (1992).
Quill, Jeffrey, *Birth of a Legend: The Spitfire*, Quiller Press, London 1986, (1987).
Robson, Martin, *The Spitfire Pocket Manual*, Conway, London, 2010.
Robson, Martin, *The Hurricane Pocket Manual*, Conway, London, 2016.
Scoullar, J. L., *Official History of New Zealand in the Second World War 1939–45: Battle for Egypt The Summer of 1942*, War History Branch, Wellington, 1955.
Shores, Christopher and Thomas, Chris, *2nd Tactical Air Force: Volume 2 Breakout to Bodenplatte, July 1944 to January 1945,* Classic Publications, Surrey, 2005.
Shores, Christopher, Massimello, Giovanni and Guest, Russell, *A History of the Mediterranean Air War 1940-1945 Volume One: North Africa June 1940–January 1942*, Grub Street, London, 2012.
Shores, Christopher, *Dust Clouds in the Middle East*, Grub Street, London, 1996, (2016).
Showell, Jak P. Mallmann, *Companion to the German Navy 1939–1945*, The History Press, Stroud, 1999, (2009).
Smith, Graham, *Norfolk Airfields in the Second World War*, Countryside Books, Newbury, 1994, (2014).
Smith, Richard C., *Hornchurch Eagles: The Life Stories of Eight of the Airfield's*

Distinguished WWII Fighter Pilots, Grub Street, London, 2002.
Terraine, John, *The Right of the Line*, Wordsworth, 1985, (1997).
Thomas, Andrew, *Osprey Aircraft of the Aces: Volume 87, Spitfire Aces of Burma and the Pacific*, Osprey, Oxford, 2009.
Thomas, Chris, *Osprey Combat Aircraft: Volume 86, Typhoon Wings of 2nd TAF 1943–45*, Osprey, Oxford, 2010.
Thomas, Graham A., *Firestorm: Typhoons over Caen, 1944*, Spellmount, Stroud, 2006.
Wilson, Stewart, *Spitfire*, Aerospace Publications, Fyshwick, 1999.
Watts, W. Ken, *One Airman's War: An Australian Fighter Pilot's Experience of a Lifetime*, Perfect Print, 1988.

JOURNALS AND MAGAZINES

J.P. Pallud, 'The Invasions of Elba Island', *After the Battle*, No. 173, August 2016.
S. Handsaker, 'Wirraways', in *Spitfire News: Journal of the Spitfire Association*, No. 86, March 2007.

UNPUBLISHED SOURCES AND CORRESPONDENCE WITH THE AUTHOR

451 Squadron Association, 451 Squadron R.A.A.F. Middle East Forces 1941–1946 Anecdotes, (2002).
Wartime diary—Jim Ferguson.

PILOTS' FLYING LOGBOOKS

Don Andrews
Norman Baker
Joe Barrington
John Carmichael
Bob Clemesha
Sidney Handsaker
Vern Lancaster
Alan Lane
James Lynch
Colin 'Rusty' Leith

Clifford Alan Murray (CAM) Taylor
Jack Olver
Numerous phone calls and emails with the families and veterans of these two squadrons.

WEBSITES

320th Bomb Group: www.320thbg.org
Air of Authority—A History of RAF Organisation: www.rafweb.org/index.html
Australians at War Film Archive (AWFA): http://australiansatwarfilmarchive.unsw.edu.au/ (Interviews with: Joe Barrington, Herbert Biggs, John Culbert, Sid Handsaker, Leonard Hayman, Charles Hulls, Bob Milner, George Purdy and Edward Smith)
Australian War Memorial: www.awm.gov.au/
Barth City History: http://rathaus.stadt-barth.de/geschichte.php
Canadian Military Headquarters (CMHQ) reports 1940 to 1948: www.canada.ca/en/department-national-defence/services/military-history/history-heritage/official-military-history-lineages/reports/military-headquarters-1940-1948.html
Commonwealth War Graves Commission (CWGC): www.cwgc.org/
Helton's Hellcats 493rd BG(H) Debach: www.493bgdebach.co.uk/index.php
National Library of Australia (NLA): www.trove.nla.gov.au
North East Medals: www.northeastmedals.co.uk/britishguide/hmso/campaign_stars_defence.htm
Old Spitalfields Market (London): www.oldspitalfieldsmarket.com/the-market/the-history-of-the-market
Spitfire Aircraft Production: www.airhistory.org.uk/spitfire/
United States Holocaust Memorial Museum: https://encyclopedia.ushmm.org/content/en/article/ravensbrueck
WWII Aircraft Performance: www.wwiiaircraftperformance.org/

ACKNOWLEDGEMENTS

Thanks to:

The following museums and archives: Australian War Memorial (especially Jennifer Wilward), Imperial War Museum (London), National Archives of Australia, South Australian Aviation Museum, The National Archives (UK—Kew).

The veterans and their families who gave interviews and access to their private collections: Alec Arnel, Joe Barrington, Sidney Handsaker and Lindsay Richards.

The families of the veterans who preserved their history in boxes and folders and entrusted me with them: Andrews, Baker, Clemesha, Cowpe, Ferguson, Lancaster, Lane, Leith, Lynch, Olver, Purdy and Taylor.

The only Dutchman I know who loves shopping as much as history—Hennie van der Salm.

Martin Jackson, Secretary of the RAAF/Rhodesia Association.

Group Captain David Fredericks and Flight Sergeant Darryll Fell of the RAAF History and Heritage Branch.

My father Peter Lunney, who, despite being picky, found fewer errors than my best proofer and editor:

My darling wife Heather, who really would like to read something apart from books on aeroplanes.

INDEX